REMEMBERING
# THE END

## Radical Traditions
## Theology in a Postcritical Key

Series Editors: Stanley M. Hauerwas, Duke University,
and Peter Ochs, University of Virginia

*Radical Traditions* cuts new lines of inquiry across a confused array of debates concerning the place of theology in modernity and, more generally, the status and role of scriptural faith in contemporary life. Charged with a rejuvenated confidence, spawned in part by the rediscovery of reason as inescapably tradition constituted, a new generation of theologians and religious scholars is returning to scriptural traditions with the hope of retrieving resources long ignored, depreciated, and in many cases ideologically suppressed by modern habits of thought. *Radical Traditions* assembles a promising matrix of strategies, disciplines, and lines of thought that invites Jewish, Christian, and Islamic theologians back to the word, recovering and articulating modes of scriptural reasoning as that which always underlies modernist reasoning and therefore has the capacity—and authority—to correct it.

Far from despairing over modernity's failings, postcritical theologies rediscover resources for renewal and self-correction within the disciplines of academic study themselves. Postcritical theologies open up the possibility of participating once again in the living relationship that binds together God, text, and community of interpretation. *Radical Traditions* thus advocates a "return to the text," which means a commitment to displaying the richness and wisdom of traditions that are at once text based, hermeneutical, and oriented to communal practice.

Books in this series offer the opportunity to speak openly with practitioners of other faiths or even with those who profess no (or limited) faith, both academics and nonacademics, about the ways religious traditions address pivotal issues of the day. Unfettered by foundationalist preoccupations, these books represent a call for new paradigms of reason—a thinking and rationality that is more responsive than originative. By embracing a postcritical posture, they are able to speak unapologetically out of scriptural traditions manifest in the practices of believing communities (Jewish, Christian, and others); articulate those practices through disciplines of philosophic, textual, and cultural criticism; and engage intellectual, social, and political practices that for too long have been insulated from theological evaluation. *Radical Traditions* is radical not only in its confidence in nonapologetic theological speech but also in how the practice of such speech challenges the current social and political arrangements of modernity.

# REMEMBERING
# THE END

~

*Dostoevsky as*
*Prophet to Modernity*

P. TRAVIS KROEKER
BRUCE K. WARD

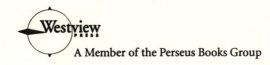

A Member of the Perseus Books Group

Copyright © 2001 by Westview Press, A Member of the Perseus Books Group

Published in 2001 in the United States of America by Westview Press, 5500 Central Avenue, Boulder, Colorado 80301–2877, and in the United Kingdom by Westview Press, 12 Hid's Copse Road, Cumnor Hill, Oxford OX2 9JJ

Find us on the World Wide Web at www.westviewpress.com

Library of Congress Cataloging-in-Publication Data
Kroeker, P. Travis (Peter Travis), 1957–
    Remembering the end : Dostoevsky as prophet to modernity / by P. Travis Koeker and
    Bruce K. Ward.
        p.    cm.—(Radical traditions)
    ISBN 0-8133-6608-9 (pbk.)
1. Dostoyevsky, Fyodor, 1821–1881—Philosophy.    2. Dostoyevsky, Fyodor, 1821–1881.
Brat§'ì Karamazovy.    3. Dostoyevsky, Fyodor, 1821–1881—Religion.    I. Ward, Bruce.
Kinsey.    II. Title.    III. Series.

PG3328.Z7 P5456    2001
891.73'3—dc21

                                                                                    00-066087

The paper used in this publication meets the requirements of the American National Standard for Permanence of Paper for Printed Library Materials Z39.48–1984.

PERSEUS
**POD**
ON DEMAND    10    9    8    7    6    5    4    3    2

*This book is dedicated to children and to parents*

~

*To Sarah, Miriam, and Peter Stewart-Kroeker*

~

*To Helen Ward*
*and*
*Donald K. Ward*
*(February 16, 1923 – March 28, 2000)*

~

*"memory eternal . . . unto ages of ages"*

# Contents

# Credits and Acknowledgments

Although we bear joint responsibility for the book as a whole, we think it best to specify who wrote which parts: Chapters 1, 4, 6, and the second section of Chapter 7 ("The Silent Christ: A Theological Coda") were written by Travis Kroeker; Chapters 3 and 5, the first section of Chapter 7 ("Identifying the Silent Christ: Sources, Parallels, and Contrasts"), and the introductory section of Chapter 2 were written by Bruce Ward.

An earlier version of a portion of Chapter 3 was published previously under the title "Dostoevsky and the Problem of Meaning in History," in *Dostoevsky and the Twentieth Century: The Ljubljana Papers*, ed. Malcolm Jones (Nottingham, U.K.: Astra, 1993). Part of Chapter 5 also reflects an earlier article, "Dostoevsky and the Hermeneutics of Suspicion," published in *Literature & Theology*, vol. 11, no. 3 (September 1997). We wish to acknowledge the editors of these publications.

We thank Vintage Books for permission to reprint Dostoevsky's "The Grand Inquisitor" from Fyodor Dostoevsky, *The Brothers Karamazov*, trans. Richard Pevear and Larissa Volokhonsky (New York: Vintage, 1990), pp. 246–264.

We are particularly grateful to Stanley Hauerwas, coeditor of the Radical Traditions series, and to the three anonymous readers who scrutinized our manuscript for Westview Press. Their thoughtful and constructive comments were a great help.

We wish also to thank the following people, who have helped to support, stimulate, or enrich our thinking about Dostoevsky: Roger Anderson, Fred Bird, Harold Coward and the Centre for Studies in Religion and Society at the University of Victoria, David Jasper and the Centre for the Study of Literature and Theology at the University of Glasgow, David Jeffrey, Joel Marcus, Carl Ridd, John Robertson, Stephen Westerholm, the faculty and students who participated in the

1993–1994 Dostoevsky Seminar at Lonergan College of Concordia University, and the participants in the Dostoevsky seminar at McMaster University. Thanks also to Paul Corey, for help in preparing the manuscript, and to David Penner for compiling the index.

Special personal thanks are also extended to friends and family: from Bruce to Susan Srigley, for her encouragement and her own ideas about prophecy and literature, and to his sons Ian and Graeme, for our ongoing dialogue about matters political and historical; and from Travis to Cathy Stewart-Kroeker, for all manner of support and companionship—spiritual, intellectual, emotional—and to friends at St. Cuthbert's.

*P. Travis Kroeker*
*Bruce K. Ward*

# Introduction

Tormented with a spiritual thirst
I trampled through a somber desert,
And a seraph with six wings
To me appeared across the way . . .
And with sword he clove my chest,
And my trembling heart plucked out,
And a coal, aflame with fire,
Thrust into my gaping breast.
Like a desert's corpse I lay,
And God's voice called out:
"Arise, O prophet, and see and hear,
And fulfill my will,
And as you circle sea and land
With my word burn human hearts."

— PUSHKIN, "THE PROPHET"

Nearing the end of a lifetime of formidable misfortune, in June 1880, Dostoevsky enjoyed a rare, spontaneous outburst of public acclaim. The occasion was a speech he delivered in Moscow at the unveiling of a monument to the poet Pushkin. In an excited letter to his wife, written later that day, Dostoevsky described the extraordinary response of the large crowd: "And when, at the end, I proclaimed the *universal oneness of mankind,* the hall seemed to go into hysterics, and when I finished there was . . . elation. People in the audience who had never met before, wept, sobbed, embraced each other. . . . They kept calling me back for half an hour, waving their handkerchiefs. . . . 'Prophet, prophet!' people were shouting in the crowd."[1]

Dostoevsky evidently took particular note of the accolade "prophet" *(prorok)*, with good reason: The speech that had evoked this response was focused on the prophetic aspect of Pushkin's poetry; and later that day, in the final event of the festivities, Dostoevsky was to give a dramatic reading of Pushkin's poem "The Prophet." The judgment of Dostoevsky's Russian audience, that *his own* words and work were prophetic, has since been taken up and confirmed, to the point of becoming a truism, by generations of readers throughout the world. This judgment is affirmed also in the subtitle of this book—not by rote, but because we think that the prophetic significance of Dostoevsky's art has neither been exhausted by scholarly commentary nor overtaken and rendered superfluous by the events of the twentieth century. Dostoevsky's prophetic word, properly understood, retains the power to "burn the hearts" of those who hear it. But what is the nature of this power?

Many examples of Dostoevsky's foresight into the twentieth century may be cited: visions of tyranny, terror, and large-scale warfare endured by human masses; and of widespread alienation, and frequently desperate quests for meaning, among individuals. However, it is possible also to cite historical developments that belie Dostoevsky's prognostications, especially those involving the destiny of his native Russia and its supposed mission of regenerating modern Western civilization. The power of Dostoevsky's word cannot be assessed by tallying his correct or incorrect predictions about the future, as if he were a clairvoyant or a diviner.

The prophetic role in modernity is more profoundly expressed in Heidegger's image of the poet (specifically in relation to Hölderlin) as "exposed to the divine lightnings" as he stands attentively in the realm of the Between—between the gods and human beings. Heidegger would have it that the poet *is* the prophet of our era, the only one we can have. In a postreligious age such as ours, the word of the poet, Dostoevsky's included, has come to be regarded with a certain earnest reverence as a spiritual unveiling. Yet, what is sought so avidly is a new spiritual word, a word of *novelty*; Heidegger's poet, after all, also stands between the No-more of "the gods that have fled" and the Not-yet of the "god that is coming."[2] The prophet—the visionary poet who names the "new god"—is the author of novelty.

The novelty of Dostoevsky's art of the novel has been noted from the beginning. Bakhtin's heralding of the open-ended dialogic or polyphonic world of Dostoevsky's novels laid the foundations of a rich and fruitful reading that continues to ensure Dostoevsky a central place in the modern (and postmodern) consciousness. It is our view, however, that the characteristic modern focus on the prophet as the author of novelty—even if of spiritual novelty—is based on an incomplete appreciation of the nature of Dostoevsky's prophetic art: The power of Dostoevsky's word is not primarily a matter of novelty. The word in Dostoevsky that still can burn the hearts of his readers is a *remembered* word.

The insistent intertextuality of Dostoevsky's literary art is one of its chief features. His final masterpiece, *The Brothers Karamazov,* in particular, appears to have swallowed an entire library, ranging from Dante, Shakespeare, Voltaire, Goethe, and Pushkin, to now all-but-forgotten Western and Russian minor authors and stories from the Russian folkloric tradition. These multitudinous literary echoes, however, are overpowered by the utterly pervasive reverberation of the Bible—all of it, from Genesis to Revelation. But the biblical sonority, is not strident or doctrinaire; if it were, Dostoevsky's art would not have been so frequently hailed as a harbinger of postmodern indeterminacy. Although Dostoevsky's allusions to particular biblical passages are myriad, the Bible serves primarily to anchor the overall vision—especially the ethical vision. The principal characteristic of Dostoevsky's prophetic art, then, is neither historical prognostication nor spiritual novelty but remembered ethical vision that speaks to the present. His word is prophetic in the manner of the genuine prophet as characterized by Martin Buber: the one who, rather than announcing an immutable decree, "speaks into the power of decision lying in the moment."[3]

The prophet has been aptly described as one who stands with "one foot in the *kronos,* the other in *kairos* . . . ear to eternity and mouth toward the city."[4] This stance imposes a necessary balance between remembered vision and present engagement. We have attempted to read Dostoevsky as a writer who is thoroughly engaged with the modern present—not just "from the outside" but from within his own inner experience, thinking, and instincts—and at the same time, rooted in the remembered word—both of the written Book and of the "Living Book" of the Word incarnate.[5] Few would assert that *The Divine Comedy* of Dante can be fully appreciated without taking into account both its concerned engagement with the poet's secular present and its remembered Christian vision. We believe that a complete understanding of the prophetic art of Dostoevsky can be attained only by using the same approach: One must forget neither how engaged with the consciousness of the secular present his art is nor how Christian it is. The parallel between *The Divine Comedy* and *The Brothers Karamazov* breaks down only in that the remembered religious Word of Dostoevsky's modern present is far more fragmented and distorted than that of Dante's present.

In addition to furthering a deeper reading of Dostoevsky, our primary goal in writing this book was one that would have interested Dostoevsky more: Through his work we have sought insight into the nature of the present moment in which we find ourselves, as individuals and as a society, required to decide. There is no shortage of modern thinkers who advise that we decide *resolutely;* but we especially wish to heed those who might help us decide *well.*

~

Dostoevsky was both a literary artist and a religious thinker; we did not write this book on the assumption that we *must* treat him as either one or the other. Given our overriding concern with the prophetic nature of his art, our reflection is preponderantly focused on his religious thinking. Yet it is also rooted in a close reading of Dostoevsky's art. That art serves always as the touchstone for our interpretation of his thought. Our reading of Dostoevsky is not primarily a reading of the prose works—critical essays, journalism, and correspondence—in which he speaks in his own name. Without any doubt, the significant expression of his prophetic word—and certainly of the word that can burn hearts—is his art. For us, the novels themselves constitute the litmus test for our understanding of his thought. The measure of that understanding is the degree to which it is confirmed by Dostoevsky's art and enhances its appreciation.

The principal source for our reflection on Dostoevsky's prophetic thought is his last novel, *The Brothers Karamazov,* which he was just finishing when he delivered his speech on Pushkin. He regarded this novel as the culmination of his work; perhaps he indeed saw it as the modern equivalent to *The Divine Comedy* that he believed needed to be written.[6] In it, he strove to say all that he had in him to say, as artist and religious thinker. This immense novel is a recapitulation as well as a culmination of Dostoevsky's prophetic word, and it therefore serves appropriately as our chief source (though other works will be referred to as required for the elaboration of particular themes).

Dostoevsky's culminating novel finds its "culminating point" (Dostoevsky's own words) in the chapter entitled "The Grand Inquisitor." This single chapter is probably most responsible for Dostoevsky's reputation as a prophetic voice for modernity. We have therefore chosen to include the whole of "The Grand Inquisitor" in our book (see Chapter 2).

Our book contains seven chapters in all: Chapter 1 introduces the salient features of Dostoevsky's religious thought in its prophetic engagement with modernity, and explores the relationship between prophecy and poetics in his art. Both in terms of literary genre and theological vision, Dostoevsky's prophetic art may be defined as apocalyptic. It points toward the mysterious disclosure of the divine Word present in the hidden life of all material reality, as its fundamental principle of movement—the radical meaning of divine love unveiled in Christ's self-giving movement even unto death. Like the prophets of old, Dostoevsky brings together ancient memories of divine address and decisive contemporary challenges in order to clarify our spiritual and moral discernment into the meaning of justice, history, and happiness. The central question we address here is: How does Dostoevsky's artistic embodiment of apocalyptic poetics enable him to narrate the decisive personal, political, and moral questions in modernity with such illuminating power?

Chapter 3 explores the remarkable meditation on the problem of meaning in history expressed in "The Grand Inquisitor." This meditation operates on two levels—those of the author and of the character(s) (Ivan Karamazov and the Inquisitor). Whereas the Inquisitor appeals to the Bible, particularly the book of Revelation, as the framework for an interpretation of world history that is intended to verify his solution to the problem of human order, Dostoevsky himself is engaged with the problem of modern historicism (especially in its Hegelian version). The key question addressed in this chapter is: Might Dostoevsky be a prophetic figure for our age not only in his insight into the destructive implications of the modern historical consciousness but also as an example of how difficult it is for him as a Christian to avoid these same implications?

Revelation can be a two-edged sword: Although the Inquisitor *mis*uses the book of Revelation, the same text plays a prominent, positive role in the critique of modernity articulated by Dostoevsky through "The Grand Inquisitor." Chapter 4 discusses the role played by the book of Revelation in Dostoevsky's art—particularly in "The Grand Inquisitor," where several significant references to the biblical text are explicitly made. The context of Ivan's prose poem *(poemka)* about the Inquisitor is his rebellion against the world as created by God, on the grounds of Ivan's earthly, Euclidean measure of justice (articulated in the chapter entitled "Rebellion," immediately preceding "The Grand Inquisitor"). Ivan's collection of stories of the grotesque suffering of innocent children constitutes a legal brief against God's justice. The *poemka* is Ivan's poetic attempt to work out the implications of his rebellion by bringing heavenly powers (namely, Christ) down to earth. In form and content, it is an apocalyptic parable that parodies the symbolism of the book of Revelation. The most important question we addressed in Chapter 4 is: Why and how does Dostoevsky find in the book of Revelation a symbolic context for interpreting the problem of modern justice?

Chapter 5 subjects to critical scrutiny the professed motivation underlying the Grand Inquisitor's solution to the problem of justice: his "love of humanity." Dostoevsky's demystification of modern humanist love is contrasted with that of another modern prophet, Nietzsche. The dialogue set up between these two reveals areas of convergence and divergence: the former, apparent in a shared suspicion of a secular humanism that affirms love of humanity at the same time as it repudiates religious faith; the latter, apparent in their ultimately different understandings of love and its relation to God and immortality. The principal question is this: What finally comes of the modern humanist affirmation of freedom, equality, and especially love of humanity, when God and immortality are denied?

Chapter 6 reflects on the conflicting ethical-political visions presented in *The Brothers Karamazov*. One is the vision of the Grand Inquisitor, expressed through his interpretation of the third temptation (Matthew 4), in which he proposes the establishment of a universal and homogeneous state, founded upon the "noble lie" of immortality. This solution functions as a parodic mimesis of the heavenly city imaged poetically in the book of Revelation. The alternative vision is that of Dostoevsky, who like the author of the biblical apocalypse is engaging in a prophetic critique of global empire from the standpoint of "God and immortality"—a hidden, divine justice founded upon the slain Lamb who rules in the heavenly city, a city mediated on earth in the suffering church. These conflicting political theologies with their attendant moral logics inhabit the same worldly space. The question is, which is true and which is founded upon a lie? This chapter explores the ways in which this question is addressed throughout the novel—especially in the contrasting practices of retributive and restorative justice.

Dostoevsky's portrayal of the silent Christ in "The Grand Inquisitor" might well be the most dramatically prophetic moment of his art. It is perhaps inevitable and self-explanatory, then, that our book culminates with a chapter (7) titled "Christ in 'The Grand Inquisitor.'"

Although the book follows the structure outlined here, the reader will not find in it a strictly linear narrative development. This is partly because of the nature of the primary source on which our reflections are focused. Interpreting "The Grand Inquisitor," or for that matter, *The Brothers Karamazov*, is something like peeling an onion; one layer is peeled away only to reveal another. Our discussion thus moves in spiral fashion: One returns to certain themes and passages, but with a sense of ever deepening understanding. As T. S. Eliot once so beautifully described this sort of movement (in "Little Gidding"): "We shall not cease from exploration / And the end of all our exploring / Will be to arrive where we started / And know the place for the first time."

The reader will not find a strictly linear development in the book also because it has two authors. Certain themes and passages come under discussion more than once—for differing reasons and with differing outcomes. We share a common, high estimation of the significance of Dostoevsky's prophetic art, but our interpretations of his writing were developed independently. Indeed, when we began to consider this collaboration, our understanding was that we would each bring to the project a particular emphasis (though always with the whole in view), in accord with the twofold thrust of Dostoevsky's prophetic art: One emphasis would be on the remembered biblical vision, and the other, on the engagement with modern thought. After agreeing on the overall structure of the book, we each did our own work, and then brought it together. The result was sometimes surprising, always interesting; above all, we found that the result was neither repetition nor conflict but a richer understanding—in keeping with the spiral-like and dialogic movement of Dostoevsky's art itself. We hope that our readers will make a similar discovery.

# Notes

1. Letter of 8 June 1880 to Anna G. Dostoevsky, *Selected Letters of Fyodor Dostoevsky*, eds. Joseph Frank and David I. Goldstein, trans. Andrew R. MacAndrew (London: Rutgers University Press, 1987), p. 506.

2. See Martin Heidegger, "Hölderlin und das Wesen der Dichtung," translated as "Hölderlin and the Essence of Poetry," in *Existence and Being*, ed. Werner Brock, trans. R.F.C. Hull and Alan Crick (Chicago: H. Regnery, 1949).

3. Martin Buber, *The Prophetic Faith* (New York: Harper and Row, 1960), p. 103.

4. David Lyle Jeffrey, *People of the Book* (Grand Rapids, Mich.: William B. Eerdmans, 1996), p. 26. Jeffrey's discussion of the nature of prophecy (chapter 2) is insightful.

5. The expression "Living Book" is Jeffrey's (see Ibid., p. 20). In a letter of 1 January 1868 to his niece, Sofya A. Ivanov, Dostoevsky writes: "The whole of the Gospel of Saint John is a statement to that effect; he finds the whole miracle in the Incarnation alone."

6. With Victor Hugo explicitly in mind, Dostoevsky pointed to "the idea of raising up the lowly" as the "historic testament of modern times, so often unjustly accused of contributing nothing to compare with the great literary works of the past." He then expressed the hope that "by the end of the [nineteenth] century, it [the idea of raising up the lowly] will become embodied, completely, clearly, and powerfully, in some great work of art that will express the profound character of the time as fully and lastingly as, for example, *The Divine Comedy* expressed its epoch of medieval Catholic beliefs and ideals" (as quoted in Joseph Frank, *Dostoevsky: The Stir of Liberation 1860–1865* [Princeton: Princeton University Press, 1986], p. 198). As Joseph Frank observes, *The Brothers Karamazov* "comes closer than any other work at the end of the century to fulfilling this prophecy of a great masterpiece of Christian art" (Ibid.).

# one

# *Prophecy and Poetics*

Dostoevsky has often been called a prophet, both by his Russian contemporaries and by many of his subsequent readers in the Western world. How is it that Dostoevsky's art might be viewed as "prophetic" for the modern (and postmodern) era? There are two respects in which the term might function generally to depict Dostoevsky's engaged social criticism: (1) his incisive portrayal of the movement from socialism to totalitarian political order, as famously expressed in "The Grand Inquisitor"; and (2) his unmasking of liberal conceptions of justice and moral psychology as inadequate to the complexities of human nature. Both critiques proved prophetic in regard to the dominant political ideologies of the twentieth century, the consequences of which remain with us as a critical challenge now and for the foreseeable future.

Yet another reason for describing Dostoevsky's voice as prophetic is the central importance of apocalyptic symbolism to his artistic vision. Unlike his compatriot Tolstoy—whose translation of the New Testament gospel into a liberal, pacifist moral creed had its own influence—for Dostoevsky the Christ of the Gospels is a cosmic, apocalyptic figure who tears open the hidden meaning of everyday life, exposing it as spiritual crisis (*krisis,* in the literal sense of judgment or decision—in a metaphysical and theological, not just sociopolitical or moral, sense).[1] Dostoevsky's art portrays the spiritual crisis of modern/postmodern culture with reference to the question of God and immortality. Like apocalyptic prophets of old, Dostoevsky is passionately concerned with the question of worldly justice in its immediate context, but always with reference to the ultimate context—the cosmic pathos of divine justice.

In this respect Dostoevsky's work defies Martin Buber's distinction (which has been very influential both in literary and in social-political theory) between prophecy—defined by Buber as engaged, morally responsible social criticism in history—and apocalyptic writing—defined as escapist and inactive in history, and hence morally irresponsible both in the present and for the future.[2] Dostoevsky brings together practical, historical engagement and the dialogue with God, but always with reference to the cosmic canvas on which apocalyptic images are drawn. For him the prophetic "life-task" receives its living inspiration from its connection with the strange otherness of apocalyptic vision. Far from "speaking into his notebook" (Buber's characterization of the apocalyptic writer), Dostoevsky speaks to particular persons, who recognize in his words "their situation's demand for decision and to act accordingly."[3]

## The Pushkin Speech

The occasion on which Dostoevsky was perhaps most famously and most publicly hailed as a prophet by his own people took place in June 1880, when he gave a speech on Pushkin at a meeting of the Society of Lovers of Russian Literature— a speech in which he described the "prophetic significance" of Pushkin's art. Pushkin, said Dostoevsky, was prophetic for Russia in two central respects:[4] Firstly, Pushkin was the first to capture in artistic form the essential negative and positive types of the Russian character. On the negative side, his characters Aleko and Onegin represent the rootless detachment of the educated classes, whose abstraction from "the People" leaves them restless and spiritually disoriented. They seek the truth outside themselves and the heartland of their native culture, hoping to find it somehow in the external trappings of European success: in science and in technological and economic "progress." Such self-interested and restless dreams lead quickly to violence, greed, and the appeal to abstract rights in order to redress personal grievances. These people have lost contact with the skilled labor of love in relation to their native culture and traditional obligations, having traded these lived, spiritual connections for a mess of modern abstractions that bring them only greater disharmony and unhappiness. Pushkin's Tatiana, in contrast, is a strong, positive character, rooted in the wisdom of her native soil. Her spiritual rootedness and depth give her insight into the soul of Onegin, whereas his spiritual blindness allows him to attend only to external abstractions. Hence, despite her attraction to him, he cannot see her beauty of soul so long as she appears, humbly and simply, in a provincial backwater; when he meets her again in fashionable Petersburg society, that changes. But now it is too late—she is the wife of an elderly general, to whom she will be faithful even though she loves Onegin, because of the promises she has made.

    At this point in his speech, Dostoevsky offers his own interesting interpretation of this contrast in characters, in relation to the question of happiness, and he does so by developing an image made famous in *The Brothers Karamazov*, which he was completing at the time of his Pushkin speech:

> Can you imagine that you are erecting the edifice of human destiny with the goal of making people happy in the end, of giving them peace and rest at last? And now imagine as well that to do this it is essential and unavoidable to torture to death just one human creature. . . . Will you consent on those terms to be the architect of such an edifice? That is the question. And can you admit, even for a moment, the idea that the people for whom you were building this edifice would themselves agree to accept such happiness from you if its foundations rested on the suffering of, say, even one insignificant creature, but one who had been mercilessly and unjustly tortured—and, having accepted this happiness, would they remain happy ever after?[5]

No, says Dostoevsky, human happiness cannot be so conceived. The happiness of one is intricately related to the happiness of all, and so also the suffering of one to that of all. Tatiana sees this and is prepared to sacrifice her individual happiness for the happiness of the whole. Dostoevsky goes further: Even were she free to do so, she would not have gone off with Onegin. Why? Because she has divined the essence of his character, she knows what he is—a restless dreamer who sees her only when she gains prominence in fashionable society (in which she herself is not truly at home). She sees that he loves only yet another novel fantasy of his restless, rootless imagination, that he lacks the discipline and humility to cultivate true love. His image of happiness lacks substance; it is an "illusion of happiness"[6] that lacks a complete and true foundation. Such edifices crumble. Her happiness, to the contrary, is rooted in the spiritual soil of the People and their spiritual beauty, to which she sees true happiness is ultimately tied. Hence the significance of the other positive type to which Dostoevsky refers in Pushkin's art, also rooted in the spiritual soil of the Russian people—the "chronicler-monk," about whom "one could write a whole book."[7] In *The Brothers Karamazov* Dostoevsky himself had done precisely that, and had answered his own negative type (Ivan), and the poetic legend of the Grand Inquisitor, with the "life of the Russian monk," chronicled by the odd monastic hero of the novel (Alyosha). We shall return to this contrast below, for it represents the prophetic heart of Dostoevsky's artistic vision.

The second key aspect of Pushkin's prophetic significance highlighted in the speech by Dostoevsky was that Pushkin—unlike many other noble Russian belletrists of the time—did not identify the happiness of his people with the European ideals of progress and sophistication. Instead, he identified happiness with the spiritual simplicity and depth of the Russian soul. This latter identification, Dostoevsky suggests, is what enabled Pushkin so successfully to incarnate through his poetic artistry the poetic genius of other nations. It is clear that on this point Dostoevsky links Pushkin's prophetic significance to the prophetic power of the Russian soul. He audaciously asserts that not even the greatest European poets (in his own estimation, Shakespeare, Cervantes, and Schiller) could match Pushkin's ability to embody the spiritual identities of alien peoples: The Europeans usually interpreted the spirit of other peoples from their own point of view (Shakespeare's Italians, for example, seem very English).

This spiritual capacity, which is tied to the ultimate aspiration toward the "universal brotherhood of peoples," is the prophetic strength of the Russian people. Thus, says Dostoevsky: "Having become completely a national poet, Pushkin at once, as soon as he came in contact with the force of the People, at once senses the great future mission of this force. Here he is a visionary; here he is a prophet."[8] But here Dostoevsky addresses himself to "one great misunderstanding"—a misunderstanding that not only afflicted Russians of his day but that has affected interpretations of Dostoevsky's prophetic message ever since—the conflict between Westernizers and Slavophiles. It is, says Dostoevsky, a historically necessary misunderstanding, for it concerns precisely the question of which vision for the future Russia will choose to be guided by: secular European modernity or traditional Russian Christianity? And yet it remains precisely a misunderstanding when interpreted only on the level of political ideology, for it is really a question of the truth about the human soul and its historical destiny, about happiness and the just society. Here Dostoevsky's speech grows impassioned:

> To become a genuine Russian will mean specifically: to strive to bring an ultimate reconciliation to Europe's contradictions, to indicate that the solution to Europe's anguish is to be found in the panhuman and all-unifying Russian soul, to enfold all our brethren within it with brotherly love, and at last, perhaps, to utter the ultimate word of great, general harmony, ultimate brotherly accord of all tribes through the law of Christ's Gospel![9]

Dostoevsky knows that these words will strike his hearers as "ecstatic, exaggerated, and fantastic." What would it mean for Russia to play such a prophetic role among the nations? Certainly it cannot mean the "light" of economic prosperity or scientific or military glory. Human unity, in which all particular peoples dwell together harmoniously in their difference, is neither constituted nor preserved by external forces for homogenization. Only the power of the word of Christ "in serf's garb," the Christ who traverses the impoverished land with blessing, can fulfill this prophetic task. In his letters to his wife Anna, Dostoevsky describes the pandemonium that broke out in response to his speech, the crowd hailing *him* as their prophet.[10] Many of those in the audience, it seems, were also avid readers of his serialized novel, *The Brothers Karamazov*, and saw immediately the connections between Dostoevsky's interpretation of prophetic elements in Pushkin and Dostoevsky's own prophetic art.

## *The Brothers Karamazov* as Prophecy

The hero of Dostoevsky's famous novel is Alexei (Alyosha) Karamazov, "a strange man, even an odd one," the narrator tells us in the preface, whose odd significance is related to his particularity precisely insofar as he "bears within himself the heart of the whole, while the other people of his epoch have all for some reason been torn away from it for a time by some kind of flooding wind."[11] The flooding wind is a reverse *mistral*, blowing European fantasies, desires, and habits into Russia, along with the latest scientific and economic developments, uprooting the people from their spiritual soil and alienating them from one another. By contrast, Alyosha's odd path, as "an early lover of mankind" (18), is shaped by Christian monasticism and the commission given him by his spiritual father, the unconventional monastic elder Zosima, to "sojourn in the world like a monk" (285). Dostoevsky's hero, then, comes to embody a prophetic form of Christian ascetic theology in the world, in imitation of the suffering Christ "in serf's garb."

In book 6 of *The Brothers Karamazov*, entitled "The Russian Monk," Dostoevsky develops (in the voice of Alyosha) his poetic, prophetic answer to Ivan Karamazov's powerfully articulated rejection (in the Grand Inquisitor) of the Christian vision of God's creation. As his letters make clear, Dostoevsky wrote these pages in fear and trembling, concerned that in this "culminating point" of the novel, for the sake of which "the whole novel is being written," he would be unable to communicate in persuasive artistic form the practical realism of "pure" Christian existence.[12] Not surprisingly, it is Ivan's poem of the Grand Inquisitor, not Alyosha's life of the elder Zosima, that has become the most famous of Dostoevsky's prophetic texts in the twentieth century. As Dostoevsky feared, Christian asceticism—even in the form of "sojourn in the world"—failed to capture the imagination and commitment of his Russian readers (despite the adulation of the Muscovite crowd). This too is foretold in the narrator's preface to the novel: Modern, realist critics, he speculates, will judge the hero "unrealistic," the representative of an isolated, otherworldly path that cannot be recommended as a model of social and cultural responsibility for our time. Yet the narrator insists that to the contrary, Alyosha was "even more of a realist than the rest of us" (25) and surely less isolated in the sense expressed by Jesus, in the words that serve as epigraph to the entire novel (John 12:24): "Verily, verily, I say unto you, Except a corn of wheat fall into the earth and die, it abideth alone; but if it die, it bringeth forth much fruit."

How does Dostoevsky's novel envision the ascetic path that leads out of the darkness of falsehood and isolation into the light of truth? How might death unite us with "the heart of the whole"? For Dostoevsky this can only be understood in relation to the dramatic biblical—and in particular, the Johannine—cosmology: God's higher, "spiritual" truth is embodied in the world as the pattern of self-giving, suffering love. It is a pattern prophetically and poetically revealed in a dramatic reversal imaged in Revelation 5: the messianic Lion that conquers the world and saves it from violent destruction is unveiled as a slain Lamb. Precisely this image of the slain Lamb appears at the climax of the famous conversation between Ivan and Alyosha Karamazov that leads into Ivan's "The Grand Inquisitor." Having unleashed the retributive fury piled up in his dossier of grotesque punishment stories in which innocent young children are violated, Ivan questions Alyosha:

> Tell me straight out, I call on you—answer me: imagine that you yourself are building the edifice of human destiny with the object of making people happy in the finale, of giving them peace and rest at last, but for that you must inevitably and unavoidably torture just one tiny creature . . . and raise your edifice on the foundation of her unrequited tears—would you agree to be the architect on such conditions? (245)

Alyosha replies that he would not agree; however, he then responds with his own image of innocent suffering, the Lamb slain before the foundation of the world: "You've forgotten about him, but it is on him that the structure [of human destiny, happiness, and harmony] is being built, and it is to him that they will cry out: 'Just art thou, O Lord, for thy ways have been revealed!'" (246). But Ivan has not forgotten; indeed, he has been waiting for precisely this opportunity to recite his counterprophecy, "The Grand Inquisitor," which he has conceived as a corrective to the botched anthropology and politics of the Christian mythos. There is nothing redemptive in suffering servanthood, and the "higher harmony" toward which it points is achieved at an exorbitant price—namely, vast human unhappiness and injustice.[13] Here we find the central prophetic pro and contra of the entire novel.

Dostoevsky, like Pushkin, images in poetic form the fateful historical decision facing the Russian people (but certainly not Russians alone) through his two central prophetic characters, Ivan and Alyosha. Ivan is Dostoevsky's rootless, abstract intellectual. He writes learned articles and powerful prose poems that explore the fashionable cultural implications of the dominant European ideologies: secular humanism, atheistic socialism, and scientistic cosmologies. His apocalyptic prophecies have to do with the nihilistic and violently destructive future of European humanism. He does not flinch from laying out the base logic of its Euclidean earthly realism, in propositions such as the following:

- "There exists no law of nature that man should love mankind"; this is a religious proposition rooted in belief in God and immortality, without which "the moral law of nature ought to change immediately into the exact opposite of the former religious law," namely the egoism of "all is permitted" (69).
- Egoism nevertheless must be restrained if human happiness and political order are to be realized. Hence, religious and moral ideologies must be used in the service of taming human nature, but they must be politically controlled and managed via extensive technological, ideological, and military networks of external power. *Used as controlled.*
- When the idea of God has been destroyed in human beings, a "new man" will arise, a nature-conquering man-god who will remake the world in the image of a virtual reality and "will thereby every hour experience such lofty delight as will replace for him all his former hopes of heavenly delight" (649). Ivan's sidekick Rakitin, the socialist seminarian, is especially enamored of the glorious possibilities for social and mental engineering, which will solve all moral problems.

Onegin's fantasies are nothing, compared to the earthly dreams of Ivan. Ivan, however, is as unable as Onegin to act decisively and meaningfully. He remains trapped in his divided conscience (old habits die hard), mired in self-isolating, retributive fantasies—although his liberated "Licharda" (Smerdyakov) becomes a nihilistic instrument of Ivan's prophetic teachings. Dostoevsky powerfully depicts the modernist European realism "from within," with an artistic insight that has caused many to believe he sided with Ivan; but it is clear (as Mikhail Bakhtin[14] and others have pointed out) that the dramatic dialogue of diverse spiritual types in the novel is governed by a quite different prophetic voice—that of Christ.

There is a stark opposition between the Euclidean materialist cosmology of Ivan's prophetic vision ("earthly realism") and the spiritual cosmology of Alyosha's Christian realism, a traditional teaching that Alyosha receives from his elder. While the rootless Ivan plays with modern ideological abstractions, Alyosha binds himself in loyal obedience to the authority of a traditional Russian institution—Christian monasticism, and the personal spiritual authority of the ascetic monk Zosima. Nothing stands in greater contrast to liberal European humanism than this path, although it too is subject to potential abuse, as Dostoevsky is aware.[15] It is in the particular character of the relationship between the elder and Alyosha that Dostoevsky's prophetic stance between past and future can be discerned. And that stance has everything to do with the apocalyptic reversal imaged in Revelation 5, between the conquering Lion and the suffering Lamb.

This radically traditional reversal of meaning—of how meaning is to be measured and how truth is to be discerned from lies—is cultivated in the ascetic spiritual disciplines. To those captured by a slavishly materialist vision of human freedom and fulfillment that truly isolates selves (as "rights-bearers") and kills community, the monastic way may seem isolating and constricted. The elder Zosima begs to differ:

> Obedience, fasting, and prayer are laughed at, yet they alone constitute the way to real and true freedom: I cut away my superfluous and unnecessary needs, through obedience I humble and chasten my vain and proud will, and thereby, with God's help, attain freedom of spirit and, with that, spiritual rejoicing! Which of the two is more capable of upholding and serving a great idea—the isolated rich man or one who is liberated from the tyranny of things and habits? (314)

Only one freed from the isolation of self-love can truly love others. Such freedom is made possible through spiritual rebirth in the image of Christ—that is, conformity to the "form of the servant" or "serf's garb" that builds up human community through deeds of humble love. The justice of this human community, moreover, is not to be found in the mechanics of procedural justice or "rights"—it is situated in the "consciousness of one's own conscience" (64), cultivated above all in the disciplined dialogical intimacy of personal relationship. Moral education is a matter of beautiful and good personal memories, especially in childhood and one's familial home,[16] not ideological lectures and technical scientific instruction. The justice of a community of conscience, the politics of this spiritual vision, is likewise understood, not in terms of the abstract procedural techniques of legal investigation and forensic courtroom psychology, but rather in familial, organic terms. As we shall explore in detail in Chapter 6, the elder's discussion of criminal justice defines this as paternal guidance, mother-love, brotherhood, and sonship (64–65)—a pattern he embodies in the very act of mediating as "elder" an intense familial dispute in his monastic cell, in what is effectively the opening scene of the novel's central drama (book 2).

Thus, in answer to the question raised above, it is not ascesis per se that saves—after all, *The Brothers Karamazov* also gives us the cramped, judgmental asceticism of *ressentiment* in the character of Father Ferapont, who is captured by a crudely materialist religious cosmology; and the false prophet, Ivan's Grand Inquisitor, is also a rigorous ascetic. Rather, it is ascesis in the service of the truth of

Christ that saves, a cultivation of the penitential consciousness whereby one be-comes "also guilty before all people, on behalf of all and for all, for all human sins, the world's and each person's, only then will the goal of our unity be achieved. . . . This knowledge is the crown of the monk's path, and of every man's path on earth" (164). Only conscious solidarity with the world's sin and guilt can move human hearts to participate in the divine love that seeks to reconcile the world in a peaceable harmony. This form of asceticism does not seek other-worldly purity, nor, as the elder reiterates (164, 318f.), is it afraid of human evil and injustice. It rather "keeps close company" with the heart where the measure of active love—the image of Christ—presides, taking the penitential path of con-tinual confession and suffering servanthood in which the re-creative mystery of divine love is powerfully enacted. "And what is the word of Christ without an ex-ample?" asks the elder. Alyosha's biography recollects a series of examples of the penitential life, taken from the elder's memory. They follow a common pattern: an existential revelation of the "whole truth" of life, the confession of solidarity in human guilt, repentance, forgiveness, and a turn to the path of community brought about through active, embodied love. To quote Father Zosima once again:

> Every action has its law. This is a matter of the soul, a psychological matter. In or-der to make the world over anew, people themselves must turn onto a different path psychically. Until one has indeed become the brother of all, there will be no broth-erhood. No science or self-interest will ever enable people to share their property and their rights among themselves without offense. Each will always think his share too small, and they will keep murmuring. (303)

This vision of "the truth alone," and "not earthly truth, but a higher one" (308), dies to the pursuit of retributive, mechanical justice and its alienating, isolating claims (which underlie Ivan's and the Inquisitor's rebellion), in order to be re-born into the suffering solidarity of human-divine community, where God's presence is lovingly served in all its created likenesses on the earth. It is this prophetic path, psychically and socially, that Alyosha represents. But before one can understand that this is the "heart of the whole," one must consider further the relation between prophecy and poetics in Dostoevsky's art.

## Prophecy and Poetics[17]

In her excellent monograph *The Brothers Karamazov and the Poetics of Memory,* Diane Thompson offers an illuminating interpretation of how the categories of prophecy and poetics are connected in Dostoevsky's work. Citing Aristotle's observation in *De Poetica* that causality is the distinctive feature of a good tragedy—that a tragic plot should account for action and life, happiness and misery, in its representation of discoveries and reversals (peripeties) and the motives of characters in acting as they do—Thompson, following Mikhail Bakhtin, distinguishes between the "pragmatic plot" or external side of Dostoevsky's novel (the murder mystery emplotment) and the "ideological plot."[18] The murder of the Karamazov brothers' father has to do not only with external circumstances and immediate motives (rivalry for money and love, vengeful hatred, and personal loathing) but with the worldviews or ideas of the characters, as expressed in the pro and contra of the novel. It is here that the causality of Dostoevsky's poetic art makes reference to Christian memory and moves from the genre of classical tragedy to prophetic Christian realism. In order to account for the action of the novel as a whole, including the inner and outer causality of the central event—the murder of Fyodor—it is not enough to examine the characters' ideas. It is also necessary to attend to the spiritual vision, the "higher realism" as Dostoevsky called it, of Christian memory, which structures the action of the novel. According to Thompson, this takes us beyond "ordinary causality" to the mysterious agency of divine speech and action, above all as disclosed in Scripture and preeminently in the voice of the Word made flesh. Indeed, as the epigraph signals, the mysterious pattern of death and resurrection structures the entirety of this Dostoevskian tragedy. The action in Dostoevsky's novel does not provide the "completed whole" sought by Aristotle's poetics of tragedy, as it remains open and incomplete, not yet being finished. The model it presents for imitation, then, is not transparently vindicated by ordinary, temporal causality; it requires another sort of education and confirmation, structured by faith and hope in Christ as the truth.[19]

In contrast to Thompson—who suggests that we abandon language of causality for the language of "figural meaning" (Auerbach) and symbolic pattern in order to understand Dostoevsky's prophetic art—we would argue that his poetics bears testimony to a spiritual causality characterized by the mysterious enactment of the extraordinary in the world.[20] This is in fact what the realism of biblical prophecy, in which Dostoevsky's poetics is rooted, is all about. It does not claim that faith is somehow beyond reason or that sacred history is detached from secular, mundane history or from nature.[21] Rather, it claims that the truth about the world is made, named, and sustained by divine agency—an agency that human action (in keeping with its created status *in imago dei*) is to imitate in certain regards, if it is to find happiness and true life. Yet to see this or to hear it requires a transformation of perception and attention that gives access to what is hidden and inaudible to conventional, fallen humanity. Prophecy gives expression to this transformation in the form of address—it seeks to unveil and enact what is hidden so as to reorient human thought and action with reference to the "whole truth" of God.

Let us explore the nature of this spiritual causality by following up another of Diane Thompson's suggestive observations, namely, that "Christ's parable of the sower is the master metaphor of the novel."[22] This is evident not only from the seed metaphor in the novel's epigraph but also from Father Zosima's centrally important reference to the "seed of the word of God" planted in the soul as life-giving memories, memories that bear fruit in perception and in discernment, which enacts this truth in the world.[23] For Zosima this spiritual causality of the divine word is a great mystery: "In the face of earthly truth [pravda], the enacting of eternal truth is accomplished." This word addresses us in the stories of Scripture: "Lord, what a book, what lessons! What a book is the Holy Scripture, what miracle, what power are given to man with it! Like a carven image of the world, and of man, and of human characters, and everything is named and set forth unto ages of ages. And so many mysteries resolved and revealed" (292).

Zosima goes on to exhort his fellow priests to spread this word by reading and teaching Scripture to the people, whose hearts will be shaken in response: "Only a little, a tiny seed is needed," and it will serve as a hidden reminder of the true meaning of life. Yet this word is not simply a verbal sign or moral, doctrinal "information" given by God. All creation witnesses the beauty of divine mystery by ceaselessly enacting it, "for the Word is for all, all creation and all creatures, every little leaf is striving towards the Word, sings glory to God, weeps to Christ, unbeknownst to itself, doing so through the mystery of its sinless life" (295). The spiritual causality of the divine word is present in the hidden life of all material reality, as its fundamental principle of movement. To discern this—and it can only be discerned by the eye of love ("If you love each thing, you will perceive the mystery of God in things") (319)—is to be enlightened by "the whole truth" that life itself is paradise. The connection here with the Prologue of John's gospel, the wisdom Christology of Colossians 1:15f. (cf. Hebrews 1:3), and II Corinthians 3–5 is obvious. The Word revealed in Christ is tied to the cosmic causality of all creation. The poetry of the divine Word holds together the cosmic causal structure, not Euclidean geometry or any other purely immanent principle of interpretation. Yet what is unveiled continues to be a mystery; hence the difficulty of perceiving it and being reconciled fully with it. It is not a causality under human control or mastery—scientific, artistic, or philosophical. This brings us to the climax of Zosima's seminal vision, which underlies the novel:

> Much on earth has been concealed from us, but in place of it we have been granted
> a secret, mysterious sense of our living bond with the other world, with the higher
> heavenly world, and the roots of our thoughts and feelings are not here but in other

worlds. That is why philosophers say it is impossible on earth to conceive the
essence of things. God took seeds from other worlds and sowed them on this earth,
and raised up his garden; and everything that could sprout sprouted, but it lives and
grows only through its sense of being in touch with other mysterious worlds; if this
sense is weakened or destroyed in you, that which has grown up in you dies. Then
you become indifferent to life, and even come to hate it. So I think. (320)

This is, in fact, the central prophetic claim of the novel: that only by dying to the
isolation of immanent earthly realism can one become alive to life itself and thus
"bear fruit." It is a vision that reverses the cosmologies and ideologies of modernity no less than it did the expectations of Jews and Greeks in Jesus' time.

The elder speaks here out of a deep internalization of the biblical word, and
this is worth pondering further. The word that stands for "secret" or "mystery"
*(mysterion)* is used in the synoptic gospels in only one context—the parable of
the sower and the seed (Matthew 13; Mark 4; Luke 8), which concerns the mystery of the kingdom of God as proclaimed by Jesus. Parable is the characteristic
form of speech in Jesus' proclamation, as Matthew's gospel points out: "Indeed
he said nothing to them without a parable" so as to bring to prophetic utterance
"what has been hidden since the foundation of the world" (Matthew 13:34–35).
Of course, there is something highly ironic about unveiling what is hidden by
means of parabolic speech, which is itself designed to preserve the hiddenness of
its meaning. As the parable about the form and process of parabling (both as
speech and as a way of life), the parable of the sower and the seed brings this
irony into explicit focus: "so that seeing they may not perceive, and hearing they
may not understand."[24] There is an attempt here to reflect on the mystery of spiritual causality—why some see and others do not, despite their living in a common, shared reality; what it means to understand what is hidden in experience
and in speech; and how to respond to the strong resistance to (not merely passive
ignorance of) prophetic parabolic speech and action.

Dostoevsky's novel, we suggest, is also a reflection on this mystery. As in the
gospel interpretations of the parable, Dostoevsky places his reflection in an apocalyptic setting: the "realism" of faith and its response to the divinely given miracle
that faith alone can see; the authority of the image and law of Christ in the cosmos
but also in the heart, which makes proper discernment of the truth possible; the
mysterious cosmic struggle between God and the devil that goes on in the ordinary events of daily life and makes human choice so fateful. For Dostoevsky, as for
the gospels, the hiddenness is *necessary* for divine unveiling to occur—the light is
being revealed in the darkness and yet it cannot be discerned by those who continue to dwell in the darkness of the old order of death. Hence the resistance to the
Word by those who dwell in the old order and refuse to die to it.[25]

The hiddenness of apocalyptic realism can also be seen in the indirectness of speech that bears witness to it. We see this, for example, in the highly mediated relay of witnesses in the book of Revelation (1:1–2): "The revelation of Jesus Christ, which God gave him to show to his servants what must soon take place; and he made it known by sending his angel to his servant John, who bore witness to the word of God and to the testimony of Jesus Christ, even to all that he saw." A similar relay of witnesses is present in the remembered "Life of the Hieromonk and Elder Zosima," which is introduced by a fictional narrator; consists of Alyosha's written retrospective taken from previous conversations and addresses; and focuses upon the elder's memories of conversations and events, many of which took place long ago in his own life, in response to Scripture, prophetic messengers, and mysterious visitors.[26] To participate in the unveiling of the hidden truth requires patient dialogue and the disciplines entailed in a difficult quest, on which is staked nothing less than the whole of life. It cannot be had directly—God's mysterious, hidden love seeks to "form a heart," as Kierkegaard puts it in *Works of Love,* from which proceed the visible fruits that bear witness to its truth.

The parable of sower and seed is here explicitly connected to the death and resurrection pattern expressed in John 12:24. Both sower and seed must die in order to be reborn into new life, new vision—what John Dominic Crossan rightly calls the "self-abnegation of the sower."[27] This is not, however, simply a rhetorical, aesthetic, or even moral requirement. The *mysterion* of God, as Paul asserts in I Corinthians 2, cannot be proclaimed in lofty rhetoric of worldly wisdom, for it is ultimately (and materially) expressed in the crucified Christ; its causal power is tied to a mysterious, hidden wisdom, which must be spiritually discerned.[28] This wisdom is visible in the world as death, and yet for those with eyes to see, it lives even now, beyond death. The *mysterion* of the bodily transformation from death (the man of dust) to life (the man from heaven) is, for Paul, at the heart of divine causality—the end of all things (I Corinthians 15). Paul uses the agricultural (not mechanistic or artistic) metaphor of seed to express this mysterious transformation from death to life in the cosmic drama. The mysterious meaning and end of human existence in the world is of a piece with the order created by God, the dynamism of which is the continual self-giving gift of God's creative Spirit (not mechanism, not human making or rhetoric—"for the kingdom of God is not in talk but in power") that enlivens the world through love.

By now it should be evident why Dostoevsky's poetics cannot conform to Aristotle's requirements. The action "as a whole" that Dostoevsky's art imitates (and in which it elicits the reader's imitative participation) has as its end the completion of all things in the life and action of God. It cannot therefore be fully disclosed by any one event or story, since it concerns the whole of the whole, which is a length too great to be "taken in by the memory"[29] or comprehended by a human causal account. It can only be unveiled by a willing participation in the action itself, whereby the Word is enacted and takes root in the particularities of the here and now. Dostoevsky's novel is intended to witness to this spiritual motion and its causality: "All is like an ocean, all flows and connects; touch it in one place and it echoes at the other end of the world" (319).

Also present in *The Brothers Karamazov* is another kind of seed, indicative of another kind of agency and spiritual causality—seeds of evil action, darkness, and forgetting. As the devil suggests to Ivan: "I will sow just a tiny seed of faith in you, and from it an oak will grow—and such an oak that you, sitting in that oak, will want to join the desert fathers and the blameless women" (645). The seeds sown by principalities and powers of darkness also have real effects in the world: They take root in the heart and give rise to lying parodies of the truth and to destructive deeds. As the elder puts it:

> See, here you have passed by a small child, passed by in anger, with a foul word, with a wrathful soul; you perhaps did not notice the child, but he saw you, and your unsightly and impious image has remained in his defenceless heart. You did not know it, but you may thereby have planted a bad seed in him, and it may grow . . . because you did not nurture in yourself a heedful, active love. Brothers, love is a teacher, but one must know how to acquire it, for it is difficult to acquire, it is dearly bought, by long work over a long time. (319)

The earthly father of the brothers Karamazov, Fyodor, literally sows the seeds of his own destruction by fathering in the same year the two sons—Ivan and Smerdyakov—responsible for his murder.[30] This is not simply a genetic or biological "sowing"; it is also, above all, a spiritual begetting. As Smerdyakov comments to Ivan in their third and final meeting, when the truth is finally spoken between them:

> You love money, that I know, sir, you also love respect, because you're very proud, you love women's charms exceedingly, and most of all you love living in peaceful prosperity, without bowing to anyone—that you love most of all, sir. . . . You're like Fyodor Pavlovich most of all, it's you of all his children who came out resembling him most, having the same soul as him, sir. (632)

Of course, Smerdyakov most craves the affirmation and approval of Ivan. The two of them (to Ivan's disgust and outrage) have much in common, as rivals and co-conspirators. Smerdyakov confronts Ivan with their complicity: "You killed him, you are the main killer, and I was just your minion, your faithful servant Licharda, and I performed the deed according to your word" (623). Ivan's atheistic teachings have taken effective root in Smerdyakov's receptive, murderous heart; unlike Ivan, who reserves murderous latitude only in his wishes, Smerdyakov carries them out in action. The two form a symbiotic community in horrible fulfillment of Ivan's parody of Paul's statement (in I Corinthians) that "everything is permitted":

> "It's true what you taught me, sir, because you told me a lot about that then: because if there's no infinite God, then there's no virtue either, and no need of it at all. It was true. That's how I reasoned."
> "Did you figure it out for yourself?" Ivan grinned crookedly.
> "With your guidance, sir." (632)

The power of an example of the word, whether of light or of darkness, of life or of death, is poetically enacted in the novel. It comes to explicit focus in the courtroom, where the question of exemplary fatherhood is taken up at the level of motivational psychology and moral (criminal) responsibility. As the novel makes clear, however, the question cannot be properly answered in the modern courtroom, precisely because of its inadequate assumptions about spiritual causality. Human moral psychology and agency must be considered within the larger cosmic canvas of divine causality if they are to be properly discerned. This cosmic context is the apocalyptic struggle between the kingdom of light and the kingdom of darkness. Prophecy, as an unveiling of the truth about God, is also an unveiling (and judgment) of idols—false images of divine purpose and truth, and a false naming of reality. Indeed, as both John of Patmos and Dostoevsky emphasize, demonic powers of darkness often perform their mysterious and seductive arts through concealment. The proclamation of the prophetic word seeks to reveal the "god of this world" who has blinded the minds of people and deceived the nations, in the light of Christ who is "the likeness of God" (II Corinthians 4:4).

I have suggested that Dostoevsky's apocalyptic poetics is more than a matter of literary form or artistic representation—it is rooted in what might be called a "metaphysics of apocalypse."[31] Liza Knapp begins her fine monograph, *The Annihilation of Inertia: Dostoevsky and Metaphysics,* by citing a famous passage from Dostoevsky's private journal, written on Holy Thursday, 1864, in the presence of his first wife's corpse: "Masha is lying on the table. Will I see Masha again?"[32] The question is followed by a lengthy meditation on the conflict between the law of individual egoism, which answers the question in the negative, and the law of Christ that commands love of another person "as one's own self," which is the "highest goal" of individual selfhood and the "final goal" of all humanity—the "paradise of Christ." Only the latter path, which overcomes the resistance of the

law of fallen human nature, can answer the question affirmatively in the hope of
resurrection beyond death. History is characterized by the struggle between these
two laws—one of death and one of life. The real metaphysical or philosophical
question is which law is ultimately true: that life must end in death as the final
transition, or that death to the individual, mortal "I" can lead to a transition beyond death, to life eternal? What law fundamentally governs the transition?

In his meditation, Dostoevsky connects the law of Christlike love to the openness of human nature. He surmises that human life on earth is in a transitional
state, striving to attain its goal, a goal that remains hidden and unknown just as
God's nature remains unknown. However, according to "the law of our history,"
Christ revealed one important trait of the future paradisal state of resurrected
humanity: "They neither marry nor are given in marriage, but are like angels in
heaven" (Matthew 22:30). This eschatological trait is "profoundly significant," not
in suggesting that mortal relationships and bodily continuity are insignificant. To
the contrary, "the family is the most sacred thing of man on earth" in preserving
human openness to the future and in fostering the transition from egoism to
other-love. And yet it too remains egoistic and exclusivist, it cultivates isolation
from the whole, it seeks a private peaceful prosperity that loves only what is
"one's own." Within this most sacred of natural institutions, then, the cosmic
conflict of laws also rages, a conflict from which the attainment of the goal of life
through full participation in the divine nature will free us. This "rebirth" into the
form of divine life will entail the end of family life and its temporal struggles:
"There, being is a full synthesis, eternally taking pleasure and being fulfilled, and
therefore, time will no longer exist." The law of this divine nature stands in contrast to fallen human nature above all in the quality of love, which dwells in the
perfection of eternal harmony even in multiplicity—in contrast to human love,
which clings to its divided partiality even as it seeks unity (a tragic struggle).
Likewise, the ordered truth of divine wisdom stands in contrast to the multiplicity and partiality of human science, which tries to build up an account of the
whole from partial fragments of knowledge (an endless struggle).

The law of Christ, states Dostoevsky, is the earthly incarnation of the divine
law of nature and thus imprints a temporal memory of the goal or end of human
life, of its final, completed nature. What form this nature will take, of course, "is
difficult for man to imagine definitely," not least because it has not yet fully become our nature. For it to become our nature requires the ongoing sacrifice of
one's "I" to others, in the ongoing context of suffering and human fallenness.
Hence Christ brings no easy, consoling peace but the prophetic sword; he clarifies
the conflictual truth of the transitional character of earthly life. As *The Brothers
Karamazov* makes abundantly clear, and we argue in the chapter on "The Third
Temptation," Dostoevsky was not a defender of the traditional Russian family as

the solution to modern social problems. Instead, he sought to discern the tragic character of the family's earthly struggle in the light of apocalyptic causality.

Throughout his meditation, Dostoevsky conducts a polemical debate with those he terms "the antichrists," who attack Christian teaching at certain crucial points. They mistakenly think they refute Christianity by pointing to the lack of fulfillment of its hopes for universal community, not realizing that Christ himself clarifies the transitional character of earthly existence prior to its eternal fulfillment beyond death. Further, "they say that man is destroyed and dies *completely*," and yet human experience of biological procreation and memory, the complex processes of human personality and its historical development, contradict such an assertion. That Christ has entered and left a definitive memory of the human end is a part of this natural process, and clarifies it prophetically. Finally, Dostoevsky ends his reflection by starkly juxtaposing the metaphysical alternatives: "The teaching of the materialists—universal inertia and the mechanization of matter—means death. The teaching of true philosophy is the annihilation of inertia, that is thought, that is the center and Synthesis of the universe and its outer form—matter, that is God, that is eternal life." The account of nature and its laws that is dead to the spiritual causality of divine life, that reduces nature to matter, has as its last word for human beings (as for all forms of life) death. Such forms of naturalism—whether Newtonian inertia, Euclidean geometry, or the determinism of Claude Bernard's materialism—are mired in an understanding that Paul the Apostle called *psychikos* ("natural human being"), which attends in its fallenness only to outer material form or the "things of the flesh." Indeed the naturalism of the unregenerate *psychikos* is more accurately called *sarkikos* or "material human being," incapable of spiritual discernment (see I Corinthians 2–3) and ultimately tied to "this body of death" (Romans 7:24).

By contrast, "true philosophy"—spiritual wisdom given by God—annihilates such inertial abstractions with reference to a living image of spiritual discernment, a memory of the end as the "all in all" of divine being. This wisdom stands in conflict with the "law of sin and death" and claims the power to free human beings from "bondage to decay," by life-giving love. The higher realism of Christian faith is put painfully to the test in the presence of corpses—as is evident in the tears of Jesus at Lazarus's tomb, Alyosha's lament over the stinking decomposition of the elder Zosima's body, and the copious weeping at the child Ilyusha's funeral. The natural process of putrefaction provides powerful sensory evidence of the material disintegration of human selves, and Dostoevsky was not one to romanticize it. The question of bodily, material reality and how it is related to the spiritual causality of "life itself" is therefore a crucial question for Christian faith, and especially for its apocalyptic teaching of the resurrection. The question of which law finally governs reality is at the heart of the pro and contra of Dostoevsky's novel: the external law of nature and the egoistic self-assertion of the fallen natural will, or the spiritual law of divine providence and the "unnatural" law of Christ, which recreates the world in order to bring about the goal of living union with the divine Creator.

This eschatological tension is beautifully embodied in Dostoevsky's poetics. It is foreshadowed in *The Brothers Karamazov*, in a chapter entitled "Father Ferapont," after a materialist religious ascetic, who no less than the proponents of atheistic materialism is depicted as "an extremely dangerous adversary" of the elder Zosima and his vision of penitential love. The chapter begins with the elder "pouring out his heart" to all the monks:

> Love one another, fathers . . . . Love God's people. For we are not holier than those
> in the world because we have come here and shut ourselves within these walls, but,
> on the contrary, anyone who comes here, by the very fact that he has come, already
> knows himself to be worse than all those who are in the world. . . . But when he
> knows that he is not only worse than all those in the world, but is also guilty before
> all people, on behalf of all and for all, for all human sins, the world's and each per-
> son's, only then will the goal of our unity be achieved. . . . Only then will our hearts
> be moved to a love that is infinite, universal, and that knows no satiety. Then each
> of us will be able to gain the whole world by love and wash away the world's sins
> with his tears. (164)

Here we have a clear expression of the penitential consciousness that sacrifices the "I" in order to participate in the loving movement of the whole; it is the prophetic path of the monk. Immediately following this ecstatic homily (afterward, the narrator tells us, "they all remembered these words"), great excitement is generated among the monks by news that one of the elder's prophetic words to a peasant woman the day before (that her son, from whom she had no news for a year, was still alive and would either come or send a letter shortly) has literally come true. The news of this "miracle of prediction" is taken as a great sign of the elder's prophetic power, and many of the monks wish to rush out and tell everyone about it.

So begins the chapter depicting Father Ferapont, that "great ascetic" and keeper of silence who "rarely appeared at liturgy," cultivating an eccentric and intriguing regime of monastic solitude. Despite his advanced age and "undoubtedly great fasting," Ferapont appears vigorous and healthy (in contrast to the frail and ailing Zosima). Though a keeper of silence, Ferapont occasionally engages curious visitors in conversations in which he is "brief, curt, strange, and almost always rude." His speech also betrays that he is in constant communication with "heavenly spirits," which presumably accounts for his ability to see devils everywhere—"I see, I see throughout"—and especially among the less ascetic monks who "can't do without their bread here." There is a marked contrast between Ferapont's fearmongering and mystification and, at the end of the chapter, the prophetic words of Father Paissy (elder Zosima's associate, who "adopts" Alyosha from his dying mentor) to Alyosha, words that "made a rather strong and unexpected impression" on him:

> Remember, young man, unceasingly . . . that the science of this world, having united itself unto a great force, has, especially in the last century, examined everything heavenly that has been bequeathed to us in sacred books, and, after hard analysis, the learned ones of this world have absolutely nothing left of what was once holy. But they have examined parts and missed the whole, and their blindness is even worthy of wonder. Meanwhile the whole stands before their eyes as immovably as ever, and the gates of hell shall not prevail against it. . . . Even in the movements of the souls of those same all-destroying atheists, it lives, as before, immovably! For those who renounce Christianity and rebel against it are in their essence of the same image of the same Christ, and such they remain, for until now neither their wisdom nor the ardor of their hearts has been able to create another, higher image of man and his dignity than the image shown of old by Christ. (171)

These prophetic words are intended to prepare Alyosha for "the temptations of the world"—not so much in the naive form of distorted religious apocalypticism as in the form of rational scientific materialism, which has become powerful among the institutional and technological authorities of modern secular culture. Modern science of this sort cultivates isolation, for it methodologically excludes the spiritual whole. By contrast, Alyosha's monasticism in the world will point to an alternative, life-giving vision of the meaning and end of human existence—a vision founded on the model of worthiness of the slain Lamb.

Alyosha's prophetic embodiment of this spiritual type is foretold in the elder's commissioning: "You will go forth from these walls, but you will sojourn in the world like a monk. You will have many opponents, but your very enemies will love you. Life will bring you many misfortunes, but through them you will be happy, and you will bless life and cause others to bless it—which is the most important thing" (285). The elder declares that Alyosha's face has been both a reminder (a memory) and a prophecy (an expectation) of the spiritual path to the heart of the whole for all people. Alyosha's "brotherly countenance" will resurrect others and build community wherever he goes.

We appropriately conclude this introductory chapter with a word about the beginning and end of *The Brothers Karamazov* (as we know, beginnings and endings are always intimately related in apocalyptic literature): In the prefatory note from the author (3–4), we are told that there are really "two novels"—one concerning the memory of things past, and the "main novel," the second one, about the hero "in our time, that is, in our present, current moment." This cunning comment has occasioned all manner of speculation on Dostoevsky's possible plans for another novel having been precluded by his untimely death. But such Euclidean speculation remains tone deaf to Dostoevsky's prophetic voice, which warns and beckons to the reader: "Having acquainted himself with the first story, the reader can decide for himself whether it is worth his while to begin the second" (4). The first novel itself will judge the reader's response by whether or not she or he can echo the children's ecstatic cry at the end of the first novel: "Memory eternal! . . . And eternally so, all our lives hand in hand! Hurrah for Karamazov!" And thus might it become possible to take up the second novel, the drama of our own lives, in a manner that shapes the future of this present moment by remembering the end. That, in any case, is the possibility explored in this book.

# Notes

1. See George Steiner, *Tolstoy or Dostoyevsky: An Essay in the Old Criticism* (New York: Penguin, 1959), especially chapter 4.

2. Martin Buber, "Prophecy, Apocalyptic, and the Historical Hour," in *Pointing the Way*, ed. and trans. M. Friedman (New York: Schocken, 1957), pp. 192–207. See also Douglas Robinson, "Literature and Apocalyptic," in *The Encyclopedia of Apocalypticism*, vol. 3 (New York: Continuum, 1998), pp. 360–391.

3. Buber, "Prophecy, Apocalyptic, and the Historical Hour," p. 200.

4. In his explanatory note to the Pushkin speech (also published in the August 1880 issue of *A Writer's Diary*), Dostoevsky states that he wanted to make "four points about Pushkin's significance for Russia." I have conflated the first two (negative and positive types of the Russian character) and the second two (Pushkin's capacity to reincarnate the genius of other nations, a capacity that is unique to the Russian spirit). See Fyodor Dostoevsky, *A Writer's Diary*, vol. 2: *1877–1881*, trans. K. Lantz (Evanston, Ill.: Northwestern University Press, 1994), pp. 1271–1295.

5. Ibid., pp. 1287–1288.

6. Ibid., p. 1289.

7. Ibid., p. 1290.

8. Ibid., p. 1293.

9. Ibid., p. 1294.

10. See letters 871, 872, and 875 in Fyodor Dostoevsky, *Complete Letters*, vol. 5: *1878–1881*, ed. David Lowe (Ann Arbor, Mich.: Ardis, 1991).

11. Fyodor Dostoevsky, *The Brothers Karamazov*, trans. Richard Pevear and Larissa Volokhonsky (New York: Vintage, 1990), p. 3. Hereafter, references to this work appear within the narrative, inside parentheses.

12. See Dostoevsky, *Complete Letters*, vol. 5, letters 784, 785, 791, and 807.

13. See the superb discussion of Ivan's *poemka* in Robert Louis Jackson, *The Art of Dostoevsky: Deliriums and Nocturnes* (Princeton: Princeton University Press, 1981), chap. 14.

14. Mikhail Bakhtin, *Problems of Dostoevsky's Poetics*, ed. and trans. Caryl Emerson (Minneapolis: University of Minnesota Press, 1984), p. 97f. As has been shown in several important recent studies, Bakhtin's approach is itself rooted in the Johannine theology of the Russian Orthodox tradition and the Christological formulations of conciliar theology. See especially Alexander Mihailovic, *Corporeal Words: Mikhail Bakhtin's Theology of Discourse* (Evanston, Ill.: Northwestern University Press, 1997); Charles Lock, "Carnival and Incarnation: Bakhtin and Orthodox Theology," in *Critical Essays on Mikhail Bakhtin*, ed. Caryl Emerson (New York: G. K. Hall, 1999).

15. His narrator states, "It is also true, perhaps, that this tested and already thousand-year-old instrument for the moral regeneration of man from slavery to freedom and to moral perfection may turn into a double-edged weapon, which may lead a person not to humility and ultimate self-control but, on the contrary, to the most satanic pride—that is, to fetters and not to freedom" (29). There is for Dostoevsky no formulaic path to harmony and happiness, since the path is mediated by human freedom.

16. Such memories pervade the novel, and this theory of moral education is thematized both by the elder and by Alyosha. The elder states: "No memories are more precious to a man than those of his earliest childhood in his parental home, and that is almost always so, as long as there is even a little bit of love and unity in the family. But from a very bad family, too, one can keep precious memories, if only one's soul knows how to seek out what is precious. With my memories of home I count also my memories of sacred history" (290). In his address to the boys, at the novel's end, Alyosha repeats this teaching: "My dear children, perhaps you will not understand what I am going to say to you, because I often speak very incomprehensibly, but still you will remember and some day agree with my words. You must know that there is nothing higher, or stronger, or sounder, or more useful afterwards in life, than some good memory, especially a memory from childhood, from the parental home. You hear a lot said about your education, yet some such beautiful, sacred memory, preserved from childhood, is perhaps the best education" (774).

17. For good discussions of this relation and the history of interpretation, see Abraham J. Heschel, *The Prophets*, vol. 2 (New York: Harper and Row, 1962), chapter 11: "Prophecy and Poetic Inspiration"; and David Jeffrey, *People of the Book* (Grand Rapids, Mich.: William B. Eerdmans, 1996).

18. Diane Oenning Thompson, *The Brothers Karamazov and the Poetics of Memory* (Cambridge: Cambridge University Press, 1991), chap. 3. See also Bakhtin, *Problems of Dostoevsky's Poetics*. Bakhtin's important thesis is that Dostoevsky's "internally dialogic" approach to the represented consciousness of his characters is tied to "a dialogicality of the ultimate whole" (Ibid., p. 18), which is not formed by a single, unified monological consciousness but by polyphonic openness to endless dialogue. Hence Dostoevsky's poetics is not tied to a "mono-ideational framework" such as characterizes post-Enlightenment representational theories of human consciousness but to the embodiment of the plurality of voices—the dialogue—in which consciousness itself is thoroughly dialogical. Dostoevsky's art, then, is not an attempt to represent an ideal or even an idea of the real; it is an act of dialogical address in which dialogue is "not a means but an end, not threshold to action but the action itself, not a means for self-revelation but becoming who one is" (Ibid., p. 252).

19. This is in keeping with David Jeffrey's account of the literary "grammar" of the Old Testament prophets, in which the subtext continually interrupts and overlaps the surface text of historical narrative. Regarding this subtext of divine speech, Jeffrey suggests: "This text is not, in any wooden way, the literal codex of the Torah, but its incorporated sub-

stance as ethical vision. It is the psychological memory, the story within that comments upon and interprets the story without. It is not simply the record of unfolding present historical events but rather the playbook of sacred memory and dream" ("How to Read the Hebrew Prophets," in *Mappings of the Biblical Terrain: The Bible as Text,* eds. V. Tollers and J. Maier [Lewisburg, Pa.: Bucknell University Press, 1990], p. 293).

20. Our argument here is not so much with Eric Auerbach's description of "figural interpretation" as with Thompson's view of it—though the two are related. Auerbach says of the figural connection between the sacrifice of Isaac and the sacrifice of Christ that "a connection is established between the two events which are linked neither temporally nor causally"—that is, they are not linked on a horizontal plane (*Mimesis: The Representation of Reality in Western Literature,* trans. Willard Trask [Princeton: Princeton University Press, 1953], p. 73). Their linkage is vertical—to Divine Providence. In contrast to Auerbach's insistence on the concurrence of both levels, Thompson divides them, succumbing to one of the pitfalls of figural interpretation in the modern context, as described in Hans W. Frei, *The Eclipse of Biblical Narrative: A Study in Eighteenth- and Nineteenth-Century Hermeneutics* (New Haven: Yale University Press, 1974), p. 29f. In Auerbach's account of figural interpretation, to comprehend mimetically is a spiritual act: "The two poles of a figure are separated in time, but both, being real events or persons, are situated within temporality. They are both contained in the flowing stream which is historical life, and only the comprehension, the *intellectus spiritualis,* of their interdependence is a spiritual act" (Auerbach, *Mimesis,* p. 73; cf. Auerbach, "Figura," in *Scenes from the Drama of European Literature* [Minneapolis: University of Minnesota Press, 1984], p. 57). Figural interpretation is thus understood as a spiritual act that deals with real events experientially rather than in conceptual abstraction. It differs from allegory and myth in its emphasis on the historical, but it does not accede to the self-sufficient provisionality of modern historicism, which treats historical events as "steps in an unbroken horizontal process" ("Figura," p. 59). In contrast, figural history points to the spiritual depth of reality for its causal meaning. This is precisely what makes it prophetic: "Figural prophecy implies the interpretation of one worldly event through another; the first signifies the second, the second fulfills the first. Both remain historical events; yet both, looked at in this way, have something provisional and incomplete about them; they point to one another and both point to something in the future, something still to come, which will be the actual, real, and definitive event. . . . Thus history, with all its concrete force, remains forever a figure, cloaked and needful of interpretation" ("Figura," p. 58). That is, the temporal participates in and points toward the eternal for its meaning—a meaning that requires spiritual attentiveness and imitation if it is to be understood. This view is compatible with a Christological understanding of Bakhtin's important concept of the "unfinalizability" of the living Word that echoes in Dostoevsky's dialogical art.

21. These are Thompson's claims, it seems—though they are subtly stated. We are indebted to her very fine interpretation, and agree with her claim that: "The Christian redemptive pattern is a complete inversion of the classical plot, structurally and semantically. It begins from a fallen state (sin, pride, wrongdoing). The keystone of its structure rests on its definition of discovery as a recognition (a memory) of 'eternal verity', and peripety as a spiritual renewal upon acceptance of that truth. It culminates in a fundamental spiritual change in one's life, in the way one lives in the world. The Christian pattern is reversible, or is always potentially so, in that while a tragedy cannot be undone, it can be atoned. The classical tragedy is irreversible. In the Christian view, suffering is re-

demptive, in the classical, it is irreducible" (Thompson, *The Brothers Karamazov*, p. 70). However, we do not accept that the classical pattern is the only way to define rational causality and that (therefore) "the Christian memory structure" offers a symbolic pattern that transcends "the limitations of reason" (Ibid.). Nor do we agree that Dostoevsky "aimed to transcend the mundane world of cause and effect into a world of art where the divine can be poetically represented" (Ibid., p. 72). This leads inevitably to a separation between history and nature, as in Thompson's stated agreement with Ernst Cassirer's comment, "Nature can offer no support to the prophetic consciousness" (Ibid., p. 261). This approach ultimately must concede reason and nature—indeed, the realm of "causality"— to what is humanly measured and controlled. Dostoevsky wanted to show the moral and spiritual bankruptcy of such forms of humanism, and to place causality (and reason and nature) into the context of divine action and speech. This critical point may be overly subtle, but I believe it is important, especially in the realm of political morality.

22. Ibid., p. 13.

23. See especially section (b) of Alyosha's "Life of Elder Zosima," in Dostoevsky, *The Brothers Karamazov*, trans. Pevear and Volokhonsky, p. 290f.

24. Luke 8:10. There are many good studies of parables in the New Testament, many of which (not surprisingly) are in disagreement. One disagreement, in particular, directly affects our interpretation of Dostoevsky's poetics as "prophetic realism," and more specifically, as apocalyptic. Our interpretation is in keeping with those who view Jesus's parables as apocalyptic—see especially Joel Marcus, *The Mystery of the Kingdom of God* (Atlanta: Scholars Press, 1986); also N. T. Wright, *Jesus and the Victory of God* (Minneapolis: Fortress Press, 1996). There are those, foremost among them John Dominic Crossan, who read the eschatology of the parables as *anti*-apocalyptic (see Crossan, *Cliffs of Fall: Paradox and Polyvalence in the Parables of Jesus* [New York: Seabury Press, 1980]; idem, *In Parables: The Challenge of the Historical Jesus* [New York: Harper and Row, 1973]). At issue here is the definition of *apocalyptic*, which has been disputed in New Testament studies ever since Albert Schweitzer's groundbreaking *The Quest of the Historical Jesus*. How one defines *apocalyptic* will shape one's assumptions about the nature of reality, and in particular, of historical and natural causality. When *apocalyptic* is interpreted as crude, otherworldly literalism that seeks to predict (in determinist, monolithic fashion) the imminent "end of history" in complete discontinuity with "ordinary" human experience, it will remain a difficult category to appropriate in anything other than a rather far-fetched literary genre suitable for cranks and fundamentalists. When apocalyptic is treated purely as a literary genre in which human beings unveil the poetic structures of their own imagination, as in the Romantic tradition of William Blake and Northrop Frye, it will have as its primary reference the inner life of human consciousness and its imaginative constructs. In the first case, the apocalyptic is an externalized, transcendent literalism having to do with extrinsic, divine agency; in the second, it is an internalized, allegorical process of the divine human imagination. Dostoevsky's writing permits neither of these interpretations, although his artistic position contains elements of both. Although he was influenced by the Romantic tradition and its attention to embodied human feeling, passion, and consciousness, Dostoevsky rejected its immanent humanism—the view that the human imagination is itself divine and capable of self-salvation through aesthetic creativity and erotic self-purification. It is not the agency of human consciousness that dramatically animates nature; it is the agency of God. Dmitri must repent of his self-actualizing romanticism if he is to be saved from cynicism and despair. As I have already suggested, the figure of Fa-

ther Ferapont is sufficient evidence of the spiritual bankruptcy of literalist apocalypticism. Yet Dostoevsky is convinced that divine agency and its spiritual counterparts are a reality that transcends human imagination. The claims of the Bible concerning the beginning and end of all creation provide a definitive framework—points of orientation, and standards of judgment or discernment—for interpreting history and human experience in the world "as a whole." These claims are not simply human constructs but represent the unveiling of the underlying or ultimate meaning of reality by divine speech and action, in terms that lie beyond human control and capacity. They exert real causal power, both in word and in deed, though not in any mechanical or arbitrary or univocal manner. This is in keeping with the hermeneutics of apocalyptic prophetic realism.

25. Paul also refers to the hardening process in Romans 11—the violent resistance and opposition to the revelation of divine mystery—as a *mysterion* (11:25). Paul speaks of this, as does Matthew (13:14f.), in language borrowed from the prophet Isaiah (Isaiah 6), with the assurance that even blasphemous resistance to the divine Word nevertheless bears witness to divinely given spiritual causality and the critical judgment evoked by its presence. This view is also evident in Alyosha's first response to Ivan's "The Grand Inquisitor": "Your poem praises Jesus, it doesn't revile him . . . as you meant it to" [p. 52 below].

26. Sergei Hackel takes this indirectness and "distancing" as a sign of Dostoevsky's religious doubt and reticence about Orthodox Christianity, and believes that Dostoevsky's art may in fact be a thin Christian veneer for a kind of pagan natural mysticism. At the very least, in Hackel's view, it *reduces* the eschatological intensity of the biblical teaching on the kingdom of God (Hackel, "The Religious Dimension: Vision or Evasion? Zosima's Discourse in *The Brothers Karamazov*," in *Fyodor Dostoevsky*, ed. H. Bloom [New York: Chelsea House, 1989], pp. 211–235). Hackel misreads the theological meaning of indirectness and reticence here (just as so many have misunderstood the silence of Christ)—namely, that no one can see God "face to face" and live, that the approach to God entails a richly mediated and disciplined path, and the "unveiling" requires patient waiting and active love. Divine truth resists the lust for immediate gratification and easy fulfillment.

27. Crossan, *Cliffs of Fall*, p. 50f. However, we fail to see why such self-abnegation necessarily implies, as Crossan suggests, the priority of text over author (Ibid., p. 58). It would seem that precisely such attempts to detach form from content, speech from action, and proclamation from person, contradict prophetic parabolic causality.

28. "For the kingdom of God does not consist in talk but in power," says Paul in I Corinthians 4:20. This power consists in the humility of following in the path of the crucified Christ, and seeking understanding through the difficult practice of suffering love. In Dostoevsky's novel, this is embodied in the often inarticulate, tongue-tied Alyosha, who nevertheless is the powerful hero of the story—in deed, but also at the end, in an inspired word, inspired by the example of his elder, who is in turn inspired by Markel and by Scripture. In contrast, Dmitri can only begin to live with purpose and meaningful direction once his seductive rhetorical excess (expressed above all in the poetry of the Romantics) has been humbled by repentance and confession. Ivan the articulate intellectual, the artful writer of articles and prose poems, is unable to act decisively throughout the novel, despite his high-flown rhetoric. He suffers from an illness that only Alyosha begins (in prayer) to understand at the end of the novel: "The torments of a proud decision, a deep conscience! God, in whom he did not believe, and his truth were overcoming his heart, which still did not want to submit" (655).

29. See Aristotle, *De Poetica*, trans. Ingram Bywater, in *Introduction to Aristotle*, ed. Richard McKeon (New York: Modern Library, 1947), p. 634 [1451].

30. See the discussion in Thompson, *The Brothers Karamazov*, p. 129f.

31. This is the language used in David Toole, *Waiting for Godot in Sarajevo: Theological Reflections on Nihilism, Tragedy, and Apocalypse* (Boulder: Westview, 1998), chap. 7.

32. Liza Knapp, *The Annihilation of Inertia: Dostoevsky and Metaphysics* (Evanston, Ill.: Northwestern University Press, 1996), p. 2. Joseph Frank offers a description and an analysis of the vigil and journal entry in his *Dostoevsky: The Stir of Liberation, 1860–1865* (Princeton: Princeton University Press, 1986), chap. 20. An English translation of the passage may be found in *The Unpublished Dostoevsky: Diaries and Notebooks (1860–81)*, ed. Carl Proffer (Ann Arbor, Mich.: Ardis, 1973), vol. 1, pp. 39–41.

# two

# Dostoevsky's
# "The Grand Inquisitor"

In Russia, Dostoevsky's reputation as a prophet initially owed most to the speech on Pushkin that he delivered shortly before his death; in the West, however, that reputation has always rested primarily on the chapter in *The Brothers Karamazov* entitled "The Grand Inquisitor." The list of major Western thinkers of the twentieth century who have attested to the great significance "The Grand Inquisitor" had for them is long and includes Freud, Wittgenstein, Heidegger, Sartre, and Camus. The relative absence of theologians from the list is notable, and seemingly indicates an opportunity missed by modern Western religious thinkers. In contrast, the Russian religious thinker Berdyaev, writing early in the century, not only considered Dostoevsky's art "extraordinarily fruitful as a prophetic presentation of the highest spiritual possibilities" but also insisted that "The Grand Inquisitor" specifically contains "the best of the constructive part of Dostoevsky's religious ideas."[1]

Dostoevsky himself called "The Grand Inquisitor" the "culminating point" of *The Brothers Karamazov.*[2] As such, it could also be considered the culminating point of both his art and his religious thought, the text in which his prophecy and his poetics come together in the most compact intensity. It is the axis around which our reflection in this book revolves. For this reason, and because there is no substitute for the text itself, we have included the entire chapter in our book. Readers thus will be able more easily to reflect with us on Dostoevsky's most prophetic text rather than being always at the third remove of reflecting on our reflection.

The obvious convenience for readers outweighs, in our view, the equally obvious risk that our secondary interpretation will appear even paler when placed directly beside Dostoevsky's prose. This risk is heightened, moreover, by the excellence of the English translation by Richard Pevear and Larissa Volokhonsky. This translation fulfills admirably George Steiner's observation that a great translation "bestows on the original *that which was already there*"—not as imitation, but as "creative echo" or "metamorphic mirroring."[3] In this translation, the generative presence of Dostoevsky's original text has indeed been preserved.

The separate publication of "The Grand Inquisitor" is meant to be helpful, but it might be misleading if it encourages readers to interpret the chapter in isolation from the whole novel. Neither the Inquisitor nor Christ appears directly elsewhere in *The Brothers Karamazov*, but Ivan and Alyosha Karamazov certainly do; and Dostoevsky's meaning will be lost or distorted if it is forgotten that Ivan is the author of the prose poem "The Grand Inquisitor," and that Ivan's listener—prior to any readers—is his younger brother Alyosha. "The Grand Inquisitor" points *back* to Ivan's rebellion against God on behalf of suffering humanity. Ivan indicts God for unwillingness or inability to alleviate the unjust suffering of the innocent, thereby eliciting Alyosha's response that this indictment has not taken into account the God of self-emptying love manifested in the Incarnation and Crucifixion. Ivan, who has already prosecuted God, then undertakes, through the Inquisitor, the prosecution of Christ. "The Grand Inquisitor" also points *forward* to the response of Alyosha's Christian realism, expressed through his authorship of the "Life of the Hieromonk and Elder Zosima," and through his actual living out of his (and Zosima's) way of thought—in contrast to Ivan's actual living out of *his* intellectual stance in the rest of the novel. Although our reflections in this book begin and (frequently) end with "The Grand Inquisitor," they of necessity range through the whole of *The Brothers Karamazov* and sometimes beyond, to Dostoevsky's other writings. There is no substitute for reading the major novels.

"The Grand Inquisitor" divides naturally into three parts: Ivan's "literary preface" to his poem; the Inquisitor's lengthy indictment of the silent prisoner, culminating in the verdict and sentence of death by burning at the stake; and the reflections of both author (Ivan) and listener (Alyosha) on how the poem, including the prisoner's kissing of the Inquisitor, should be interpreted.

The first part establishes the setting and introduces the protagonists. The Grand Inquisitor is a cardinal of the Roman Catholic Church in sixteenth-century Spain. He represents Roman Catholicism not at its apogee in the high Middle Ages but in its desperately militant efforts to counter the Protestant Reformation by means of the Spanish sword. The Inquisitor, near death himself, stands near the end of Roman Catholic order in the West and at the beginning of the modern quest for a new order. It should be emphasized that although thus identified with a particular time and place, the Inquisitor's vision extends in both directions to encompass the entire history of Western civilization, from the ancient Roman Empire to the new Rome that he anticipates after the fall of modern liberalism and socialism. The identity and significance of the other main character, the silent prisoner, is less exactly defined. Although Ivan's "literary preface" treats this figure as Christ returned to the earth, this identification is rapidly qualified, prior to the Inquisitor's monologue, as possibly just an old man's fantasy. Yet the prisoner at the very least evokes the image of Christ and is therefore evidently meant to signify an alternative to the Inquisitor's account of history, politics, religion, and human nature. However, the meaning of this alternative, and even the degree to which it *is* an alternative—after all, the Christ-figure is Ivan's character no less than the Inquisitor—is peculiarly difficult to determine, as is the import of the prisoner's silence or his kissing of the Inquisitor. Insofar as this silence does constitute a response to the Inquisitor's indictment, it points, on the one hand, to the Christianity of Alyosha and Zosima elsewhere in the novel, and on the other hand, to the self-betraying speech and actions of the Inquisitor and Ivan. For a more direct interpretation of the Christ of "The Grand Inquisitor," we refer the reader to the final chapter of this book.

The second part of "The Grand Inquisitor" presents the Inquisitor's (hence, Ivan's) indictment of Christ, in the course of which he puts forward his own teaching about the best human order—his final social formula. The Inquisitor's teaching is set out within the framework provided by the biblical account of Christ's temptation in the wilderness (Matthew 4:1–11). He claims that the "real, thundering miracle" of the story of the three temptations lies in the fact that the questions posed in them should have come to be articulated among human beings at all, especially at such an early time in history; for the posing of these questions demonstrates an insight into all that is most fundamentally at issue in the problem of human happiness, an insight arrived at prior to the centuries of historical experience that have since borne it out. The Inquisitor's social formula is founded on his own exegesis of the three temptations recorded in Matthew, which provide the reader with a basic map through the maze of his words. In relation to each of the three temptations, the Inquisitor's interpretation focuses on three questions: What fundamental human need is revealed? What is the means to the satisfaction of this need? How does history itself verify the truth of this interpretation of the temptation? In each case, according to the Inquisitor, Christ rejected what he should have accepted. The "should" is rooted in three assumptions: that the three temptations contain the fundamental principles of the best human order; that order or complete social unity is what human beings most need for the alleviation of their suffering; and that if Christ had truly loved humanity, he would have given the highest priority to this alleviation. The Inquisitor's exegesis of the Gospel passage clearly constitutes an indictment of Christ for insufficient and/or ineffective love of human beings.

In the third and last part of "The Grand Inquisitor," Ivan and Alyosha together reflect on the meaning of the poem. Alyosha asks pointed questions: Does the poem actually praise rather than disparage Jesus? Is "freedom" understood properly? What is the Inquisitor's "secret"? How does the poem end? Why does it end this way? These questions, in turn, elicit revealing responses, both from Ivan and potentially from the attentive reader, who is invited to join the commentary on the poem already begun in the conversation of the brothers. We have accepted this invitation, and we invite readers to enter with us into the ongoing commentary.

No other part of Dostoevsky's oeuvre has inspired so large and so diverse a body of interpretation. Is it an utterly devastating attack on Christianity; or, as Berdyaev would have it, an expression of Dostoevsky's entire "Christian metaphysic"? Is the Inquisitor's argument unanswerable; or is a sufficient, albeit hidden, response already embodied in the silent Christ-figure? If the Grand Inquisitor is indeed an atheist, why is he presented as a member of the Roman Catholic hierarchy of the sixteenth century? If the silent prisoner is indeed Christ, is he the Christ of Protestantism? Or of Orthodoxy? Or is he Ivan's version of the "historical Jesus"? Who *does* love humanity more? Where does "The Grand Inquisitor" cease to be Ivan's "poem" and become Dostoevsky's religious-political apocalypse? As the latter, how prophetic does it remain for us? This is but a short sample of the seemingly endless questioning engendered by "The Grand Inquisitor." When faced with such a challenge, it is good to be reminded that questioning can be the "piety of thought."

The particular questions to which we have devoted our reflection in this book, and the manner in which the questions are addressed, have everything to do with the overriding question that we bring to the text. This question could be expressed by quoting the words of the Christian philosopher Vladimir Solovyov, a close friend of Dostoevsky's: "The general meaning of Dostoevsky's entire activity, the meaning of Dostoevsky as a social figure, consists in the resolution of this two-fold question: about the highest idea of social order and the genuine way to the actualization of this idea."[4] In our view, this twofold question fundamentally informs Dostoevsky's prophetic elucidation of the crisis of modernity.*

◞

"But here, too, it's impossible to do without a preface, a literary preface, that is—pah!" Ivan laughed, "and what sort of writer am I! You see, my action takes place in the sixteenth century, and back then—by the way, you must have learned this in school—back then it was customary in poetic works to bring higher powers

---

*The version of "The Grand Inquisitor" that appears below is excerpted from Fyodor Dostoevsky, *The Brothers Karamazov,* trans. Richard Pevear and Larissa Volokhonsky (New York: Vintage, 1990), pp. 246–264, and is reprinted by permission of Vintage Books, a Division of Random House, Inc. Translation copyright © 1991 by Richard Pevear and Larissa Volokhonsky.

down to earth. I don't need to mention Dante. In France, court clerks, as well as monks in the monasteries, gave whole performances in which they brought the Madonna, angels, saints, Christ, and God himself on stage. At the time it was all done quite artlessly. In Victor Hugo's *Notre Dame de Paris,* in the Paris of Louis XI, to honor the birth of the French dauphin, an edifying performance is given free of charge for the people in the city hall, entitled *Le bon jugement de la très sainte et gracieuse Vierge Marie,* in which she herself appears in person and pronounces her *bon jugement.* With us in Moscow, in pre-Petrine antiquity, much the same kind of dramatic performances, especially from the Old Testament, were given from time to time; but, besides dramatic performances, there were many stories and 'verses' floating around the world in which saints, angels, and all the powers of heaven took part as needed. In our monasteries such poems were translated, recopied, even composed—and when?—under the Tartars. There is, for example, one little monastery poem (from the Greek, of course): *The Mother of God Visits the Torments,* with scenes of a boldness not inferior to Dante's. The Mother of God visits hell and the Archangel Michael guides her through 'the torments.' She sees sinners and their sufferings. Among them, by the way, there is a most amusing class of sinners in a burning lake: some of them sink so far down into the lake that they can no longer come up again, and 'these God forgets'—an expression of extraordinary depth and force. And so the Mother of God, shocked and weeping, falls before the throne of God and asks pardon for everyone in hell, everyone she has seen there, without distinction. Her conversation with God is immensely interesting. She pleads, she won't go away, and when God points out to her the nail-pierced hands and feet of her Son and asks: 'How can I forgive his tormentors?' she bids all the saints, all the martyrs, all the angels and archangels to fall down together with her and plead for the pardon of all without discrimination. In the end she extorts from God a cessation of torments every year, from Holy Friday to Pentecost, and the sinners in hell at once thank the Lord and cry out to him: 'Just art thou, O Lord, who hast judged so.' Well, my little poem would have been of the same kind if it had appeared back then. He comes onstage in it; actually, he says nothing in the poem, he just appears and passes on. Fifteen centuries have gone by since he gave the promise to come in his Kingdom, fifteen centuries since his prophet wrote: 'Behold, I come quickly.' 'Of that day and that hour knoweth not even the Son, but only my heavenly Father,' as he himself declared while still on earth. But mankind awaits him with the same faith and the same tender emotion. Oh, even with greater faith, for fifteen centuries have gone by since men ceased to receive pledges from heaven:

Believe what the heart tells you,
For heaven offers no pledge.

Only faith in what the heart tells you! True, there were also miracles then. There were saints who performed miraculous healings; to some righteous men, according to their biographies, the Queen of Heaven herself came down. But the devil never rests, and there had already arisen in mankind some doubt as to the authenticity of these miracles. Just then, in the north, in Germany, a horrible new heresy appeared. A great star, 'like a lamp' (that is, the Church), 'fell upon the fountains of waters, and they were made bitter.' These heretics began blasphemously denying miracles. But those who still believed became all the more ardent in their belief. The tears of mankind rose up to him as before, they waited for him, loved him, hoped in him, yearned to suffer and die for him as before. . . . And for so many centuries mankind had been pleading with faith and fire: 'God our Lord, reveal thyself to us,' for so many centuries they had been calling out to him, that he in his immeasurable compassion desired to descend to those who were pleading. He had descended even before then, he had visited some righteous men, martyrs, and holy hermits while they were still on earth, as is written in their 'lives.' Our own Tyutchev, who deeply believed in the truth of his words, proclaimed that:

> Bent under the burden of the Cross,
> The King of Heaven in the form of a slave
> Walked the length and breadth of you,
> Blessing you, my native land.

It must needs have been so, let me tell you. And so he desired to appear to people if only for a moment—to his tormented, suffering people, rank with sin but loving him like children. My action is set in Spain, in Seville, in the most horrible time of the Inquisition, when fires blazed every day to the glory of God, and

> In the splendid auto-da-fé
> Evil heretics were burnt.

Oh, of course, this was not that coming in which he will appear, according to his promise, at the end of time, in all his heavenly glory, and which will be as sudden 'as the lightning that shineth out of the east unto the west.' No, he desired to visit his children if only for a moment, and precisely where the fires of the heretics had begun to crackle. In his infinite mercy, he walked once again among men, in the same human image in which he had walked for three years among men fifteen centuries earlier. He came down to the 'scorched squares' of a southern town where just the day before, in a 'splendid auto-da-fé,' in the presence of the king, the court, knights, cardinals, and the loveliest court ladies, before the teeming populace of all Seville, the Cardinal Grand Inquisitor had burned almost a hundred heretics at once *ad majorem gloriam Dei*. He appeared quietly, inconspicuously, but, strange to say, everyone recognized him. This could be one of the best passages in the poem, I mean, why it is exactly that they recognize him. People are drawn to him by an invincible force, they flock to him, surround him, follow him. He passes silently among them with a quiet smile of infinite compassion. The sun of love shines in his heart, rays of Light, Enlightenment, and Power stream from his eyes and, pouring over the people, shake their hearts with responding love. He stretches forth his hands to them, blesses them, and from the touch of him, even only of his garments, comes a healing power. Here an old man, blind from childhood, calls out from the crowd: 'Lord, heal me so that I, too, can see you,' and it is as if the scales fell from his eyes, and the blind man sees him. People weep and kiss the earth he walks upon. Children throw down flowers before him, sing and cry 'Hosanna!' to him. 'It's he, it's really he,' everyone repeats, 'it must be he, it can be no one but he.' He stops at the porch of the Seville cathedral at the very moment when a child's little, open, white coffin is being brought in with weeping: in it lies a seven-year-old girl, the only daughter of a noble citizen. The dead child is covered with flowers. 'He will raise your child,' people in the crowd shout to the weeping mother. The cathedral padre, who has come out to meet the coffin, looks perplexed and frowns. Suddenly a wail comes from the dead child's mother. She throws herself down at his feet: 'If it is you, then raise my child!' she exclaims, stretching her hands out to him. The procession halts, the little coffin is lowered down onto the porch at his feet. He looks with compassion and his lips once again softly utter: '*Talitha cumi*'—'and the damsel arose.' The girl rises in her coffin, sits up and, smiling, looks around her in wide-eyed astonishment. She is still holding the bunch of white roses with which she has been lying in the coffin. There is a commotion among the people, cries, weeping, and at this very moment the Cardinal Grand Inquisitor himself crosses the square in front of the cathedral. He is an old man, almost ninety, tall and straight, with a gaunt face and sunken eyes, from which a glitter still shines like a fiery spark. Oh, he is not wearing his magnificent cardinal's robes in which he had displayed himself to the people the day before, when the enemies of the Roman faith were burned—no, at this moment he is wearing only his old, coarse monastic cassock. He is followed at a certain distance by his grim assistants and slaves, and by the 'holy' guard. At the sight of the crowd he stops and watches from afar. He has seen everything, seen the coffin set down at his feet, seen the girl rise, and his face darkens. He scowls with his thick, gray eyebrows, and his eyes shine with a sinister fire. He stretches forth his finger and orders the guard to take him. And such is his power, so tamed, submissive, and tremblingly obedient to his will are the people, that the crowd immediately parts before the guard,

and they, amidst the deathly silence that has suddenly fallen, lay their hands on
him and lead him away. As one man the crowd immediately bows to the ground
before the aged Inquisitor, who silently blesses the people and moves on. The
guard lead their prisoner to the small, gloomy, vaulted prison in the old building
of the holy court, and lock him there. The day is over, the Seville night comes,
dark, hot, and 'breathless.' The air is 'fragrant with laurel and lemon.' In the deep
darkness, the iron door of the prison suddenly opens, and the old Grand Inquisitor himself slowly enters carrying a lamp. He is alone, the door is immediately
locked behind him. He stands in the entrance and for a long time, for a minute
or two, gazes into his face. At last he quietly approaches, sets the lamp on the
table, and says to him: 'Is it you? You?' But receiving no answer, he quickly adds:
'Do not answer, be silent. After all, what could you say? I know too well what you
would say. And you have no right to add anything to what you already said once.
Why, then, have you come to interfere with us? For you have come to interfere
with us and you know it yourself. But do you know what will happen tomorrow?
I do not know who you are, and I do not want to know: whether it is you, or only
his likeness; but tomorrow I shall condemn you and burn you at the stake as the
most evil of heretics, and the very people who today kissed your feet, tomorrow,
at a nod from me, will rush to heap the coals up around your stake, do you know
that? Yes, perhaps you do know it,' he added, pondering deeply, never for a moment taking his eyes from his prisoner."

"I don't quite understand what this is, Ivan," Alyosha, who all the while had
been listening silently, smiled. "Is it boundless fantasy, or some mistake on the old
man's part, some impossible *qui pro quo*?"

"Assume it's the latter, if you like," Ivan laughed, "if you're so spoiled by modern realism and can't understand anything fantastic—if you want it to be *qui pro
quo*, let it be. Of course," he laughed again, "the man is ninety years old, and
might have lost his mind long ago over his idea. He might have been struck by the
prisoner's appearance. It might, finally, have been simple delirium, the vision of a
ninety-year-old man nearing death, and who is excited, besides, by the auto-da-
fé of a hundred burnt heretics the day before. But isn't it all the same to you and
me whether it's *qui pro quo* or boundless fantasy? The only thing is that the old
man needs to speak out, that finally after all his ninety years, he speaks out, and
says aloud all that he has been silent about for ninety years."

"And the prisoner is silent, too? Just looks at him without saying a word?"

"But that must be so in any case," Ivan laughed again. "The old man himself
points out to him that he has no right to add anything to what has already been
said once. That, if you like, is the most basic feature of Roman Catholicism, in my
opinion at least: 'Everything,' they say, 'has been handed over by you to the pope,
therefore everything now belongs to the pope, and you may as well not come at

all now, or at least don't interfere with us for the time being.' They not only speak this way, they also write this way, at least the Jesuits do. I've read it in their theologians myself. 'Have you the right to proclaim to us even one of the mysteries of that world from which you have come?' my old man asks him, and answers the question himself: 'No, you have not, so as not to add to what has already been said once, and so as not to deprive people of freedom, for which you stood so firmly when you were on earth. Anything you proclaim anew will encroach upon the freedom of men's faith, for it will come as a miracle, and the freedom of their faith was the dearest of all things to you, even then, one and a half thousand years ago. Was it not you who so often said then: "I want to make you free"?' 'But now you have seen these "free" men,' the old man suddenly adds with a pensive smile. 'Yes, this work has cost us dearly,' he goes on, looking sternly at him, 'but we have finally finished this work in your name. For fifteen hundred years we have been at pains over this freedom, but now it is finished, and well finished. You do not believe that it is well finished? You look at me meekly and do not deign even to be indignant with me. Know, then, that now, precisely now, these people are more certain than ever before that they are completely free, and at the same time they themselves have brought us their freedom and obediently laid it at our feet. It is our doing, but is it what you wanted? This sort of freedom?'"

"Again I don't understand," Alyosha interrupted. "Is he being ironic? Is he laughing?"

"Not in the least. He precisely lays it to his and his colleagues' credit that they have finally overcome freedom, and have done so in order to make people happy. 'For only now' (he is referring, of course, to the Inquisition) 'has it become possible to think for the first time about human happiness. Man was made a rebel; can rebels be happy? You were warned,' he says to him, 'you had no lack of warnings and indications, but you did not heed the warnings, you rejected the only way of arranging for human happiness, but fortunately, on your departure, you handed the work over to us. You promised, you established with your word, you gave us the right to bind and loose, and surely you cannot even think of taking this right away from us now. Why, then, have you come to interfere with us?'"

"What does it mean, that he had no lack of warnings and indications?" Alyosha asked.

"You see, that is the main thing that the old man needs to speak about."

"'The dread and intelligent spirit, the spirit of self-destruction and non-being,' the old man goes on, 'the great spirit spoke with you in the wilderness, and it has been passed on to us in books that he supposedly "tempted" you. Did he really? And was it possible to say anything more true than what he proclaimed to you in his three questions, which you rejected, and which the books refer to as "temptations"? And at the same time, if ever a real, thundering miracle was performed on earth, it was on that day, the day of those three temptations. The miracle lay precisely in the appearance of those three questions. If it were possible to imagine, just as a trial and an example, that those three questions of the dread spirit had been lost from the books without a trace, and it was necessary that they be restored, thought up and invented anew, to be put back into the books, and to that end all the wise men on earth—rulers, high priests, scholars, philosophers, poets—were brought together and given this task: to think up, to invent three questions such as would not only correspond to the scale of the event, but, moreover, would express in three words, in three human phrases only, the entire future history of the world and mankind—do you think that all the combined wisdom of the earth could think up anything faintly resembling in force and depth those three questions that were actually presented to you then by the powerful and intelligent spirit in the wilderness? By the questions alone, simply by the miracle of their appearance, one can see that one is dealing with a mind not human and transient but eternal and absolute. For in these three questions all of subsequent human history is as if brought together into a single whole and foretold; three images are revealed that will take in all the insoluble historical contradictions of human nature over all the earth. This could not have been seen so well at the time, for the future was unknown, but now that fifteen centuries have gone by, we can see that in these three questions everything was so precisely divined and foretold, and has proved so completely true, that to add to them or subtract anything from them is impossible.'

"'Decide yourself who was right: you or the one who questioned you then? Recall the first question; its meaning, though not literally, was this: You want to go into the world, and you are going empty-handed, with some promise of freedom, which they in their simplicity and innate lawlessness cannot even comprehend, which they dread and fear—for nothing has ever been more insufferable for man and for human society than freedom! But do you see these stones in this bare, scorching desert? Turn them into bread and mankind will run after you like sheep, grateful and obedient, though eternally trembling lest you withdraw your hand and your loaves cease for them. But you did not want to deprive man of freedom and rejected the offer, for what sort of freedom is it, you reasoned, if obedience is bought with loaves of bread? You objected that man does not live by bread alone, but do you know that in the name of this very earthly bread, the spirit of the earth will rise against you and fight with you and defeat you, and everyone will follow him exclaiming: "Who can compare to this beast, for he has given us fire from heaven!" Do you know that centuries will pass and mankind will proclaim with the mouth of its wisdom and science that there is no crime, and therefore no sin, but only hungry men? "Feed them first, then ask virtue of them!"—that is what they will write on the banner they raise against you, and by which your temple will be destroyed. In place of your temple a new edifice will be raised, the terrible Tower of Babel will be raised again, and though, like the former one, this one will not be completed either, still you could have avoided this new tower and shortened people's suffering by a thousand years—for it is to us they will come after suffering for a thousand years with their tower! They will seek us out again, underground, in catacombs, hiding (for again we shall be persecuted and tortured), they will find us and cry out: "Feed us, for those who promised us fire from heaven did not give it." And then we shall finish building their tower, for only he who feeds them will finish it, and only we shall feed them, in your name, for we shall lie that it is in your name. O, never, never will they feed themselves without us! No science will give them bread as long as they remain free, but in the end they will lay their freedom at our feet and say to us: "Better that you enslave us, but feed us." They will finally understand that freedom and earthly bread in plenty for everyone are inconceivable together, for never, never will they be able to share among themselves. They will also be convinced that they are forever incapable of being free, because they are feeble, depraved, nonentities and rebels. You promised them heavenly bread, but, I repeat again, can it compare with the earthly bread in the eyes of the weak, eternally depraved, and eternally ignoble human race? And if in the name of heavenly bread thousands and tens of thousands will follow you, what will become of the millions and tens of thousands of millions of creatures who will not be strong enough to forgo earthly bread for the sake of the heavenly? Is it that only the tens of thousands of the great and strong are dear to you, and the remaining millions, numerous as the sands of the sea, weak but loving you, should serve only as material for the great and the strong? No, the weak, too, are dear to us. They are depraved and rebels, but in the end it is they who will become obedient. They will marvel at us, and look upon us as gods, because we, standing at their head, have agreed to suffer freedom and to rule over them—so terrible will it become for them in the end to be free! But we shall say that we are obedient to you and rule in your name. We shall deceive them again, for this time we shall not allow you to come to us. This deceit will constitute our suffering, for we shall have to lie. This is what that first question in the wilderness meant, and this is what you rejected in the name of freedom, which you placed above everything. And yet this question contains the great mystery of this world. Had you accepted the "loaves," you would have answered the universal and everlasting anguish of man as an individual being, and of the whole of mankind together, namely: "before whom shall I bow down?" There is no more ceaseless or tormenting care for man, as long as he remains free, than to find someone to bow down to as soon as possible. But man seeks to bow down before that which is indisputable, so indisputable that all men at once would agree to the universal worship of it. For the care of these pitiful creatures is not just to find something before which I or some other man can bow down, but to find something that everyone else will also believe in and bow down to, for it must needs be *all together*. And this need for *communality* of worship is the chief torment of each man individually, and of mankind as a whole, from the beginning of the ages. In the cause of universal worship, they have destroyed each other with the sword. They have made gods and called upon each other: "Abandon your gods and come and worship ours, otherwise death to you and your gods!" And so it will be until the end of the world, even when all gods have disappeared from the earth: they will still fall down before idols. You knew, you could not but know, this essential mystery of human nature, but you rejected the only absolute banner, which was offered to you to make all men bow down to you indisputably— the banner of earthly bread; and you rejected it in the name of freedom and heavenly bread. Now see what you did next. And all again in the name of freedom! I tell you that man has no more tormenting care than to find someone to whom he can hand over as quickly as possible that gift of freedom with which the miserable creature is born. But he alone can take over the freedom of men who appeases their conscience. With bread you were given an indisputable banner: give man bread and he will bow down to you, for there is nothing more indisputable than bread. But if at the same time someone else takes over his conscience—oh, then he will even throw down your bread and follow him who has seduced his conscience. In this you were right. For the mystery of man's being is not only in living, but in what one lives for. Without a firm idea of what he lives for, man will not consent to live and will sooner destroy himself than remain on earth, even if there is bread all around him. That is so, but what came of it? Instead of taking over men's freedom, you increased it still more for them! Did you forget that peace and even death are dearer to man than free choice in the knowledge of good and evil? There is nothing more seductive for man than the freedom of his conscience, but there is nothing more tormenting either. And so, instead of a firm foundation for appeasing human conscience once and for all, you chose everything that was unusual, enigmatic, and indefinite, you chose everything that was beyond men's strength, and thereby acted as if you did not love them at all—and who did this? He who came to give his life for them! Instead of taking over men's freedom, you increased it and forever burdened the kingdom of the human soul with its torments. You desired the free love of man, that he should follow you freely, seduced and captivated by you. Instead of the firm ancient law, man had henceforth to decide for himself, with a free heart, what is good and what is evil, having only your image before him as a guide— but did it not occur to you that he would eventually reject and dispute even your image and your truth if he was oppressed by so terrible a burden as freedom of choice? They will finally cry out that the truth is not in you, for it was impossible to leave them in greater confusion and torment than you did, abandoning them to so many cares and insoluble problems. Thus you yourself laid the foundation for the destruction of your own kingdom, and do not blame anyone else for it. Yet is this what was offered you? There are three powers, only three powers on earth, capable of conquering and holding captive forever the conscience of these feeble rebels, for their own happiness—these powers are miracle, mystery, and authority. You rejected the first, the second, and the third, and gave yourself as an example of that. When the dread and wise spirit set you on a pinnacle of the Temple and said to you: "If you would know whether or not you are the Son of God, cast yourself down; for it is written of him, that the angels will bear him up, and he will not fall or be hurt, and then you will know whether you are the Son of God, and will prove what faith you have in your Father." But you heard and rejected the offer and did not yield and did not throw yourself down. Oh, of course in this you acted proudly and magnificently, like God, but mankind, that weak, rebellious tribe—are they gods? Oh, you knew then that if you made just one step, just one movement towards throwing yourself down, you would immediately have tempted the Lord and would have lost all faith in him and been dashed against the earth you came to save, and the intelligent spirit who was tempting you would rejoice. But, I repeat, are there many like you? And, indeed, could you possibly have assumed, even for a moment, that mankind, too, would be strong enough for such a temptation? Is that how human nature was created—to reject the miracle, and in those terrible moments of life, the moments of the most terrible, essential, and tormenting questions of the soul, to remain only with the free decision of the heart? Oh, you knew that your deed would be preserved in books, would reach the depths of the ages and the utmost limits of the earth, and you hoped that, following you, man, too, would remain with God, having no need of miracles. But you did not know that as soon as man rejects miracles, he will at once reject God as well, for man seeks not so much God as miracles. And since man cannot bear to be left without miracles, he will go and create new miracles for himself, his own miracles this time, and will bow down to the miracles of quacks, or women's magic, though he be rebellious, heretical, and godless a hundred times over. You did not come down from the cross when they shouted to you, mocking and reviling you: "Come down from the cross and we will believe that it is you." You did not come down because, again, you did not want to enslave man by a miracle and thirsted for faith that is free, not miraculous. You thirsted for love that is free, and not for the servile rapture of a slave before a power that has left him permanently terrified. But here, too, you overestimated mankind, for, of course, they are slaves, though they were created rebels. Behold and judge, now that fifteen centuries have passed, take a look at them: whom have you raised up to yourself? I swear, man is created weaker and baser than you thought him! How, how can he ever accomplish the same things as you? Respecting him so much, you behaved as if you had ceased to be compassionate, because you demanded too much of him—and who did this? He who loved him more than himself! Respecting him less, you would have demanded less of him, and that would be closer to love, for his burden would be lighter. He is weak and mean. What matter that he now rebels everywhere against our power, and takes pride in his rebellion? The pride of a child and a schoolboy! They are little children, who rebel in class and drive out the teacher. But there will also come an end to the children's delight, and it will cost them dearly. They will tear down the temples and drench the earth with blood. But finally the foolish children will understand that although they are rebels, they are feeble rebels, who cannot endure their own rebellion. Pouring out their foolish tears, they will finally acknowledge that he who created them rebels no doubt intended to laugh at them. They will say it in despair, and what they say will be a blasphemy that will make them even more unhappy, for human nature cannot bear blasphemy and in the end always takes revenge for it. And so, turmoil, confusion, and unhappiness—these are the present lot of mankind, after you suffered so much for their freedom! Your great prophet tells in a vision and an allegory that he saw all those who took part in the first resurrection and that they were twelve thousand from each tribe. But even if there were so many, they, too, were not like men, as it were, but gods. They endured your cross, they endured scores of years of hungry and naked wilderness, eating locusts and roots, and of course you can point with pride to these children of freedom, of free love, of free and magnificent sacrifice in your name. But remember that there were only several thousand of them, and they were gods. What of the rest? Is it the fault of the rest of feeble mankind that they could not endure what the mighty endured? Is it the fault of the weak soul that it is unable to contain such terrible gifts? Can it be that you indeed came only to the chosen ones and for the chosen ones? But if so, there is a mystery here, and we cannot understand it. And if it is a mystery, then we, too, had the right to preach mystery and to teach them that it is not the free choice of the heart that matters, and not love, but the mystery, which they must blindly obey, even setting aside their own conscience. And so we did. We corrected your deed and based it on *miracle, mystery,* and *authority.* And mankind rejoiced that they were once more led like sheep, and that at last such a terrible gift, which had brought them so much suffering, had been taken from their hearts. Tell me, were we right in teaching and doing so? Have we not, indeed, loved mankind, in so humbly recognizing their impotence, in so lovingly alleviating their burden and allowing their feeble nature even to sin, with our permission? Why have you come to interfere with us now? And why are you looking at me so silently and understandingly with your meek eyes? Be angry! I do not want your love, for I do not love you. And what can I hide from you? Do I not know with whom I am speaking? What I have to tell you is all known to you already, I can read it in your eyes. And is it for me to hide our secret from you? Perhaps you precisely want to hear it from my lips. Listen then: we are not with you, but with *him*, that is our secret! For a long time now—eight centuries already—we have not been with you, but with *him*. Exactly eight centuries ago we took from him what you so indignantly rejected, that last gift he offered you when he showed you all the kingdoms of the earth: we took Rome and the sword of Caesar from him, and proclaimed ourselves sole rulers of the earth, the only rulers, though we have not yet succeeded in bringing our cause to its full conclusion. But whose fault is that? Oh, this work is still in its very beginnings, but it has begun. There is still long to wait before its completion, and the earth still has much to suffer, but we shall accomplish it and we shall be caesars, and then we shall think about the universal happiness of mankind. And yet you could have taken the sword of Caesar even then. Why did you reject that last gift? Had you accepted that third counsel of the mighty spirit, you would have furnished all that man seeks on earth, that is: someone to bow down to, someone to take over his conscience, and a means for uniting everyone at last into a common, concordant, and incontestable anthill—for the need for universal union is the third and last torment of men. Mankind in its entirety has always yearned to arrange things so that they must be universal. There have been many great nations with great histories, but the higher these nations stood, the unhappier they were, for they were more strongly aware than others of the need for a universal union of mankind. Great conquerors, Tamerlanes and Genghis Khans, swept over the earth like a whirlwind, yearning to conquer the cosmos, but they, too, expressed, albeit unconsciously, the same great need of mankind for universal and general union. Had you accepted the world and Caesar's purple, you would have founded a universal kingdom and granted universal peace. For who shall possess mankind if not those who possess their conscience and give them their bread? And so we took Caesar's sword, and in taking it, of course, we rejected you and followed *him*. Oh, there will be centuries more of the lawlessness of free reason, of their science and anthropophagy—for, having begun to build their Tower of Babel without us, they will end in anthropophagy. And it is then that the beast will come crawling to us and lick our feet and spatter them with tears of blood from its eyes. And we shall sit upon the beast and raise the cup, and on it will be written: "Mystery!" But then, and then only, will the kingdom of peace and happiness come for mankind. You are proud of your chosen ones, but you have only your chosen ones, while we will pacify all. And there is still more: how many among those chosen ones, the strong ones who might have become the chosen ones, have finally grown tired of waiting for you, and have brought and will yet bring the powers of their spirit and the ardor of their hearts to another field, and will end by raising their *free* banner against you! But you raised that banner yourself. With us everyone will be happy, and they will no longer rebel or destroy each other, as in your freedom, everywhere. Oh, we shall convince them that they will only become free when they resign their freedom to us, and submit to us. Will we be right, do you think, or will we be lying? They themselves will be convinced that we are right, for they will remember to what horrors of slavery and confusion your freedom led them. Freedom, free reason, and science will lead them into such a maze, and confront them with such miracles and insoluble mysteries, that some of them, unruly and ferocious, will exterminate themselves; others, unruly but feeble, will exterminate each other; and the remaining third, feeble and wretched, will crawl to our feet and cry out to us: "Yes, you were right, you alone possess his mystery, and we are coming back to you—save us from ourselves." Receiving bread from us, they will see clearly, of course, that we take from them the bread they have procured with their own hands, in order to distribute it among them, without any miracle; they will see that we have not turned stones into bread; but, indeed, more than over the bread itself, they will rejoice over taking it from our hands! For they will remember only too well that before, without us, the very bread they procured for themselves turned to stones in their hands, and when they came back to us, the very stones in their hands turned to bread. Too well, far too well, will they appreciate what it means to submit once and for all! And until men understand this, they will be unhappy. Who contributed most of all to this lack of understanding, tell me? Who broke up the flock and scattered it upon paths unknown? But the flock will gather again, and again submit, and this time once and for all. Then we shall give them quiet, humble happiness, the happiness of feeble creatures, such as they were created. Oh, we shall finally convince them not to be proud, for you raised them up and thereby taught them pride; we shall prove to them that they are feeble, that they are only pitiful children, but that a child's happiness is sweeter than any other. They will become timid and look to us and cling to us in fear, like chicks to a hen. They will marvel and stand in awe of us and be proud that we are so powerful and so intelligent as to have been able to subdue such a tempestuous flock of thousands of millions. They will tremble limply before our wrath, their minds will grow timid, their eyes will become as tearful as children's or women's, but just as readily at a gesture from us they will pass over to gaiety and laughter, to bright joy and happy children's song. Yes, we will make them work, but in the hours free from labor we will arrange their lives like a children's game, with children's songs, choruses, and innocent dancing. Oh, we will allow them to sin, too; they are weak and powerless, and they will love us like children for allowing them to sin. We will tell them that every sin will be redeemed if it is committed with our permission; and that we allow them to sin because we love them, and as for the punishment for these sins, very well, we take it upon ourselves. And we will take it upon ourselves, and they will adore us as benefactors, who have borne their sins before God. And they will have no secrets from us. We will allow or forbid them to live with their wives and mistresses, to have or not to have children—all depending on their obedience—and they will submit to us gladly and joyfully. The most tormenting secrets of their conscience—all, all they will bring to us, and we will decide all things, and they will joyfully believe our decision, because it will deliver them from their great care and their present terrible torments of personal and free decision. And everyone will be happy, all the millions of creatures, except for the hundred thousand of those who govern them. For only we, we who keep the mystery, only we shall be unhappy. There will be thousands of millions of happy babes, and a hundred thousand sufferers who have taken upon themselves the curse of the knowledge of good and evil. Peacefully they will die, peacefully they will expire in your name, and beyond the grave they will find only death. But we will keep the secret, and for their own happiness we will entice them with a heavenly and eternal reward. For even if there were anything in the next world, it would not, of course, be for such as they. It is said and prophesied that you will come and once more be victorious, you will come with your chosen ones, with your proud and mighty ones, but we will say that they saved only themselves, while we have saved everyone. It is said that the harlot who sits upon the beast and holds *mystery* in her hands will be disgraced, that the feeble will rebel again, that they will tear her purple and strip bare her "loathsome" body. But then I will stand up and point out to you the thousands of millions of happy babes who do not know sin. And we, who took their sins upon ourselves for their happiness, we will stand before you and say: "Judge us if you can and dare." Know that I am not afraid of you. Know that I, too, was in the wilderness, and I, too, ate locusts and roots; that I, too, blessed freedom, with which you have blessed mankind, and I, too, was preparing to enter the number of chosen ones, the number of the strong and mighty, with a thirst "that the number be complete." But I awoke and did not want to serve madness. I returned and joined the host of those who have *corrected your deed*. I left the proud and returned to the humble, for the happiness of the humble. What I am telling you will come true, and our kingdom will be established. To-morrow, I repeat, you will see this obedient flock, which at my first gesture will rush to heap hot coals around your stake, at which I shall burn you for having come to interfere with us. For if anyone has ever deserved our stake, it is you. To-morrow I shall burn you. *Dixi*.'"

Ivan stopped. He was flushed from speaking, and from speaking with such enthusiasm; but when he finished, he suddenly smiled.

Alyosha, who all the while had listened to him silently, though towards the end, in great agitation, he had started many times to interrupt his brother's speech but obviously restrained himself, suddenly spoke as if tearing himself loose.

"But . . . that's absurd!" he cried, blushing. "Your poem praises Jesus, it doesn't revile him . . . as you meant it to. And who will believe you about freedom? Is that, is that any way to understand it? It's a far cry from the Orthodox idea . . . It's Rome, and not even the whole of Rome, that isn't true—they're the worst of Catholicism, the Inquisitors, the Jesuits . . . ! But there could not even possibly be such a fantastic person as your Inquisitor. What sins do they take on themselves? Who are these bearers of the mystery who took some sort of curse upon themselves for men's happiness? Has anyone ever seen them? We know the Jesuits, bad things are said about them, but are they what you have there? They're not that, not that at all . . . They're simply a Roman army, for a future universal earthly kingdom, with the emperor—the pontiff of Rome—at their head . . . that's their ideal, but without any mysteries or lofty sadness . . . Simply the lust for power, for filthy earthly lucre, enslavement . . . a sort of future serfdom with them as the landowners . . . that's all they have. Maybe they don't even believe in God. Your suffering Inquisitor is only a fantasy . . . ."

"But wait, wait," Ivan was laughing, "don't get so excited. A fantasy, you say? Let it be. Of course it's a fantasy. But still, let me ask: do you really think that this whole Catholic movement of the past few centuries is really nothing but the lust for power only for the sake of filthy lucre? Did Father Paissy teach you that?"

"No, no, on the contrary, Father Paissy once even said something like what you . . . but not like that, of course, not at all like that," Alyosha suddenly recollected himself.

"A precious bit of information, however, despite your 'not at all like that.' I ask you specifically: why should your Jesuits and Inquisitors have joined together only for material wicked lucre? Why can't there happen to be among them at least one sufferer who is tormented by great sadness and loves mankind? Look, suppose that one among all those who desire only material and filthy lucre, that one of them, at least, is like my old Inquisitor, who himself ate roots in the desert and raved, overcoming his flesh, in order to make himself free and perfect, but who still loved mankind all his life, and suddenly opened his eyes and saw that there is no great moral blessedness in achieving perfection of the will only to become convinced, at the same time, that millions of the rest of God's creatures have been set up only for mockery, that they will never be strong enough to manage their freedom, that from such pitiful rebels will never come giants to complete the tower, that it was not for such geese that the great idealist had his dream of harmony. Having understood all that, he returned and joined . . . the intelligent people. Couldn't this have happened?"

"Whom did he join? What intelligent people?" Alyosha exclaimed, almost passionately. "They are not so very intelligent, nor do they have any great mysteries and secrets . . . Except maybe for godlessness, that's their whole secret. Your Inquisitor doesn't believe in God, that's his whole secret!"

"What of it! At last you've understood. Yes, indeed, that alone is the whole secret, but is it not suffering, if only for such a man as he, who has wasted his whole life on a great deed in the wilderness and still has not been cured of his love for mankind? In his declining years he comes to the clear conviction that only the counsels of the great and dread spirit could at least somehow organize the feeble rebels, 'the unfinished, trial creatures created in mockery,' in a tolerable way. And so, convinced of that, he sees that one must follow the directives of the intelligent spirit, the dread spirit of death and destruction, and to that end accept lies and deceit, and lead people, consciously now, to death and destruction, deceiving them, moreover, all along the way, so that they somehow do not notice where they are being led, so that at least on the way these pitiful, blind men consider themselves happy. And deceive them, notice, in the name of him in whose ideal the old man believed so passionately all his life! Is that not a misfortune? And if even one such man, at least, finds himself at the head of that whole army 'lusting for power only for the sake of filthy lucre,' is one such man, at least, not enough to make a tragedy? Moreover, one such man standing at its head would be enough to bring out finally the real ruling idea of the whole Roman cause, with all its armies and Jesuits—the highest idea of this cause. I tell you outright that I firmly believe that this one man has never been lacking among those standing at the head of the movement. Who knows, perhaps such 'ones' have even been found among the Roman pontiffs. Who knows, maybe this accursed old man, who loves mankind so stubbornly in his own way, exists even now, in the form of a great host of such old men, and by no means accidentally, but in concert, as a secret union, organized long ago for the purpose of keeping the mystery, of keeping it from unhappy and feeble mankind with the aim of making them happy. It surely exists, and it should be so. I imagine that even the Masons have something like this mystery as their basis, and that Catholics hate the Masons so much because they see them as competitors, breaking up the unity of the idea, whereas there should be one flock and one shepherd . . . However, the way I'm defending my thought makes me seem like an author who did not stand up to your criticism. Enough of that."

"Maybe you're a Mason yourself!" suddenly escaped from Alyosha. "You don't believe in God," he added, this time with great sorrow. Besides, it seemed to him that his brother was looking at him mockingly. "And how does your poem end," he asked suddenly, staring at the ground, "or was that the end?"

"I was going to end it like this: when the Inquisitor fell silent, he waited some time for his prisoner to reply. His silence weighed on him. He had seen how the captive listened to him all the while intently and calmly, looking him straight in the eye, and apparently not wishing to contradict anything. The old man would have liked him to say something, even something bitter, terrible. But suddenly he approaches the old man in silence and gently kisses him on his bloodless, ninety-year-old lips. That is the whole answer. The old man shudders. Something stirs at the corners of his mouth; he walks to the door, opens it, and says to him: 'Go and do not come again . . . do not come at all . . . never, never!' And he lets him out into the 'dark squares of the city.' The prisoner goes away."

"And the old man?"

"The kiss burns in his heart, but the old man holds to his former idea."

"And you with him!" Alyosha exclaimed ruefully. Ivan laughed.

"But it's nonsense, Alyosha, it's just the muddled poem of a muddled student who never wrote two lines of verse. Why are you taking it so seriously? You don't think I'll go straight to the Jesuits now, to join the host of those who are correcting his deed! Good lord, what do I care? As I told you: I just want to drag on until I'm thirty, and then—smash the cup on the floor!"

"And the sticky little leaves, and the precious graves, and the blue sky, and the woman you love! How will you live, what will you love them with?" Alyosha exclaimed ruefully. "Is it possible, with such hell in your heart and in your head? No, you're precisely going in order to join them . . . and if not, you'll kill yourself, you won't endure it!"

"There is a force that will endure everything," said Ivan, this time with a cold smirk.

"What force?"

"The Karamazov force . . . the force of the Karamazov baseness."

"To drown in depravity, to stifle your soul with corruption, is that it?"

"That, too, perhaps . . . only until my thirtieth year maybe I'll escape it, and then . . . "

"How will you escape it? By means of what? With your thoughts, it's impossible."

"Again, in Karamazov fashion."

"You mean 'everything is permitted'? Everything is permitted, is that right, is it?"

Ivan frowned, and suddenly turned somehow strangely pale.

"Ah, you caught that little remark yesterday, which offended Miusov so much . . . and that brother Dmitri so naively popped up and rephrased?" he grinned crookedly. "Yes, perhaps 'everything is permitted,' since the word has already been spoken. I do not renounce it. And Mitenka's version is not so bad."

Alyosha was looking at him silently.

"I thought, brother, that when I left here I'd have you, at least, in all the world," Ivan suddenly spoke with unexpected feeling, "but now I see that in your heart, too, there is no room for me, my dear hermit. The formula, 'everything is permitted,' I will not renounce, and what then? Will you renounce me for that? Will you?"

Alyosha stood up, went over to him in silence, and gently kissed him on the lips.

"Literary theft!" Ivan cried, suddenly going into some kind of rapture. "You stole that from my poem! Thank you, however. Get up, Alyosha, let's go, it's time we both did."

They went out, but stopped on the porch of the tavern.

"So, Alyosha," Ivan spoke in a firm voice, "if, indeed, I hold out for the sticky little leaves, I shall love them only remembering you. It's enough for me that you are here somewhere, and I shall not stop wanting to live. Is that enough for you? If you wish, you can take it as a declaration of love. And now you go right, I'll go left—and enough, you hear, enough. I mean, even if I don't go away tomorrow (but it seems I certainly shall), and we somehow meet again, not another word to me on any of these subjects. An urgent request. And with regard to brother Dmitri, too, I ask you particularly, do not ever even mention him to me again," he suddenly added irritably. "It's all exhausted, it's all talked out, isn't it? And in return for that, I will also make you a promise: when I'm thirty and want 'to smash the cup on the floor,' then, wherever you may be, I will still come to talk things over with you once more . . . even from America, I assure you. I will make a point of it. It will also be very interesting to have a look at you by then, to see what's become of you. Rather a solemn promise, you see. And indeed, perhaps we're saying goodbye for some seven or ten years. Well, go now to your Pater Seraphicus; he's dying, and if he dies without you, you may be angry with me for having kept you. Good-bye, kiss me once more—so—and now go . . . "

Ivan turned suddenly and went his way without looking back. It was similar to the way his brother Dmitri had left Alyosha the day before, though the day before it was something quite different. This strange little observation flashed like an arrow through the sad mind of Alyosha, sad and sorrowful at that moment. He waited a little, looking after his brother. For some reason he suddenly noticed that his brother Ivan somehow swayed as he walked, and that his right shoulder, seen from behind, appeared lower than his left. He had never noticed this before. But suddenly he, too, turned and almost ran to the monastery. It was already getting quite dark, and he felt almost frightened; something new was growing in him, which he would have been unable to explain. The wind rose again as it had yesterday, and the centuries-old pine trees rustled gloomily around him as he entered the hermitage woods. He was almost running. "Pater Seraphicus—he got that name from somewhere—but where?" flashed through Alyosha's mind. "Ivan, poor Ivan, when shall I see you again . . . ? Lord, here's the hermitage! Yes, yes, that's him, Pater Seraphicus, he will save me . . . from him, and forever!"

Several times, later in his life, in great perplexity, he wondered how he could suddenly, after parting with his brother Ivan, so completely forget about his brother Dmitri, when he had resolved that morning, only a few hours earlier, that he must find him, and would not leave until he did, even if it meant not returning to the monastery that night.

# Notes

1. Nicholas Berdyaev, *Dostoevsky*, trans. Donald Attwater (New York: World, 1957), pp. 204, 210, 226. Berdyaev's study of Dostoevsky was first published in English translation in 1934.

2. Letter of 10 May 1879 to his publisher, Nikolai A. Lyubimov, in *Selected Letters of Fyodor Dostoevsky*, eds. Joseph Frank and David I. Goldstein, trans. Andrew R. MacAndrew (London: Rutgers University Press, 1987), p. 464.

3. George Steiner, "An Exact Art," in *No Passion Spent* (New Haven: Yale University Press, 1996), pp. 203, 206. The italics are Steiner's.

4. Vladimir Solovyov, "Tri rechi v pamyat' Dostoevskago," in *Sobranie sochinenii* (Brussels, 1966), vol. 3-4, p. 193. See also idem, *Lectures on Godmanhood* (London, 1948) for a philosophical exposition of the three temptations of Christ. It is probable that Solovyov's account of the temptations reflects his discussions with Dostoevsky himself about the meaning of "The Grand Inquisitor."

# three

# *Breaking the Seals*

## *Dostoevsky and Meaning in History*

Dostoevsky and other writers of the nineteenth century (such as Nietzsche) whom we now consider prophetic fascinate us in part because of their ability to discern an underlying sense to history—so much so, that they were able to extrapolate from the events and trends of their century to make remarkably accurate predictions about the one to come. Our fascination with these prophetic voices can be seen as an aspect of what Hannah Arendt has called "the unprecedented historical consciousness" of the modern age. Whatever the differences among the dominant ideologies of the twentieth century, they manifest a common orientation toward mastery of the future that is rooted in a certain conception of meaning in history. The word *history,* no less than words such as *freedom* and *creativity,* lies at the core of the contemporary consciousness.[1]

In his concern with the crisis of modernity, Dostoevsky did not fail to notice its unprecedented historical sensibility. His Grand Inquisitor duly exhibits this sensibility, appealing repeatedly to history as a verification of his formula for final human happiness. The Inquisitor's vision is both global and world-historical, and in this he is thoroughly modern.

Yet, insight into the hidden patterns of history can easily be superseded by history itself. "The Grand Inquisitor" offers a remarkable meditation on the meaning of world history, but just how remarkable does it remain today? As a prophetic discernment of the advent of twentieth-century totalitarianism by a writer living in the latter nineteenth century, does it remain remarkable—other than as a historical curiosity—for those living in the twenty-first century? If Dostoevsky's "Grand Inquisitor" continues to be prophetic for us, then it should reveal a possibility that has not yet been foreclosed by intervening historical events.

In his book *The End of History and the Last Man,* Francis Fukuyama has argued that despite the fact that *the* human experience of much of this century has been that of living under totalitarianism, this experience is finally to be interpreted as a detour (albeit enormous) from the goal toward which the "locomotive of History" is clearly headed—the global realization of liberal democratic order. The totalitarian temptation is not a permanent human possibility but an aberration explicable in terms of specific and temporary historical/cultural circumstances, a "disease of the transition" to global liberal democracy:

> At the end of the twentieth century, Hitler and Stalin appear to be bypaths of history that led to dead ends, rather than real alternatives for human social organization. While their human costs were incalculable, these totalitarianisms in their purest form burned themselves out within a lifetime—Hitlerism in 1945, and Stalinism by 1956. . . . Of course . . . we have no guarantee and cannot assure future generations that there will be no future Hitlers or Pol Pots . . . . On the other hand, a Universal History need not justify every tyrannical regime and every war to expose a meaningful, larger pattern in human evolution. The power and long-term regularity of that evolutionary process is not diminished if we admit that it was subject to large and apparently unexplainable discontinuities, any more than the biological theory of evolution is undermined by the fact of the sudden extinction of the dinosaurs . . . . It is not sufficient to simply cite the Holocaust and expect discourse on the question of progress or rationality in human history to end, much as the horror of this event should make us pause . . . . It is possible to understand nazism as another, albeit extreme, variant of the "disease of the transition," a byproduct of the modernization process that was by no means a necessary component of modernity itself . . . . *Fascism is a pathological and extreme condition, by which one cannot judge modernity as a whole.*[2]

Egregiously complacent though these assurances might seem, especially when one thinks of the human suffering caused by totalitarianism, Fukuyama does not make the mistake of simply equating historical success with truth and right. His view that liberal democracy represents the ultimate goal of modernity, whereas totalitarianism is but a temporary detour, is justified by what he takes to be the superior philosophical truth of liberalism (particularly in its Hegelian version)—that human beings can and will be satisfied in their essence only by the social order based on *equality of recognition.*

If Fukuyama's argument is valid, then Dostoevsky's "Grand Inquisitor" offers prophetic insight into certain major events of the twentieth century, but not into the historical destiny of modernity itself. We can retrospectively acknowledge

Dostoevsky's insight into the looming threat of twentieth-century totalitarianism, but this insight is historically limited; it is not an insight into an ongoing or permanent possibility on a world-historical scale. Dostoevsky was prophetic for his time, but not for ours, as we have now emerged from the nightmare of defeated and discredited totalitarian regimes.

Is "The Grand Inquisitor" still required reading for those who seek insight into the problem of human order as we enter the next millennium? Do Hitlerism and Stalinism exhaust the totalitarian possibilities revealed through "The Grand Inquisitor," or were they merely partial embodiments of a human temptation discerned by Dostoevsky and still concealed within the global success of liberal democracy? With these questions in mind, let us turn to the Inquisitor's meditation on the problem of meaning in history.

## The Grand Inquisitor's Account of Meaning in History

The Gospel story of Christ's temptation in the wilderness (Matthew 4:1–11) provides the framework for the Inquisitor's interpretation of world history:

"If it were possible to imagine . . . that those three questions of the dread spirit had been lost from the books without a trace, and it was necessary that they be restored, thought up and invented anew . . . and to that end all the wise men on earth— rulers, high priests, scholars, philosophers, poets—were brought together and given this task: to think up . . . three questions such as would not only correspond to the scale of the event, but, moreover, would express in . . . three human phrases only, the entire future history of the world and mankind—do you think that all the combined wisdom of the earth could think up anything faintly resembling in force and depth those three questions that were actually presented to you then by the powerful and intelligent spirit in the wilderness? . . . For in these three questions all of subsequent human history is as if brought together into a single whole and foretold; three images are revealed that will take in all the insoluble historical contradictions of human nature over all the earth. This could not have been seen so well at the time, for the future was unknown, but now that fifteen centuries have gone by, we can see that in these three questions everything was so precisely divined and foretold, and has proved so completely true, that to add to them or subtract anything from them is impossible."[44]*

---

*Here and below, references appearing inside parentheses in the narrative—unless otherwise indicated—are page numbers in Fyodor Dostoevsky, *The Brothers Karamazov,* trans. Richard Pevear and Larissa Volokhonsky (New York: Vintage, 1990). References inside square brackets are page numbers in "The Grand Inquisitor," reprinted from the aforementioned edition, in Chapter 2 of the present volume.

The Inquisitor regards the biblical account of Christ's temptation in the wilderness as prophetic in the popular sense of foretelling the future. Fifteen centuries of world history, as he interprets it, have already confirmed the accuracy of much of what was "divined and foretold" in the Bible. This historical confirmation justifies the sense of certainty with which he speaks of the future yet to unfold: "What I am telling you will come true, and our kingdom will be established"[51].

Yet the Inquisitor is also concerned with prophecy in the more authentic sense. The three questions posed to Christ illumine the unknown future not through some inexplicable magical divining but through their insight into the reality underlying the transient moments of history, the reality of human nature, or more precisely, "the historical contradictions of human nature." The Inquisitor wishes to speak, with the philosophers, about a political order that satisfies humanity *qua* humanity, a permanent order "over all the earth." According to him, although the three questions made their appearance within a particular cultural horizon, if they are properly interpreted, their import is universal; they concern all the wise on earth, "rulers, high priests, scholars, philosophers, poets."

The Inquisitor is not explicit about his understanding of the relation between the particularities of history and human nature "over all the earth." His emphasis on the "*historical* contradictions" of human nature implies that what is essential to humanity, although it might be present potentially always and everywhere, is actualized in and through the historical process. Subsequent human history thus not only confirms the insight of the three questions; it unfolds the chief elements of that insight.

Among the philosophers, it is Hegel, especially, to whom the Inquisitor appears close—a closeness only more apparent when we consider his account of world history as a three-stage development. According to the Inquisitor, each of the three questions posed in Matthew's Gospel reveals a fundamental inclination of human nature, and at the same time, a historical epoch.

The aspect of essential human nature expressed in the first temptation is the need for obedience:

> "Recall the first question; its meaning, though not literally, was this: 'You want to go into the world, and you are going empty-handed, with some promise of freedom, which they in their simplicity and innate lawlessness cannot even comprehend, which they dread and fear—for nothing has ever been more insufferable for man and for human society than freedom! But do you see these stones in this bare, scorching desert? Turn them into bread and mankind will run after you like sheep, grateful and obedient . . . .' But you did not want to deprive man of freedom and rejected the offer, for what sort of freedom is it, you reasoned, if obedience is bought with loaves of bread?"[44]

The historical epoch corresponding to the human need for obedience was long since underway when Jesus appeared with his "promise of freedom"—the epoch of tribal unity based on "communality of worship" and strict adherence to the "firm ancient law"[46]. This corresponds to the first stage in Hegel's philosophy of history, the ancient "Oriental World," in which "the individual never comes to the consciousness of independence," not even among the Hebrews, where the individual was subsumed within the family and a nationality rooted in an exclusive religious faith.[3]

Although the idea of individual freedom first made its appearance in the ancient world, among the Greeks, even Plato and Aristotle "knew only that *some* are free," not human beings as such.[4] For the Inquisitor—as, again, for Hegel—it is Christianity that brings fully to light that other aspect of essential human nature, revealed in the second temptation—the desire for freedom:

> He alone can take over the freedom of men who appeases their concience....There is nothing more seductive for man than the freedom of his conscience, but there is nothing more tormenting either....The dread and wise spirit set you on a pinnacle of the Temple and said to you: "If you would know whether or not you are the Son of God, cast yourself down, for it is written of him that angels will bear him up...and then you will know whether you are the Son of God, and will prove what faith you have in your Father." But you heard and rejected the offer and did not yield and did not throw yourself down....But, I repeat, are there many like you? And, indeed, could you possibly have assumed, even for a moment, that mankind, too, would be strong enough for such a temptation? Is that how human nature was created—to reject the miracle, and in those terrible moments of life, the moments of the most terrible, essential, and tormenting questions of the soul, to remain only with the free decision of the heart?[46–47]

It is clear that the human attraction to freedom is not understood by the Inquisitor as primarily a matter of political liberty, though this could be one of its appropriate ramifications; nor is the Inquisitor thinking of the freedom to satisfy material desires. If the latter were the case, then freedom would pose little challenge to human unity, for obedience can easily be "bought with loaves of bread." The freedom at issue in the Inquisitor's interpretation of the second temptation is above all an internal experience of consciousness, a sense of one's independence not only from external authority but also from natural impulse and desire. It is the inner sense of moral responsibility, or in the Inquisitor's words, "freedom of conscience." Nothing, the Inquisitor maintains, has been more seductive to human beings than this "freedom of conscience"—and nothing has been more tormenting. The "seduction" and the "torment" together have shaped the second great epoch of human history, stretching from Jesus to Luther (in the Inquisitor's own time) and beyond, into the modern age. Jesus, the "great idealist"[53], was right in his estimation that human beings will throw away "earthly bread" for the sake of the "heavenly bread" of freedom of conscience; but he was wrong in his failure to provide also the means of appeasing the moral conscience once it has been aroused: "It was impossible to leave them in greater confusion and torment than you did . . . "[47].

It was the task of those who organized the church bearing Jesus's name to appease and to tame the individual's awakened consciousness of moral independence. This, according to the Inquisitor, was the great historical accomplishment of medieval Roman Catholicism, which transformed the church from a spiritual community into an ecclesiastical power based on "miracle, mystery, and authority"[48]. The human need for obedience was given precedence over the desire for freedom, and a semblance of the unified community enjoyed by pre-Christian society was restored. It could, of necessity, only be a "semblance," because once "freedom of conscience" had made its appearance in history, it became an aspect of essential human nature that could not be ignored. It could, however, be appeased by deception, and moreover, by self-deception: "For fifteen hundred years we have been at pains over this freedom, but now it is finished, and well finished . . . . Know, then, that now, precisely now, these people are more certain than ever before that they are completely free, and at the same time they themselves have brought us their freedom and obediently laid it at our feet. It is our doing, but is it what you wanted? This sort of freedom?"[43] Human credulity, the desire for obedience that is fundamental to essential human nature, nostalgia for the lost unity of the "firm ancient law"—all facilitated the "correction" of Jesus's work that was accomplished by the Inquisitor and his allies. Let us refer yet again to Hegel's *Philosophy of History:*

> Thus the Church took the place of *Conscience:* it put men in leading strings like children, and told them that man could not be freed from the torments which his sins had merited by any amendment of his own moral condition, but by outward actions, *opera operata*—actions which were not the promptings of his own goodwill, but performed by command of the ministers of the Church . . . actions which are unspiritual, stupefy the soul, and which are not only mere external ceremonies, but are such as can be even vicariously performed . . . . Thus was produced an utter derangement of all that is recognized as good and moral in the Christian Church . . . . A condition the very reverse of Freedom is intruded into the principle of Freedom itself.[5]

The Inquisitor, who announces that we are now "finished" with the free individual, might well consider himself therefore to be standing at the end of history.

That he is actually standing at the beginning of the modern era must strike the reader as ironic, though the irony is mitigated greatly by the Inquisitor's own sense of the troubles yet to come. Another "great idealist," Luther, has recently appeared "in the north, in Germany," and just the day before his encounter with the Christlike prisoner, the Inquisitor himself had supervised the burning of "almost a hundred heretics at once"[41]. He knows, therefore, that freedom of conscience is not entirely finished, that there is rebellion everywhere, and that this rebellion might even "tear down" the temple of ecclesiastical power. He anticipates, further, that Protestantism will inaugurate "centuries more" of "freedom, free reason, and science," which will end with the rejection of the image of Christ, even in its Protestant form. And he anticipates that this extended rebellion will finally provoke another counterreaction toward unity, this time of an entirely secular sort: "In place of your temple a new edifice will be raised, the terrible Tower of Babel will be raised again"[45].

With the aid of Dostoevsky's hindsight, the medieval Inquisitor is able to divine, without naming them explicitly, the Protestant Reformation, the rise of modern science and the Enlightenment, the French Revolution, and the nineteenth-century liberal-socialist experiments in reconciling individual freedom with social unity on the basis of reason alone. To emphasize this point again, however: The Inquisitor's insight into the future is not an instance of quasi-magical divination but an inference from his penetration into the present reality of essential human nature. This reality, revealed in the first two temptations of Matthew's Gospel, is one of *contradictory* desires for obedience in unity and freedom in individuality. The historical future anticipated by the Inquisitor is simply the playing-out of this unstable tension between the nostalgia for a lost community and the attraction of free individuality.

The Inquisitor's interpretation of world history extends to the era of his creator, Dostoevsky, and then beyond. This movement of insight beyond the present of Dostoevsky into our present (and perhaps further yet?) is propelled by the Inquisitor's interpretation of the third and last temptation: "Why did you reject that last gift? Had you accepted that third counsel of the mighty spirit, you would have furnished all that man seeks on earth, that is: someone to bow down to, someone to take over his conscience, and a means for uniting everyone at last into a common, concordant, and incontestable anthill—for the need for universal union is the third and last torment of men"[49]. Nostalgia for the lost unity of ancient times, a nostalgia that has characterized the historical epoch corresponding to the second temptation, must be transformed into the hopeful expectation of a future unity, yet on a higher level. "Higher" because it will take into account and satisfy the human desire for freedom of conscience: "We shall convince them that they will only become free when they resign their freedom to us"[50]. And "higher" also because the reconciliation of social unity and individual freedom will be *global* rather than particular and exclusive, for the need for a union that is universal is the third fundamental aspect of human nature revealed in Matthew's Gospel: "Mankind in its entirety has always yearned to arrange things so that they must be universal"[49]. Although intimations of this yearning for a global order have always been present in history, its fulfillment belongs to the third epoch, the final epoch of human history. The desires for obedience in unity, for freedom in individuality, and for a global order that resolves these historical contradictions of human nature will find total satisfaction in the future anticipated by the Inquisitor. With this final satisfaction, the rebellious impulse that drives the transformations of history will cease: "The flock will gather again...and this time once and for all"[50]. Although events will continue to occur, significant history will have come to an end, since the goal that conferred meaning and significance on human struggles will have been attained.

Fukuyama employs a colorful metaphor (and an appropriate one, given the American face of contemporary liberal democracy) to conclude his argument, inspired by Hegel and Hegel's most notable twentieth-century interpreter, Alexandre Kojève—to wit, that the end of history is now upon us:

> Rather than a thousand shoots blossoming into as many different flowering plants, mankind will come to seem like a long wagon train strung out along a road. Some wagons will be pulling into town sharply and crisply, while others will be bivouacked back in the desert, or else stuck in ruts in the final pass over the mountains. Several wagons, attacked by Indians, will have been set aflame and abandoned along the way. There will be a few wagoneers who, stunned by the battle, will have lost their sense of direction and are temporarily heading in the wrong direction, while one or two wagons will get tired of the journey and decide to set up permanent camps at particular points back along the road . . . . But the great majority of wagons will be making the slow journey into town, and most will eventually arrive there . . . . Alexandre Kojève believed that ultimately history itself would vindicate its own rationality. That is, enough wagons would pull into town such that any reasonable person looking at the situation would be forced to agree that there had been only one journey and one destination.[6]

The town into which the wagons are pulling and will continue to pull is named Capitalist Liberal Democracy. It is not a town entirely free of problems such as unemployment, pollution, drugs, crime, and the especially vexatious issues of social policy generated by the competing claims of freedom and equality within a liberal democratic order. Such difficulties, however, Fukuyama assures us, are a matter of fine-tuning rather than a goad to undertaking a new journey, because liberal democracy constitutes the best possible solution to the human problem. It alone, of all possible human orders, fulfills our essential humanity by satisfying the desire of free individuals for equal recognition:

> The success of democracy in a wide variety of places and among many different peoples would suggest that the principles of liberty and equality on which they are based are not accidents or the results of ethnocentric prejudice, but are in fact discoveries about the nature of man as man, whose truth does not diminish but grows more evident as one's point of view becomes more cosmopolitan . . . . If we are now at a point where we cannot imagine a world substantially different from our own . . . then we must also take into consideration the possibility that History itself might be at an end.[7]

If the Inquisitor and Hegel converge remarkably in their accounts of the major stages of humanity's historical journey, they diverge dramatically in their visions of the final destination. For Hegel and his progressivist interpreters Kojève and Fukuyama, the freedom and equality vouchsafed in theory to humanity by Christianity are realized in historical actuality within global liberal democracy. The Inquisitor, on the contrary, asserts that the order that will finally satisfy "man as man" represents a fundamental *modification* rather than a *realization* of freedom and equality: freedom diverted into an illusion, and equality only within the flock that has submitted "once and for all" to its shepherds. The town into which the wagons are pulling is a tyranny—the most complete tyranny conceivable—because it is one that most completely satisfies our fundamental desires: "Then we shall give them quiet, humble happiness, the happiness of feeble creatures, such as they were created . . . . And everyone will be happy, all the millions of creatures, except for . . . those who govern them"[50, 51].

From the liberal progressivist perspective, the Inquisitor's vision of the end of History can only be an error that mistakes a temporary and unfortunately all-too-possible detour for the final goal itself. That the Inquisitor actually *prefers* tyranny as the final solution to the human problem must be simply perverse and symptomatic of his historical position; after all, he is a leading member of the authoritarian Roman Catholic hierarchy, which substituted ecclesiastical power for the spiritual power preached by Jesus. In thus situating his character, Dostoevsky seems actually to confirm the progressivist thesis that twentieth-century totalitarianism is a "disease of the transition" to liberal democracy, made possible by the persistence of religious, nationalist, ethnic, and other fanaticisms of the past. It might well be argued that in offering "The Grand Inquisitor" as a prophetic judgment on modernity as a whole, Dostoevsky was being far too pessimistic.

This, or something like it, would be the liberal progressivist perspective on "The Grand Inquisitor" as prophecy for today's world. But what if we turn the tables and ask about the Inquisitor's perspective on the modern progressivist interpretation of history? "The Grand Inquisitor" is the culmination of a sustained meditation on the modern idea of history as progress that is to be found throughout Dostoevsky's major writings.

## Dostoevsky's Account of Modern Progressivism

Let us turn our attention, first, to *Notes from the Underground,* where Dostoevsky broached many themes that were to became central in his later work. In the course of his assault on the pretensions of modern reason, the underground-man ridicules the argument of one H. T. Buckle that humankind mellows under the influence of civilization and "becomes less bloodthirsty and less inclined to war."[8] In his three-volume *History of Civilization in England* (published in a Russian edition in 1864), Buckle had offered a philosophy of history in which he equated advancing scientific knowledge with advancing humaneness. As promising evidence of the steady progress of European civilization, he cited two developments: the virtual disappearance of religious persecution and the steady decline of warfare, which "must be evident to the most hasty reader of European history."[9] The hearty optimism of Buckle's philosophy of history has hardly been borne out by the subsequent facts of modern history. A century later, if he is remembered at all, it is primarily as the hapless object of the underground-man's caustic wit. Yet he was an extremely influential spokesman for a doctrine of progress that captivated the nineteenth-century consciousness and that clearly continues, in various forms, to exercise a powerful influence today.

Dostoevsky was fascinated by the mysterious process whereby ideas, once launched by their authors into the world, take on a life of their own and come to dominate the consciousness of people who have little or no awareness of their original source. The underground-man cites Buckle as a source for the idea of history as progress. There were, of course, many others who had given expression to the same idea with varying degrees of assurance and subtlety: Russian contemporaries of Dostoevsky, such as Belinsky, Herzen, Bakunin, and Chernyshevsky; and the Western progressivist philosophers who most influenced them, such as Voltaire, Saint-Simon, Fourier, Schelling, Hegel, and Marx. When Dostoevsky was writing *Notes from the Underground,* the left-Hegelian interpretation of history was dominant among Russia's Westernized intelligentsia. Dostoevsky's chief concern, however, was not intellectual history but the inner meaning and the implications of the modern faith in progress, whatever its particular variant.

According to the underground-man, modern progressivism places great emphasis on the notion that world history is ultimately rational.[10] We might add that the assumption that human reason has the capacity to grasp the final meaning of history is apparent in the very phrase *philosophy of history,* which was invented by Voltaire.[11] However, does this overt appeal to rationality perhaps mask a more deeply rooted impulse? For the underground man, reason is merely the tip of the iceberg, amounting to "perhaps one-twentieth" of what constitutes human being. Under his scrutiny, the modern idea of progress is revealed not as the expression of dispassionate reason but as the symptom of fervent hope—hope for the "Crystal Palace" of the future.[12] The "Crystal Palace" is one of a set of images—the Inquisitor's "Tower of Babel" is another—that function in Dostoevsky's art as signifiers of the modern hope that human history is progressively advancing toward its fulfillment in a new kind of social order.

This hoped-for order, though often associated in Dostoevsky's writing with the French revolutionary slogan of *liberté, égalité, fraternité,*[13] is far more than "political" in the ordinary sense. As the narrator of *The Brothers Karamazov* asserts in his introductory words about Alyosha, "socialism is not only the labour question ... but first of all ... the question of the modern embodiment of atheism, the question of the Tower of Babel built precisely without God ... to bring heaven down to earth" (26). This expresses the essentially religious dimension of the modern progressivist expectation. Indeed, Dostoevsky's work as a whole lends powerful support to the argument that modern civilization should be understood not as something essentially novel but as somehow engendered by the same religious faith that it ostensibly rejects.

Dostoevsky was not the first to interpret the modern idea of progress as a secularized expression of biblical faith. After all, the most philosophically profound of nineteenth-century liberal progressivists, Hegel, understood his thought as the rational fulfillment of the truth contained embryonically in Christianity. What is of special significance in Dostoevsky is his depiction of the inner moral dynamic of the secularizing process, a dynamic embodied most memorably in Ivan Karamazov's rebellion. Through Ivan's rebellion, Dostoevsky responds to the truly interesting question: How could Christianity produce such anti-Christian consequences? Ivan, whom Dostoevsky described in a letter as a "present-day, serious socialist,"[14] gives voice to that ancient, intractable question of the Western theological tradition: How can the idea of a perfect God be reconciled with the affliction of human beings? The special feature of Ivan's well-known argument against religious faith is usually considered to be his willingness to accept God but not the "world ... created by God" (235). Ivan dismisses all of the logical proofs for or against the existence of God generated by Western philosophy and focuses on theodicy, the issue that he finds most existentially compelling. He opens his argument with an appeal to the sentiment that provides the common space where believer and nonbeliever can meet as human beings—the sentiment of compassion for the suffering neighbor. After affirming the importance of such compassion, Ivan proceeds to catalogue various "facts" of the world, with particular emphasis on the affliction of children. The pain evoked in the listener—Alyosha, and generations of readers of *The Brothers Karamazov*—prepares emotional ground into which the logic of Ivan's argument can insinuate itself. Despite Ivan's early claim that it is God's world, rather than God, that he is rejecting, it is clear that his entire argument leads ultimately to the rejection of God and that this was his intention all along. The logic of his argument is not original; indeed, it is at least as old as the book of Job. It was given its classic rational expression by eighteenth-century philosopher David Hume: "Is God willing to prevent evil but not able? Then he is impotent. Is he able but not willing? Then he is malevolent. Is he both able and willing? Whence then evil?" Yet the driving force of this argument, as developed in Ivan's rebellion, is not so much logical as moral: Those who genuinely love their suffering neighbor *ought* not, at the same time, to love God, who is responsible, directly or indirectly, for their neighbor's suffering.

In the New Testament (Matthew 22:37–39, for instance), love of God and love of neighbor are presented as inseparable. Ivan's strategy is to affirm the second part of the Christian love-commandment, the love of neighbor, but then to argue that it is incompatible with the love of God. One must choose whether to love God or humanity:

> For the hundredth time I repeat: there are hosts of questions, but I've taken only the children, because here what I need to say is irrefutably clear. Listen: if everyone must suffer, in order to buy eternal harmony with their suffering, pray tell me what have children got to do with it? It's quite incomprehensible why they should have to suffer, and why they should buy harmony with their suffering. Why do they get thrown on the pile, to manure someone's future harmony . . . . I don't want harmony, for love of mankind I don't want it . . . . I'd rather remain with my unrequited suffering and my unquenched indignation, *even if I am wrong*. Besides, they have put too high a price on harmony; we can't afford to pay so much for admission. And therefore I hasten to return my ticket. (244–245)

According to Ivan, the traditional theological response (the one emanating from the "they" above)—attempting to reconcile the apparent contradiction between the perfection of God and the affliction of human beings by means of the doctrine of divine providence—too readily abandons any truthful witness to the facts as they are, calling good evil and evil good. He therefore rejects traditional theodicy in the name of intellectual honesty and compassionate love for suffering humanity. This Ivan-like "metaphysical rebellion" is revealed in Dostoevsky's art as the animating source of the modern project of bringing heaven down to earth.[15] Modern progressivism shares the traditional biblical hope for the final overcoming of evil by good; but on moral grounds it refuses any longer to await obediently the transcendent overcoming promised in the doctrine of divine providence. Instead it envisages the process of earthly history, hastened by human action, as the sphere of this overcoming. As Karl Löwith has put it: "The irreligion of progress is still a sort of religion, derived from the Christian faith in a future goal, though substituting an indefinite and immanent *eschaton* for a definite and transcendent one."[16] This irreligious/religious notion of humanity bringing good out of evil through its own progressive shaping of history is the binding idea that, in the words of Versilov in *The Adolescent,* "underlies all contemporary civilization."[17]

We would do well to remind ourselves at this point that the author of "The Grand Inquisitor" is the same Ivan Karamazov whose powerful repudiation of faith in divine providence immediately precedes the recitation of his prose poem *(poemka)* about the Inquisitor. In this context, it would be natural to identify the Inquisitor as a man ahead of his time, who is involved in the shaping of history for the sake of actualizing heaven on earth. Yet, again, we find ourselves up against his apparently perverse anticipation of a heaven on earth that will be a tyranny rather than the liberal-socialist society of freedom and equality envisaged by Hegel, Marx, and the other modern proponents of a progressive, human shaping of history. Dostoevsky's general categorization of Ivan as a "present-day socialist" adds to readers' perplexity. Why would Ivan, immediately following his enucleation of the moral impulse inspiring the modern shift from faith in providence to faith in progress, choose a character like the Inquisitor as his prophet of the future?

Perhaps the answer lies in the fact that Ivan's metaphysical rebellion might in the end justify the repudiation of modern progressivism no less than Christian providentialism. This possibility is underlined particularly by the strong resemblance between Ivan's return of his "ticket of admission" to the future harmony and Vissarion Belinsky's famous retort to Hegel (well-known to Dostoevsky):

No thank you, Egor Fedorych [Hegel], with all due respect to your philosophical cap; let me inform you . . . that if I did succeed in reaching the top of your evolution ladder, I would demand even there an account from you of all the victims of the conditions of history . . . of accident, superstition, the Inquisition . . . etc., etc.,: otherwise I will throw myself headlong from the top rung . . . . Disharmony is said to be a condition of harmony: that may be very profitable and pleasant for megalomaniacs, but certainly not for those whose fates are destined to express the idea of disharmony.[18]

If Ivan is to refuse the transcendent *eschaton* out of love of humanity, then must he not refuse the immanent *eschaton* for the same reason? In the space of conflicting ideas opened up by Dostoevsky's art, no perspective stands unopposed. In the case of Ivan, both the moral justification of modern progressivism *and* its most fatal inadequacies are revealed through the same character.

Ivan's rebellious challenge to the promise of future harmony, even an immanent secular one, should be seen in the light of objections to the idea of progress voiced by other characters throughout Dostoevsky's work. Perhaps the most obvious of these objections is that of the underground-man, who in response to the notion of the "reasonableness" of the historical process, simply appeals to the facts accessible to common sense:

> Just take a look at the history of mankind—and what do you see? Majesty? Perhaps even majesty . . . . Variety? Perhaps even variety; one need only collect the ceremonial uniforms, both military and civilian, of all nations, of all ages . . . and if you include the uniforms of the civil service then you really will get lost . . . . Monotony? Well, perhaps monotony too: fighting and fighting, they are fighting now, they fought before, and they fought after—you'll agree this is already too monotonous. In short, anything can be said about world history . . . . The only thing that cannot be said is that it's rational. You'd choke on the first word.[19]

As for the notion of "progress," again, according to the underground-man, the facts speak loudly to the contrary: "And what is it in us that is mellowed by civilization? All it does, I'd say, is to develop in man a capacity to feel a greater variety of sensations. And nothing, absolutely nothing else. . . . Civilization has made man, if not always more bloodthirsty, at least more viciously, more horribly bloodthirsty."[20] Ivan's painful cataloguing of the cruelties that modern, civilized human beings remain capable of inflicting upon one another constitutes a graphic elaboration of the underground-man's observation. The more sophisticated philosophies of history are, of course, cognizant of such "facts"; but one suspects that the underground-man would not be swayed by references, for instance, to Hegel's emphasis on the role of negation in historical development. For where Hegel sees the necessary labor of the dialectic, the underground-man sees the chronic perversity of human nature—a perversity that casts doubt upon the whole notion of a new order of freedom, equality, and brotherhood.[21]

"Chronic perversity" or the "labor of the dialectic": These are two different readings of the negative facts of history. Yet even if the latter reading were to be granted, it would still face, in Dostoevsky's art, extremely powerful objections. Perhaps most damaging is the observation that the idea of progress is inherently contradictory. The underground-man notes that according to the modern philosophy of history the final order of good, free, and happy human beings is the inevitable product of historical necessity; people will find themselves "obliged to do good." Yet, he asks, in the absence of a free, personal choice, can one speak of genuine moral goodness?[22] This difficulty can perhaps be mitigated by understanding "goodness" as a kind of indifferent peaceableness (niceness) brought about through social adjustment rather than the outcome of what Kant called a "morally good disposition." Such a "lowering of the sights" in regard to human goodness would certainly be in keeping with the tendency of liberal progressivism to build its edifice on the reliable human desires, whether for comfortable self-preservation (Locke) or for recognition (Hegel). And insofar as freedom itself can be understood merely as the absence of external obstacles to the fulfillment of such natural desires, it might be possible to mitigate, to some extent, the embarrassing contradictoriness of the notion that people can be forced to become free by some sort of automatic mechanism called "history." Most acute, however, is the contradiction between the idea of progress and the idea of personal happiness, and it is not at all clear how this contradiction can be softened by some lowering of expectations in defining "happiness." If final happiness—in Fukuyama's language, the complete satisfaction of human beings in their essential humanity (however this satisfaction is precisely understood)—can be located at some future point in history, then what becomes of those individuals now, and throughout history, who by sheer bad luck do not happen to live at the right moment? To quote Ivan: "Is it possible that I've suffered so that I . . . should be manure for someone's future harmony?" (244) There does not appear to be much consolation in the thought that one's life, viewed from the perspective of history, can be regarded as fertilizer for the happiness of others.

Even allowing that some individuals might rise above the self-centered concern with personal satisfaction to an altruistic concern with the happiness of humanity in general, there remains a final inadequacy in the idea of progress. This is the fact of finitude; not so much one's own death, which is perhaps no longer of primary concern, but the inevitable death of those living within the future order, and moreover, the inevitable death of that order itself as part of a universe subject to the law of entropy. Hence the question posed by Arkady Dolgorukov in *The Adolescent:* "Why must I inevitably love my neighbor or your future humanity, which I'll never see, which I'll never know, and which will eventually also disintegrate without leaving a trace . . . when the earth will turn into an icy rock and float in airless space amidst an infinite number of other such icy rocks? . . . Why must I behave so nobly when nothing is going to last more than a moment?"[23]

All of the above objections to the doctrine of progress focus on the problem of ensuring the consent of those who are asked to serve as raw material for the future edifice. But the perspective can also be reversed to focus on those fortunate enough to inhabit that edifice. Would they be able to accept a happiness based on the suffering of so many? Could a just person consent to a happiness founded on the innocent tears of even one "tiny creature"? This is Ivan's question: "Answer me: imagine that you yourself are building the edifice of human destiny with the object of making people happy in the finale . . . but for that you must inevitably and unavoidably torture just one tiny creature . . . and raise your edifice on the foundation of her unrequited tears—would you agree to be the architect on such conditions?" (245)

Is one's own happiness possible if it presupposes the suffering of others (or even *another*)? This question takes us to the heart of Dostoevsky's moral concern; indeed, here we can assert without hesitation that character and author are at one. Dostoevsky's art here and elsewhere shows itself as the poetic expression—perhaps unparalleled—of Kant's supreme moral principle that every person must be treated as an end, never merely as a means.[24]

Up to this point, Ivan's challenge to liberal progressivism comes from within liberalism itself.[25] Kant, too, defended the infinite value of the individual, though this did not stop him from asking whether it might be possible to write a Universal History from a cosmopolitan point of view; and Hegel, who attempted to do just that, was nonetheless sensitive to the way in which any interpretation of history as a forward movement might appear callously indifferent to the trampling of many an innocent "flower" along the way.[26] The horror of the Holocaust is enough to make even Fukuyama "pause and contemplate" before affirming that, nevertheless, the "locomotive of History" is still on track toward its goal.

Yet, instances of hesitation arising from within liberal progressivism tend to be overcome by faith in the ultimate future goal, as the crushing of innocent flowers is given at least some redemptive meaning by reference to the future universal flowering. The logic of a progressivist interpretation of history, even a sensitive one, inevitably entails the tendency to sanction force, since force is the principal mechanism of historical change. At the same time, the very ideal of the future goal counters this tendency, functioning as a moral restraint on human actions in the present. Although modern progressivism repudiates the notion of a moral absolute beyond space and time, it retains the notion of a moral absolute within history. This moral concern can be the bad conscience of modernity, causing it to pause in its forward movement, and at the same time the necessary good conscience, sustaining and renewing the advance toward freedom, equality, and happiness for all. We detect a similar ambiguity in Ivan, who rejects the future harmony out of compassion for the suffering of "one tiny creature," and at the same time confesses his thirst to see with his own eyes the hind lie down with the lion, and the murdered man rise up and embrace his murderer (244).

However, what if it is no longer possible to believe in the future goal that gives meaning and justification to the historical process? This question can have an empirical sense, expressing doubt that the events of history really do indicate movement toward a global order of freedom and equality. Skepticism about the realizability of the goal can and does generate much debate even among progressivists. The same question can be posed in a far more radical manner: *Even if* history is now moving inexorably toward a global order of freedom and equality, is this desirable? Will this fully satisfy the most fundamental human longing? Would it really signify the fulfillment of our essential humanity? Or would it still be possible to conceive of a world order that is substantially different from, and better than, that conceived of by liberal-socialist progressivism? "The Grand Inquisitor" is Ivan's response to this more radical set of questions. Rather than representing a reactionary throwback, a "disease of the transition," this response can be understood as a further advance into the logic of modern thought. One might see it as a Nietzschean correction of Hegel.

In historicist progressivism, the fundamental principles of human thought and action are interpreted as successive worldviews determined by the historical milieu. Yet when the belief that this succession has a final goal weakens and disappears, only a radical historical relativism remains. Humanity is left face to face, in Nietzsche's ironic phrase, with only "the finality of becoming." Nietzsche made philosophically explicit what was already implicit in modern historicism: If there is no permanent truth transcending historical process, then there is finally no stable basis for concepts such as good and evil, or justice and injustice. Liberal progressivism was more than willing to employ the weapon of historical relativism against the dogmas and certainties of the past; Nietzsche turns the same weapon against the cherished values of liberalism itself. As Fukuyama acknowledges: "Relativism is not a weapon that can be aimed selectively at the enemies one chooses . . . . If nothing can be true absolutely, then cherished principles like human equality have to go by the wayside as well."[27]

Nietzsche's attack on the liberal principle of equality is based on something more than the logic of relativism, since he is willing to exempt certain privileged "truths"—for instance, that life is will to power—from this logic. Because logical *certainty* concerning the absolute truth of any principle is impossible according to Nietzsche, the scrupulous thinker should at least strive for an *understanding* of the principle sufficient to warrant its affirmation or rejection.[28] In regard to the principle of human equality, even its proponents have acknowledged the difficulty posed by the empirical evidence, which tends to show that nature has bestowed its gifts unequally. The principle of equality becomes even more doubtful when one understands its genealogical origins; it is readily explicable in terms of all-too-human motivations—especially the resentment of the weak toward those more generously endowed by nature—that have led people to invent and embrace it.

Nietzsche would insist that even if history could be interpreted as a movement toward a global order of human equality, this order is not desirable, for it would not fulfill the most fundamental human longing. Or to put it more precisely, it would satisfy only the weak—those who ask nothing more from life than comfort and entertainment as well as their modest share of recognition. The end of history envisaged by liberal progressivism is, for Nietzsche, the triumph of the "last man," the lowest common denominator of human possibility. To quote from *Thus Spoke Zarathustra:* "'What is love? What is creation? What is longing? What is a star?' thus asks the last man, and he blinks. The earth has become small, and on it hops the last man, who makes everything small . . . . 'We have invented happiness,' say the last men, and they blink. They have left the regions where it was hard to live, for one needs warmth . . . . No shepherd and one herd! Everybody wants the same, everybody is the same: whoever feels different goes voluntarily into a madhouse."[29]

An existence devoted to "rational consumption" will not, however, satisfy the deepest longing of the stronger or more spirited, who demand more from life and from themselves. Even in the absence of nobler ideas by which to live and die, they will find ways to express their will to power. The domination of the "last man" at the end of history will thus be put in question by the "nihilists," who will pursue power for its own sake, even to the point of precipitating immensely destructive wars and tyrannies, for they would rather "will *nothingness* than *not* will."[30] Nietzsche does not affirm as an end unto itself the destructive nihilism he envisages, but he is willing to affirm it as a means of ensuring that liberal democratic equality will not constitute the end of history, that the future will remain a possibility open to a higher vision of human life.

Dostoevsky's prophetic significance for our time was defined by Albert Camus as follows: "I have loved Dostoevsky as the one who most profoundly lived and expressed our historical destiny. For me, Dostoevsky is, above all, the writer who, well before Nietzsche, knew how to discern contemporary nihilism, to define it, to predict its monstrous consequences, and to attempt to point out the way of salvation from it."[31] Dostoevsky might not have used the word *nihilism* in precisely the same way as Nietzsche and Camus—in nineteenth-century Russia it had a particular, relatively limited usage[32]—but the phenomenon he depicted was the same. Before Nietzsche's annunciation of the death of God, Dostoevsky in Russia had already explored some of the consequences of the awareness that life is without any final meaning, that all the gods, all the moral ends—whether beyond history or within the historical future—to which human beings have devoted themselves are human inventions. Stavrogin, in *Demons*, for whom the distinction between good and evil is "just a prejudice," who perceives no difference in beauty between "some voluptuous and brutish act, and any great deed, even the sacrifice of life for the good of humanity," is perhaps the most compelling result of Dostoevsky's exploration of nihilism on the level of the individual.[33] However, he knew also that the nihilist insight, once sufficiently widespread, would have profound implications also for society as a whole.

Dostoevsky discerned on the horizon a profound social crisis precipitated by the loss of faith in the doctrine of progress, which had been the guiding idea of modernity. The modern world is confronted by him with this fundamental question: What will become of human society in the absence of any shared idea of the meaning of existence? Responses to this question expressed in his work bear a notable resemblance to Nietzsche's prophecies. There is, for instance, the possibility that many modern people will simply cling to a debased version of the final human happiness promised in the idea of progress. Lebedev, in *The Idiot,* foresees a universal decline into "flabbiness," the inevitable consequence of an exclusive concern with material consumption.[34] This vision of the trivialization of human life through a triumphant materialism finds several echoes throughout Dostoevsky's writing. Yet Lebedev's evocation of future materialism is closely associated with a story about cannibalism, which hints at another possibility: that of the complete disintegration of social life—portrayed, for instance, in Raskolnikov's chilling dream in the epilogue to *Crime and Punishment,* in which human beings who could no longer "agree on what to regard as evil, what as good . . . killed each other in some sort of meaningless spite."[35] The boundless trivialization of human life and/or its wholesale destruction: these remain *possibilities*—"trial balloons" launched by Dostoevsky's art[36]—rather than *certainties.* They signify attempts to give some shape to what Dostoevsky, speaking in his own name in *A Writer's Diary,* called the "enormous upheavals" *(ogromnye perevoroty)* on the horizon of modern civilization.[37]

Yet another possibility is that such "enormous upheavals" will drive a desperate humanity toward the final fulfillment envisaged by the Inquisitor: "Freedom, free reason, and science will lead them into such a maze . . . that some of them, unruly and ferocious, will exterminate themselves; others, unruly but feeble, will exterminate each other; and the remaining third, feeble and wretched, will crawl to our feet and cry out to us: 'Yes, you were right . . . and we are coming back to you—save us from ourselves'"[50].

The "unruly" who demand more of life than rational consumption might in their despair, as the Inquisitor anticipates, "exterminate themselves"; but some might seek political power. We are told that Ivan might choose to "smash the cup on the floor," or out of compassion for the weak, he might join those who are completing the new Tower of Babel[54]. Although there is no inherent conjunction between nihilism and political power, it is certainly one possibility. Is there any reason to believe that this possibility has been exhausted by the events of the twentieth century? Hitler and Stalin were indeed "unruly and ferocious," but it is doubtful that they took to completion in reality the possibility imaginatively embodied by Dostoevsky in the Inquisitor. Their regimes lacked, for instance, a central feature of the Inquisitor's tyranny—its philanthropic nature. The old Inquisitor has "loved mankind all his life," just as his creator, Ivan, loves humanity to the point of returning his ticket to the future harmony.

Perhaps the closest historical approximation to the philanthropic tyranny prophesied in "The Grand Inquisitor" was that achieved in East Germany during the era of the Wall (1961 to 1989), when Erich Mielke was in charge of the Ministry for State Security (the Stasi). Out of humanitarian love, the Inquisitor and his fellow rulers purport to take possession of people's freedom, giving them in exchange "miracle, mystery, and authority" (a quasi-religious system of meaning) and "bread" (material comfort). The East Germans were given Marxist ideology and cheap food, free medical care, and apartments. In the Stadtmuseum of Dresden (the German city where Dostoevsky lived for a year, while writing *Demons*) hang protest banners used in the mass demonstrations of October 1989, which precipitated the opening of the Berlin Wall in November. One of these banners reads:

> **"Ich liebe euch doch alle [I love you all]."**
> **—Mielke**

> **Was sagt der Gross Inquisitor!**
> **[What the Grand Inquisitor says!]**

If Dostoevsky's "Grand Inquisitor" does remain prophetic, that is because it conjoins political power with a nihilism that has exchanged its "ferocious" aspect for a humanitarian face. This compels us to question our usual conception of what a tyranny is, to entertain the possibility of a tyranny *incognito*. Indeed, any image of the tyrant—whether Hitler, Stalin, Mielke, or the Inquisitor himself—might be far too literal, when the actual danger is the subtle tyranny that never appears to be such—the tyranny of bureaucracies and corporations gradually becoming oblivious of human equality (as evidenced, for instance, by their questioning the equal value of every human life in the name of "quality of life"). It was Nietzsche's argument against the liberal principle of equality that human beings are so evidently unequal in quality that to some of them less is due; and if many still hesitate before this conclusion, that is merely testimony to the long shadow still cast by the archaic Christian worldview. As he puts it in *Thus Spake Zarathustra*:

"'We are all equal.—Man is but man, before God—we are all equal.' Before God! But now this God has died."[38]

It was Dostoevsky's insight that the "present day" liberal or socialist (Ivan) could be the Inquisitor of tomorrow, that progressivism harbors within itself its undermining by nihilism, that Hegel would be followed by Nietzsche. It was his insight that human equality could not be sustained by the very liberalism that trumpets it with such fanfare, because its overt basis is reason alone, and this finally provides more arguments for inequality than for equality. Dostoevsky, unlike Nietzsche, took no satisfaction from this insight. His critique of modernity did not include a rejection of the principle of equality but a warning as to its vulnerability in the face of the fundamental question: What is it about human beings that makes equal justice their due? The inability of liberal progressivism convincingly to answer this question gives rise to the danger that the town where Fukuyama's wagons eventually arrive will be the smooth, humanitarian tyranny of which Dostoevsky warns in "The Grand Inquisitor."[39]

## Speaking for Christ: The Elder Zosima's Account of Meaning in History

Prophetic warning presupposes the human power to decide between alternatives. But what viable alternative to the Inquisitor's vision does Dostoevsky offer modern people? Within "The Grand Inquisitor" itself this alternative is embodied in the silent figure of Christ, with all that this portends. Dostoevsky might well have intended access to the meaning of this silent figure to depend ultimately on the condition of the reader's heart; even the Inquisitor, after experiencing the prisoner's kiss of forgiving love, decides to release him. Nevertheless, the old man does not change his mind: "The kiss burns in his heart, but [he] holds to his former idea"[54]. A change of heart is necessary, but it is not sufficient by itself, in the absence of an alternative "idea." In order to get sight of this alternative Christian idea, we must descend from the silent Christ to the Russian monk Zosima.

Just as the Grand Inquisitor is Ivan Karamazov's prophetic creation, so is Zosima, in a sense, the prophetic creation of Alyosha Karamazov. As the narrator informs us, the life and teachings of Zosima (constituting book 6 of the novel, "The Russian Monk," following immediately after book 5, which contains "Rebellion" and "The Grand Inquisitor") are based on a manuscript by Alyosha, who "wrote it all down from memory some time after the elder's death" (286). "The Russian Monk," then, represents Alyosha's written response to Ivan's "Grand Inquisitor." It is also Dostoevsky's apologia for the silent Christ. It might be that

Dostoevsky invested all of his more memorable characters with some facet of himself; however, Zosima is unique in his explicit designation as spokesman for the author's most "cherished" ideas. In him we find embodied the religious vision of the mature Dostoevsky, though expressed in "another language and another form," as demanded by the artistic presentation of a Russian monk.[40]

Why did Dostoevsky choose a Russian monk for the breaking of Christ's silence in the face of the Inquisitor? The answer to this question might appear obvious given the appropriate symmetry between the two old men, both of whom play a leadership role in their respective churches, Roman Catholic and Russian Orthodox. Yet we already know that the obvious impression is misleading in the case of the Inquisitor, whose mind is closer to modern historicism and nihilism than to medieval theology. The question—who precisely is Zosima?—is likewise both more complicated and more significant than it might at first appear. Let us consider, first, the common temptation to identify Zosima as the Russian Orthodox response to the Roman Catholic Inquisitor. This suggests the equation: Roman Catholicism, the West, rationalism, and atheism on one side; and Orthodoxy, Russia, and faith on the other side—with Dostoevsky, of course, condemning the former and defending the latter. This oft-cited equation has the merit of simplicity, but it diverts us from a fuller understanding of Dostoevsky, who in his writings almost always chooses the ambiguous and paradoxical over the simple and straightforward. To note one example of the sort of nuance this equation ignores: Zosima is on one occasion called "Pater Seraphicus," a name more striking in the original Russian text because of the contrast between the Roman letters in which it appears and the surrounding Cyrillic script. It is also striking because this was the name sometimes given to St. Francis of Assisi, a Western spiritual figure, with whom Zosima seems to have more in common than with many Russian Orthodox saints.

In order to understand Zosima properly, we must be prepared to make more careful distinctions than the common equation permits. Dostoevsky goes out of his way to assist his readers by deliberately situating Zosima within a particular religio-historical milieu—that of the *startsy* ("elders" or "spiritual directors") of nineteenth-century Russian Orthodox monasticism. In an early chapter describing this milieu, the narrator offers this definition of *elder:*

> An elder is one who takes your soul, your will into his soul and into his will. Having chosen an elder, you renounce your will and give it to him under total obedience and with total self-renunciation. A man who dooms himself to this trial, this terrible school of life, does so voluntarily, in the hope that after the long trial he will achieve self-conquest, self-mastery to such a degree that he will, finally, through a whole life's obedience, attain to perfect freedom—that is, freedom from himself—

and avoid the lot of those who live their whole lives without finding themselves in themselves. (27–28)

The emphasis in this definition on practice rather than theory reflects the view, for instance, of a thirteenth-century Eastern theologian, Gregory Palamas, who once said: "To say something about God is not equivalent to meeting with God."[41] The elder, by precept and example, guides others to experiencing the truth of Christianity rather than merely conceptualizing it.

Dostoevsky describes the institution of elders as having existed for more than a thousand years. To be more precise, its origins can be found in the fourth century, in St. Antony, the founder of Egyptian monasticism; however, as Kallistos Ware has suggested, the model for the institution exists in the New Testament itself, in Paul's relationship with Timothy. In Ware's (Eastern) view, it is possible to speak of two strands or two forms of apostolic succession within the Christian Church. There is the visible succession of the ecclesiastical hierarchy, the series of bishops associated with metropolitan centers such as Rome, Constantinople, and Moscow. Alongside this, existing on a charismatic rather than an official level, there is the largely invisible apostolic succession of the spiritual fathers and mothers of each generation associated with remote monasteries in the desert, forests, or mountains, such as Athos in Greece, the countryside of Assisi in Italy, and Optina Pustyn in Russia.[42] Sometimes the hierarchical and the spiritual strands overlap or coexist with some harmony, but just as often they conflict. For instance, Zosima's spirituality is juxtaposed with the dogmatic, external piety embodied in his rival, Ferapont, an enemy of the practice of elders and a heroic keeper of fasts, who sees devils everywhere. Ferapont is vivid testimony to the fact that Dostoevsky did not uncritically affirm the Russian Orthodox tradition; he was aware of its darker side, and in his chapter on elders it is noted by the narrator that the rigid hierarchical strand eclipsed the spiritual strand throughout most of Russian history, and that the latter had enjoyed a renaissance only within the previous hundred years:

> [The institution of elders] was revived again in our country at the end of the last century by one of the great ascetics (as he is known), Paissy Velichkovsky, and his disciples, but even to this day, after almost a hundred years, it exists in rather few monasteries, and has sometimes been subjected almost to persecution as an unheard-of innovation in Russia. The institution flourished especially in one celebrated hermitage, Kozelskaya-Optina. (27)

Dostoevsky himself visited the Optina monastery and its elder, Father Amvrosy, while in the planning stages of *The Brothers Karamazov*.

To sum up, then: Zosima is a Russian Orthodox monk, but more importantly, he embodies a spiritual practice that predates the schism between Western and Eastern Christianity. The primary difference between him and the Inquisitor is not identical with the divide between Roman Catholicism and Russian Orthodoxy but rather with that between the hierarchical and spiritual strands of Christianity.

Zosima's participation in a spiritual tradition originating in the fourth century—and of course, his own advanced age—might tempt readers into another misrepresentation: that he is an essentially archaic figure. It is important to note that Zosima is accused by many of his fellow monks of being a modern innovator who does not properly observe the fasts and does not take the sacrament of confession and penance seriously enough. More importantly, Zosima seems to take to heart Fyodor Karamazov's criticism that monks expect to save themselves by shutting themselves up in monasteries, "looking at each other and eating cabbage" (37). This monk commands, with all the authority of an elder over his disciple, that Alyosha leave the monastery in order to live in the world "like a monk" (285). Zosima's spirituality may have ancient roots, but it is explicitly oriented toward engagement with the modern world.

In "The Russian Monk" the reader is presented with no systematic theology, let alone any point-by-point, Euclidean response to Ivan-Inquisitor.[43] Dostoevsky presents, instead, an artistic "form of life" bodying forth an alternative way of seeing and responding to the world.[44] This world, for both Zosima and Ivan, is the same one in which innocent human beings suffer. Indeed, Zosima would hardly constitute a serious response to Ivan were we to believe that as a monk cloistered away from the world, he is inevitably less aware of the extent to which it is soaked through, "from crust to core," with human tears. A careful reading of the novel leaves no reason to doubt that Zosima is acutely aware of human suffering—an awareness, moreover, based on his own experience in the world and on many years of receiving the confessions of others, whereas the twenty-four-year-old Ivan bases his argument on cases he has read about in the newspapers.

Ivan-Inquisitor's compassion for human suffering, as we have seen, justifies his questioning of the principles of freedom and equality, insofar as these principles are obstacles to whatever measure of happiness is possible for such "unfinished, trial creatures created in mockery"[53]. Zosima, too, expresses fundamental doubts about human freedom and equality in the modern era. He argues that the liberal notion of freedom as the right of the individual to satisfy her/his desires, with only the minimum restraint necessary to allow others to do the same, has eventuated in the competitive materialism that pervades modern social life. The modern self has, as he puts it, condemned itself to the "tyranny of material things and habits." Modern people have "succeeded in amassing more and more things, but have less and less joy" (314). In this climate of all-consuming materialism, the notion of equality can be little more than an expression of envy and resentment: "But what of this right to increase one's needs? For the rich, *isolation* and spiritual suicide; for the poor, envy and murder, for they have been given rights, but have not yet been shown any way of satisfying their needs" (313).

The Russian monk's observations might seem close to a Marxist critique of the merely formal equality of capitalist liberalism—except that for Zosima, the socialist insistence on substantive equality remains entirely within the materialist interpretation of the human self, which pervades modern society. "Feed them first, then ask virtue of them!"—thus the Inquisitor sums up the actual meaning of modern freedom and equality. He and Zosima are at one in their argument that a materialist conception of human happiness is incompatible with freedom and equality. Says the Inquisitor: "They will finally understand that freedom and earthly bread in plenty for everyone are inconceivable together, for never, never will they be able to share among themselves"[45]. These are Zosima's echoing words: "They [the rich] live only for mutual envy, for pleasure-seeking and self-display . . . while the poor, so far, simply drown their unsatisfied needs and envy in drink. But soon they will get drunk on blood instead of wine" (314).

Unlike the Inquisitor, however, Zosima does not reject the principles of freedom and equality. Indeed, he defends them vehemently; his critical observations about liberal-socialist materialism preface an appeal to a different thinking about freedom and equality, a thinking that affirms the higher, spiritual dimension of human being. The self of modern liberalism, as a social and narrative construction out of the raw materials of desire and will, can ultimately find its satisfaction only in terms of these raw materials, in the "tyranny of material things and habits." According to Zosima, only the reality of the higher self makes genuine freedom possible. Human freedom, as he understands it, is the reverse image of modern materialism: Rather than an aggrandizement of the self, it is a freedom *from* the self. The way to fulfillment for human beings is not through the acquisition of things but through an ascesis that seeks to find the self within the self: "Obedience, fasting, and prayer are laughed at, yet they alone constitute the way to real and true freedom: I cut away my superfluous and unnecessary needs, through obedience I humble and chasten my vain and proud will, and thereby, with God's help, attain freedom of spirit, and with that, spiritual rejoicing!" (314)

Zosima certainly raises the sights for human beings. For, although he is speaking particularly of the monk, he also asserts clearly that anyone can be open to such self-discovery, and that no immanent natural gift of intellect or talent is required. It is by virtue of this spiritual possibility that *every* human being is owed respect: "Equality is only in . . . spiritual dignity" (316). For Zosima, the principle of equality derives its legitimacy and meaning from the eternal destiny of each person. But does it derive therefrom any force in regard to actual human life—and especially human suffering—in this world? Does Zosima's rethinking of human equality on Christian foundations really constitute an alternative to the Inquisitor's rejection of equality out of compassion for human suffering? It should be kept in mind that the Inquisitor has already charged the silent Christ with demanding too much of humanity; and it might be argued that Zosima's appeal to the transcendent destiny of human beings likewise raises the sights so high as to be inapplicable to life in this world. This inapplicability would be twofold: It demands too much in its asceticism and too little in its tendency to become a doctrine of consolation that discourages constructive action. If the genuine freedom and equality envisaged by Zosima are to find fulfillment only in a "higher, heavenly" world (320), then it would seem that we are presented in this Russian monk merely with an appeal to an otherworldly doctrine of providence.

Zosima has frequently been read in this manner, especially by those who understand Dostoevsky to be opposing Ivan's metaphysical rebellion with an appeal to a doctrinaire Christianity. Given this reading, it is little wonder that the monk can seem an "intolerable old bore" beside the impassioned young rebel.[45] This, however, is a misreading that fails to do justice to Dostoevsky as an artist or a thinker. Because it is contradicted by the text itself, one can only surmise that it is a willful misreading according to some preconceived notion of what Christianity "must" have to say.

In the face of human suffering, Zosima does indeed appeal to the mystery of the providential "enacting of eternal truth," especially as revealed in the book of Job (292). Yet in response to Ivan's demand for justice on earth, he does not stop at reaffirming the mystery of eternal justice; instead, he invokes an alternative vision of justice on earth—one founded not on Euclidean reason alone but on Christ. This Russian monk insists repeatedly that "life is paradise," that we need only want to understand, and "it will come at once in all its beauty" (299). Whatever the precise meaning of this insistence, it testifies against any easy dismissal of Zosima's orientation as "otherworldly." Clearly, his raising of the sights concerning the principles of freedom and equality does not preclude for him their enactment in the world. His concern with engaging the world is everywhere evident, in his words and his actions, from his stricture against child labor (315) to his commission to Alyosha to live as a monk *in the world* (285). Although freedom and equality in Zosima's Christian understanding might find their initial realization in the monastic community, he does not envisage this community as a spiritual elite separate from a hopelessly corrupt world; monasticism is to function, rather, as a leavening force within the world, working toward the latter's transformation. In response, however, to those who work for a transformation of the political or socioeconomic structures, Zosima points to a different sort of transformation: "In order to make the world anew, people themselves must turn onto a different path psychically. Until one has indeed become the brother of all, there will be no brotherhood" (303).[46] Those who would refashion the world must first begin with themselves.

This starting with oneself signifies the first step in what Dostoevsky himself once termed his "theory of practical Christianity."[47] In its engagement with the world, a "practical" Christianity can employ "impractical" means—obedience, fasting, and prayer, for instance—because these can foster the sort of psychic transformation needed if people are going to be capable of forming communities in which they actually feel and live according to the idea that "everyone is really responsible for everyone" or that "each of us is guilty before everyone and for everyone" (298). In a world given over to external technique, Dostoevsky's practical Christianity can appear highly uncertain in its results. A genuinely transformative movement of the heart is indeed a chancy and mysterious thing (as few have appreciated better than Dostoevsky himself); but if such an emphasis is to be considered "otherworldly," then self-knowledge and personal responsibility must be accounted of little importance in this world.

With this emphasis on personal responsibility in the service of freedom and equality, we are faced with a feature of Zosima's teaching that is too often overlooked—his willingness to use the language of liberal thought. The Russian monk can at times sound remarkably like a modern Western progressive. This is, in part, a matter of rhetorical strategy. One aim of Dostoevsky's practical Christianity was to persuade; and he knew well that most of his readers, especially the young, were attracted by the claims of liberal-socialist progressivism. He was willing to invite these readers to consider the possibility—albeit a strange one at first encounter—that the freedom and equality they sought was really to be found in the vision of the Russian monk. Yet Dostoevsky's use of secular progressivist language and his evocation of its purer aspirations are more than stratagems. Dostoevsky took no satisfaction from his prophetic insight that human equality was vulnerable to being undermined within the very bosom of the secular progressivism that promoted it in the modern world. Against the common tendency to categorize him as a conservative in social and political matters, it must be emphasized that his critique of modernity was not aimed simply at the rejection of liberal progressivism but at its redemption.

This aim is evident in one of the most memorable of all Dostoevsky's characters, Stepan Trofimovich Verkhovensky, of *Demons*. Stepan Trofimovich begins the novel as little more than a caricature of the nineteenth-century Russian liberal progressive.[48] He is complacently, even naively, satisfied as to his enlightened superiority to the traditions and convictions of the past, especially, of course, to those of religion; Christianity, for instance, "has never understood woman." Although he rejects historical Christianity, he is somewhat open to the idea of God, though only (in Hegelian fashion) as a "being who is conscious of himself in me."[49] Although his self-absorption is virtually total, it does leave room for some devotion to the "great thought" of a future order of human freedom and equality. Stepan Trofimovich's awakening to the nihilistic implications (embodied, appropriately, in his son Peter) of his self-satisfied liberalism is gradual and painful, but when it occurs, he reveals a beauty of character that surprises the reader (and perhaps the author himself). In the final words of his "last pilgrimage," Stepan reverts to the "Great Thought" that he has long revered. The capitalized letters in the text reflect his new awareness of this idea's necessary relation to the eternal destiny of human beings:

> The one constant thought that there exists something immeasurably more just and happy than I, fills the whole of me with immeasurable tenderness and—glory—oh, whoever I am, whatever I do! Far more than his own happiness, it is necessary for a man to know and believe every moment that there is somewhere a perfect and peaceful happiness, for everyone and for everything . . . . If people are deprived of the immeasurably great, they will not live and will die in despair. The immeasurable and infinite is as necessary for man as the small planet he inhabits . . . . My friends, all, all of you: long live the Great Thought! The eternal, immeasurable Thought! For every man, whoever he is, it is necessary to bow down before that which is the Great Thought . . . . *Petrusha* [Peter] . . . Oh, how I want to see them all again! They don't know, they don't know that they, too, have in them the same eternal Great Thought![50]

True to character, Stepan does not relinquish the conceptual language of his liberalism, but his change of heart does lend to that language a more profound (if vague) resonance. His final acknowledgment of the human need for the eternal is emblematic of Dostoevsky's hope that the movement of secular progressivism into nihilism might be forestalled, to some extent, by encouraging progressivism to recollect its spiritual origins. But for every Stepan Trofimovich, there are several Pyotr Alexandrovich Miusovs (Miusov is the archetypal, self-satisfied liberal in *The Brothers Karamazov* who remains just that); and more significantly, there is an increasing number of Ivan Karamazovs, who do not flinch before the nihilist possibility. An individual change of heart might be a necessary first step, but it is a highly uncertain hope for the future of an entire civilization. By itself, this first step of personal transformation would not seem to justify the confident expectation that marks Zosima's discourse about Christian freedom and equality:

People laugh and ask: when will the time come, and does it look as if it will ever come? But I think that with Christ we shall bring about this great deed. And how many ideas there have been on the earth, in human history, that were unthinkable even ten years earlier, and that would suddenly appear when their mysterious time had come and sweep over all the earth! So it will be with us as well. (317)

Zosima's faith is not only actively engaged with the world; it anticipates a possible historical fulfillment.

Instead of judging profane history as ultimately unimportant, Zosima appears to envisage it as having a final spiritual goal, which it is capable of containing within itself and toward which it is moving. He defines this goal as the transfiguration of society into a universal Church: "'It is true,' the elder smiled, 'that now Christian society itself is not yet ready, and stands only on seven righteous men; but as they are never wanting, it abides firmly all the same, awaiting its complete transfiguration from society as still an almost pagan organization, into one universal and sovereign Church. And so be it, so be it, if only at the end of time, for this alone is destined to be fulfilled!'" (66) The Christian society envisaged by Zosima might be labeled by some a "theocracy" (the liberal Miusov dismisses the notion as "arch-Ultramontanism"); but insofar as that term implies the rule of a priestly order representing God's will, it is a misnomer. Zosima has very little to say about priests, and what he does say is invariably tinged with criticism. He has even less to say about the sacramental functions of the Church. The universal Church on earth confidently awaited by Zosima is not primarily an ecclesiastical and sacramental institution imaging forth through symbolism and ritual the Lordship of Christ in a profane world—that is, it is not the Church as it has been and is now. It is, rather, a realized human community in which human behavior and relationships have been transformed by Christian love, in which people actually live according to the idea that "everyone is really responsible for everyone and everything" (320). This community, like that envisaged by modern progressivism, is one of freedom, equality, and brotherhood—but as understood and achieved on the basis of Christ rather than reason alone (318).

When we put together Zosima's expectation of a transfigured earthly society with his enigmatic assertion that "life is paradise," it might appear that he, no less than the most ardent progressivists, is preaching a future heaven on earth. If this is so, then Ivan's use of the Franciscan title *Pater Seraphicus* to refer to Zosima is richly and ironically suggestive. Many of the followers of St. Francis regarded him, themselves, and the events of their time as the fulfillment of the prophecy of the twelfth-century Italian abbot, Joachim of Fiore, that the third and final age of the Holy Spirit was imminent (it would begin in 1260, according to Joachim's own calculation). On the basis of insight derived from the book of Revelation,

Joachim conceived of world history as a sequence of three ages or dispensations—those of the Father, Son, and Holy Spirit—through which Christian truth is successively revealed. The age of the Spirit was to be the final, Third Realm, after which history would come to an end. With the advent of this final age, the existing church of clergy and sacraments would be replaced by a church of the Spirit, essentially an order of monks in which the mediating role of preaching and sacraments would no longer be required. When the Roman Catholic hierarchy suppressed the Franciscan Spirituals in the fourteenth century, Joachim's theology of history was forced underground—only to reemerge five centuries later, in secularized form, in modern philosophers of history such as Saint-Simon, Schelling, and Hegel.[51]

It would be ironic if Dostoevsky's acquaintance with the nineteenth-century philosophers of history had influenced unconsciously his expression of a Christianity that was intended as a response to their historicism. If Zosima's view of history signifies merely an appeal from modern Joachism to something very much like the original Joachitic theology of history, then it fails to offer a real alternative. Is Dostoevsky a prophetic figure for our age not only through his insight into the implications of the modern historical consciousness but also as an example of how difficult, or perhaps impossible, it is to think beyond this consciousness?

The obvious affinities between Zosima's future universal Church on earth and Joachim's final age of the Spirit justify the posing of the question above. It is not clear, however, that the answer must be affirmative. Although it would be inappropriate to seek anything like a systematic theology of history in Zosima's sayings, his fellow monk, the "very learned" Father Paissy, clarifies an important issue: the expectation, which he shares with Zosima, of the future universal Church on earth does *not* signify a complete immanentization of the Christian eschatological hope. Paissy, who can be regarded here as Zosima's spokesman, distinguishes between the "Kingdom of Heaven" and the kingdom of the Church on earth: "The Kingdom of Heaven, of course, is not of this world, but in heaven, but it is entered in no other way than through the Church that is founded and established on earth . . . . The Church is indeed a kingdom and appointed to reign, and in the end must undoubtedly be revealed as a kingdom over all the earth" (61–62). To Zosima, apparently, the universal Church on earth is apparently the ultimate end (both *finis* and *telos*) of human history; but *sub specie æternitatis* it is a penultimate end, to be succeeded by the eternal consummation promised in the New Testament. The relation between the historical and the eternal fulfillments is expressed by the "mysterious visitor" (who can also be regarded here as speaking for Zosima): "You ask when it will come true. It will come true, but first the period of human *isolation* must conclude . . . . There must needs come a term to this horrible isolation, and everyone will at once realize how unnaturally they have separated themselves one from another. Such will be the spirit of the time, and they will be astonished that they sat in darkness for so long, and did not see the light. Then the sign of the Son of Man will appear in the heavens" (303–304). Here the realization of the true spiritual community on earth and the end of the world are so closely associated as to merge into one eschatological hope. And in this regard, note, too, Zosima's conditional phrase: "And so be it, so be it, *if only at the end of time.*" Zosima, unlike Joachim, does not insist on a temporally enduring age of the Spirit, or millennial age, before the ultimate end. There is no hint, moreover, in Zosima of the Joachitic notion that Christian truth is unfolded successively in the historical process; for Zosima, the touchstone of meaning and truth is the one single event of Christ. Finally, unlike Joachim, Zosima does not venture down the all-too-beguiling path of predictive calculation about the end time: "There is no need to trouble oneself with times and seasons, for the mystery of times and seasons is in the wisdom of God" (66).

In these important respects, then, Zosima avoids the tendency to make truth and good, and their human appropriation, dependent on a scrutable historical process. Moreover, in these respects, at least, we can answer the question posed earlier in the negative: He (and hence Dostoevsky) does *not* simply appeal from the modern philosophy of history to a theology of history held by the same assumptions.

However, another element of Zosima's hope clearly precludes answering the question with an unqualified negative: The view that profane history is to any extent capable of embodying the freedom and equality of the City of God leads naturally to the question of how particular historical nations and events are related to this future embodiment. Zosima has very little to say about the actual events of world history, but he is emphatic about the crucial role of one historical people, the Russians: "This is a God-bearing *(bogonosets)* people" (316). The truth of the universal Christian community is preserved in its purity within the Russian monastery, and at least implicitly in the attitudes and practices of the Russian people. When the need arises, it will be revealed to the modern world: "This star will shine forth from the East" (313). In order to consider more carefully the import of Zosima's strange assertion, we must turn to other writings by Dostoevsky, in which he speaks in his own name.

In *A Writer's Diary* as well as in his notebooks and correspondence, Dostoevsky expresses more directly the salient elements of Zosima's interpretation of history, though in "another form" and within the context of a far more detailed account of European and Russian history. Vasily Zenkovsky has spoken of Dostoevsky's development of a "metaphysics of history."[52] Although this phrase is probably an overstatement, Dostoevsky's work does evince considerable reflection on the basic theoretical principles that ought to govern the interpretation of history. Dostoevsky presents himself as an advocate of the "idealist" approach to history, arguing that those who strive to define the "laws" or "necessities" determining historical development must examine, above all, the various systems of meaning that have given purpose to the lives of peoples. Civilizations are not founded on the mere need to—as he puts it—"save one's neck" but always on the basis of "a great idea."[53] This principle of the primacy of religious ideas as the animating force in the rise and fall of civilizations is applied to actual history in his journalism, and on occasion, in his novels.

In his rough notes for a projected (though never published) essay on "Socialism and Christianity," Dostoevsky sketches in broad strokes his outline of world history. Notably, as in "The Grand Inquisitor," a three-stage schema is posited. The first stage, represented in the primitive communities at the dawn of history, is characterized by the complete integration of the individual within the unity of the common life. This stage of unconscious happiness is disrupted by the appearance of individual self-consciousness. The ensuing disharmony between the individual and society results in a fundamental unhappiness that has burdened this second stage—called "civilization" by Dostoevsky—from its inception to the present: "Man in this condition feels bad . . . loses the source of living life (*zhivaya zhizn'*), doesn't know spontaneous sensations and is conscious of everything."[54] Civilized humanity has striven desperately to find a new social harmony, but the interests of society and of the individual have only become articulated into opposed, apparently irreconcilable ideas. These opposing ideas of social unity and individual freedom have been manifested in the massive and bloody conflicts that have characterized the history of civilization. In the West, for instance, the idea of compulsory social unity animated the Roman Empire and was then bequeathed to its descendants, Roman Catholicism and socialism, whereas the idea of individual freedom has been expressed in the opposing movements of Protestantism, and later, capitalist liberal and nihilist individualism.

For Dostoevsky, the crisis of order in the modern age, which he expected to become increasingly intense, was everywhere characterized by the tension between individuality and social unity, or freedom and equality. The thought and practice of the modern West appeared utterly unable to discover the way to that reconciliation of the individual and the community imagined by Dostoevsky as follows:

> If we transposed fraternity into rational . . . language, of what then would it consist? It would consist of this: each individual, of his own accord, without any external pressure or thought of profit, would say to society, "We are strong only when united; take all of me, if you need me . . . . I cede all my rights to you and beg you to dispose of me as you see fit. My greatest joy is to sacrifice everything to you, with-

out hurting you by so doing. I shall annihilate myself, I shall melt away, if only your brotherhood will last and prosper."—But the community should answer, "You offer us too much. What you offer we have no right to refuse, for you say it would be your greatest joy; but what can we do, when our constant concern is for your happiness. Take everything that is ours too. Constantly . . . we shall struggle to increase your personal freedom and self-fulfillment . . . . We are all behind you . . . we watch eternally over you."[55]

Dostoevsky observes that this sort of social harmony will remain merely a pious dream so long as freedom is understood as a principle of individualism, of "isolation, of intense self-preservation . . . of self-determination of the *I*." In a capitalist liberal society in which the personality is intent only on demanding its "rights," the socialist who wants to promote unity and equality must resort to calculated appeals to self-interest, and finally, to force: "The frantic socialist sets desperately to work on the future fraternity, defining it, calculating its size and weight, enticing you with its advantages, explaining, teaching, telling of the profit each stands to gain . . . . And driven to the final stage of desperation . . . ends by proclaiming '*liberté, égalité, fraternité, ou la mort.*'"[56] We have seen how the Inquisitor would propose that the contradictory human desires for unity and freedom be resolved in a third and final stage of world history. Dostoevsky, too, looks to a third stage that would supersede the contradictions of historical civilization, but through a genuine reconciliation rather than an illusory one that undermines the true meaning of both opposing terms. This difference is related to their assessments of what Christianity means in world history. According to the Inquisitor, the unity attained in the Roman Empire was undermined by the new religion, with its idea of personal freedom; but for Dostoevsky, in contrast, Christianity did not signify exclusively the idea of freedom but also a new kind of human communion—a "spiritual" rather than "compulsory" one, aiming to preserve and enhance the free personality in unity.

Dostoevsky applied his interpretation of world history to the contemporary relationship between Russia and the West frequently and in detail in *A Writer's Diary*. He suggested, for instance, that the intense struggle between France and Germany for European hegemony in the latter nineteenth century had to be understood in terms of the more fundamental, antithetical ideas of compulsory unity and isolating freedom:

Germany's objective is one; so it was before, and so it was always. It is her *Protestantism*—meaning not just the expression of the Protestantism that took shape in Luther's time but her chronic protestantism, her chronic tendency to *protest*— against the Roman world . . . against everything that was Rome and Roman in its objective; and then against everything that was passed on from ancient Rome to the new Rome and to all those peoples who took the idea of Rome . . . against the heirs of Rome and everything that makes up this legacy.[57]

Immense nationalist struggles, which will eventually draw in the Anglo-American world, lie in the West's future. Yet, according to Dostoevsky, even these elemental conflicts are overshadowed in significance by the possibility of a "colossal revolution" posed by the diffusion of socialism throughout the West. He predicts that, following an era of great wars, communist revolution "will surely come and triumph," though, "after a bit, it will fall."[58] The precise configuration of national struggle, war, and revolution tends to shift in his various speculations, but his insistence on the decisive role that could be played by Russia does not vary. Just as he tends to associate the idea of compulsory unity with France—the modern heir to Rome (both Imperial and Catholic)—and the idea of individualism with Germany—the heir of Protestantism—so he associates the reconciling Christian idea with the Orthodoxy of Russia. The inevitable involvement of Russia in the conflicts of the modern West implied the possibility of a final resolution of the problem of human order. Dostoevsky's account of meaning in history comes to its most extreme expression in an article written in 1877 on the Balkan question, which was then agitating the Western powers and Russia:

> This terrible Eastern Question is virtually our entire fate for years to come. It contains, as it were, all our goals and, mainly, our only way to move out into the fullness of history. It contains as well our final collision with Europe and our final uniting with her, but now on new, powerful, productive principles. Oh, how is Europe now to grasp all the fateful, vital significance the solution of this question has for us . . . . In short . . . sooner or later, *Constantinople must be ours,* even if it be only in the next century![59]

Faced with such a proclamation, it is customary for embarrassed interpreters of Dostoevsky to refer to his xenophobic Russian chauvinism as a kind of ideological virus that overmastered him all too frequently in *A Writer's Diary* but that fortunately did not fatally infect the artistic genius of the novels. This virtually obligatory separation of Dostoevsky the artist from Dostoevsky the political polemicist does not, however, satisfy. For there *is* clearly a relation between the art and the concern with Russia's world-historical mission. Dostoevsky's "Constantinople must be ours" can be seen as a translation into more specific terms of Zosima's "This [the Russian people] is a God-bearing people." The quick and easy "explanation" according to Dostoevsky's prejudices, even if justified, precludes exploration of the more interesting questions that might attend his hope in a Russian spiritual mission to the modern world.

Characteristically, the most significant question along these lines is posed by Dostoevsky himself in his art, at a pivotal moment during a conversation in *Demons* between Shatov and Stavrogin. First, Shatov expounds his interpretation of history:

> "Not one nation," he began, as if reciting line by line, and at the same time still looking menacingly at Stavrogin, "not one nation has ever set itself up on the principles of science and reason; there has never been an example of it, unless perhaps only for a moment, out of foolishness . . . . Nations are formed and moved by another ruling and dominating force, whose origin is unknown and inexplicable . . . . It is the force of a ceaseless and tireless confirmation of its own being and a denial of death. The Spirit of life, as Scripture says, the 'rivers of living water,' whose running dry is so threatened in the Apocalypse . . . . The aim . . . of every nation and in every period of its existence, is solely the seeking for God, its own God, entirely its own, and faith in him as the only true one. God is the synthetic person of the whole nation, taken from its beginning and to its end . . . . It is a sign of the nation's extinction when there begin to be gods in common. When there are gods in common, they die along with the belief in them and with the nations themselves. The stronger the nation, the more particular its God . . . . But the truth is one, and therefore only one among the nations can have the true God, even if the other nations do have their particular and great gods. The only 'god-bearing' nation is the Russian nation. . . . "

Stavrogin, in response, poses his question:

> "I simply wanted to know: do you yourself believe in God, or not?"
> "I believe in Russia, I believe in her Orthodoxy . . . I believe in the body of Christ . . . I believe that the second coming will take place in Russia . . . I believe . . . ," Shatov babbled frenziedly.
> "But in God? In God?"
> "I . . . I will believe in God."[60]

Although Shatov is portrayed sympathetically elsewhere in the novel, his stammering confusion here clearly reflects the author's dim view of his religious historicism. Since Shatov (from *shatkii*, "unsteady") is unable to affirm the existence of a God who transcends history, and since according to him the Russians are the true God-bearing people, then the final measure and demonstration of this truth can only be found in the future historical destiny of Russia. Unless it can some-

how be shown that peaceful persuasion rather than force is the primary mechanism of historical success, Shatov's views ultimately imply little more than the
worship of sheer force. Given this vision of history, the trampling of "many an innocent flower" would appear both inevitable and justified. Shatov's religious interpretation of history is therefore open to precisely the same objections expressed in Dostoevsky's work to the modern secular doctrine of history as
progress. As expressed in Shatov, the notion that the Russian people (or any other
people) can be "God-bearing" amounts merely to a variant of the most extreme
historicist reduction of God to a product of cultural development. As the Inquisitor puts it: "In the cause of universal worship, they have destroyed each other
with the sword. They have made gods and called upon each other: 'Abandon your
gods and come and worship ours, otherwise death to you and your gods!'" [46]

Shatov is certainly a prophetic instance of the difficulty, not to say impossibility, of escaping the modern historical consciousness, even when one is attempting to repudiate it in the name of Christian faith. To repeat the question raised
earlier: Is Dostoevsky himself such an instance? An affirmative answer would
seem strange in the face of his clear-sighted analysis, in Shatov, of what we might
call Christian historicism. Yet we are also faced with his own "Constantinople
must be ours," written a few years after *Demons,* and with Zosima's assertion,
identical to Shatov's, a decade later. One can only speculate as to why Dostoevsky
retained this "God-bearing" assertion, transferring it from the Slavophile nationalist to the Russian monk who embodied his mature religious thought. One
could, of course, revert to the explanation that Dostoevsky had a chauvinist tendency. But a more thoughtful explanation might point to the notion of Russia's
"historical mission" as a kind of second-order strategy: Aware of the ultimate
shortcomings of the notion, Dostoevsky nevertheless was willing to promote it
for the sake of reuniting an increasingly fragmented Russian culture around a
higher, Christian ideal—thereby staving off the worst consequences of Western
materialism.[61] This might be considered a "second step" in his "practical Christianity," encouraging individuals who have already worked on themselves to work
also toward a more historical-social expression of Christian faith.

Such a second step appears a natural one for Dostoevsky; for even a Christianity acutely aware of the dangers of historicism cannot refuse to take history seriously. The classical Christian idea of divine providence implies that history in the
fullest sense is, as Oliver O'Donovan puts it, the story of "what has happened in
God's good providence to the good world which God made."[62] In the New Testament given to Dostoevsky on his way to penal servitude in Siberia (his only permitted reading during four years in a hard-labor camp), "N.B." appears in the
margin, written in Dostoevsky's own hand beside a verse in Christ's farewell dis-

course to his disciples in the Gospel of John (16:33), of which the last three words, *Ya pobedil mir* ("I have overcome the world"), are underlined.[63] It would seem that Dostoevsky looked to the history of Russia and the West for hopeful signs that the darkness of the modern world might indeed be overcome by "God's good providence." In response to Ivan's charge that God does not actually care about human suffering and that the Inquisitor loves humanity more, how can the person of faith refrain from the attempt to vindicate the ways of a good God to the world?

The inscrutability of divine providence causes the prophet of the book of Revelation to weep (5:4). In attempting to discern the traces of God in history and in contemporary events, Dostoevsky certainly risked calling good evil and evil good. Yet it must be asked: Was this risk uniquely his, or does it belong to the Christian faith itself, insofar as the good God is also conceived of as the Lord of history? In its posing of this question, Dostoevsky's prophetic art addresses itself to Christians, confronting them with the difficult imperative of refusing modern historicism without refusing to engage in history.

## Notes

1. Hannah Arendt, *The Human Condition* (Chicago: University of Chicago Press, 1958), p. 296. See also George Grant, *Time As History* (Toronto: University of Toronto Press, 1995) for an illuminating discussion of the meaning and implications of the modern belief that we are essentially historical beings.

2. Francis Fukuyama, *The End of History and the Last Man* (New York: Free Press, 1992), pp. 127–129. The italics are ours.

3. G.W.F. Hegel, *The Philosophy of History*, trans. J. Sibree (New York: Dover, 1956), p. 197.

4. Ibid., p. 18. The italics are in the original.

5. Ibid., p. 379.

6. Fukuyama, *The End of History and the Last Man*, pp. 338–339.

7. Ibid., p. 51. Fukuyama's more recent book, *The Great Disruption: Human Nature and the Reconstitution of Social Order* (New York: Free Press, 1999), is somewhat less sanguine about the current situation and prospects of global liberal democracy. In it he acknowledges that the individualism promoted by political and economic liberalism has tended to undermine the social and moral values that made liberal democracy work in the West: "A society dedicated to the constant upending of norms and rules in the name of expanding individual freedom of choice will find itself increasingly disorganized, atomized, isolated, and incapable of carrying out common goals and tasks." Yet despite his concern about the rise of "moral individualism" and the consequent "miniaturization of community," Fukuyama remains fundamentally convinced of the "upward direction of the arrow of History" toward liberal democracy. The reason for his continued optimism in the face of all the evidence he amasses of a ubiquitous breakdown in family and community is what he calls the human "instinct" for reconstituting "social capital." It is in-

structive that Fukuyama's faith in this instinct is based on the latest research in neurophysiology, genetics, animal ethology, primatology, and evolutionary psychology. He does not, though, ignore the possibility and even desirability of religious faith playing some role in the "renorming" of society, so long as that role is strictly secondary: "Some religious conservatives hope, and liberals fear, that the problem of moral decline will be resolved by a large-scale return to religious orthodoxy—a Western version of the Ayatollah Khomeini returning to Iran on a jetliner. . . . A return to religiosity is far more likely to take a more benign form, one that in some respects has already started to appear in many parts of the United States. Instead of community arising as a by-product of rigid belief, people will come to religion because of their desire for community . . . , not necessarily because they accept the truth of revelation. . . . In this sense they will not be taking religion seriously on its own terms but will use religion as a language with which to express their moral beliefs" (Fukuyama, *The Great Disruption,* as quoted in *Atlantic Monthly,* May 1999, vol. 283, no. 5, pp. 55–80). One would be hard-pressed to find a clearer example than this of the contemporary liberal progressivist view of the place of religion in a secular world.

8. Fyodor Dostoevsky, *Notes from the Underground,* trans. Jane Kentish (Oxford: Oxford University Press, 1991), p. 24.

9. Henry Thomas Buckle, *History of Civilization in England* (London: Longmans, Green, and Co., 1885), p. 190. This work appeared in a Russian edition in 1864, an edition that Dostoevsky had in his own library. See Leonid Grossman, *Biblioteka Dostoevskago* (Odessa, 1919), p. 145.

10. Dostoevsky, *Notes from the Underground,* p. 30.

11. Voltaire used this phrase to describe his *Essai sur les moeurs et l'esprit des nations* (1756).

12. Dostoevsky, *Notes from the Underground,* chaps. 8, 10.

13. See, for instance, Fyodor Dostoevsky, *Winter Notes on Summer Impressions,* trans. R. L. Renfield (N.p.: Criterion, 1955), pp. 109–110.

14. Letter of 19 May 1879 to Konstantin Pobedonostsev, in *Selected Letters of Fyodor Dostoevsky,* eds. Joseph Frank and David I. Goldstein, trans. Andrew R. MacAndrew (London: Rutgers University Press, 1987), p. 467.

15. The term "metaphysical rebellion" is Albert Camus's. For his insightful commentary on Ivan's rebellion, see Albert Camus, *The Rebel,* trans. Anthony Bower (New York: Alfred A. Knopf, 1956), pp. 55–61.

16. Karl Löwith, *Meaning in History* (Chicago: University of Chicago Press, 1949), p. 114.

17. Fyodor Dostoevsky, *The Adolescent,* trans. Andrew R. MacAndrew (New York: Doubleday, 1972), p. 212. It should be noted that this progressive human shaping of history has been directed especially toward enhancing human equality by overcoming the deficiencies of nature (through technology) and society (through political reform, and on occasion, revolution).

18. Vissarion G. Belinsky, *Selected Philosophical Works* (Moscow, 1948), pp. 149–150. Belinsky was an extremely influential literary critic and popular philosopher of the 1840s. He acted, in effect, as mentor to that generation of aspiring writers to which Dostoevsky belonged. It was Belinsky who "discovered" Dostoevsky, ensuring his early fame by celebrating with such enthusiasm the young writer's first novel, *Poor People.* See also the discussion in Chapter 7 about Dostoevsky's later recollection of Belinsky's attitude toward Christ.

19. Dostoevsky, *Notes from the Underground,* p. 30.

20. Ibid., p. 25.

21. Ibid., p. 30.

22. Ibid., p. 22.

23. Dostoevsky, *The Adolescent,* p. 55.

24. See Immanuel Kant, *Groundwork of the Metaphysic of Morals,* trans. H. J. Paton (New York: Harper and Row, 1964), p. 96.

25. It has not been forgotten that Dostoevsky refers to Ivan as a "socialist" rather than a "liberal" of today. However, for him, the terms are generally interchangeable; although he was well aware of the debate between modern liberals and socialists—especially that about the relative importance of individual liberty and social equality—he nevertheless tended to view them as predicates of the same subject: historicist progressivism.

26. "So mighty a form must trample down many a flower . . . crush to pieces many an object in its path" (Hegel, *The Philosophy of History,* p. 32). See also Immanuel Kant, *On History,* trans. Lewis White Beck (New York: Bobbs-Merrill, 1963), pp. 24–26.

27. Fukuyama, *The End of History and the Last Man,* p. 32.

28. See Richard Schacht, *Nietzsche* (London: Routledge and Kegan Paul, 1983), pp. 122–130.

29. Friedrich Nietzsche, *Thus Spoke Zarathustra,* trans. Walter Kaufmann (New York: Penguin, 1978), pp. 17–18.

30. Friedrich Nietzsche, *On the Genealogy of Morals,* trans. Walter Kaufmann (New York: Random House, 1989), p. 163.

31. Albert Camus, "Pour Dostoïevski," in *Théâtre, récits, nouvelles* (Paris: Gallimard, 1962), p. 1888.

32. Dostoevsky would already have encountered the term *nihilist* in Russian intellectual circles of the 1860s, where, in reflection of its usage by Turgenev in *Fathers and Sons,* it generally signified a radical rejection of traditional bonds of family, society, and religion for the sake of a future order based on modern science. See Andrzej Walicki, *A History of Russian Thought: From the Enlightenment to Marxism* (Stanford: Stanford University Press, 1979), pp. 209–215. What particularly concerned Dostoevsky, however, was the person who had rejected traditional gods but also did not believe in those of the future. This is a concern with nihilism in the broader, Nietzschean sense.

33. Fyodor Dostoevsky, *Demons,* trans. Richard Pevear and Larissa Volokhonsky (New York: Alfred A. Knopf, 1994), p. 254.

34. Fyodor Dostoevsky, *The Idiot,* trans. David Magarshack (New York: Penguin, 1955), pp. 416–417.

35. Fyodor Dostoevsky, *Crime and Punishment,* trans. Richard Pevear and Larissa Volokhonsky (New York: Vintage, 1993), p. 547.

36. See Fyodor Dostoevsky, *The Notebooks for The Brothers Karamazov,* ed. and trans. Edward Wasiolek (Chicago: University of Chicago Press, 1971), p. 75.

37. Fyodor Dostoevsky, *A Writer's Diary,* vol. 2, trans. Kenneth Lantz (Evanston, Ill.: Northwestern University Press, 1994), p. 1213.

38. Nietzsche, *Thus Spoke Zarathustra,* p. 286.

39. Oliver O'Donovan makes a suggestive distinction between *state*-totalitarianism and "recent liberal *culture*-totalitarianism," in his *Resurrection and Moral Order* (Grand Rapids, Mich.: William B. Eerdmans, 1986), pp. 73–74. See also George Grant's elaboration of the remark once made by Huey Long, "When fascism comes to America, it will

come in the name of democracy," in his *English-Speaking Justice* (Notre Dame, Ind.: University of Notre Dame Press, 1985). One of the first modern Western philosophers to offer a non-Christian justification of equality, based on reason alone, was Hobbes. He argued that human beings were fundamentally equal in their ability to kill one another, for the physically weaker could always resort to cunning. This emphasis on the human fear of violent death, and the roughly equal ability of humans to inflict it on one another, certainly represents a telling and ominous "lowering of the sights" concerning the basis of human community. In the tradition of political philosophy derived from Hobbes and Locke, the emphasis on calculating self-interest makes it extremely difficult to say why equal rights should continue to be extended to every person if such an extension is not congruent with the comfortable self-preservation (as they see it) of the majority or of a powerful minority. Hegel thought the society of rational consumption exalted by bourgeois liberalism an incomplete answer to the problem of human order, because it fails to take account of the fact that there exists a "spiritedness" in human beings (akin to the *thymos* recognized in Plato's *Republic*) that frequently inspires the sacrifice of material desire for the sake of something less tangible—such as recognition. He would thus modify Hobbes and Locke to add the desire for recognition to the desire for comfortable self-preservation. But again, the question to which there seems no clear answer in Hegel is: Why should equal recognition be extended to each and every person simply because this is what they desire? What if such an extension contradicts the desire for *a greater* recognition on the part of those in a position to satisfy their excessive "spiritedness" at the expense of the weaker? The liberalism of Hobbes, Locke, and Hegel, in its emphasis on the self-regarding desires, might explain what every individual wants; but it does not explain why the powerful should be obliged to give them what they want, especially if such action runs counter to the similar desires of the powerful. Among the liberal philosophers, it is Kant who most powerfully addressed this problem of obligation to others, by asserting that all human beings, irrespective of natural inequalities, are equally worthy of respect, because all are equally open to the possibility of rationally willing the moral good. The basis of Kant's moral affirmation of human equality is that morality is an indisputable "fact" of human reason. According to Nietzsche, Kant deserves to be called the "great delayer," for having persuaded so many for so long that reason supports the fact of the moral law, whereas in reality, reason tells us that there are no moral facts at all but only moral *interpretations* of facts—interpretations rooted in historical circumstances and in the instincts. In regard to the philosophical origins of liberalism, and the current vulnerability of the liberal idea of equality in the face of Nietzschean historicism, I have found particularly helpful Grant's *English-Speaking Justice;* and Leo Strauss, *Natural Right and History* (Chicago: University of Chicago Press, 1953).

40. For Dostoevsky's own comments on the function of Zosima as spokesman for his religious thought, see his letter of 7 August 1879 to Nikolai A. Lyubimov, in *Selected Letters of Fyodor Dostoevsky,* p. 477.

41. Quoted in John Meyendorff, *A Study in Gregory Palamas* (London: Faith Press, 1962), p. 168. Palamas was attempting to express the difference between his mystical theology and the scholastic theology of his Western contemporary Thomas Aquinas.

42. See Bp. Kallistos Ware, "The Spiritual Father in Orthodox Christianity," *Cross Currents* (Summer/Fall 1974); and Joseph J. Allen, *Inner Way: Towards a Rebirth of Eastern Christian Spiritual Direction* (Grand Rapids, Mich.: William B. Eerdmans, 1994). One can see from these studies how Dostoevsky's chapter "Elders" in *The Brothers Karamazov* has become an important source for scholars of Eastern Christian spirituality.

43. For Dostoevsky's own hyphenated identification of the two, see *The Notebooks for The Brothers Karamazov*, p. 23.

44. For an insightful explanation of how Zosima's alternative "form of life" constitutes a philosophically significant response to Ivan, see Stewart Sutherland, *Atheism and the Rejection of God* (Oxford: Basil Blackwell, 1977), chapter 6.

45. For this and other responses of critics to "The Russian Monk," see George Panichas, *The Burden of Vision* (Grand Rapids, Mich.: William B. Eerdmans, 1977), pp. 166, 170.

46. The words are actually spoken by Zosima's "mysterious visitor," but they represent his own thinking, just as other expressions—such as "life is paradise" or "we are all responsible"—are first given to Zosima through his elder brother Markel. This transmission of ideas finds its mirror image in the manner in which Ivan's expressions—for instance, "everything is permitted"—are taken up by characters such as Smerdyakov and Rakitin.

47. See Fyodor Dostoevsky, *The Notebooks for The Idiot*, ed. Edward Wasiolek, trans. Katherine Strelsky (Chicago: University of Chicago Press, 1967), p. 222.

48. We know from Dostoevsky's rough notebooks that the model for his character was the liberal historian Timofey Granovsky, a leading figure among Russian "Westernizers" of the 1840s. See Fyodor Dostoevsky, *The Notebooks for The Possessed [Demons]*, ed. Edward Wasiolek, trans. Victor Terras (Chicago: University of Chicago Press, 1968), p. 82.

49. Dostoevsky, *Demons*, p. 37.

50. Ibid., pp. 664–665.

51. For a fascinating account of Joachim's theology of history and its subsequent permutations in modern historicism, see Karl Löwith, *Meaning in History*, chapter 8 and appendix 1.

52. Vasily V. Zenkovsky, "Dostoevsky's Religious and Philosophical Views," in *Dostoevsky: A Collection of Critical Essays*, ed. Rene Wellek (Englewood Cliffs, N.J.: Prentice-Hall, 1962), p. 144.

53. See, for instance, Dostoevsky's reply to Alexander Gradovsky's criticism of his speech on Pushkin, in Dostoevsky, *A Writer's Diary*, vol. 2, pp. 1312–1323.

54. Fyodor Dostoevsky, *The Unpublished Dostoevsky*, vol. 1, ed. C. R. Proffer (Ann Arbor, Mich.: Ardis, 1973), pp. 95–96.

55. Dostoevsky, *Winter Notes on Summer Impressions*, p. 113.

56. Ibid., pp. 110, 114, 116.

57. Dostoevsky, *A Writer's Diary*, vol. 2, pp. 1003–1007.

58. Dostoevsky, *The Unpublished Dostoevsky*, vol. 2, p. 101.

59. Dostoevsky, *A Writer's Diary*, vol. 2, p. 900. The italics are in the original.

60. Dostoevsky, *Demons*, pp. 250–253.

61. For an interpretation along these lines, see Ellis Sandoz, *Political Apocalypse: A Study of Dostoevsky's Grand Inquisitor* (Baton Rouge: Louisiana State University Press, 1971), pp. 231–233.

62. See O'Donovan, *Resurrection and Moral Order*, p. 60.

63. Geir Kjetsaa, *Dostoevsky and His New Testament* (Atlantic Highlands, N.J.: Humanities Press, 1984), pp. 8, 42.

# four

# The Inquisition of the Lamb

## Dostoevsky, Revelation, and Justice

Dostoevsky's writings are replete with references to memory and remembering (both personal and cultural) and to the apocalyptic end of all things. The same is true of the book of Revelation—it is a vision of the end of the world; but at the same time it is full of references to biblical memory, and it prophetically addresses the churches of the time about the critical significance of current affairs. The "end" is present, then, not only as the future "end of history" or "end of the world," but also—and indeed primarily—as a matter of *telos*, the inner purpose and ultimate meaning of human life in the world. This is presented in dramatic fashion in order to unveil the spiritual causality that underlies not only the moral psychology of individual agents but of various forms of social and political organization that structure human experience. As a prophet, then, it is important to note that Dostoevsky does not offer an exegetical reading of Revelation or a learned and systematic reflection on the significance of its vision of history, ethics, and politics for our time. Rather, his dramatic art *echoes* the theological poetry of the apocalypse in order to unveil the significance of the end—revealed in the death and resurrection of Jesus—for Dostoevsky's (and our) time and place.

A theology of justice and peace that passes through the crucible of Dostoevsky's apocalyptic art will be quite different from the liberal pacifism and moralism of Tolstoy, as George Steiner has argued.[1] Dostoevsky's prophetic art portrays the movement of the human soul in the crisis of cosmic fall and redemption, yet within the portentous particularity of late-nineteenth-century Russia, struggling over its future identity. Will Russia become a modern Western secular power, or remain a God-bearing people serving the reconciliation of nations in the image of Christ? What role does Revelation play in Dostoevsky's depiction of this existential and cultural struggle?

*The Brothers Karamazov* is a novel about justice, and its most famous passage, Ivan's prose poem of "The Grand Inquisitor," puts the Christian account of divine justice itself on trial. Ivan's Inquisitor accuses Christ of betraying human solidarity and the possibility of worldly justice by refusing the three temptations of the devil and siding with the divine justice that has made the world as it is. Many commentators have discussed the structure of the Inquisitor's case against Christ with reference to his reinterpretation of the three temptations of Jesus in Matthew 4.[2] The larger symbolic context of the poem, however, is the cosmic conflict depicted in the book of Revelation, which concerns the nature and destiny of human history and addresses the problem of evil and divine justice. Several important references to Revelation are explicitly made in "The Grand Inquisitor," and various interpreters have noted these, but no sustained attention has been given to this symbolic context and its importance for understanding the religio-ethical framework of *The Brothers Karamazov*.[3] This chapter explores these references and shows how the symbolism of the biblical text is used by Dostoevsky to illuminate Ivan's (and the Inquisitor's) rebellion against God in the name of retributive justice and to develop a Christian response to this rebellion in the novel as a whole. Though the two functions cannot be neatly separated, this chapter focuses primarily on Dostoevsky's use of the symbolism of Revelation to depict the moral and psychological dynamics of his characters in relation to the question of divine justice, and Chapter 6 concentrates on the sociopolitical implications of Dostoevsky's apocalyptic Christian construal of spiritual causality.

It is surely no accident that Ivan's poem brings the heavenly powers to earth, to be judged by a Euclidean mind, in contrast to the revelatory vision given to St. John of Patmos, in which John was raised up in the Spirit to the throne of heaven. In an important article written some years ago, Paul Minear makes the point that John's cosmology in the book of Revelation is not dominated by the (Euclidean) categories of time and space but rather by heaven and earth, with primacy accorded to the heavenly realm.[4] Furthermore, there is not merely a "first" heaven and earth (*ta prota,* 21:4, which ultimately pass away), but also a "new" heaven and earth, which constitute the decisive frontier of the old—not in terms of temporal succession (though the new heaven and earth do not pass away) but as an alternative cosmic order and community in which God dwells and is worshiped as Sovereign. Though they coexist in time and space, then, the saints as citizens of the heavenly Jerusalem live under a different rule, order, and ethic than do the earth-dwelling citizens of Babylon. These two orders, however, do not coexist peacefully—they are engaged in cosmic conflict over the meaning of human happiness, peace, and justice. The decisive role in this conflict is played by the slain Lamb, who constitutes, seals, and leads this "new" community to its victorious end.

The meaning of divine justice (and of human happiness and fulfillment), then, depend upon the cosmic framework in which it is understood. So too in *The Brothers Karamazov*. In the conversation leading up to Ivan's poem, Ivan confesses to Alyosha that, created as he is, with a "Euclidean earthly mind" (235),* he cannot resolve the "universal" or "eternal" questions they are discussing with reference to the mind of God. Thus, he says, "while I am on the earth, I hasten to take my own measures" (244). This measure judges God's "higher harmony" not to be worth the suffering of innocent children. The factual accounts of human injustice that Ivan has compiled in his dossier are used to pass judgment on divine justice. He cannot accept the world as it has been created by God. Ivan's earthly measure of justice demands *retribution* for human injustice—not in some remote, infinite realm but in the Euclidean dimensions of earthly time and space in which he—Ivan—dwells.

There is another side to Ivan, revealed in his earlier profession to his brother of his erotic "thirst for life," a basic love of life experienced with his insides, his guts (230). This is a love that he cannot explain; indeed, it stands in conflict with his Euclidean logic and his rebellion against the created order of things. Ivan's torment is rooted in an inner division between his heart—his love of life, which is the source of his "faith in the woman I love" and "faith in the order of things"—and his intellect,[5] which is oriented toward the "graveyard" of modern Europe, which represents death—death of the traditional God, and death of faith in a spiritual moral order alive in the nature of things. The question, stated dramatically by Alyosha both at the beginning and at the end of their conversation, is: Will Ivan's basic, erotic love of life be salvifically "resurrected," or will he, at age thirty, dash the cup of life to the ground in self-destructive, rebellious despair (230–231,[54])*? By the end of his recitation of "The Grand Inquisitor," Ivan has convinced himself that the latter will occur. Alyosha identifies this as the consequence of his inner "hell," the torment of a divided conscience.[6]

The novel makes clear that Ivan's atheism is not merely an abstract, intellectual phenomenon but has a personal, spiritual root: the inability to love his father, and furthermore, the desire for retribution against that father for his forgetfulness and neglect of Ivan as a child.[7] We see the first expression of Ivan's wish for

---

*Here and below, references appearing inside parentheses in the narrative are page numbers in Fyodor Dostoevsky, *The Brothers Karamazov*, trans. Richard Pevear and Larissa Volokhonsky (New York: Vintage, 1990). References inside square brackets are page numbers in "The Grand Inquisitor," reprinted from the aforementioned edition, in Chapter 2 of the present volume.

his father's death in part 1: "As for my wishes ... there I reserve complete freedom for myself" (143); but he gives in to the hateful thing that is "gnawing his
soul, as if he were about to take revenge on someone" (276), when he sends an indirect signal to Smerdyakov, preparing the way for his father's murder. Ivan's inability to love and his clinging to a desire for retributive justice cause him to remain in the hell of inner division.[8] The social vision of the Inquisitor, then, is not
simply a political theory—it represents a state of the soul in rebellion against divine love.

The specific form of higher harmony against which Ivan rebels is identified by
Alyosha at the end of the chapter entitled "Rebellion," as the Lamb slain before
the foundation of the world (Revelation 13:8; cf. I Peter 1:19–20), who "can forgive everything, forgive all *and for all,* because he himself gave his innocent blood
for all and for everything" (246). This vision and the accompanying, worshipful
refrain of the heavenly community—"Just art thou, O Lord, for thy ways have
been revealed!" (repeated both in the book of Revelation[9] and in the Grand Inquisitor)—are directly challenged by Ivan and the Inquisitor. Out of his professed
love for humanity (245), Ivan rejects the biblical conception and teaching of
Christ and expresses poetically in the mouth of the Grand Inquisitor his conception of a truer image of human nature and a more realistic image of the good and
just social order. Divine grace will be replaced by the reign of earthly justice,
which cannot atone for injustice but can at least mitigate human evil and suffering. Miracle, mystery, and authority, as parodically articulated by the Inquisitor,
closely parallel the dragon and the two beasts in Revelation, which are (like the
Inquisitor) symbolically allied with the earthly powers of Babel/Babylon and the
Holy Roman Empire.

Four other important allusions to Revelation in the novel confirm and expand
the moral significance of John's Apocalypse for Dostoevsky's art. On the positive
(pro) side, these include references to images of the "heavenly Jerusalem" (Revelation 3:12; 21), in the rebirth visions of Alyosha and Mitya, and, in Snegiryov's
lament over the imminent death of his son Ilyusha; and on the negative (contra)
side, the alternative cosmology depicted in Ivan's anti-rebirth vision of the devil.
The second section of this chapter explores how Dostoevsky used these references to answer the challenge posed by Ivan/the Inquisitor to the meaning and
nature of divine justice in the world, to which we now turn.

## The Inquisition Scene

"The Grand Inquisitor" can be read as a legal trial concerning the true meaning
of human nature and history, where the God revealed in Christ is in the dock.
That is why the poem is structured on the model of the three temptations in

Matthew 4[43]. The real miracle of the New Testament, says the Inquisitor, is not Christ's offer of salvation but the three questions posed to Christ by the devil in the wilderness:

> By the questions alone, simply by the miracle of their appearance, one can see that one is dealing with a mind not human and transient but eternal and absolute. For in these three questions all of subsequent human history is as if brought together into a single whole and foretold; three images are revealed that will take in all the insoluble historical contradictions of human nature all over the earth. . . . Decide for yourself who was right: you or the one who questioned you then?[44]

The wilderness temptation story, like the Gospel accounts of the crucifixion, takes the form of a legal trial concerning the truth about the human condition, political authority, and historical justice. The larger symbolic context in which to understand these trials is the cosmic battle, depicted in the book of Revelation, between the power of light or divine rule and the rebellious powers of darkness headed by the great spirit of rebellion in the heavenly court, Satan or the Devil.

It is worth noting here that the longest section of the novel is also a criminal trial—the trial of Dmitri Karamazov, falsely accused of the murder of his father. The trial is set in a modern courtroom operating according to the secularizing innovations of legal reform introduced in Russia in 1864, an adversarial system based on rights and the objective presentation of forensic evidence, similar to the current systems used in North America.[10] This section of the novel provides a deep critique of the contemporary system of justice, insofar as neither the facts of the murder nor the psychology and character of the accused are or can be accurately construed or understood within the nondialogical, clinical, "Euclidean" courtroom, whose authorities have no insight into "spiritual causality." We shall return to this point in Chapter 6. The Inquisitor's case, in contrast, is not prosecuted within the terms of modern liberal justice—and this is no accident. The Inquisitor is conducting a religious inquisition within the cell of a "gloomy, vaulted prison in the old building of the holy court" (250); and *he* has insight into spiritual causality—even as he stands in explicit rebellion against its Creator.

Indeed, the inquisition scene is staged precisely to lay bare the spiritual roots of rebellion. As Albert Camus argued in his important study of modern culture, *The Rebel:* "Metaphysical rebellion is the movement by which man protests against his condition and against the whole of creation. It is metaphysical because it contests the ends of man and of creation."[11] The staging in Dostoevsky's novel is important, because unlike John of Patmos, who is "raised up" by the Spirit "on the Lord's day" to the worship scene in the heavenly city, Ivan puts this heavenly city and its Ruler on an earthly stage. The inquisition of divine rule is conducted by one of the ugliest representatives of earthly Christian authority—a sixteenth-century Spanish Grand Inquisitor—and the representative for the defense is a romanticized and mostly silent Christ, Ivan's literary fantasy of the slain Lamb. Ivan offers a description and critical evaluation of this setting in his "literary preface":

> He appeared quietly, inconspicuously, but, strange to say, everyone recognized him. This could be one of the best passages in the poem, I mean, why it is exactly that they recognize him. People are drawn by an invincible force, they flock to him, surround him, follow him. He passes silently among them with a quiet smile of infinite compassion. The sun of love shines in his heart, rays of Light, Enlightenment, and Power stream from his eyes and, pouring over the people, shake their hearts with responding love. He stretches forth his hands to them, blesses them, and from the touch of him, even only of his garments, comes a healing power.[41]

Ivan's artistic creation both resembles and differs from the biblical portraits of the incarnate Christ in crucial respects: The deeds of miraculous power are unaccompanied by word—only "a quiet smile of infinite compassion"—and the light he brings is described in terms of the power of personality, the "invincible force" of inner beauty. There is nothing here of the divine incognito, the "form of the servant" in serf's garb, nothing of the sword of judgment embodied in the words of Jesus. Indeed, the only words Jesus speaks publicly in Ivan's account are the words he spoke privately in the Gospel—*Talitha cumi* (Mark 5:41). In Ivan's account they become magical, romantic words of earthly miracle. Hence, though Ivan's description of the "sun of love" shining in the face of Christ mimics certain elements of John of Patmos's description of the heavenly "son of man" in his vision,[12] what is left out (the "sharp sword" of the prophetic word, for example) and how those elements are construed significantly alter the portrait. Ivan's romantic poetics offer a secular replacement for the liturgical poetics of the Apocalypse and in this respect parody biblical prophecy.

Yet another parodic reversal in Ivan's setting makes this even clearer: The Grand Inquisitor appears incognito, "not wearing his magnificent cardinal's robes in which he had displayed himself to the people the day before, when the enemies of the Roman faith were burned," but attired in "his old, coarse monastic cassock"[41]. This staged effect heightens the sense of rivalry between the two religious figures and conceals the Inquisitor's true public identity. (The cardinal's robes as well as the monk's cassock also conceal the Inquisitor's rebellious disbelief in the God he claims to represent.) He begins his inquisition with John the Baptist's question, "Is it you?" but quickly adds, "Do not answer, be silent," because "you have no right to add anything to what you already said once"[42]. Ivan here parodies the closing warning in the book of Revelation (22:18f.), not to add to (or take away from) the words of the prophecy, again raising the fundamental question of how God's truth and justice are revealed in history. This question has already been raised in Ivan's literary preface[39] with reference to another of Revelation's closing phrases: "Behold I come quickly" (Revelation 22:7, 12, 20).

These words from the final chapter of Revelation clearly raise an obstacle to faith, not only because of the time elapsed since the prophetic promise but especially because believers must now rely for confirmation only on the promptings of the heart, having no external signs or miracles or "additional words." According to Ivan and the Inquisitor, Christ's reliance on his followers' inner faith reveals excessive confidence in the human heart. Hence the significance of another of Ivan's prefatory literary allusions, his reference to the falling star Wormwood (Revelation 8:10–11) in connection with a new, miracle-denying heresy that has arisen in the sixteenth century in northern Germany[40]. The reference is important in two respects: Firstly, the Inquisitor, representing the ideology of papal monarchy, seeks the earthly political establishment of divine rule through the unity of the Holy Roman Empire and the Roman Catholic Church. The union of church and empire requires the civil religious display of heavenly legitimacy and power via impressive earthly miracles. The second point has to do with the substance of the allusion to the "great star" Wormwood, representing Babylon (Isaiah 14:12f.; Jeremiah 51), which has fallen from heaven upon the waters, poisoning and embittering them. Like subsequent references to Revelation (and to Babel/Babylon in particular) in Dostoevsky's art, this one is a parodic reversal: Wormwood/Babylon represents the poisoning power of idolatry, of service to false religious authority or power, which has destructive consequences, not the least of which are the fiery Inquisitorial *autos-da-fé*. Although putatively a criticism of the heretical denial of miracles represented in early modern ideas of faith, the Grand Inquisitor's understanding of miracles—conscripting religious mystery and authority in the service of purely temporal ends—is ultimately revealed to be idolatrous in Dostoevsky's portrayal.

Thus, the staging of Ivan's poetic prophecy is important, and it is consistent with the larger poetic background of Dostoevsky's novel, which in turn parallels the symbolism and the setting of the poetic prophecy of the Apocalypse. G. B. Caird comments helpfully on the eschatological context of the book of Revelation: "John's book begins on the Lord's day and ends in eucharistic worship; and it is in the setting of worship that his eschatology is to be understood. He and his fellow Christians had no difficulty in believing that the end could come to meet them in the midst of time."[13] The revelatory power of what has been revealed in the person of Christ continues to accomplish its meaning and purpose whenever it is remembered for what it is—namely, a vision of God's rule, enacting the full meaning of worship.[14] This might be called the "liturgical consciousness." As

Caird points out, the providential pattern of divine sovereignty is unsealed by the slain Lamb in Revelation 5 "in order to involve those whom he has made 'a royal house of priests in God's service' (5:10), and . . . nothing less is intended than the bringing of the whole creation into the worship and service of God (5:13). But apart from the Cross this purpose can be neither known nor implemented."[15] Hence the purpose of worship is to "lift up" the eucharistic community by the way of the cross[16] to a vision of the holy God (and God's purposes) mirrored in the worship of the heavenly community.

The meaning of liturgical worship here obviously extends far beyond cultic ritual. It includes the meaning and direction of the whole of life, as might be suggested in the original sense of *leitourgia,* a work of public service. This broader meaning, which is also central to the liturgical theology of Eastern Orthodoxy, is evident in the artistic structure of *The Brothers Karamazov.*[17] Vigen Guroian comments further on the liturgical location of Orthodox Christian tradition and ethics:

> It is a eucharistic and eschatological science, a eucharistic and eschatological way of knowing. In the final analysis, the continuity of tradition is not located in theological texts, creeds, liturgical forms, or ecclesiastical offices. The continuity that contemporary writers such as Pelikan, Zizioulas, and Schmemann have identified is a product of the eucharistic *anamnesis* of the gathered worshiping community. The collective remembrance of this community, in the power of the Holy Spirit, makes Christ and his sacrifice present and also affords a passage into and a proleptic experience of God's eschatological kingdom.[18]

The characters and actions (or inaction) of the Karamazov brothers and others in the novel are linked, positively and negatively, to liturgical images and settings that reveal the connections between heaven and earth and thus unveil the meaning of spiritual causality.[19] Ivan's poetic tale of "The Grand Inquisitor" is clearly an antiliturgical setting, a deliberate parody of the poetics of Christian liturgical theology.

In order to understand fully how the Inquisitor's account of the three temptations parodies the Christian messianic conception of divine justice and rule, one must understand the central symbols of Revelation 12–18: the dragon, the two beasts, and Babylon the whore. References to these figures appear in all three temptations. The context of this symbolism is the cosmic battle between the true, eternal ordering of divine rule and the false, diabolical rule, the power of which is rooted in the ability to deceive by manipulating external appearances. Revelation 12 introduces the battle with reference to the cosmic birth of the anointed Son (a messianic interpretation of Psalms 2:7–9), a birth that refers not to the nativity of Christ but to his crucifixion. The mother giving birth can be read as the messianic community (cf. Galatians 4:26: "Jerusalem above who is our mother"), and the agony of delivery, as the suffering of redemptive love. The enthronement of the anointed Son that is accomplished by his death (cf. Revelation 3:21; John 12:30f.) conquers the dragon's power to kill, a power that extends only to the outer realm, not the inner spirit.[20] This act of enthronement initiates the war in heaven between the angels and the dragon, now identified as Satan or the Devil, "the deceiver of the whole world" (Revelation 12:9). The Devil here, as elsewhere in the Bible, is identified as the accuser in the heavenly court, the chief prosecutor of legal demands for retributive justice (Revelation 12:10; cf. Job 1; Zechariah 3). We now see that the cosmic battle is also a legal one, over the meaning of justice itself. The dragon's attempt to devour the messianic child includes the temptations of Christ (the great dragon is also the "ancient serpent"—Revelation 12:9, 13–17), but its ultimate background is the cosmic drama of redemption as a reenactment of the creation, in which the dragon of chaos must be defeated by the Creator. In this battle, clearly, retributive justice is not the final word. Justice must be related to a more profound understanding of the Creator's purposes and of the goodness of the creation as it is.

Deposed from heaven, the dragon/serpent/devil then unleashes his power on earth. In Revelation 13 it becomes evident that this power is rooted in the ability to deceive. Part of the dragon's deception, it would seem, is the misrepresentation of God's rule strictly in terms of retributive justice, thereby distorting the true meaning of good and evil, life and death.[21] The subsequent chapters detail the tremendously destructive rebellion unleashed by the thwarted and defeated dragon and his minions—a rebellion that those who are faithful to divine rule experience as suffering and martyrdom. The nature of diabolical rule is given further expression in the two beasts of Revelation 13. Just as the dragon parodies the Creator, the first beast (the "antichrist") is a clear parody of Christ. This beast, who arises out of the sea (the bottomless abyss, Revelation 11:7) and is given the power and authority of the dragon, elicits a following by producing a miracle— the healing of an apparently mortal wound. His subsequent blasphemous and destructive authority is rooted in the delusive power of idolatry. This first beast is implicitly present in the Inquisitor's discussion of the second temptation.

The second beast, who arises from the land (i.e., a human prophet) and who imitates both the false "lamb" and the dragon (Revelation 13:11), seeks to establish the worship of the first beast. This it does through the working of "great signs"—the very miracles that Christ refused to perform, "making fire come down from heaven to earth in the sight of men" (13:13; cf. Luke 9:54; 11:29–36). It is not insignificant that the Inquisitor quotes this verse in the context of the first temptation[44], where Christ is tempted to put an end to earthly suffering by satisfying his bodily hunger at the expense of the spiritual freedom of human beings. Although the Inquisitor recognizes the spiritual dimension of human nature (in contrast to scientific socialism, for example, which simply denies it), he argues that Christ resolved the question wrongly—he should have used miraculous powers to coerce spiritual conformity through material means. By doing so, implies the Inquisitor, Christ could have taken away not only the torment of physical hunger but also the burden of spiritual freedom.

This brings us to the relation of the first beast to the second and third temptations. The task of the second beast is to solicit worship of the first beast (Revelation 13:14f.). The idolatrous claims of the first beast (based on the mysterious and miraculous overcoming of a mortal wound) are "given breath" by the second beast through the performance of miraculous signs, backed with the coercive power of the sword (13:15) in order to establish a community based on political religion. In his retelling of the second temptation, the Inquisitor criticizes Christ for not capturing the human conscience through the powers of (1) miraculous works ("for man seeks not so much God as miracles"[47]); (2) blank, impenetrable mystery (not the mystery of the human heart and the freedom of love) that requires "blind obedience"[48]; and (3) the authority of the sword, the "fire from heaven" that eliminates opposition through coercive punishment. The nature and exercise of this authority in the service of a universal religious state constitutes the substance of the third temptation, to which we will return. The importance of the second temptation is that it represents a parody of the mystery of divine love, rooted in a lower view of human nature and the worship of a less transcendent, visible god—which is more "realistic" in its demands:

> I swear, man is created weaker and baser than you thought him! How, how can he ever accomplish the same things as you? Respecting him so much, you behaved as if you had ceased to be compassionate, because you demanded too much of him— and who did this? He who loved him more than himself! Respecting him less, you would have demanded less of him, and that would be closer to love, for his burden would be lighter.[48]

The 144,000 martyrs sealed in the first resurrection (Revelation 7:20; cf. 14:1; 20:4f.), says the Inquisitor, "were not like men, as it were, but gods"[48].[22] The premise is that human beings are not created in the image of God and therefore cannot be guided in freedom by the image of the crucified Lamb. Human beings do not seek God, or the offer of divine love accepted in the free decision of the heart, so much as they seek miracles—the immediate gratification of their bodily desires, without responsibility.

Appropriately, then, the Inquisitor's monologue ends with a parody of Christ the sin-bearing mediator of salvation and of the 144,000 martyrs who follow him in death. Based on the anthropological premises implicit in the Devil's temptations, the Inquisitor will "correct" the work of Christ[51] and solve the problem of evil in a manner that realizes justice and human happiness on the earth. The cost of this remediation, says the Inquisitor, will be borne by those who govern in conscious alliance with the Devil:

> We will tell them that every sin will be redeemed if it is committed with our permission; and that we allow them to sin because we love them, and as for the punishment of these sins, very well, we take it upon ourselves. . . . And everyone will be happy, all the millions of creatures, except for the one hundred thousand of those who govern them. For only we, we who keep the mystery, only we shall be unhappy. There will be thousands of millions of happy babes, and a hundred thousand sufferers who have taken upon themselves the curse of the knowledge of good and evil. Peacefully they will die, peacefully they will expire in your name, and beyond the grave they will find only death. But we will keep the secret, and for their own happiness we will entice them will a heavenly and eternal reward.[51]

In contrast to the 144,000 martyrs in whose mouths "no lie was found" (Revelation 14:5) but whose lives on earth were cut short by violent death, these 100,000 seek to complete the human project by securing bodily life on earth by means of a lie. The Inquisitor sees death as the last word for mortals—that is his "secret." Eternal life and happiness are religious constructs that may be used for political purposes. This is a parodic reversal of Revelation, where the power to kill the body is exposed as penultimate and under the judgment of the eternal God. It is this judgment, in the Inquisitor's view, that must be called into question: "We, who took their sins upon ourselves for their happiness, we will stand before you and say: 'Judge us if you can and dare'"[51].

The Inquisitor then shifts from accusation to personal confession, revealing that he too was once "preparing to enter the number of your chosen ones, the number of the strong and mighty, with a thirst 'that the number be complete.' But I awoke and did not want to serve madness"[51]. The reference to the "completed number" is taken from Revelation 6:11, where in response to the loud cry from the martyred souls under the altar ("O Sovereign Lord, holy and true, how long before thou wilt judge and avenge our blood?") God gives them white robes (the promise of immortal glory[23]) and tells them to wait "a little longer" until the number of martyred saints is complete—that is, until the redemptive purposes of God obtained through suffering love are accomplished. It is against this "madness" of divine love—which does not cut short the suffering of the innocent, in order that all may be saved—that both Ivan and the Inquisitor rebel, in the name of retributive justice and a less grand (less transcendent or cosmic) harmony.

Perfect poetic consistency, then, is displayed in the last words of the Inquisitor, which stand in defiant opposition to the *Marana tha* ("Come, our Lord!") of Revelation 22:20: "Go and do not come again . . . do not come at all . . . never, never!"[54]—even as the Inquisitor has silenced Christ from the beginning of his monologic tirade, ironically titled an "inquisition."

## Echoes of the New Jerusalem

The answer to Ivan's (and the Inquisitor's) rebellion in the novel is the revelation of a divine measure beyond retributive justice, a love of the created order as it is. Such a love of creation gives up its own finite perspective as the place where judgment of the goodness of the created order or of divine justice occurs. It gives up its own divided knowledge of good and evil as the place where true understanding is found, in order to be lifted up to participate in the reconciling action of divine love in the world, according to the image of Christ. All of this is elaborated in the life and teachings of Elder Zosima as recorded by Alyosha—not as a point-by-point refutation of Ivan's and the Inquisitor's charges but as the dramatic development of an alternative perspective rooted in a very different spiritual orientation. To attempt a point-by-point refutation of the Inquisitor would of course be to accept the tempter's turf; it would be to succumb to another form of disordered desire—the desire to win the intellectual battle of the gods. It would be another idolatry parodying the divine truth, the truth that communicates itself in another manner altogether. Dostoevsky's response to Ivan's prose poem, then, is not a counterargument but an embodiment of the truth of the Gospel parodied by Ivan.

Dramatic references to the symbolism of Revelation in answer to Ivan and the Inquisitor occur in the rebirth experiences of Alyosha and Mitya, both of whom give up the claim to retributive justice in order to love the world as it is, despite unjust suffering. They renounce earthly human measures for a saving faith in God. Both men's conversions follow the penitential pattern of death and resurrection signaled in the novel's epigraph; and both rebirths are accompanied by visions that bear allusions to the vision of the new Jerusalem at the end of Revelation. These visions are no mere doctrinal abstractions or literary allusions; rather, they are dramatic enactments of the penitential consciousness modeled after the image of Christ. The prominence of penitence in John's Apocalypse might be noted here as well. As Richard Bauckham points out, Revelation 11:1–13 offers the fullest treatment of the manner in which the church's witness secures the witness and faith of the nations in the cosmic war of the Lamb.[24] The two witnesses of chapter 11 represent the church as a continuation of the prophetic witness of Jesus to the nations. They are clothed in sackcloth, the symbol of repentance (cf. Jonah 3:4f.; Matthew 11:21), and their proclamation of the judgment of God is in fact a call to repentance—as are also the letters to the seven churches, with which the book of Revelation begins (2–3). Take, for example, these words to the church in Sardis: "Awake, and strengthen what remains and is on the point of death. . . . Remember then what you received and heard; keep that, and repent" (Revelation 3:2–3). The faithful power of witness that conquers the powers of evil is closely tied to penitence and the remembered offer of divine forgiveness.

To awaken and remain attentive to the restoration of true humanity by the slain Lamb who rules in the heavenly city—a rule mediated on earth by the suffering, servant church—requires rebirth. It requires the obedient practice of the disciplines of the penitential life, for it is a truth that is transparent neither in the fallen human soul nor in fallen human familial and societal relationships. The cosmic struggle between divine truth and its false, parodic copies defines the terms of human existence in Dostoevsky's novel; to serve the truth is an *agon* for which only the reborn are equipped. Rebirth and awakening are not simply matters of the inner heart (as Ivan's portrait of Christ imagines) or of individual experience. Only rebirth into the true inner-outer nature of divine love can bind the world together in an ordering of love. This rebirth becomes visible in the world through embodied, relational expression—the *mimesis* of the spiritual motion of humble love incarnated by Christ. If the pattern is true, then its nature cannot be an abstract or formal or "otherworldly" ideal; it must hold in all aspects of existence as the underlying, causal structure.

Contrary to Ivan's assertion, then, such love is not a "miracle impossible on the earth" or possible only through the "strain of a lie, out of love enforced by duty, out of self-imposed penance" (237). The love of neighbor taught and enacted by Christ cannot be an abstract or formal or "otherworldly" ideal "staged" by the Gospel stories and the Christian church for dramatic, inspiring effect.[25] It is indeed tied to faith in God and immortality, but not in a doctrinal or rhetorical sense; rather as a demanding way of life, and one for which human beings have been made. Faith in God and immortality is not a matter for intellectual proof, says the elder, but is causally connected with the experience of active earthly love—"The more you succeed in loving, the more you'll be convinced of the existence of God and the immortality of your soul" (56). As the elder goes on to say to that sentimental dreamer Madame Khokhlakov, who like Ivan lacks faith in immortality and in the pattern of humble love and admits it with "deep sincerity": "You have already done much if you can understand yourself so deeply and so sincerely! But if you spoke with me so sincerely just now in order to be praised, as I have praised you, for your truthfulness, then of course you will get nowhere with your efforts at active love; it will all remain merely a dream, and your whole life will flit by like a phantom."

This point is crucial to Dostoevsky's prophetic vision, tied here to the prophetic insight of the elder. Cosmic causality is not discerned through the external observation of nature and society and their visible motion; it is discerned in the soul, that *organon,* as Plato calls it, with which one sees the truth and which must be "turned around" *(periagoge)* from the stage show of temporal motion to the eternal realm of divine goodness (*The Republic* 518cd). For Dostoevsky this true pattern of the soul's end is learned by practicing the difficult disciplines of neighbor-love modeled by Christ. In the words of the elder:

> I am sorry that I cannot say anything more comforting, for active love is a harsh and fearful thing compared with love in dreams. Love in dreams thirsts for immediate action, quickly performed, and with everyone watching. Indeed, it will go as far as the giving even of one's life, provided it does not take long but is soon over, as on stage, and everyone is looking on and praising. Whereas active love is labor and perseverance, and for some people, perhaps, a whole science. (58)

The dramatic motion of *The Brothers Karamazov* follows this pattern of "turning around" from earthly dreams and stage-shows, the idols and rivalries of human life "underground"—the pattern we refer to here as the penitential consciousness.

The decisive spiritual shift that brings about penitential consciousness is modeled prominently in Dostoevsky's art, as has been noted by many commentators. Yet another of his most famous works, *Notes from the Underground* (1864), revolves around this shift—a conversion to the image of Christ, catalyzed by a revelation of the contrast between that image and the idolatrous fallenness of the human condition (expressed so self-consciously by the underground man). René Girard provides an extensive analysis of the prophetic power of Dostoevsky's depiction of the "underground."[26] The underground is the law of fallen human desire—that is, of desire divided against itself. On the one hand the self is created for life with others in an ordering of love; on the other hand the self seeks to be the center of that ordering. Thus, although it needs and desires others (no self can come to self-consciousness without the mediation of another), it turns that very desire to the self-asserting domination of the other. The other becomes both model and rival, the object of desire and of domination and therefore of both love and hatred. This struggle reflects the separation and isolation of selves not only from one another but also from the source of reconciling, divine love. The need and desire for God is likewise falsely externalized, as the dependent, relational self seeks its independent fulfillment through the possession of objects of desire, and even more importantly (and more ironically), through the imitation of "successful" models and mediators of possessive desire in the world. The *imitatio dei* becomes the *imitatio alteri* that creates the endless and increasingly violent cycles of mimetic rivalry between competing, desiring egos—especially when the process is willfully repressed and hidden. Girard comments: "One goes 'underground' as a result of frustrated mimetic desire. All underground people carefully hide their imitations, even from themselves, so as not to give their models the psychic reward of seeing themselves imitated, not to humiliate themselves by being revealed as imitators."[27]

Yet this very egoism intensifies desire and requires ever greater external mediation of that desire. As one seeks self-confirmation and fulfillment through others, the underground self becomes increasingly enslaved to the objects and external mediations of desire. This enslavement causes tremendous hatred and *ressentiment,* which gives rise eventually to demonic self-laceration or revenge against others, as so penetratingly depicted in *The Brothers Karamazov,* even in the novel's very structure.[28]

Thus we come full circle to Ivan's lament of protest against the God revealed in Christ: "I need retribution, otherwise I will destroy myself." It is a protest against a God who makes a world in which children suffer and are "in solidarity with their fathers in all the fathers' evildoings" (244). This mimetic rivalry is the central dynamic of the novel, as is the question of how humans might free themselves of it: murder? suicide? or forgiveness and the higher harmony of suffering love? The pattern of each of the brothers (including the bastard son of "stinking Lizavetta," fathered by Fyodor) is different, yet all have to do with their role in and responses to the death of a father. Can the basic erotic desire, the earthy, raw life-force of the Karamazovs be raised up by the Spirit of God to a higher harmony (220, 230–231), or will it consume itself and others in violent death, the "hell" of isolation?

Fatherhood clearly plays a central role in this novel. As Paul Ricoeur shows in his analysis of the movement of the father figure from phantasm to symbol, fatherhood is a complex relational and cultural designation that traverses a variety of semantic levels—all of which are to be found in Dostoevsky's novel.[29] The level of the phantasm, or the idol, centers upon the economy of desire. The father models and mediates the desires of the son, and hence becomes both an admired and a feared power-figure—indeed, a mimetic rival.[30] The father possesses privileges of power desired by the son in order to realize himself; this gives rise to the desire to murder the father. We surely see that desire in all of Fyodor's sons—except perhaps Alyosha, who stands outside this particular mimetic rivalry but not altogether outside the mimetic struggle, as we shall see. Both the father and mimetic desire are transfigured at the cultural level through the self-conscious education or sociocultural formation of desire by way of ethical roles and responsibilities. Ricoeur shows that for Hegel the threshold between *Moralität* (the moral will) and *Sittlichkeit* (the ethical community) is the family, a relation that is social but not purely contractual; it is also a spiritual community, but not voluntary.[31] At the cultural level, fatherhood has become a symbol, but not yet a religious symbol—it remains at the level of law. In *The Brothers Karamazov* this level is explicitly represented in the legal trial of Dmitri for the crime of parricide—a violation of the highest order, and not merely a contractual violation but also a spiritual one. We examine this representation more closely in Chapter 6.

There remains the third level: that of religious symbol and the connection of fatherhood to God. There is, says Ricoeur, great reserve in the biblical language of God as father—given the potential for great idolatry, and possible confusion with the immediacies and reified forms (phantasms) of fatherhood in the other levels. In Israel's tradition the return of the father is found in God *adopting* Israel in an affective bond (not kinship)—a relation most pronounced in the prophets, where it is often tied to explicitly eschatological promises. The affective bond between God as father and his human children is also often compared to that between spouses (see, for example, Jeremiah 3:19–20). Ricoeur comments: "By means of this strange mutual contamination of two kinship figures, the shell of literality of the image is broken and the symbol is liberated. A father who is a spouse is no longer a progenitor (begetter), nor is he any more an enemy to his sons; love, solicitude, and pity carry him beyond domination and severity."[32]

The eschatological meaning of "father" is intensified by Jesus' use of it in the New Testament—fatherhood is connected to the coming reign of God in a community that can be entered only if one is like a child. It is in Jesus' address to God as his father that the biblical reserve is broken, not as a "relapse into archaism" but as a prophetic direction toward the fulfillment of all things in intimate relation with their source and end. It is a form of address that breaks through the distance of transcendent judgment into the reconciling community of spiritual love.

This breakthrough, however, can be accomplished only through death, the unjust death of the Just One, present in the prophetic image of the Suffering Servant. His meek willingness to undergo death is a countermovement to the murderous desire to possess the immortality and power of the father. It is all the more striking because he already shares in everything the father has, as expressed in the liturgical hymn in Philippians 2:5–8: "Have this mind *(phroneite)* among yourselves, which was in Christ Jesus, who, though he was in the form of God, did not count equality with God a thing to be grasped, but emptied himself, taking the form of a servant. . . . He humbled himself and became obedient unto death." In contrast to Freud and Nietzsche, who interpret this as an ingenious Christian twist on the old, eternal power struggle, Dostoevsky (like Ricoeur and Girard) sees it as a decisive end to the cycle of violent enmity. The pattern of God's rule, of God's nature, is not the self-asserting imposition of power—creating a world of suffering in order to enhance the glory of higher harmony and transcendent justice—but rather the free offering of self in the service of a wider reconciliation in which love fulfills all.

There is a fundamental difference in *The Brothers Karamazov* between the self-asserting murder of Fyodor Karamazov—a "just" rebellion that is nevertheless rooted in a mimesis of Fyodor's own pattern of instinctual, egoistic desire and in revenge—and the death of the son Ilyusha, which becomes the occasion for mediating the spiritual motion of dying to self and being reborn into a reconciling community of children at the end of the novel. The death of Ilyusha, and its wider spiritual meaning (as in the "dying to self" displayed in the "turning around" of Alyosha and Mitya), is artistically linked by Dostoevsky to the pattern of Christ, the God-man, in which it participates—and into which those with eyes to see are invited as participants. This form of participation, however, requires that the death-dealing violent and retributive pattern of fallen desire be "put to death," in order for the self to be reborn into a community where even kinship relations are transfigured into nonrivalrous, nonegoistic relations of love. This rebirth is an enactment and embodiment of the penitential pattern, the expression in speech and deeds of a new mind and a new nature. At the motivating heart of this participation in the kenotic pattern of Christ is neither dazzling miracle nor forensic transaction—it is the transformation of all of life by holy, erotic, divine love. The culminating image here is the celebratory assembly of the marriage feast of the Lamb, a wedding feast that ties together earthly joy and its heavenly completion. Let us chart the "pro and contra" responses of the brothers Karamazov to this salvific pattern, following the order in which they are presented in the novel: Alyosha (book 7), Mitya (book 8), and Ivan/Smerdyakov (book 11).

The youngest of the Karamazov brothers is described as "simply an early lover of mankind" (18)[33] who is "strange" from the cradle—that is, he displays ascetic and monastic traits including a "wild, frantic modesty and chastity" (20) and a lack of concern about "who was supporting him." Because he refuses to participate in the various triangulations of desire, with their accompanying rivalries and lacerations, he becomes a confidant and mediator of healing love to his father, his brothers, and other characters. It is no surprise that he throws himself into the monastic path as an "ideal way out for his soul struggling from the darkness of worldly wickedness towards the light of love" (18, 26). He does not share in the "instinctual" forms of mimetic rivalry modeled by Fyodor and the other sons, but this is not to say that his "monastic" path is free of disordered desire and the false externalization of desire. Among other things, Alyosha will have to struggle with his idolatrous representation of his earthly spiritual father (his "Pater Seraphicus," as Ivan calls him), the elder Zosima, whose life he seeks above all to imitate in his own. Early in the novel Alyosha is described as having "unquestioning faith in the miraculous power of the elder" (30), and he shares the popular dream that the elder's death will be accompanied by many miracles confirming his spiritual power and glory. Alyosha's idolatry is evident in his veneration of Zosima:

> He was not at all troubled that the elder . . . stood solitary before him: "No matter, he is holy, in his heart is the secret of renewal for all, the power that will finally establish the truth on earth, and all will be holy and will love one another, and there will be neither rich nor poor, neither exalted nor humiliated, but all will be like the children of God, and the true kingdom of Christ will come." That was the dream in Alyosha's heart. (30–31)

Alyosha's dream of a unifying spiritual power that will transfigure reality is focused rapturously on this father to whom he has bound himself in obedience. Thus, when Zosima undergoes a death accompanied by none of the anticipated miracles but rather by the premature putrefaction of his body, Alyosha experiences a crisis of faith and questions the divine justice that allows the public humiliation of this most righteous man (339f.). The religious authority and spiritual power of his elder are called radically into question by an external sign (the stinking corpse); and Alyosha, like Ivan, is tempted to rebel, judging God's creation to be unjust. Not only is the order of providence, of spiritual causality, hidden; it is blatantly reversed in this unusual acceleration of the material processes of bodily putrefaction. The stinking humiliation of the elder's prematurely decomposing body tempts Alyosha to respond as Ivan did to the filthy stench of God's world. The intensity of Alyosha's spiritual desire, mocked by the humiliating disgrace of his elder's image, is drawn toward the memory of his brother Ivan's impassioned thirst for visible justice:[34] "Where was Providence and its finger? Why did it hide its finger 'at the most necessary moment' (Alyosha thought), as if wanting to submit itself to the blind, mute, merciless laws of nature?" (340)

Alyosha's "virgin heart" is wounded in this personal experience of injustice, and he is suddenly open to the fleshly inducements offered by his tempter, Rakitin: sausage, vodka, and the seductive Grushenka (the object of erotic attention and rivalry among him, his father Fyodor, and his brother Mitya). Unlike Ivan's intellectualist "underground," Alyosha, like Mitya, is lured toward the sins of the flesh, his own "back lane" where he can enjoy the shame of depravity (109). In his ordeal of temptation, however, Alyosha experiences an unexpected miracle from an unexpected source. Instead of "falling," he is "raised up" by the "fallen"

Grushenka, who upon hearing that the elder has just died, jumps off Alyosha's lap and crosses herself. This act restores Alyosha's soul: He sees that Grushenka begins to respond as if the elder himself were present—that is, she begins to display sisterly love, attuned to conscience—precisely the authority appealed to by the elder's teachings (64). Alyosha comes to see that the authority of the elder, the "secret of renewal for all" and the "power of the kingdom," is not carried around in the body of one man. Instead, it is available to all in the form of a conscience guided by the "law" or "image" of Christ and embodied in experiences of active love. There is a discovery here of an inner solidarity in which "all are responsible for all" not only in guilt but also in atoning love.

Their exchange shakes the souls of both Alyosha and Grushenka, and it causes Grushenka to remember a folktale from childhood about salvation from hell afforded by an act of love (the gift of an onion, which symbolizes saving grace), in which the outcome depends on what one does with the opportunity—whether one shares it with others or selfishly attempts to possess it for oneself. Her sharing of an onion, to which Alyosha has responded with loving gratitude, evokes an act of penitential confession. She confesses her evil intentions, her intense desire to "ruin" the pure Alyosha (and his "wild chastity"[35]): "I was determined: I'll eat him up. Eat him up and laugh. See what a wicked bitch I am, and you called me your sister!" The encounter causes her also to confess her retributive, vengeful feelings regarding the man who wronged her, her Polish suitor who has recently made another overture toward her after five years. She bursts into penitential tears, wondering whether her heart can truly forgive (and confessing further that she has grown fond of her tears of self-pity over the years), and Alyosha is moved to make his own confession, "with tears in his voice."[36]

This change in Alyosha's heart is represented artistically by Dostoevsky in what Diane Thompson has appropriately called an "icon" of immortality, the chapter entitled "Cana of Galilee."[37] Alyosha returns to the elder's cell to pray after his miraculous turnaround; and later, as Father Paissy reads the Gospel—John's, of course—over the coffin of the dead elder, Alyosha has a vision. It is a vision structured by the Gospel reading of the wedding at Cana, where Christ performed his first miracle to "help men's joy" (360). It is also a marriage, a wedding feast, and Alyosha's vision is of the heavenly wedding feast where all earthly loves culminate in joyful worship of the divine maker. This is the celebration of the marriage of the Lamb described in St. John's vision (Revelation 19:7f.; 21:2f.). Arriving at the feast, Alyosha is greeted by the dead elder, and directed by him toward the focus of worship, identified as "our Sun" (361). This is the sun that shines in the new Jerusalem: "And the city has no need of sun or moon to shine upon it, for the glory of God is its light, and its lamp is the Lamb. By its light shall the nations walk . . . and there shall be no night there" (Revelation 21:23f.; cf. 1:16). In

Alyosha's vision, then, the holy city has "come down" from heaven, symbolizing the dwelling of God with human beings in a new, reconciled order of creation. It is a vision of the Alpha and Omega, the beginning of all things and the end toward which they move for completion. The way to completion is the one taught by the elder, and modeled in the suffering, active love of Christ. The ascetic vision of humble, serving love has as its final aim the inclusion of all reality in the joyful feast of the remembering people of God and in the descent out of heaven of the holy Jerusalem, lit by the Lamb in whose light walk all the nations, each bringing their particular gift of glory to it.

It is no accident that Dostoevsky places this vision of the eschatological banquet in the new Jerusalem at the culminating point of Alyosha's existential rebirth. He has experienced for himself the full inner-outer meaning of the elder's teachings, an experience that now equips him spiritually for the ascetic "sojourn in the world" to which he has been called. It is a penitential rebirth characterized by weeping, erotic confession:

> It was as if threads from all those innumerable worlds of God all came together in his soul, and it was trembling all over, "touching other worlds." He wanted to forgive everyone and for everything, and to ask forgiveness, oh, not for himself! but for all and for everything, "as others are asking for me," rang again in his soul. But with each moment he felt clearly and almost tangibly something as firm and immovable as this heavenly vault descend into his soul. Some sort of idea, as it were, was coming to reign in his mind—now for the whole of his life and unto ages of ages. He fell to the earth a weak youth and rose up a fighter, steadfast for the rest of his life. (362–63)[38]

Alyosha's ecstatic vision in the monastery garden occurs at roughly the same time that his brother Dmitri finds himself in another garden, the garden of their father, Fyodor—the hated father who neglected him as a child, who has cut off his inheritance money, and (the last straw) who has become his erotic rival in relation to Grushenka. Whereas Alyosha is praying for the world, Dmitri finds himself in the dark, boiling with vengeful anger against his vile father, whom he is observing through a window (392). His personal loathing and desire for retribution become so intense that he is tempted to kill his father. But at this moment he experiences a "miracle": "'God was watching over me then,' Mitya used to say afterwards" (393).[39] This miracle is not only an inner event, and it is no abstraction: Grigory, Fyodor's servant, who served as a surrogate father to Mitya the neglected child (and his abandoned brothers), plays an important role in it.[40] He absorbs the blow intended for the abusive father, Fyodor, and thus provides a redemptive opportunity for Dmitri: The spilled blood of the innocent Grigory marks Mitya's guilt (396–397). Dmitri's conviction that he has killed Grigory, even as he discovers he has apparently lost his beloved Grushenka to her erstwhile Polish lover, causes him to become "drunk in spirit" (401). Waving his pistols and threatening suicide, this Schiller-spouting lover of beauty still speaks in romantic terms about loving life—"I want to live, I love life! Believe me. I love golden-haired Phoebus and his hot light" (402)—as he prepares to flee to Mokroye ("moist mother earth") to see Grushenka once more, presumably at *her* wedding feast, to which he brings costly refreshments and rare wine. He wishes to drink to life and to bless God's creation, but he also wants to exterminate "one foul insect" (406)—himself. The only question now is how he will do it: By physical suicide, or by spiritual death to self-assertion?[41]

This crisis of death and life is evident in the narrator's repeated phrase "Mitya's soul was troubled" (cf. John 12:27), which anticipates the crisis as Mitya journeys to Mokroye (409f.). This crisis ends in religious conversion and in death to self-assertion, a movement that begins in Mitya's conversation with the peasant coachman Andrei, who reminds Mitya of the crucified Son of God who frees sinners suffering in hell. It is in this conversation that the symbolism in Mitya's speech shifts from romantic lyricism (Phoebus the sun god) to the crucified Son of God, prayer for forgiveness, and the petition "let me also finish with loving" (412).[42] The order of love to which he is now being conformed cannot be accomplished without suffering, as he increasingly sees in the light of Grushenka's response of love to him:[43] "By her eyes he could now see clearly whom she loved. So now all he had to do was live, but . . . but he could not live, he could not, oh, damnation! 'God, restore him who was struck down at the fence! Let this terrible cup pass from me! You worked miracles, O Lord, for sinners just like me!'" (437)

Though Mitya quotes only the first half of Jesus' prayer on the Mount of Olives (Matthew 26:37), to be spared the cup of suffering, he nevertheless remains open to the will of God. We cannot trace here the complex journey of Mitya's soul through the three torments of spiritual purification (book 9, chapters 3 to 5), except to note that they are occasioned by being accused of a crime he did not commit even as he discovers that his blow did *not* kill old Grigory (458–459).[44] The miracle he earlier requested, which seems to have been granted by the "resurrecting" news that Grigory is alive and which leads him to begin speaking the truth in humble confession, turns instead into a more humiliating death. Not only is his true statement that he did not kill his father disbelieved, but he is stripsearched in front of his prosecutors, exposing his dirty underclothes (484). He then makes a full confession of his inner, secret disgrace regarding his duplicitous amatory and monetary dealings with Katya, dealings rooted in pride and vengefulness.[45] Though he has not sought torments for himself as the elder prescribes for those afflicted with desires for revenge (321), they have been given him by the hand of providence—to the will of which his heart has been opened, leading him to confess even his "private life" (468), which turns out to be relevant to the case (even though his legal prosecutors continue to think it is not).

Following upon this confession, Mitya has his strange dream of "the wee one" (507) who opens him to the experience of spiritual rebirth, an image that will grow in his consciousness and enable him later to overcome temptation. The vision is of poor, burnt-out, starving peasants on the Russian steppe, one of whom holds a crying baby. Especially significant in the dream are the questions Mitya asks the peasants: "Tell me: Why are these burnt-out mothers standing here, why are the people poor, why is the wee one poor, why is the steppe bare, why don't they embrace and kiss, why don't they sing joyful songs, why are they blackened with such misery, why don't they feed the wee one?" (507)

These questions are related to love of life "as it is," prior to logic (cf. 231), and they initiate a loving (rather than retributive) quest in Mitya for understanding of life's meaning. They lead him in his dream to an experience of heart-felt compassion for the suffering ones and the desire to "do something for them" (508), an "immediate deed" (cf. 26) "so that there will be no more tears in anyone from that moment on" (508). It is not far-fetched to see in this dream a reference to the "new Jerusalem" that comes down out of heaven, after the dragon and the sea of chaos have been conquered, when God comes to dwell permanently with human beings: "And God himself will be with them; he will wipe away every tear from their eyes, and death shall be no more, neither shall there be mourning nor crying nor pain any more, for the former things have passed away" (Rev. 21:3–4).

The vision ends with Mitya's whole heart "blaz[ing] up and turn[ing] towards some sort of light, and he wanted to live" (508). It is this vision that keeps Mitya from falling into retributive despair over his unjust fate, and from succumbing to Rakitin the tempter's image of the "new man," which reduces conscience to environmental stimulus, the soul to a chemical synapse, and ethics to social and chemical engineering (588–589). Instead Mitya is sustained by a very different "new man" that has arisen in his soul, who is capable of suffering love because he is nurtured by God's gift of joy, "without which it's not possible for man to live" (592). This is the hymn-singing "underground man" born anew, who knows the transcendent sun of the new Jerusalem: Even "if I don't see the sun, still I know it *is*. And the whole of life is there—in knowing that the sun *is*" (592).

Mitya's hymn has been transformed from the romantic "Glory to the Highest in the world, Glory to the Highest in me" (103) and Schiller's hymn in praise of Nature, *An die Freude,* to the underground hymn: "Hail to God and his joy! I love him!" This indicates the shift in Mitya's orientation from anthropocentric humanism (which cannot address or resolve the lacerating cycles of the underground man) to the God of the Bible. And yet, the new Jerusalem has not descended from heaven, and Mitya must continue to wrestle with the conflict of new and old desires in his heart. Though he has responded in openness to the providential "blow" that has jolted him out of his directionless movement from passion to passion—"Never, never would I have arisen by myself!"(509)—and that has offered him a path of purifying suffering, the struggle remains.

Mitya's struggle is strikingly symbolized in the chapter entitled "A Hymn and a Secret," in which different approaches to moral responsibility, causality, and community are presented. Rakitin and Mitya have been discussing ideas about the nature of ethics. Rakitin's ideas are taken from Claude Bernard, famous for his development of the experimental scientific method rooted in what W. M. Simon calls "the one article of faith he regarded as necessary to any science," that the principle of causal determinism is operative everywhere in "factual" nature.[46] This narrowly defined science, and the methodological reduction of movement to physicochemical processes, stand in stark contrast to the "whole science" of active love proclaimed by the elder. Rakitin rejects the elder's religious naïveté, but he also modifies Ivan's thesis that without God and immortality "all is permitted" to "all is permitted to the intelligent man." The egoism of enlightened self-interest will not allow the passions to control the mind; it will stay out of legal trouble even while getting what it wants. Rakitin is a socialist and therefore ideologically pure. He is beyond the sensualism of scoundrels, and believes that contrary to Ivan's "stupid theory," "mankind will find strength in itself to live for virtue, even without believing in the immortality of the soul! Find it in the love of liberty, equality, fraternity" (82). Yet Rakitin's scientific socialism, as the Inquisitor's exposé shows, lacks insight into the spiritual causality of human action and fails to see the incompatibility between egoistic freedom and sharing equally with all. Distributive justice cannot satisfy the spiritual demands of retributive justice. Rakitin himself is the most mercenary of careerists, transparently motivated by the desire for money and critical literary fame; he is filled with *ressentiment*. If Ivan is a grave, as Mitya claims, Rakitin is the whitewash on it.

Mitya is not truly tempted by Rakitin's theories, and he sees through the shallowness of his intelligence. And yet he recognizes his own weak ability to follow the prophetic path of suffering shown him in the vision of the "wee one" and the "new man" that has arisen within him. He wants to sing the underground man's tragic hymn to God, in whom there is joy, but "all these philosophies are killing me, devil take them!" (592). The real tempter for Mitya (as for Alyosha) is brother Ivan, who "hides his idea" and remains silent as a sphinx. Ivan's tormented struggle over God and immortality goes beyond the battle between ideological and doctrinal slogans so characteristic of liberalism: "European liberalism in general, and even our Russian liberal dilettantism, has long and frequently confused the final results of socialism with those of Christianity" (69), precisely because it reduces both to moralism—that is, to social morality devoid of substantive spiritual and theological depth. There is a confusion here about the law of nature, as if nature itself entails the moral injunction to love humankind. Ivan does not hold to this view. The law of love does not derive from natural law but from the command of God, the religious law that challenges the egoism of human nature. Without God and immortality, the egoistic "all is permitted," even to the point of crime, is the most reasonable conclusion.

Ivan's idea—"there is no virtue if there is no immortality"—catches the attention of Mitya from the outset: "I'll remember" (70). It is a thought that continues to plague Mitya even after his resurrecting vision, just as it continues to torment Ivan in his secret heart.[47] It is a secret identified by Alyosha in response to Ivan's claim that the Inquisitor's dream of harmony is joined to "the intelligent people": "What intelligent people? . . . They are not so very intelligent, nor do they have any great mysteries and secrets . . . Except maybe for godlessness, that's their whole secret. Your Inquisitor doesn't believe in God, that's his whole secret!"[53] The secret in "A Hymn and a Secret" concerns something more particular, related to the larger secret of godlessness, and it too is suggested by Ivan—a plan for Mitya to escape to America with Grushenka in order to make a "new start." Mitya links this secret plan to his conscience: "What about my conscience? I'll be running away from suffering! I was shown a path—and I rejected the path; there was a way of purification—I did an about-face. . . . Well, and where will our underground hymn take place? Forget America, America means vanity again!" (595) This struggle in Mitya's conscience has already been noted by Grushenka, who comments on his mood swings. When he talks about the "wee one" and the hymn, oriented by the liturgical vision of the new Jerusalem ruled by the slain Lamb, he weeps and laughs "as if he were a child himself" (570). The darker side to Mitya's moods, the side of fear and anxiety, is connected to the secret plan suggested and insisted upon by Ivan and Katya. Both brothers try above all to keep the secret from Alyosha—the "cherub" (595, cf. 651) in their conscience—whose life judges the plan a lie. It will not bring freedom for a new beginning (that is to be found only in the path of Christ—not my will but thine be done—as testified to in the hymn); it will instead require a secretive life supported by external, mechanical fabrication, and will bring torments of conscience and self-condemnation that cannot be escaped.[48] What is most needed in this whole tragic affair is the repentance, confession, and forgiveness of the triangulated rivals trying to escape the "problem" of Mitya's having been falsely accused, in which they are all spiritually implicated. Mitya is finally able to speak out of this redemptive knowledge of the loving source of human solidarity when he calls his hated rival sibling "brother Ivan"; his last words in the conversation with Alyosha are "love Ivan" (597).

We note, by contrast, Ivan's parting words to Alyosha concerning his brother Dmitri: "I hate the monster, . . . I hate the monster! I don't want to save the monster, let him rot at hard labor! He's singing a hymn!" (654) These words of Ivan's occur at the end of his own "three torments"—his visits to Smerdyakov, during which his complicity in the parricide is gradually unveiled; but his journey represents a contrasting movement of "truth" to Mitya's. Mitya is publicly accused of a murder he did not commit, even as he discovers that he has not murdered Grigory and is therefore not legally a "murderer." Mitya, however, recognizes his murderous heart and takes free responsibility for it in a full, life-changing confession that leads him to accept the path of suffering love. Ivan, by contrast, who has reserved full latitude for murderous hatred in his "wishes" (143, 611), is brought face to face with his actual complicity in the murderous deed in his meetings with Smerdyakov—at the end of which he too has a dream, not of a "wee one" or of "Cana of Galilee," but a "nightmare" of "the devil." His has been a very different spiritual journey. The visitation by the devil in Ivan's apocalyptic dream is a fitting parody of John's vision, and it represents Ivan's state of soul. The devil "comes down" to Ivan; and yet it would seem that Ivan has "called him up" as his worst side, his inner illness. Whereas Alyosha's and Mitya's salvific visions resurrect them in joyful worship of divine truth after they have died to themselves in confession, Ivan's hellish nightmare plunges him further into despair and mental illness.

In Ivan's third and final meeting with Smerdyakov, during which Smerdyakov accuses Ivan of being the "main killer" of his father (623), Ivan expresses the fearful hope that this is all a dream or that Smerdyakov is in fact a ghost. Smerdyakov replies, "There's no ghost, sir, besides the two of us, sir, and some third one." This mediating "third" that exists "between" Ivan and Smerdyakov "is God, sir, Providence itself, sir, it's right here with us now, sir, only don't look for it, you won't find it." Indeed, the mediating presence (to faith) of loving divine Providence is replaced by its absence—the cold, murderous fear of the devil. In Ivan's nightmare this chilling presence is articulated by the shabby liberal "sponger" of a devil in the language of modern scientific cosmology. The living spiritual—and inherently moral—cosmos envisioned by Zosima (as well as Alyosha and Mitya) is here replaced by freezing, dark, dead space and the external motion of material objects in a morally neutral universe. Here the calculations of movement with reference to the sun can be replaced (in a humorous adaptation of a macabre folktale) by the "rising and setting of the axe" (640); thus, the novel's central religious symbol radiating warmth and light is replaced by a humanly made instrument for chopping, splintering, and destroying. There is a double cosmological reduction in this parody of the devil. The first is that the sun is no longer a material symbol representing a higher, divine, and spiritual light; it is here but a physical object.[49] The second, allowed for by the first, is the replacement of a divinely created thing signifying benevolent purposes by a humanly fashioned artifact, here signifying destructive purposes.

Spiritual causality and the notion of providence are not simply cosmological visions or theories. These cosmic powers and movements are closely related to movements of soul and their worldly mediation in human relationships. The chilling demonic "bond" between Ivan and his "double"—his illegitimate half-brother born the same year, of the same father—is evident early on. Leaving for home after his conversation with Alyosha about "The Grand Inquisitor," Ivan experiences a sudden, unbearable, undefinable anguish in his soul that grows worse as he gets closer to home. It seems to be related to something external, and as he approaches his father's house "he at once realized what was tormenting and worrying him so"—Smerdyakov: "Ivan Fyodorovich realized at the first sight of him that the lackey Smerdyakov was also sitting in his soul, and that it was precisely this man that his soul could not bear" (266). The special interest Ivan at first takes in Smerdyakov, finding him entertainingly original in philosophical and religious discussions, quickly turns to an intense loathing. In their conversations, it becomes clear to Ivan that Smerdyakov is interested in something more than ideas, and a certain "boundless vanity" appears, accompanied by a growing "loathsome and peculiar familiarity," as if Smerdyakov considers the two of them as somehow "in league." Despite this, perceiving that Smerdyakov wants to have a "special conversation," Ivan stops to talk with him. What follows is the indirect discussion of signals and plans having to do with the possible murder of Fyodor, a strange conversation punctuated with Ivan's exclamations, "How the devil!," "What the devil!," and "Devil take you!" These two intelligent men share a common, loathsome understanding in their souls—a shared desire, which Ivan tries to hide and projects onto the "double" that mediates it to him, but to which he is equally bound by inner intention.

By the end of their third meeting, Ivan has had to face this desire: "God knows ... perhaps I, too, was guilty, perhaps I really had a secret desire that my father ... die" (631). He resolves that together he and Smerdyakov will confess to the court the next day. Upon leaving, his tormenting hesitations about how to testify in court have left him. "It was as if a sort of joy now descended into his soul. He felt an infinite firmness in himself" (633). His newfound resolve equips him to perform a "Good Samaritan" deed (albeit for a peasant that he himself has earlier beaten), and this awareness gives him inner delight. At that moment he is stopped by a sudden question: "And shouldn't I go to the prosecutor right now at once and tell him everything?" He resolves the question negatively: "Tomorrow . . . ." And immediately his joy vanishes, to be replaced by an icy reminder of something loathsome and tormenting in his room—the devil. This scene portrays Dostoevsky's recurrent theme that faith requires immediate obedience if it is to take root. Delay reinforces the division and scattering of the divided conscience.[50]

Ivan's devil identifies himself by a parody of the divine name revealed in Revelation—"I am the Alpha and the Omega, the beginning and the end" (1:8; 21:6; 22:13)—when he says: "I am an x in an indeterminate equation. I am some sort of ghost of life who has lost all ends and beginnings, and I've finally even forgotten what to call myself" (642).[51] The devil is also described as "a sort of sponger," parasitic, isolated, and a dreamer. His power lies purely in negation. In each of these ways he represents the opposite of the divine being who actively creates what is good "out of nothing," who seeks to restore to the community of love all who are fallen and isolated, and who acts in the world to do so. The devil's "realism" parodies God's—Ivan identifies the devil as the opposite of the real truth: "You are a lie, you are my illness, you are a ghost. . . . You are my hallucination. You are the embodiment of myself, but of just one side of me . . . of my thoughts and feelings, but only the most loathsome and stupid of them" (637).

The vision ends with the devil reminding Ivan of another of his literary creations, "The Geological Cataclysm," in which Ivan speculates on the anthropological consequences of a modern scientific apocalypse—namely, the appearance of a "new man" (quite different from Dmitri's) in whom the slavish, tormenting, and violent idea of God has been destroyed, making possible the emergence of a titanic, nature-conquering "man-god": "Man, his will and his science no longer limited, conquering nature every hour, will thereby every hour experience such lofty delight as will replace for him all his former hopes of heavenly delight. Each will know himself utterly mortal, without resurrection, and will accept death proudly and calmly, like a god" (649).

This new man-god will be able to leap lightheartedly over the moral obstacles of the old "slave-man," enjoying the freedom of godlike autonomy, the "all is permitted." Yet it is clear in the novel that the tormenting question of conscience cannot be resolved in such a manner: This kind of freedom is alienated, a freedom divided against itself and its own consciousness, which is never truly independent but always in relation. Ivan dwells in division, the division between his heart (his "guts," his erotic love of life, the order of desire in the will) and his head (logic, Euclidean reason, which will take its own measures on the basis of "facts"). Such freedom cannot integrate itself, and ends up in rebellion against the order of things as well as its Orderer, upon whom created human freedom is in fact de-

pendent for its measure and fulfillment. This willful turning away from God requires the invention of a new order, a "second reality" that confirms the new, self-
centered orientation of the will. This second reality is a parody of the truth.

Oliver O'Donovan nicely describes the same dynamic with reference to Milton's portrayal of Satan in *Paradise Lost*:

> Satan's absolute and irreparable rejection of God becomes, in Milton's treatment, a
> representation of what man is ultimately capable of doing—not within the confines
> of time, of course, but eschatologically. . . . The famous line which Milton puts on
> Satan's lips, 'Evil, be thou my good!' perfectly captures the double movement of the
> soul which is the essence of the Satanic gesture: in the first place, the convulsive
> turning of the will to evil in place of the good which is its natural orientation; in the
> second place the veiling of the reality of evil under the guise of good.[52]

Dostoevsky depicts this confusion of soul in *The Brothers Karamazov* with reference to another classic, Goethe's *Faust,* in which Mephistopheles identifies himself to Faust as the one who desires evil but does only good. "Well," says Ivan's
devil, "it's quite the opposite with me," and yet his role keeps the reconciling good
a secret, and "until the secret is revealed, two truths exist for me: one is theirs,
from there, and so far completely unknown to me; the other is mine." This too is
Ivan's "humble confession" to Alyosha: the earthly human mind cannot comprehend the secret of God's goodness and divine justice; hence "while I am on earth,
I hasten to take my own measures" (244).

We shall examine in Chapter 6 the kind of politics in which such "liberal humility" eventuates. Here, as we are focusing on the personal, individual level, let
us take a closer look at the courtroom "confession" it evokes from Ivan. The devil
has taunted Ivan about confessing the truth in the courtroom even though he
doesn't believe in conscience or in virtue except as socially contructed conventions. "You're going out of pride," the devil tells Ivan, and in order to be praised
for virtue in which he does not believe. This is the source of Ivan's anger. The
confession portrays this mind-set. Immediately after tersely stating on the stand
that Smerdyakov killed their father on instructions from him, Ivan asserts, "Who
doesn't wish for his father's death?" A pre-Freudian slip? In response, an inadver-
tent comment slips from the judge, "Are you in your right mind?" Ivan's response:
"The thing is that I'm precisely in my right mind . . . my vile mind, the same as
you. . . . Everyone wants his father dead. Viper devours viper" (686). Ivan's vile
mind is rooted in his proud, egoistic "freedom" and his unwillingness to make a
penitent confession. Ivan continues to want, as the narrator puts it at the beginning of the chapter entitled "The Devil," to "vindicate himself to himself" (635).
He is hardened, like the father he has helped kill out of vengeful hatred, and yet

he remains tormented by his self-enclosed conscience—"the call to the unity of man with himself," as Bonhoeffer puts it.[53] This call comes from beyond the self and beyond the law, and only in obedient response to it is the self liberated to act.

One other allusion to the book of Revelation remains for discussion: the reference to the heavenly Jerusalem with which the novel ends. This image is the dramatic culmination of the contrast developed earlier in the novel between the nice little bourgeois family Karamazov, broken down by neglect and isolation, violent rivalry and parricide, and the family Snegiryov, which despite its affliction by poverty, illness, and ignominy, images a higher moral order of love—a family from which, as Alyosha informs the arrogant and precocious Kolya, one can learn to know the good and be "remade" (556). Of particular importance are the events surrounding the death of Ilyusha Snegiryov, which becomes the focal point for the redemptive message taught by Alyosha in the concluding pages of the novel. The love between father and son is movingly displayed in the exchange following their realization that Ilyusha will die. Ilyusha implores his father to find another boy to love as his own son, and yet not to forget him, to visit his grave. The father responds with a remembered biblical image: "If I forget thee, O Jerusalem, let my tongue cleave . . . " (562). The reference is to Psalm 137, the lament for lost Jerusalem by Israelites held in Babylonian captivity, expressing their longing to return to the city ruled by God and to be established in freedom and peace. In the novel this image is clearly linked via "memory eternal" (774–776) to the hope of the consummation of all precious loves in the new Jerusalem described in Revelation 21.

The novel ends with the community of children, transformed from the pattern of strict, retributive justice founded by the dictatorial Kolya and modeled on the Inquisitor's parodic use of miracle, mystery, and authority, to a community founded upon humble love. The transformation occurs through the mediation of the hero of the novel: Alyosha's Christlike authority, rooted in humble wisdom, punctures vanity and the cleverness that parodies spiritual authority. At the end of the novel, in the epilogue, Kolya accepts Alyosha as the founder of a truer spiritual community, one that can accept the "unnatural" conjunctions of the Christian religious vision. In his parting "Speech at the Stone" on the occasion of Ilyusha's funeral, Alyosha addresses the boys on the truth of existence as revealed by the slain and resurrected Lamb, which joins in a life-giving union what seems so opposed: unjust suffering and the joy of life, pain and yet praise of creation as it is. Kolya remarks: "It's all so strange, Karamazov, such grief, and then pancakes [bliny] all of a sudden!" (773). It bears notice that in the "Speech at the Stone," in which Alyosha names the virtues that he implores them all to remember, justice is not mentioned. Justice is left to God; it is not within human power or prerogative. Given the primacy of the theme of justice in the novel, the implication is that these other virtues—kindness, generosity, honesty, courage, humility, and above all love—will replace the reign of retributive justice (and its alienating claims) with the all-forgiving, reconciling harmony of restorative justice that looks for its authority to the slain Lamb and for its fulfillment to the heavenly Jerusalem.

# Notes

1. See George Steiner, *Tolstoy or Dostoyevsky: An Essay in the Old Criticism* (New York: Penguin, 1959), chapter 4.

2. See Bruce K. Ward, *Dostoyevsky's Critique of the West: The Quest for the Earthly Paradise* (Waterloo, Ont.: Wilfrid Laurier University Press, 1986), chap. 4; and Ellis Sandoz, *Political Apocalypse: A Study of Dostoevsky's Grand Inquisitor* (Baton Rouge: Louisiana State University Press, 1971), chap. 5.

3. See, for example, Sandoz, *Political Apocalypse.* The title leads one to expect an extensive analysis of apocalyptic symbols in "The Grand Inquisitor", including those taken from the book of Revelation (Sandoz promises as much on p. 84). However, aside from a few brief references (e.g., pp. 88–89, 136, 151), the complex substance and interpretive implications of the symbolic parallels are left unexplored. See also Roger L. Cox, *Between Earth and Heaven: Shakespeare, Dostoevsky and the Meaning of Christian Tragedy* (New York: Holt, Rinehart and Winston, 1969), chaps. 8, 9; Bruce K. Ward, "Dostoevsky and the Problem of Meaning in History," in *Dostoevsky and the Twentieth Century,* ed. Malcolm V. Jones (Nottingham, U.K.: Astra, 1994), pp. 49–65. For evidence that Dostoevsky closely studied the book of Revelation, see Geir Kyetsaa, *Dostoevsky and His New Testament* (Atlantic Highlands, N.J.: Humanities Press, 1984).

4. Paul S. Minear, "The Cosmology of the Apocalypse," in *Current Issues in New Testament Interpretation,* eds. W. Klassen and G. Snyder (New York: Harper and Row, 1962), pp. 23–37.

5. We see the same division represented in Ivan's Inquisitor, whose response to Christ's silent kiss at the end of the Inquisitor's monologue is described by Ivan thus: "The kiss burns in his heart, but the old man holds to his former idea"[54].

6. This view of hell is given substance in the "Talks and Homilies" of Father Zosima: "Fathers and teachers, I ask myself: 'What is hell?' And I answer thus: 'The suffering of being no longer able to love.'" Zosima goes on to relate this to the parable of the rich man and Lazarus (322f.). The implication is that Ivan, like the rich man, will despise the gift of active love as exemplified in the suffering love of Christ. He will dash the cup of living water to the ground and suffer eternal thirst for resurrected love—out of prideful rebellion. The torment of punishment is not external, but inner—it is willful and resides in the conscience (see the diagnosis by Alyosha, 655).

7. This is evident in Ivan's impassioned speech in the chapter "Rebellion": "I need retribution, otherwise I will destroy myself. And retribution not somewhere and sometime in infinity, but here and now, on earth, so that I see it myself. . . . Is it possible that I've suffered so that I, together with my evil deeds and sufferings, should be manure for someone else's future harmony?" "I understand solidarity in sin among men; solidarity in retribution I also understand; but what solidarity in sin do little children have? And if it is really true that they, too, are in solidarity with their fathers in all their fathers' evildoings, that

truth certainly is not of this world and is incomprehensible to me" (244). Smerdyakov picks up on the personal, patricidal indignation in Ivan's otherwise detached, intellectual formulation, which leads to the conclusion that if there is no God or immortality, then there is no such thing as virtue, and "all is permitted" (69, 134, 632, 649).

8. The elder Zosima addresses this as well: "If the wickedness of people arouses indignation and insurmountable grief in you, to the point that you desire to revenge yourself upon the wicked, fear that feeling most of all" (321). The only remedy for wickedness is suffering, serving love that dies to vengeful self-assertion.

9. See Revelation 15:3–4; 16:5–7; 19:2; cf. 4:11, 5:9.

10. See Richard A. Posner, *Law and Literature,* revised ed. (Cambridge: Harvard University Press, 1998), pp. 173–178. Posner states, "*The Brothers Karamazov* implies criticism of law, but criticism that has less to do with the particulars of Russian criminal justice than with the very idea of secular justice" (Ibid., p. 176).

11. Albert Camus, *The Rebel: An Essay on Man in Revolt,* trans. A. Bower (New York: Knopf, 1956), p. 23.

12. "Then I turned to see the voice that was speaking to me, and on turning I saw seven golden lampstands, and in the midst of the lampstands one like a son of man, clothed with a long robe and with a golden girdle round his breast; his head and his hair were white as white wool, white as snow; his eyes were like a flame of fire, his feet were like burnished bronze, refined as in a furnace, and his voice was like the sound of many waters; in his right hand he held seven stars, from his mouth issued a sharp two-edged sword, and his face was like the sun shining in full strength" (Revelation 1:12–16). John's vision of the heavenly Christ locates the latter "in the midst" of the earthly churches (lampstands), but in his "glorified" and not his earthly state. Hence John is not "drawn" to him by quiet charisma—"When I saw him, I fell at his feet as though dead" (1:17).

13. G. B. Caird, *The Revelation of St. John the Divine* (New York: Harper and Row, 1966), p. 301. Elsewhere Caird says about the genre of apocalyptic eschatology: "Dodd and others have spoken of eschatology as though it were concerned with the *eschaton,* the final event, that beyond which nothing can conceivably happen. About an *eschaton* John has nothing to say. Instead he introduces us to a person who says, 'I am the Alpha and the Omega, the first and the last, the beginning and the end.' Whenever in the course of time men and women come face to face, whether for judgement or for salvation, with him who is the beginning and the end, that event can be adequately viewed only through the lenses of myth and eschatology" (G. B. Caird, *The Language and Imagery of the Bible* [London, U.K.: Duckworth, 1980], p. 271). My interpretation of Revelation is heavily indebted to Caird's superb commentary, cited above. I am also reliant upon Richard Bauckham, *The Theology of the Book of Revelation* (Cambridge: Cambridge University Press, 1993); idem, *The Climax of Prophecy: Studies on the Book of Revelation* (Edinburgh, U.K.: T. and T. Clark, 1992); Austin Farrer, *A Rebirth of Images: The Making of St. John's Apocalypse* (Boston: Beacon Press, 1949); idem, *The Revelation of St. John the Divine* (Oxford: Clarendon Press, 1964); and G. R. Beasley-Murray, *The Book of Revelation* (Grand Rapids, Mich.: William B. Eerdmans, 1974).

14. Richard Bauckham states: "Revelation was designed for oral enactment in Christian worship services (cf. 1:3). Its effect would therefore be somewhat comparable to a dramatic performance, in which the audience enter the world of the drama for its duration and can have their perception of the world outside the drama powerfully shifted by their experience of the world of the drama" (*The Theology of the Book of Revelation* [Cambridge:

Cambridge University Press, 1993], p. 10). See also D. L. Barr, "The Apocalypse of John as Oral Enactment," *Interpretation* 40 (1986): 243–256.

15. Caird, *Revelation*, p. 292.

16. See the words of Jesus in John 12, the chapter from which the epigraph to *The Brothers Karamazov* is taken: "Now is the judgement of this world, now shall the ruler of this world be cast out; and I, when I am lifted up from the earth, will draw all people to myself" (John 12:31–32). See also the discussion in Chapter 6.

17. For an interesting recent reflection on the importance of the Apocalypse for a renewal and extension of contemporary Orthodox liturgical practice, see Petros Vassiliadis, "Apocalypse and Liturgy," *St. Vladimir's Theological Quarterly* 41/2–3 (1997): 95–112. He argues that the *Sanctus*, the heavenly worship hymn in Revelation 4:8 taken from the temple vision and calling of Isaiah (6:1–3), far from "de-historicizing" Christian worship or separating it from worldly realities, reveals the true relation between heavenly and earthly liturgy. Liturgical form (hymns, prayers, images, and symbols) unveils the true meaning of history and political order—not only theoretically but in the practices it fosters. See also T. F. Torrance, "Liturgie et Apocalypse," *Verbum Caro* 11 (1957): 28–40.

18. Vigen Guroian, *Ethics After Christendom: Toward an Ecclesial Christian Ethic* (Grand Rapids, Mich.: William B. Eerdmans, 1994), p. 47. See also idem, *Incarnate Love: Essays in Orthodox Ethics* (Notre Dame, Ind.: University of Notre Dame Press, 1987), chaps. 1, 3.

19. Positively: in icons, most significantly in Alyosha's childhood iconic memory of his mother, Sophia, on "a quiet summer evening, an open window, the slanting rays of the setting sun (these slanting rays he remembered most of all), an icon in the corner of the room, a lighted oil-lamp in front of it, and before the icon, on her knees, his mother, sobbing as if in hysterics, with shrieks and cries, seizing him in her arms, hugging him so tightly that it hurt, and pleading for him to the Mother of God, holding him out from her embrace with both arms towards the icon, as if under the protection of the Mother of God" (19); in hymns, such as Mitya's "tragic hymn" to God from the underground, which celebrates the "whole of life" illuminated by the divine sun, even if one can't see it (592); in the visions of Alyosha and Mitya; and in various other liturgical settings, formal (as in elder Zosima's death chamber) and informal (Alyosha's speech to the boys at the stone). Negatively: in Fyodor's abusive spitting on Sophia's icon, in order to "knock this mysticism out of her" (137); in Smerdyakov's secret sacrilegious rites ("as a child he was fond of hanging cats and burying them with ceremony"; see 124), and his piling up of images without memory or insight (126–127); in the many empty, romantic dreams referred to in the novel (tellingly, also the devil, who appears in Ivan's dream, says "I love to dream," and his dream "is to become incarnate, but so that it's final, irrevocable, in some fat, two-hundred-and-fifty-pound merchant's wife, and to believe everything she believes"; see 638–639); and in Ferapont's ascetic posturings.

20. This is symbolized in Revelation 11, in the vision of the measuring of the temple: John is told to measure only the inner sanctuary, not the outer court, which is "given over to the nations" (11:2). True security from the destructive ravages of evil is to be found in the inner spiritual realm, not the outer realm of the body. This theme is pervasive in the Johannine literature.

21. The theme of the devil as liar and deceiver is also common to the Johannine literature (cf. John 8:42–47; I John 2:18–27; 3:4f.). At the root of evil sits a lie, which distorts the meaning of human relationships to one another and to God by misrepresenting the truth about the created order.

22. The reader here recalls Ivan's confession at the beginning of the chapter entitled "Rebellion," that "I never could understand how it's possible to love one's neighbors," and further: "In my opinion, Christ's love for people is in its kind a miracle impossible on earth. True, he was God. But we are not gods" (236–237). The "love for humanity" that Ivan comes to endorse at the end of the chapter is rooted in retribution that takes place in this world.

23. Cf. Caird, *Revelation*, p. 85f.; Beasley-Murray, *Book of Revelation*, pp. 136–137.

24. Bauckham, *The Theology of the Book of Revelation*, p. 84f.

25. Ivan states that Christ was God but we ordinary human beings are not gods—suffering is humiliating and demeaning, and therefore both suffering and the relief of suffering should be kept faceless and out of sight: "It's still possible to love one's neighbor abstractly, and even occasionally from a distance, but hardly ever up close. If it were all as it is on stage, in a ballet, where beggars, when they appear, come in silken rags and tattered lace and ask for alms dancing gracefully, well, then it would still be possible to admire them. To admire, but still not to love" (237). Ivan here mimics the words and ideas of the sentimental "lady of little faith," Madame Khokhlakov (56f.).

26. See René Girard, *Deceit, Desire, and the Novel: Self and Other in Literary Structure*, trans. Y. Freccero (Baltimore: Johns Hopkins University Press, 1965), especially chap. 11; idem, *Resurrection from the Underground: Feodor Dostoevsky*, ed. and trans. James Williams (New York: Crossroad, 1997).

27. Girard, *Resurrection from the Underground*, p. 147.

28. Structurally, the novel begins with "a nice little family" (pt. 1, bk. 1), whose rivalrous and discordant character is revealed at "an inappropriate gathering" in the monastery (bk. 2) and in an egoistic sensuality (bk. 3, entitled "Sensualists," shows the underground intensity of mimetic erotic rivalries between Fyodor, Dmitri, and Ivan). This dynamic culminates in part 2, book 4, which is entitled "Strains" or "Lacerations" (in Russian, *Nadryv*, from the root *rvat'*, meaning "to rend, tear, split, strain, lacerate") and which depicts a twisted response to benefits received, a perversion of gratitude due to the prideful sense of one's own honor and the fear of appearing base or ignoble, tied to various forms of offense and revenge (see Robert Belknap, *The Structure of The Brothers Karamazov* [The Hague: Mouton, 1967], p. 47). "The Grand Inquisitor" (bk. 5, chap. 5) is the full-blown prophecy of this divided, isolated, demonic consciousness. Ivan's God is a projection of the egotistical underground consciousness—increasing his glory through the dependent suffering of others. Ivan's lament in the "Rebellion" chapter leading up to "The Grand Inquisitor" shows the egotistical existential root: "*I* need retribution, otherwise *I* will destroy *myself*. . . . Is it possible that *I've* suffered so that *I*, together with *my* evil deeds and sufferings should be the *manure* of someone's future harmony?" (244).

29. Paul Ricoeur, "Fatherhood: From Phantasm to Symbol," in *The Conflict of Interpretations: Essays in Hermeneutics*, ed. D. Ihde (Evanston, Ill.: Northwestern University Press, 1974), pp. 468–497.

30. I am here conflating Ricoeur's Freudian psychoanalytic account and Girard's account, which is critical of Freud (see especially Girard, *Things Hidden Since the Foundation of the World*, chap. 4); but I believe that Ricoeur's use of the Freudian categories, such as the Oedipus complex in relation to fatherhood, is more relational and dynamic—less reified—than Freud's own, and hence that Ricoeur is close to Girard on this point.

31. The educative dialectic for Hegel, Ricoeur points out, is not father and son (rooted in natural immediacy) but master and slave, which gives rise to social self-consciousness in an exchange of socially mediated roles, and which gives rise also to contractual and property relations. This is clearly at issue in Dmitri's conflict with Fyodor over inheritance matters, and it is tortuously present in Fyodor's relation to Smerdyakov, at once both lackey and bastard son.

32. Ricoeur, "Fatherhood," p. 489.

33. *Lover of mankind* is a common Orthodox liturgical phrase describing Christ.

34. We are told several times by the narrator that the conversation with Ivan about justice and the Grand Inquisitor has caused Alyosha to forget his brother Dmitri, to whom the elder Zosima has explicitly commissioned him (264, 285, 339, 342).

35. The meaning of the phrase *wild chastity* is important: For Dostoevsky, as for monastic and mystical Christianity more generally, chastity cannot be understood as the mere restraint of eros or desire (as in the virtue of moderation). To the contrary, it is a heightening of erotic tension in the higher passion of faith, whose consummation has a cosmic orientation and a divine focus.

36. "Water the earth with your tears" is often repeated by the elder, who values the "gift of tears," tears of penitence and tears of ecstatic joy, which cause the earth to bring forth fruit. This stands in contrast to Ivan's sad reference to the bitter tears of hard human suffering "that have soaked the whole earth through, from crust to core," or the tears of hysterical, strained outbreaks of emotion that punctuate the relations of distorted and demonic desire between the novel's characters.

37. See Diane Oenning Thompson's superb discussion of this "iconic triptych" in *The Brothers Karamazov and the Poetics of Memory* (Cambridge: Cambridge University Press, 1991), p. 293f.

38. Alyosha here experiences within his own soul what elder Zosima has taught: "My friends, ask gladness from God. . . . And let man's sin not disturb you in your efforts. . . . Flee from such despondency, my children! There is only one salvation for you: take yourself up, and make yourself responsible for all the sins of men. For indeed it is so, my friend, and the moment you make yourself sincerely responsible for everything and everyone, you will see at once that it is really so, that it is you who are guilty on behalf of all and for all. Whereas by shifting your own laziness and powerlessness onto others, you will end by sharing in Satan's pride and murmuring against God. . . . But on earth we are indeed wandering, as it were, and did we not have the precious image of Christ before us, we would perish and be altogether lost. . . . Much on earth is concealed from us, but in place of it we have been granted a secret, mysterious sense of our living bond with the other world, with the higher heavenly world, and the roots of our thoughts and feelings are not here but in other worlds" (320).

39. Earlier Mitya says of his distorted, rivalrous relations to his father: "I believe in a miracle . . . of divine Providence. God knows my heart, he sees all my despair. He sees the whole picture. Can he allow horror to happen? Alyosha, I believe in a miracle" (121). Later he tells his interrogators that in that moment, watching his father from the garden, "the devil was overcome" in his heart, perhaps due to someone's tears or his mother's prayers (472)—another reference to the spiritual causality that pervades the novel.

40. There is a good discussion of this in Helen Canniff de Alvarez, *The Augustinian Basis of Dostoevsky's The Brothers Karamazov* (unpublished dissertation, University of Dallas, 1977), p. 47f.

41. Mitya's life is characterized by precisely such tempestuous conflicts of desire. Earlier in the novel his strained erotic-heroic relationship to the proud Petersburg society girl Katya has evoked similar duality—he loves, admires, and despises this woman (114). When he treats her with honorable generosity—even as she expects a base, coerced seduction—thus coercing her moral love, he draws his sword and contemplates stabbing himself on the spot "from a certain kind of ecstasy. Do you understand that one can kill oneself from a certain kind of ecstasy?" (115). This is tragic romantic love, and Mitya knows its duality; he describes it with eloquence in his romantic confession to Alyosha: "I want to tell you now about the 'insects,' about those to whom God gave sensuality . . . I am that very insect, brother. . . . And all of us Karamazovs are like that, and in you, an angel, the same insect lives and stirs up storms in your blood. Storms, because sensuality is a storm, more than a storm! Beauty is a fearful and terrible thing! Fearful because it's undefinable, and it cannot be defined, because here God gave us only riddles. Here the shores converge, here all contradictions live together. . . . Beauty! . . . I can't bear it that some man, even with a lofty heart and the highest mind, should start from the ideal of the Madonna and end with the ideal of Sodom. . . . No, man is broad, even too broad, I would narrow him down. . . . The terrible thing is that beauty is not only fearful but mysterious. Here the devil is struggling with God, and the battlefield is the human heart. But, anyway, why kick against the pricks?" (108). Mitya's confession parallels his brother Ivan's, though Mitya's takes an aesthetic form (beauty) rather than a moral form (justice). Both brothers blame God for making man too broad, too free, too responsible, and without clear enough directions for how to use that nature. The struggle is more than human beings can bear; one cannot blame them for failing.

42. See the discussion in Thompson, *The Brothers Karamazov and the Poetics of Memory*, p. 275f.

43. Grushenka's open-hearted love in response to Mitya's open and freeing gesture of love toward her (he brings gifts to celebrate her reunion with the Polish suitor) also constitutes a crucial turning point for Mitya. As he later tells Alyosha, "Before it was just her infernal curves that fretted me, but now I've taken her whole soul into my soul, and through her I've become a man!" (594).

44. Mitya's response to the news that Grigory is alive is passionate as ever: "Alive? So he's alive! . . . Lord, I thank you for this greatest miracle, which you have done for me, a sinner and an evildoer, according to my prayer!" (458); "Oh, thank you, gentlemen! Oh, how you've restored, how you've resurrected me in a moment . . . ! That old man . . . he was my own father . . . !" (459).

45. From the beginning, Mitya's relations with Katya are enmeshed in the desire for revenge for her having snubbed him (111, 113–114). Mitya's horrible "stunt," and the increasingly tangled "underground" responses it triggers in himself, Katya, Ivan, and Grushenka, is a stupendous cycle of prideful, compulsively self-destructive action; and its consequences reverberate to the end of the novel. Of course, Mitya's stunt works because of Katya's own pride and her desire to "save" Mitya from his baseness (116, 147) and his shame at his baseness: "I mean, let him be ashamed before everyone and before himself, but let him not be ashamed before me. To God he says everything without being ashamed. Why, then, does he still not know how much I can endure for him? Why, why does he not know me, how dare he not know me after all that has happened? I want to save him forever." Mitya sees through this noble love—"she loves her own virtue, not me"; hence Katya's rage at her impotence in the erotic rivalry won by the "fallen" Grushenka. As Mitya

realizes early on, "there's a tragedy here" (119). The tragedy is rooted in the proud self-enclosure of fallen desire—the wish to hide one's own baseness even while everyone else's is transparent to oneself. It is the desire for the godlike control and mediation of relationships without reference to God, that is, without true penitence of the open heart and the humble love that serves freely.

46. See W. M. Simon's article on Claude Bernard (1813–1878) in *The Encyclopedia of Philosophy*, vol. 1 (New York: Macmillan, 1967), p. 304.

47. The elder prophesies this as well, in his response to Ivan's idea: "This idea is not yet resolved in your heart and torments it. . . . The question is not resolved in you, and there lies your great grief, for it urgently demands resolution. . . . Even if it cannot be resolved in a positive way, it will never be resolved in the negative way either—you yourself know this property of your heart, and therein lies the whole of its torment" (70). In the same meeting he prophesies Mitya's great future suffering (74, 285), and commissions Alyosha for "a great obedience in the world" (77). We explore this further in Chapter 6.

48. This is expressed in a chapter near the end of the novel, entitled "For a Moment the Lie Became Truth," where Alyosha engages in "Jesuitic" ethics in order to ease Mitya's conscience about the escape plan, but it doesn't work (762f.). Another escape plan, a medical-legal one, is suggested by Madame Khokhlakov, who as a result of the scandal surrounding the elder's death has given up her "little faith" for modern mathematical realism (384f.). Her plan is to stage a "legal fit of passion" for which the new courts, on medical evidence, "forgive everything"—"it's a blessing of the new courts" (577). Moral responsibility and criminal causality are here determined according to the codes and procedures established by the authorities of natural modern reason, the "Bernards." See Chapter 6.

49. Cf. the crude literalism in Smerdyakov's interpretation of the Genesis story of creation that so befuddles old Grigory (124).

50. In this case the delay is crucial, because Smerdyakov commits suicide that night, rendering Ivan's confession the next day virtually impossible and unbelievable.

51. Note Hannah Arendt's comment on modern historical consciousness, which focuses on the *process* of history (its "development" and "progress" rooted in the conditions and events or "happenings" of human action), rather than its exemplary dramatic patterns (as in the classical historiography of Augustine, for example, in which the patterns of spiritual causality that illumine the source and end of human life—not the chronological compilation of events—are offered for imitation): "The history of mankind reaches back into an infinite past to which we can add at will and into which we can inquire further as it stretches ahead into an infinite future. This twofold infinity of past and future eliminates all notions of beginning and end, establishing mankind in a potential earthly immortality. . . . So far as secular history is concerned we live in a process which knows no beginning and no end and which thus does not permit us to entertain eschatological expectations" ("The Concept of History," in *Between Past and Future: Eight Exercises in Political Thought* [New York: Penguin, 1968], 68).

52. Oliver O'Donovan, *Resurrection and Moral Order* (Grand Rapids, Mich.: William B. Eerdmans, 1986), p. 111.

53. Dietrich Bonhoeffer, *Ethics*, ed. E. Bethge (New York: Macmillan, 1955), p. 24. We return to the question of conscience in Chapter 6.

## five

# "Do You Despise or Love Humanity, You, Its Coming Saviors?"*

Since Dostoevsky wrote *The Brothers Karamazov*, we have had a century of learning in what Paul Ricoeur has dubbed the "school of suspicion," whose master teachers are Freud and Nietzsche. The critique of religious faith advanced by this school has taught theologians and philosophers of religion to ask: What is the religious meaning of atheism? If we turn to Dostoevsky's literary art—and especially *The Brothers Karamazov*—in the light of this question, we can see, first, that he anticipated it. Furthermore, what his art has to say about religious faith to our postreligious age might be more clearly heard if there is a shift of focus, away from the usual *either-or* structuring of the religious problematic to the dialectical nature of the relation between faith and atheism. In other words, we must give serious attention to Dostoevsky's own assertion that his Christian faith was "forged in the crucible of doubt"—an assertion that is not only autobiographical but also theological.[1]

The relating of Dostoevsky's art to the modern hermeneutics of suspicion can be mutually illuminating. Let us begin with Ricoeur's explanation of the nature

---

*The title of this chapter is a question posed by Dostoevsky in a letter of 11 June 1879 to Nikolai A. Lyubimov. The entire letter can be found in Fyodor Dostoevsky, *Complete Letters*, vol. 5: *1878–1881*, ed. David Lowe (Ann Arbor, Mich.: Ardis, 1991), p. 89. The wording used in this chapter title varies slightly from that in the cited edition, but it is in conformity with Dostoevsky's original Russian.

of this hermeneutic practice, which has so dominated the educated consciousness of our century:

> [It] is a type of . . . hermeneutics which is at the same time a kind of philology and
> a kind of genealogy. It is a philology, an exegesis, an interpretation insofar as the
> text of our consciousness can be compared to a palimpsest, under the surface of
> which another text has been written. The task of this special exegesis is to decipher
> this text. But this hermeneutics is at the same time a genealogy, since the distortion
> of the text emerges from a conflict of forces, of drives and counterdrives, whose ori-
> gin must be brought to light.[2]

When faced with a text—whether scripture, art, discourse, dreams, or human
consciousness itself—the concern is to "demystify," to expose "truth as lying," to
reduce the illusions of consciousness to their true origin in certain "drives and
counterdrives" (the "libido," say, or the "will to power"). This concern is aptly reflected in Nietzsche's practice of *hinterfragen*, which can be translated loosely as
"the questioning of someone's motives." As he explains it: "In everything a man
reveals we can ask: What is it supposed to hide? From what is it supposed to distract our attention? What kind of prejudice is it supposed to provoke? And then
again, how far does the refinement of this dissemblance go? And where does it go
wrong?"[3]

For readers of Dostoevsky, these words conjure up the image of the protago-
nist of *Notes from the Underground* so spontaneously and directly that it seems as
though Nietzsche must have had him in mind. Let us recall the manner in which
this first antihero of modern fiction introduces himself:

> I am a sick man . . . I'm a spiteful man. I'm an unattractive man. I think there is
> something wrong with my liver. But I cannot make head or tail of my illness and
> I'm not absolutely certain which part of me is sick. I'm not receiving any treatment,
> nor have I ever done, although I do respect medicine and doctors. Besides, I'm still
> extremely superstitious, if only in that I respect medicine. (I'm sufficiently well-
> educated not to be superstitious, but I am.) No, it's out of spite that I don't want to
> be cured. You'll probably not see fit to understand this. But I do understand it. Of
> course, I won't be able to explain to you precisely whom I will harm in this instance
> by my spite; I know perfectly well that I cannot in any way "sully" the doctors by not
> consulting them. I know better than anyone that in doing this I shall harm no one
> but myself. Anyway, if I'm not receiving medical treatment it's out of spite. If my
> liver is hurting, then let it hurt all the more! . . . I've been living like this for a long
> time—for about twenty years. . . . I used to work for the government, but I no
> longer work. I was a spiteful civil servant. I was rude and I enjoyed being rude. You

see, I didn't accept bribes so I had to reward myself in this way. (That's a lousy joke, but I won't delete it. I wrote it thinking that it would come across very wittily; but now that I can see that I only wanted to show off in a vulgar way, I'm deliberately not going to cross it out.)[4]

This *Underground* man writes as though someone is peering over his shoulder, suspiciously scrutinizing what he is writing. He introduces himself by saying, "I am a sick man"; but then he worries that the reader will think he is trying to elicit sympathy, so he adds: "I'm a spiteful man. I'm an unattractive man." He informs us that he "respects medicine and doctors"; but then he suspects that the reader will think he is naive, so he adds a little witticism: "Besides, I'm still extremely superstitious, if only in that I respect medicine." Then, however, he suspects that the reader will consider him backward or uneducated for admitting to being "superstitious," so he adds: "I'm sufficiently well-educated not to be superstitious, but I am." Finally, he defiantly asserts that it is out of spite that he does not want to be cured. Realizing by now that the reader will likely be in a state of impatient perplexity, he concedes: "You'll probably not see fit to understand this." Anticipating the next likely thought of the reader, he adds: "I know better than anyone that in doing this I shall harm no one but myself." Notice how he both anticipates and challenges the reader but at the same time wants to win the reader's approval. He shows us, for instance, that he knows he has just made a bad joke; but this obsequious currying of favor has its limits—he will not cross out the joke!

Was it not Dostoevsky, before Nietzsche and before Freud, who began to teach readers to observe what a character reveals only in order then to ask: "What is it supposed to hide? From what is it supposed to distract our attention?" The *Underground* man, himself the most striking early instance of the artistic embodiment of *hinterfragen*, prods, even bullies the reader into an attitude of suspicion: He is constantly suspicious of his own confession; the reader, encouraged at first to join him in this suspicion, goes even further, becoming suspicious of the character's suspicion, and finally, of the intentions of the author himself—just what is Dostoevsky up to? To seek meaning in Dostoevsky's work is not simply a matter of explicating the consciousness of meaning but of "attempting to *decipher its expressions*."[5]

Dostoevsky deserves to be recognized as a preeminent teacher within the "school of suspicion," along with Nietzsche and Freud; indeed, on the basis of Nietzsche's acknowledgment that Dostoevsky was "the only psychologist" from whom he had "something to learn,"[6] we might trace a lineage in the modern practice of suspicion that has its actual source in Dostoevsky. This convergence, however, should not be pushed too far: Nietzsche and Freud, after all, were Western and avowedly atheist, whereas Dostoevsky was Russian and avowedly Christian. Placing Dostoevsky in the school of suspicion is conditional upon recognizing that he employs the hermeneutics of suspicion to a different end than do these others. Whereas the hermeneutics of the other masters is one of reduction, Dostoevsky's hermeneutics could be defined as one of recollection—that is, one devoted to the *restoration* of meaning.[7]

## Deciphering Modern Humanism: The Case of Ivan Karamazov

Dostoevsky's practice of the hermeneutics of suspicion—with a Christian aim— is a formative feature of "The Grand Inquisitor." The ambiguities of the Inquisitor's discourse, in both tone and content, are designed to inspire *hinterfragen* in the reader; and the most flawed interpretations of this text are flawed precisely because their authors have failed to read suspiciously between the lines where it is most necessary to do so.

It was argued in Chapter 3 that the most unique and perplexing aspect of the Inquisitor's prophetic anticipation of modern totalitarianism is his philanthropy. The Inquisitor and his fellow rulers are not to be considered "tyrants" in the ordinary sense, because they are motivated by a profound love of humanity. Compassion for the "millions, numerous as the sands of the sea," of the "weak" and "feeble" has moved the Inquisitor to renounce private fulfillment in order to assume the burden of rule. As he declares: "Know that I, too, was in the wilderness, and I, too, ate locusts and roots . . . and I, too, was preparing to enter the number of your chosen ones, the number of the strong and mighty. . . . But I awoke and did not want to serve madness. I returned and joined the host of those who have *corrected your deed*. I left the proud and returned to the humble, for the happiness of the humble"[51]. The Inquisitor, unlike the ordinary tyrant, does not exercise power for his own satisfaction. Indeed, this exercise is for him actually a source of suffering, because it requires him deliberately to deceive those whom he loves, by means of the "noble" lies that they are free, even though they have given up their freedom for the sake of unity; that they are equal, even though their equality is that of slaves; and that they have an eternal destiny, even though there is nothing beyond the grave.

The Inquisitor's love for humanity, to the point of suffering, is not an incidental feature of his personality—it is the basis of his entire argument against the response to human suffering signified by the silent Christ. At the heart of his argument against Christ and all the other "great idealists" of history is the charge that they do not love human beings enough. He himself is well aware of the apparent perverseness of such a charge, particularly against Christ, who "came to give his life for them!"[46] He nevertheless insinuates, on the basis of his own application of suspicion to Christ, that the great idealist's rejection of the three temptations was motivated more by the desire to be loved in a certain way than by compassionate love for human beings as they actually are. This is implicit, for instance, in his interpretation of Christ's refusal to cast himself from the pinnacle of the Jerusalem temple, and at the end of his ministry, to come down from the cross when mocked: "You did not come down because, again, you did not want to enslave man by a miracle and thirsted for faith that is free, not miraculous. You thirsted for love that is free, and not for the servile raptures of a slave before a power that has left him permanently terrified"[47]. In attempting to elicit from human beings a freely given love rooted in spiritual discernment, Christ's "incognito" excluded the millions, "numerous as the sands of the sea," who are incapable of such discerning love. According to the Inquisitor, the great idealist's highly demanding form of love is limited to an elect minority, whereas the Inquisitor's realism lowers the sights sufficiently to include all within a universal, nonjudgmental compassion:

> What of the rest? Is it the fault of the rest of feeble mankind that they could not endure what the mighty endured? Is it the fault of the weak soul that it is unable to contain such terrible gifts? Can it be that you indeed came only to the chosen ones and for the chosen ones? But if so, there is a mystery here, and we cannot understand it. And if it is a mystery, then we, too, had the right to preach mystery and to teach them that it is not the free choice of the heart that matters, and not love, but the mystery, which they must blindly obey. . . . We corrected your deed and based it on *miracle, mystery,* and *authority.*[48]

The audacity of the Inquisitor's claim is astonishing: Not only is the totalitarian order he advocates based on love of humanity; it is based on a love of humanity greater than that of Christ himself. This claim is made more explicitly in the unpublished notes for the novel, where Dostoevsky has the Inquisitor declare to Christ: "I love humanity more than you do"; and where he has Ivan declare: "I am with the old man's idea, because he loves humanity more."[8] Thus, the young humanist states his chief point of accord with the old tyrant. For Dostoevsky, this is the essential self-justification of the modern progressivist rejection of Christianity—the claim to love humanity more, and more effectively.

Such a claim in the mouth of the Inquisitor serves notice of the inadequacy of understanding the rulers of the future universal state in terms of the ordinary meaning of "tyrant." Yet although the Inquisitor's love of humanity entails a voluntary assumption of suffering, which imbues his figure with a certain "lofty sadness," most readers will react, as Alyosha does, with suspicion. Alyosha suspects that the "suffering" Inquisitor is merely a deception, concealing the usual lust for power, for "filthy lucre"[53]. There is undoubtedly something in the tone of the Inquisitor's monologue that easily invites the attentive reader's suspicion about his attitude toward his "flock"; his refusal to demand too much, to esteem the "feeble creatures" too highly, treads too fine a line between loving solicitude and contempt. The old man, though a compelling figure, is not an attractive one. In contrast, Ivan Karamazov is undeniably an attractive figure, albeit an enigmatic one. As the creator of the Inquisitor, he defends his character against our suspicion:

> Look, suppose that one among all those who desire only material and filthy lucre, that one of them, at least, is like my old Inquisitor, who himself ate roots in the desert and raved, overcoming his flesh, in order to make himself free and perfect, but who still loved mankind all his life, and suddenly opened his eyes and saw that there is no great moral blessedness in achieving perfection of the will only to become convinced, at the same time, that millions of the rest of God's creatures have been set up only for mockery, that they will never be strong enough to manage their freedom . . . . Having understood all that, he returned and joined . . . the intelligent people . . ."
>
> "Whom did he join? What intelligent people?" Alyosha exclaimed . . . . "They are not so very intelligent, nor do they have any great mysteries and secrets . . . . Your Inquisitor doesn't believe in God, that's his whole secret!"
>
> "What of it! At last you've understood . . . but is it not suffering, if only for such a man as he, who has wasted his whole life on a great deed in the wilderness and still has not been cured of his love for mankind? . . . And if even one such man, at least, finds himself at the head of that whole army 'lusting for power'. . . is one such man, at least, not enough to make a tragedy?"[52]

The credibility of the Inquisitor's love of humanity clearly depends on the credibility of his creator and defender, Ivan Karamazov. That Ivan embodies a text that cries out for deciphering is explicitly recognized within the novel itself: His elder brother, Dmitri, for instance, refers to him variously as a "grave" and a "sphinx"—"he's silent, silent all the time"—a silence portending something more, a significant, unspoken secret (110, 592).* The need for a deciphering of Ivan has also been recognized from outside the novel by generations of readers and critics who have been preoccupied by the question: "Is Ivan the real hero of

---

*Here and below, references appearing inside parentheses in the narrative—unless otherwise specified—are page numbers in Fyodor Dostoevsky, *The Brothers Karamazov,* trans. Richard Pevear and Larissa Volokhonsky (New York: Vintage, 1990). References inside square brackets are page numbers in "The Grand Inquisitor," reprinted from the aforementioned edition, in Chapter 2 of the present volume.

*The Brothers Karamazov,* despite Dostoevsky's Christian intentions?" We know that Dostoevsky himself did not share Ivan's atheism and intended to refute it in the novel.[9] We know also that a number of readers (including thoughtful ones) during the century since *The Brothers Karamazov* was published remain unconvinced by this refutation. Indeed, the apparent discrepancy between Dostoevsky's intention and his art is sometimes taken to be a classic demonstration (together with Milton's *Paradise Lost*) of what has now become a truism for contemporary literary criticism: "Trust the tale, not the teller." Blake's comment about Milton might seem applicable to Dostoevsky also: "[He] was a true poet and of the Devil's party without knowing it."[10]

The question of Ivan's status remains very much alive among Dostoevsky scholars, having been given fresh impetus by the recent publication of the notebooks for the novels, which allow us to observe just how carefully Dostoevsky worked behind the scenes to orchestrate what Bakhtin called his "polyphonic" poetics. There remains much at stake in this question about Ivan Karamazov: for theologians and philosophers engaged by the problem of faith and atheism; and for literary critics concerned with the relationship between the intentions of an author and the work of art as well as that between the reader and the work of art. Beyond these significant issues, moreover, the question speaks to the very nature of modernity. Albert Camus regarded Ivan as emblematic of modern, secular humanism, because in his "metaphysical rebellion" he aimed to "replace the reign of [divine] grace" with the "reign of [human] justice."[11] As Dostoevsky intended, to ask the question about Ivan is, ultimately, to ask also about the moral meaning and implications of the whole modern enterprise. It is little wonder that the question persists; and there should be great uneasiness about answering it too quickly or definitively, one way or the other.

Any deciphering of the enigma of Ivan Karamazov must be mindful of the special complexities involved. Ivan is a literary character who does *and* does not reflect the thinking of his author, an author who himself is constrained in his presentation by the aesthetic requirements of the "polyphonic" novel-form and by the moral requirement of respect for human freedom—both that of the reader and that of the character. It has often been observed that the art of Dostoevsky can be like a mirror held up before the reader. This observation is most strikingly apt in the case of Ivan, whose destiny is so closely identified with that of the modern West. As we gaze into this mirror, it is (to paraphrase Kierkegaard) the thoughts of *our* hearts that are disclosed.[12]

Reflection upon the enigma of Ivan provides the occasion for bringing Dostoevsky the artist-philosopher into direct dialogue with Nietzsche the philosopher-artist, who is an equally suspicious interpreter of modernity. If ever two contemporaneous writers were meant for dialogue with each other, it is these two, both of whom deserve the appellation "prophet of modernity." Their dialogue, with its convergences and its divergences, is a sine qua non for those concerned with the relationship between Christian faith and the modern consciousness. The twentieth-century Russian philosopher Berdyaev once remarked that Dostoevsky knew everything Nietzsche knew . . . and more. Some might object that this judgment should be reversed. Let us turn, then, to the test case presented by the task of deciphering the sphinx-like Ivan Karamazov, focusing our attention on what makes him emblematic of modernity—his "metaphysical rebellion."

Ivan's compelling rhetoric, and certain unique features of his logic—for instance, his strategy of "accepting" God while rejecting God's world—have led some interpreters to rank his argument as *the* modern statement of antitheodicy, which may well have rendered impossible, once and for all, any rational justification of a so-called "moral world order." Having scrutinized Ivan's logic and his rhetoric in an earlier chapter, our concern at this point is with the motivation underlying his rebellion against God—his love of humanity. Here, again, is the powerful finale to his argument, which immediately precedes his tale of "The Grand Inquisitor":

> If the suffering of children goes to make up the sum of suffering needed to buy truth, then I assert beforehand that the whole of truth is not worth such a price . . . . I don't want harmony, for love of mankind I don't want it . . . . I'd rather remain with unrequited suffering and my unquenched indignation, *even if I am wrong*. Besides, they have put too high a price on harmony; we can't afford to pay so much for admission. And therefore I hasten to return my ticket. (244–245)

Ivan's avowal of love for humanity resonates with a heroic image at the ancient roots of the Western cultural imagination—the rebel Prometheus of Aeschylean tragedy, the "enemy of Zeus" because he was "too good a friend to men."[13] Ivan himself alludes to the Prometheus myth twice: first in his "Rebellion" ("So people themselves are to blame: they were given paradise, they wanted freedom, and stole fire from heaven," 244; and then through the Inquisitor ("Do you know that . . . the spirit of the earth will rise against you [Christ], and everyone will follow him exclaiming: 'Who can compare to this beast, for he has given us fire from heaven!'"[44]). Both allusions, moreover, point to another ancient source—the Bible (Genesis 2, 3, and Revelation 13). Indeed, Ivan's conflation of Greek and biblical images might well be intended to encourage in his listener an unconscious identification of the biblical God with the "tyrant" Zeus, who neglects human beings and punishes the heroic benefactor who alleviates their condition. This implicit identification—which can be extended to include, on another level, the Karamazov brothers' negligent, sensualist father—is the crucial preliminary to Ivan's appeal to the Christian virtue of compassion. It becomes clear that Ivan's avowed motive for "metaphysical rebellion" is inseparable from the logic of his argument, a logic especially effective for a Christian interlocutor: Those who truly share his love of humanity, and therefore his motivation, must also share his logical conclusion that genuine compassion for humanity is incompatible with the adoration of a God who is negligently unwilling to alleviate human affliction.

In response to Ivan, one might well take issue with the idea of God he presupposes. At this point, however, I wish to focus on the psychology rather than the theology of Ivan's argument (acceding for the moment to Nietzsche's insistence that it is psychology that offers the path to understanding the fundamental problems).[14] Let us therefore scrutinize more closely the avowed love of humanity that is so central to the motivation for and the logic of Ivan's atheism as well as to his rhetoric. Is it, in the final analysis, more rhetoric than anything else?

The novel subsequently offers a number of occasions designed to arouse suspicion in the careful reader. One such occasion is that of Ivan's wakefulness during the night immediately following the conversation with Alyosha in which he voices his rebellion against God and recites his poetic tale of "The Grand Inquisitor." To set the scene: Ivan leaves Alyosha to return to his father's house, where he is staying; on the way he encounters the sinister servant Smerdyakov; they have a conversation in which little of import is said but much is implied, though it is not clear to what extent Ivan is conscious of *all* that is implied by the devious servant. Ivan's decision during the night to go away on a trip the next day leaves his father alone, at the mercy of Smerdyakov, who murders him, thereby carrying out what he has interpreted as Ivan's wish. The implication— which becomes ever clearer to the reader and to Ivan himself as the novel progresses—is that Ivan's decision during that fateful night makes him, the self-proclaimed lover of humanity, an accomplice to the murder of his own father. At this point, Dostoevsky does not convey the implication directly. What he offers the reader, instead, is a moment—when Ivan stands at the top of the staircase listening attentively to the movements of his father below—one of those moments we have learned to call "quintessentially Dostoevskian," and which is certain to inspire *hinterfragen*. What is particularly Dostoevskian is that the moment arouses the suspicion not only of the reader, but also of the character himself:

> It was very late, but Ivan was still not asleep. He lay awake thinking . . . . But we will not describe the trend of his thoughts. . . . Even if we attempted to describe some of his thoughts, we should find it very difficult, because they were not really thoughts, but something very vague and, above all, too excited. . . . Remembering this night

> long afterwards Ivan Fyodorovich recalled . . . how he suddenly would get up from
> the sofa and quietly . . . open the door, go out to the head of the stairs, and listen to
> Fyodor Pavlovich moving around below . . . . He would listen for a long time . . .
> with a sort of strange curiosity, holding his breath, his heart pounding . . . and why
> he was doing all that . . . he, of course, did not know himself. (275–276)

Can one imagine the ancient hero, Prometheus, having a moment like this?

Whether Dostoevsky knew everything Nietzsche knew, and more—or vice versa—there is no question that Dostoevsky knew what he knew *before* Nietzsche. If one can speak at all of lines of direct influence—rather than mere coincidence of thought—the lines run from the Russian to his younger German contemporary. Dostoevsky never knew of Nietzsche; but the latter discovered Dostoevsky in 1887 when, by chance, he came upon a French translation of *Notes from the Underground* in a bookstore. In his subsequent correspondence, Nietzsche speaks of his encounter with Dostoevsky as a meeting with a "brother" to whom he is "grateful in a very special way," much as the Russian constantly "offends" his "most basic instincts." And in *Twilight of the Idols*, he pays Dostoevsky a high compliment as "the only psychologist, incidentally, from whom I had something to learn; he ranks among the most beautiful strokes of fortune in my life." With the publication of the second part of volume eight of Nietzsche's *Collected Works*, we now know that his reading of Dostoevsky was not limited to *Notes from the Underground*, nor was it haphazard; he made extensive notes, abstracts, and copies of selected passages (in his own German translation of the French) from *Crime and Punishment, The Idiot*, and *Demons*. Indeed, the available evidence indicates that Nietzsche was thoroughly familiar with all of Dostoevsky's major works except *The Brothers Karamazov*, which was not available in French or German before the onset of Nietzsche's madness.[15] There is thus no possibility of offering Nietzsche's own interpretation of Ivan's episode on the staircase. We think, however, that a *Nietzschean* interpretation is possible, and will now attempt to offer one.

Nietzsche asserted that the possession of an "intellectual conscience," the rigorous commitment to truth, is what "separates the higher human beings from the lower."[16] He might well interpret Ivan's ambiguous moment of self-awareness on the staircase in a positive sense, as a manifestation of the intellectual conscience—by this point in the novel, a pronounced trait of Ivan's. This moment could signal the tentative beginning of an emancipation from the untenable illusion, or lie, of secular humanism, which prevents Ivan from realizing his potential as a higher man.

Nietzsche, like Dostoevsky, interpreted the progressivism of the modern West as a secularized form of Christianity, especially of the New Testament command of compassionate love. Still moved by this command, the moderns come to envisage history as the arena for the overcoming of the injustices of society and nature on behalf of those who suffer from them. For Nietzsche, the idea of history as progress, in its culminating Hegelian-Marxist expression, is above all the charitable hope, now made "rational," for the realization of human equality. His critique of historicist progressivism is developed with various emphases in different contexts; let us begin with his account of the most obvious problem posed for those who possess a finely tuned intellectual conscience. Secular humanism is not tenable, according to Nietzsche, because it is riven by a fundamental theoretical contradiction: One cannot do away with the ideal of "God" while holding onto the ideal of "humanity." Or to use the language of love, since this is so important to Ivan's position, the love of humanity *depends on* belief in God. In *Beyond Good and Evil* Nietzsche argues for this dependence:

> To love humanity *for God's sake*—that has so far been the noblest and most remote feeling attained among men. That the love of man is just one more stupidity and brutishness if there is no ulterior motive to sanctify it; that the inclination to such love of man must receive its measure, its subtlety, its grain of salt and dash of ambergris from some higher inclination—whoever the human being may have been who first felt and "experienced" this, however much his tongue may have stumbled as it tried to express such *délicatesse* [a reference, apparently, to Moses] let him remain holy and venerable for us for all time as the human being who has flown highest yet and gone astray most beautifully![17]

Although Nietzsche does not in this passage foreclose the possibility of some natural inclination to love humanity, he insists that such a love cannot be sustained and made effectual without the aid of some "higher" inclination, without which it is a mere "stupidity." Thanks to his realization that love of humanity requires an "ulterior motive," Moses flies as high as Nietzsche, and higher than the modern progressivists who would patronize him. As the founding legislator of biblical morality, Moses discovered his higher sanctification of love of humanity in a divine command (a discovery still definitive for the New Testament, in which Christ also presents love [agape] of the suffering neighbor in the form of a command, as though in acknowledgment that this love is not naturally self-justifying). In this respect, then, Moses flies high; yet he goes "astray" in believing there *is* a God who issues moral commands. Nietzsche insists that those who are intellectually honest now know better; thanks to two centuries of the modern rationalist critique of biblical faith, it is no longer possible to believe in the God of Moses except out of ignorance—or worse, mendacity.[18]

According to Nietzsche, however, modern criticism has not shown the courage of its conviction, in that the effective death of God in the modern Western consciousness has yet to be directly faced in all of its consequences. One symptom of this state of denial is the persistence of a secularized biblical morality in the modern world. As he writes in *Twilight of the Idols:*

> They have got rid of the Christian God and now feel obliged to cling all the more firmly to Christian morality. . . . In England, in response to every little emancipation from theology, one has to reassert one's position in a fear-inspiring manner as a moral fanatic. That is the *penance* one pays there.—With us it is different. When one gives up Christian belief one thereby deprives oneself of the *right* to Christian morality. For the latter is absolutely *not* self-evident: one must make this point clear again and again, in spite of English shallowpates. Christianity is a system, a consistently thought out and *complete* view of things. If one breaks out of it a fundamental idea, the belief in God, one thereby breaks the whole thing to pieces: one has nothing of any consequence left in one's hands . . . . Christian morality is a command; its origin is transcendental; it is beyond all criticism, all right to criticize; it possesses truth only if God is truth—it stands or falls with the belief in God.[19]

Despite the emphasis in this particular passage, Nietzsche does not attribute only to English "shallowpates" the inconsistency of attempting to have it both ways. He would have known, after all, that George Eliot, whom he has in mind here particularly, was decisively influenced in her humanism by her study and translation of Feuerbach's *Essence of Christianity.* And elsewhere he speaks of another German, Kant, as the "great delayer" because he gave human autonomy (including the capacity to make our own history) and scientific reason their definitive philosophical justification, at the same time affirming that obedience to the moral law is the supreme fact of reason. Kant's brilliant temporizing did much to delay the realization that morality cannot exist on the basis of reason alone, without support from religious faith. Indeed, Nietzsche might well have been surprised at how persistently this delay has been extended into the present century with the burgeoning of the secular ethics industry (i.e., professional ethics, medical ethics, business ethics, and so on). If his argument is valid, however, then the untenability of secular ethics must eventually make itself felt, and this realization will coincide with the advent of popular nihilism in the modern West (a nihilism already manifest in the "killing compassion" of much contemporary ethics itself).[20]

To return to our Nietzschean reading of Ivan's moment of self-awareness on the staircase: This vignette could signal a dawning sense of the inadequacy of his humanism, which purports to reject the love of God even as it affirms the love of humanity. For Nietzsche would affirm what Ivan's humanism denies: that the two loves—of God and of the neighbor—are, as in the New Testament, inseparable. Nietzsche would place the argument of Ivan's "Grand Inquisitor" at a higher rank of intellectual honesty than the argument of his "Rebellion" precisely because the Inquisitor's so-called love of humanity is so ambiguous, so suspiciously like contempt rather than love. Indeed, the Inquisitor's attitude is decidedly unambiguous in its repudiation of at least one crucial ideal rooted in biblical morality: that of human equality. For the Inquisitor, instead, there are strong and there are weak (256, 259). Where he goes astray, from the Nietzschean perspective, is in his declaration that the strong ought then to rule over the weak *out of love for them* (261). Here we have, as in "Rebellion," that same inconsistent retention of neighbor-love after the rejection of love of God.

The ambiguous character of the Inquisitor's love, however, hints at the possibility that some other motive, some other idea, is at work. Its presence is betrayed by the Inquisitor's tone, and indeed, on one occasion at least, by Ivan's tone: "It was not for such geese *(gusey)* that the great idealist [that is, Christ] had his dream of harmony"[53]. This is not to claim that Ivan's love of humanity is nothing but a rhetorical façade, concealing a lust for power. Ambiguity is one thing and duplicity quite another; it is precisely the former that concerns Dostoevsky as artist, psychologist, and religious thinker, and it is the author's fidelity to this very human ambiguity that makes his character so compelling. Moreover, from a Nietzschean perspective, that other motive vying for precedence within Ivan need not necessarily be the ordinary lust for power. There remains still a higher possibility for someone who has broken free of the untenable lie of secular humanism. This possible higher justification of the Inquisitor's social formula, though, must be found in a different object of love—love neither of the discredited ideal of God nor of the ideal of humanity dependent upon it. In *Thus Spoke Zarathustra,* Nietzsche writes: "Do I recommend love of the neighbor to you? Sooner I should even recommend flight from the neighbor and love of the farthest . . . . Let the future and the farthest be for you the cause of your today. . . . In your friend you shall love the overman."[21]

This reference to an alternative ideal of the future brings us to a second reason for Nietzsche's rejection of secular humanism. Not only is it theoretically untenable, it is an ideal that is not salutary; it is the latest and perhaps final symptom of a sickness that has afflicted the West for two millennia—the antinaturalism of Christian morality and the Christian God. The supernatural God might be dead, but the enormous shadow cast by him persists in the secular preachers of equality who vengefully malign all that is noble, well-constituted, and life-affirming in favor of all who suffer from life. In Zarathustra's words: "I do not wish to be mixed up and confused with these preachers of equality. For, to *me* justice speaks thus: 'men are not equal.' Nor shall they become equal! What would my love of the overman be if I spoke otherwise?"22 Nietzsche's alternative ideal for the future is signified concretely in that being—the "overman" *(Übermensch)*—who, freed from the spirit of revenge, is able to affirm life as it is, as the fully natural dance of perpetual becoming, without recourse to any "higher" moral interpretation. Such a being would constitute a thisworldly justification of existence. And for Nietzsche, the development of such a being would justify the aristocratic order proposed by the Grand Inquisitor, since "every enhancement of the type 'man' has so far been the work of an aristocratic society—and it will be so again and again—a society that believes in the long ladder of the order of rank . . . and that needs slavery in some sense or other."23

## Humanism and the "Death of God": Dostoevsky Contra Nietzsche

In a Nietzschean reading, then, Ivan's moment on the staircase could signal the beginning of a journey leading from the rejection of God, through the rejection also of the humanist morality dependent on God, toward the future goal of the overman. How far is such a Nietzschean reading of Ivan supported by Dostoevsky through what he gives us in the novel?

In response to this question, we can point, first, to the clear indications in the text that Ivan is well aware of the theoretical tension between his denial of God and his love of humanity. He actually highlights this tension at the very beginning of his "Rebellion" with a story about John the Merciful, who is able to love his diseased neighbor only out of obedience to moral duty, with the strain of a "lie"—presumably the lie of belief in the God of moral prohibition and commandment:

> I must make an admission . . . . I never could understand how it's possible to love one's neighbors. In my opinion, it is precisely one's neighbors that one cannot possibly love. Perhaps if they weren't so nigh . . . . I read sometime, somewhere about "John the Merciful" (some saint) that when a hungry and frozen passerby came to him and asked to be made warm, he lay down with him in bed, embraced him, and began breathing into his mouth, which was foul and festering with some terrible disease. I'm convinced that he did it with the strain of a lie, out of love enforced by duty . . . . If we're to come to love a man, the man himself should stay hidden, be-

cause as soon as he shows his face—love vanishes . . . . It's still possible to love one's neighbor abstractly . . . but hardly ever up close." (236–237)

This admission by Ivan shows that he is not one of those whom Camus was to call "lay pharisees," who pretend to believe that Christianity is an easy matter and who demand of Christians, according to an external impression of Christianity, more than they demand of themselves.[24] Ivan appears to appreciate fully the extreme difficulty of loving one's neighbor. In this appreciation, he is subtle enough to distinguish between the love of neighbor that actually encounters the nigh-dwelling other, and the easier, more abstract love of humanity-in-general that characterizes secular progressivism. Indeed, in this passage, he sounds remarkably like Zosima, who makes a closely similar distinction between "active love" and mere "love in dreams" (56–58). For Ivan, this great difficulty of loving explains why love must be divinely commanded, why it must, even in the case of a saint, be "enforced by duty."

With this story of John the Merciful as the preface to his "Rebellion," Ivan arouses the suspicion of the attentive reader. How can someone with an avowedly Euclidean mind assert—in one and the same chapter—first the dependence of compassionate love on a belief in God, and then the incompatibility of the two? From Nietzsche's perspective, Ivan has it right the first time, when he explains the action of John the Merciful; he also has it right later in the novel, when he proposes the formula "If there is no God, there is no virtue." If Ivan is to be a higher man, he will learn finally to find his motivation somewhere other than in the love of humanity, in an alternative ideal consistent with his rejection of the supernatural God of morality. That such an alternative ideal is actually present in Ivan's consciousness is evinced in his authorship of another text, entitled "The Geological Cataclysm," the content of which is revealed later in the novel. Nowhere is Dostoevsky's anticipation of Nietzsche more striking than in Ivan's vision of the future "man-god" *(bogochelovek)*, who affirms "joy in this world only":

Once mankind has renounced God (and I believe that this period, analogous to the geological periods, will come) then the entire old world view will fall of itself . . . and, above all, the entire former morality, and everything will be new. People will come together in order to take from life all that it can give, but, of course, for happiness and joy in this world only. Man will be exalted with the spirit of divine, titanic pride, and the man-god will appear. Man, his will and science no longer limited, conquering nature every hour, will thereby every hour experience such lofty delight as will replace for him all his former hopes of heavenly delight. Each will know himself utterly mortal, without resurrection, and will accept death proudly and calmly, like a god. (648–649)[25]

This Nietzschean vision of life-affirmation is spoken in Dostoevsky by the "devil" of Ivan's nightmare. In this, obviously, the hermeneutics of suspicion of Nietzsche and Dostoevsky declare their divergence. To return to that decisive episode on the staircase: In Nietzsche's reading this ambiguous moment of awareness might have indicated the beginning of Ivan's emancipation from the last secular remnants of biblical morality. In Nietzsche's own words: "To be ashamed of one's immorality—that is a step on the staircase at whose end one is also ashamed of one's morality."[26] Yet Dostoevsky has the narrator inform us explicitly that this moment would become, in Ivan's future recollection, "the basest action of his whole life." (276) That Ivan would later—and we can assume, finally—evaluate the moment in this way provides at least a strong hint that the "torment" of his heart (to quote Zosima; see 70) will eventually be resolved in favor of a life *within* rather than *beyond* good and evil. If so, then he would be, for Nietzsche, one more instance of a superior individual who has gone astray, "torn piecemeal by some minotaur of conscience."[27] Yet what would be for Nietzsche a sad waste is for Dostoevsky a possible restoration—or to be more precise, redemption.

With the publication of the rough notebooks for *The Brothers Karamazov*, there has been a growing appreciation of the poetic means carefully employed by Dostoevsky to discredit Ivan's atheism, and further, to plant the seed of a future spiritual "turning-around" *(periagoge)* without violating his freedom or that of the responding reader.[28] It has become increasingly obvious that to regard Ivan as a character who through the power of his argument bests the Christian intention of his creator is to misread the novel. Ivan's forceful atheism is not an instance of the author's art becoming independent of the author's religious intention, but rather an *expression* of that intention, since the radical freedom enjoyed by Ivan is entirely consistent with Dostoevsky's Christian anthropology. Yet as in Dostoevsky's Christian thought, so in the novel this freedom is not unconditional, as a careful reading in conjunction with the notebooks attests. Literary critics who have wanted to interpret Dostoevsky's art without acknowledging that it is Christian art have habitually invoked Bakhtin's observation that there is finally no authoritative voice present in the novels favoring one perspective over another. In response to this fashionable Bakhtinism, it can be argued that although Dostoevsky's art is indeed polyphonic rather than monologic, this does not preclude the orchestrating presence of the author.[29]

It is legitimate, then, not only to speak of the author's concern with the possible "turning-around" of his character, but also to see that concern enacted in the novel itself. But to what *sort* of faith might Dostoevsky intend Ivan to turn? This question brings us back to the larger question with which this chapter began: What is the religious meaning of atheism? This question acknowledges that atheism has something to teach faith, an acknowledgment implicit in Ricoeur's characterization of the modern hermeneutics of suspicion as a "school" in which presumably faith itself could and should be a student. In Ricoeur's view, the school of suspicion can teach faith, even in the face of Nietzsche's declaration that "God is dead," because it remains possible to ask: "*Which* God is dead?" Or, to ask the same question in a different manner: Which symbol of the divine has shown itself inadequate to articulate and order human religious experience? The God in question might well be the one evoked in Samuel Beckett's play *Waiting for Godot,* in the manic monologue of Lucky: "Given the existence . . . of a personal God with white beard who is defined *(quaquaquaqua)* by negative attributes such as apathia, athambia, and aphasia—such a God loves us dearly with some exceptions for reasons unknown but time will tell." This is a poetic caricature of the monarchical model of God elaborated in the classical theism of the Middle Ages and the Protestant Reformation—the sovereign God of morality who both threatens and protects through the law of retribution.[30] It is evidently this God that Nietzsche has in mind when he writes in *Beyond Good and Evil:* "Why atheism today?—'The father' in God has been thoroughly refuted; ditto 'the judge,' the 'rewarder.' Also his 'free will': he does not hear—and if he heard he still would not know how to help. Worst of all: he seems incapable of clear communication: is he unclear? This is what I found to be causes for the decline of European theism, on the basis of a great many conversations, asking and listening."[31]

In our attempt to understand clearly Dostoevsky's Christian intention, we must ask: Is the "refuted" father-judge-rewarder God the same one who is the ground of virtue in Ivan's formula—"if there is no God, there is no virtue" (including the love of humanity)? The answer, we submit, is both "yes" and "no." It is "yes" in that Ivan's thinking about the relationship between faith and morality does appear always to presuppose the God of retributive judgment. This is the model of God evoked at the very beginning of Ivan's "Grand Inquisitor," in the ancient legend about the Mother of God kneeling before the throne of God and asking pardon for everyone in hell. It is the God whom the Inquisitor assumes to be essentially a God of judgment when he defiantly asserts: "Judge us if you can and dare"[51]. It is the God whose manifest unwillingness or inability to perform his retributive function of protecting the innocent and punishing their tormentors provokes Ivan's rebellion. That Ivan's argument presupposes this particular God is made explicit in the notebooks for the novel, where Dostoevsky has him declare: "I will accept God all the more readily if he is the . . . old God who cannot be understood. And so let it be *that God.*"[32]

We know from passages in *A Writer's Diary*, in which he spoke in his own name, that Dostoevsky agreed with Ivan's formula "If there is no God, there is no virtue."[33] Does this mean that the ultimate point of disagreement between the author and his character has to do with the affirmation versus negation of the existence of the God of moral retribution? And is this the crucial point of disagreement also between Dostoevsky and Nietzsche? Is the question of the existence or nonexistence of the father-judge-rewarder-God the question that determines who really does know more? It has been all too common to bring the dialogue between Dostoevsky and Nietzsche to a close in this manner, as Richard Friedman does at the conclusion of his otherwise interesting account of the convergence between the two: "Appreciating fully what the implications of the death of God were, Nietzsche was not afraid to leave Christianity . . . . Confronting the death of God really is terrifying. In the face of such fears Nietzsche took on the tension of living without God, while Dostoevsky held on tenaciously to a belief in God. In the twentieth century we see both of these responses as well: Some cling to faith. Others live with the stress."[34]

To close the dialogue at this point is to fail to recognize that while Dostoevsky would say "yes" to the formula "If there is no God, there is no virtue," he would say "no" to the manner in which Nietzsche (and Ivan) interpret it. Ivan's formula is the product of a Euclidean mind that anticipates and encourages a "yes" or "no" response, when the most fruitful response would be "What do you mean?" There is ample evidence that the dialectic of faith and atheism in *The Brothers Karamazov* is moving beyond the questions "Does God exist?" and "Can morality survive independently of religious faith?" to other questions: What sort of God are we talking about? What sort of religious faith? The manner in which the latter questions are reflected upon in the novel indicates that Dostoevsky's exploration of atheism was not only an act of confrontation but also an attempt to learn the meaning of atheism for faith.

The point that religious faith is not the monolithic phenomenon frequently imagined by its critics is made by the careful distinction that Dostoevsky draws in his novel between two characters, Ferapont and Zosima—both members of the Orthodox Church, both elderly monks, both living within the same monastery—yet each embodying a very different mode of faith. Ferapont is a dogmatic and relentless observer of fasts, silence, and solitude; an ascetic discipline that to him is an expression of the fear of the Lord. The central place that fear occupies in his religiosity is betrayed by his seeing devils everywhere: "I'm telling you—I see, I see throughout. As I was leaving the Father Superior's, I looked—there was one hiding from me behind the door, a real beefy one, a yard and a half tall or more, with a thick tail, brown, long, and he happened to stick the tip of it into the doorjamb, and me being no fool, I suddenly slammed the door shut and pinched his tail. He started squealing, struggling, and I crossed him to death with the sign of the Cross, the triple one. He dropped dead on the spot, like a squashed spider" (169). Dostoevsky's narrator makes it clear that Zosima, in contrast, belongs to a more enlightened strand of Christian spirituality having its ultimate sources in the mystical theology of the Greek Church fathers, recently revived in modern Russia through the practices of the *startsy* (elders).[35]

An encounter between Ferapont's faith and Nietzsche's suspicion is one thing; but if one substitutes Zosima for Ferapont, the encounter is very different. And it is Zosima whom Dostoevsky explicitly designates as his Christian respondent to Ivan's rebellion.[36] Zosima does not respond by invoking the God of retribution who accuses and consoles. Concerning accusation, he questions the very notion of externally imposed punishment, preferring to define hell, instead, as the suffering of no longer being able to love (322). And as for consolation, he affirms instead the mysterious and fundamentally tragic faith of the book of Job, a faith beyond all protection and assurance—even beyond the assurance that Zosima himself and what he represents will be vindicated by a divine intervention to eliminate "the odor of corruption" that emanates from his corpse so soon after his death (339–340). These are but a few examples of the manner in which Zosima's thinking implies consonance with, rather than opposition to, Ivan's denial of the God of moral retribution. The disagreement begins where Ivan would assume that this denial must entail the death of religious faith, whereas Zosima would find faith enhanced by the possibility of recollecting its more authentic nature.

Let us take stock of where we now find ourselves in relation to the question of love of humanity and the hermeneutics of suspicion. Nietzsche and Dostoevsky are both suspicious of secular humanism, which affirms the love of humanity apart from religious faith (as does Ivan). Both insist on the inseparability of the love of God and the love of one's neighbor as enunciated in the New Testament. However, they understand the connection between faith in God and love of humanity in different ways. For Nietzsche, love of humanity has its ultimate source in obedience to a divine command, obedience inspired by the fear and desire of a weak will in the face of the God who threatens and consoles. The ideal of love of humanity cannot, and should not, survive the death of this God. If Nietzsche had had the opportunity to read "The Grand Inquisitor," he might well have regarded it as prophetic—above all, in its exposure of the suspicious nature of the "godless" Inquisitor's avowed love of humanity. He himself would not have believed in this avowal, and he might well have appreciated the subtle manner in which Dostoevsky makes it difficult for other sensitive readers to believe in it.

Yet "The Grand Inquisitor" is the outcome of an impassioned "Rebellion," and Ivan's avowed love of humanity is less evidently suspicious, even to the sensitive reader. Indeed, although the hermeneutics of suspicion can be applied to Ivan's love with the aim of reducing it to its true "drives and counterdrives," something in this character resists total suspicion. Despite everything, one does not feel naive in sensing a certain love and compassion shining through Ivan's rhetoric; indeed, insofar as his secular humanism is motivated to any degree by genuine love, he has the sympathy of his author. In Dostoevsky, the hermeneutics of suspicion in the end serves a hermeneutics of recollection: He does wish to teach the reader to suspect Ivan's love of humanity—not, however, because it is nothing but an illusory mask for the will to power but because it will become this unless it recollects its bond with the Love emanating from "other mysterious worlds" (320).

The phrase "other mysterious worlds" is Zosima's, and it might well be considered the nucleus of his response to Ivan-Inquisitor as well as of a Dostoevskian response to Nietzsche. In *The Brothers Karamazov,* the idea of God is always closely associated with the idea of "other worlds" or "immortality"—so much so, that the terms appear interchangeable. Ivan's formula can be, and often is, expressed in this way: "If there is no immortality, there is no virtue."[37] This equivalence of God and immortality might help explain Alyosha's otherwise puzzling assertion, with which Ivan agrees, that the Inquisitor's "whole secret" is that he "doesn't believe in God"[53]. Nowhere in his monologue does the Inquisitor deny the existence of God; but he *does* deny immortality as anything more than a possibly salutary illusion: "Peacefully they will die, peacefully they will expire in your name, and beyond the grave they will find only death. But we will keep the secret, and for their own happiness we will entice them with a heavenly and eternal reward"[51]. The Inquisitor's repudiation of the idea of immortality, which apparently for both Alyosha and Ivan is equivalent to a repudiation of God, is yet more vehement in passages in the notebooks which were not included in the published novel: "Inquisitor: Why do we need the beyond? We are more human . . . . We love the earth . . . . Those who suffer his cross will not find anything that has been promised exactly as he himself . . . found nothing after his cross."[38]

Whether or not Dostoevsky personally was more preoccupied by the question of immortality than by the question of God, he certainly gives the former more explicit and sustained consideration in his writing. The Inquisitor's question—"Why do we need the beyond?"—is *the* question that most assuredly draws us into the heart of Dostoevsky's religious thought. Let us now shift the emphasis, then, from the symbolism of "God" to that of "immortality" in order to grasp more fully how Dostoevsky, in contradistinction to Nietzsche, understands the connection between religious faith and love of humanity.

# Humanism and the Idea of Immortality: Dostoevsky Contra Nietzsche

Hans Jonas began his 1961 Ingersoll Lecture on Immortality at Harvard University by noting as an "undeniable fact . . . that the modern temper is uncongenial to the idea of immortality."[39] Jonas's observation about this characteristic feature of the modern consciousness seems entirely valid, notwithstanding the current curiosity about near-death or "paranormal," life-after-death experiences—a cultural phenomenon that could well be interpreted as symptomatic of the loss to the modern consciousness of the serious idea of immortality.

Dostoevsky, too, would seem to endorse Jonas's observation about the modern temper. Indeed, he appears to have taken a sardonic delight in imaginatively confronting the modern skeptic with the sheer "uncongenial" fact of immortality, as in this anecdote related by the devil in Ivan's nightmare: "There was . . . a certain thinker and philosopher here on your earth, who 'rejected all—laws, conscience, faith,' and above all, the future life. He died and thought he'd go straight into darkness and death, but no—there was the future life before him. He was amazed and indignant: 'This,' he said, 'goes against my convictions.' So for that he was sentenced" (643). More common even than the modern intellectual's indignant repudiation of immortality is the general attitude of indifference noted by Mrs. Khokhlakov, the frivolous society lady in *The Brothers Karamazov,* who is "devastated" that she appears to be utterly alone in her anguish over the question of immortality: "How can it be proved, how can one be convinced? Oh, miserable me! I look around and see that for everyone else, almost everyone, it's all the same, no one worries about it anymore, and I'm the only one who can't bear it. It's devastating, devastating!" (56) Madame Khokhlakov's plaint that "no one worries" about immortality any longer might be true generally of the modern age, but it is decidedly untrue of the other characters that inhabit *The Brothers Karamazov.* Let us take note, for instance, of the questions voiced by Fyodor Karamazov to his sons Ivan and Alyosha, over cognac:

"But still, tell me: is there a God or not? But seriously. I want to be serious now."

"No, there is no God."

"Alyoshka, is there a God?"

"There is."

"And is there immortality, Ivan? At least some kind, at least a little, a teeny-tiny one?"

"There is no immortality either."

"Not of any kind?"

"Not of any kind."

"Complete zero? Or is there something? Maybe there's some kind of something? At least not nothing!"

"Complete zero."

"Alyoshka, is there immortality?"

"There is."

"Both God and immortality?"

"Both God and immortality. Immortality is in God."

"Hm. More likely Ivan is right. Lord, just think how much faith, how much energy of all kinds man has spent on this dream, and for so many thousands of years! Who could be laughing at man like that?" (134)

This exchange is only the most explicit expression of a problematic that is woven throughout the whole novel. The passage in book 6, in which Zosima speaks of the importance of the sense of "other worlds" for sustaining our love of life, can be regarded as the "master key to the philosophic interpretation, as well as to the structure, of *The Brothers Karamazov.*"[40]

Against Jonas's observation (apparently shared, on one level, by Dostoevsky himself) about the uncongeniality of immortality to the modern sensibility, we have the contrary witness of Dostoevsky's own literary art, permeated as it is by the idea of immortality. If this idea is uncongenial to modernity, Dostoevsky's art certainly is not; few among the modern novelists have more fully explored, expressed, and helped to shape the modern (and the postmodern) sensibility. Given the evidence constituted by *The Brothers Karamazov* as one of the seminal novels of modernity, Jonas's observation must be qualified. We need to understand more precisely *what* in the idea of immortality is so uncongenial to the modern sensibility. On the basis of this understanding, we will be in a position to judge with greater clarity what Dostoevsky has undertaken in *The Brothers Karamazov.*

For a clearer view of the modern repudiation of the idea of immortality, let us turn to that other master of the modern sensibility, Nietzsche, beginning with these words of Zarathustra:

I beseech you, my brothers, *remain faithful to the earth,* and do not believe those who speak to you of otherworldly hopes! Poison-mixers are they, whether they know it or not. Despisers of life are they, decaying and poisoned themselves, of whom the earth is weary: so let them go . . . . Once the sin against God was the greatest sin; but God died, and these sinners died with him. To sin against the earth is now the most dreadful thing . . . . It was suffering and incapacity that created all afterworlds . . . . Believe me my brothers: it was the body that despaired of the body and touched the ultimate walls with the fingers of a deluded spirit.[41]

Zarathustra's words are the poetic expression of a sustained philosophical argument developed throughout Nietzsche's less esoteric writings, an argument already touched on in relation to his critique of humanist love without God. The manner of this argument now needs to be outlined more explicitly. In rejecting such "metaphysical errors" as the "immortal-soul-hypothesis" or the "God-hypothesis," Nietzsche acknowledges that it cannot be demonstrated with logical certainty that there is no God and no immortality, just as it cannot be demonstrated that these exist. According to him, however, it would be a frivolous abdication of philosophical responsibility to suspend judgment on the immortal-soul hypothesis merely because its falsehood cannot be demonstrated with logical rigor, for there are other grounds for pronouncing a hypothesis untenable. If, for instance, a hypothesis has nothing in its favor but the fact that we cannot have logical certainty about it one way or the other, and at the same time there is much that is seriously doubtful about it, then honesty demands that it be repudiated.[42] The method of argumentation informing Nietzsche's hermeneutics of suspicion is thus to elicit our serious doubt by exposing the all-too-human source of the immortal-soul hypothesis and related metaphysical hypotheses of a "higher reality." His concern is to offer, through historical and psycho-physiological analysis, what he calls a "genealogy" of the belief in immortality, showing why and how it arose, and why it has had such enduring appeal. This "genealogy" is summed up in the words of Zarathustra: "It was suffering and incapacity that created all afterworlds . . . . It was the body that despaired of the body."

Nietzsche would consider the psycho-physiological dimension of his genealogy broadly applicable to all notions of an afterworld. Since his primary focus was on the Christian version of immortality, his historical analysis refers especially to the "suffering and incapacity" of the oppressed of the ancient Roman Empire who embraced the new Christian faith. According to Nietzsche, the suffering of those too weak to alleviate directly their own suffering generates images of future consolation. The observation that images of heavenly reward can make life more tolerable for those who suffer now is virtually cliché and needs no further comment. What does merit a closer look is the more malignant side of the tendency of suffering to seek relief through psychological projection. Along with consolation, the suffering of the weak generates images of accusation, which culminate in the Christian doctrine of hell. For Nietzsche, this doctrine is transparently explicable with reference to the suffering of the slaves of the Roman Empire, who lacked the capacity to act out directly their understandable desire to rise up and accuse those who oppressed them. Their impotent desire for revenge was turned inward and was satisfied by the imaginative projection of God's retributive punishment meted out to "sinners" (that is, to those who tended to possess the characteristics and ways of life of the masters). Nietzsche detects the unmistakable traces of a desire for revenge even in the later, fully developed imagination and thought of Christianity, including that of Dante and Aquinas: "Dante, I think, committed a crude blunder when, with a terror-inspiring ingenuity, he placed above the gateway of his hell the inscription 'I too was created by eternal love'—at any rate, there would be more justification for placing above the gateway to the Christian Paradise and its 'eternal bliss' . . . the inscription 'I too was created by eternal *hate*'—provided a truth may be placed above the gateway to a lie! For *what* is it that constitutes the bliss of this Paradise?" In response to his own question, Nietzsche quotes St. Thomas Aquinas: "'The blessed in the Kingdom of Heaven will see the punishments of the damned, *in order that their bliss be more delightful for them.*'"[43]

Nietzsche purports to expose what really underlies the immortality hypothesis and its attendant notions of eternal bliss and eternal punishment sanctioned by God the judge and "rewarder." It seems that like Dostoevsky, Nietzsche links closely the ideas of immortality and God; and he appears, further, to regard the former as psychologically prior, relegating God to the role of guarantor of the moral world order. To sum up his genealogical analysis, then: The psychological/historical reality underlying the immortality hypothesis is the desire for consolation and accusation on the part of a weak though imaginatively creative human will. Or to name the same reality with a different emphasis: The belief in immortality has its genesis and appeal in all-too-human egoism. Nietzsche repeatedly highlights the ridiculous aspect of this colossal egoism: "How can one make such a fuss about one's little lapses as these pious little men do! Who gives a damn? Certainly not God. Finally they even want 'the crown of eternal life,' these little provincial people; but for what? to what purpose? Presumption can go no further. An 'immortal' Peter; who could stand him? Their ambition is laughable. . . . 'Salvation of the soul'—in plain words: 'the world revolves around *me*.'"[44]

Bemusement, however, is not Nietzsche's customary attitude toward an illusion he considers to have such deadly implications. For, through its gradual spiritualization and generalization, the reaction of the weak against certain conditions of life has been transformed into a reaction against life itself on the part of those who suffer from it: "It was the body that despaired of the body." The immortality hypothesis ultimately accomplishes a revenge against the earth itself through the positing of a "higher reality" in comparison with which this reality—the only one there is—is devalued: "Why a Beyond if not as a means of befouling the Here-and-Now . . . . We *revenge* ourselves on life by means of the phantasmagoria of 'another', a 'better' life."[45] The most significant, far-reaching meaning of the immortality hypothesis is, according to Nietzsche, a despairing "no" to the earth and to life. Zarathustra, in contrast, exhorts his listeners to "remain faithful to the earth."

This brief account of Nietzsche's critique of the idea of immortality should help illumine its uncongeniality for the modern sensibility. The issue is not the logical or empirical indemonstrability of immortality but the recognition of its suspicious psychological/historical genesis and appeal. Nietzsche's genealogical method is central to the modern sensibility (one need only think of those other masters of suspicion, Freud and Marx). Central also to the modern sensibility is his repudiation of what his method apparently exposes: firstly, a morality based on egoistic incentives of eternal reward and punishment; and secondly, an other-worldly orientation that devalues this world.

Did Dostoevsky, in taking up the question of immortality in *The Brothers Karamazov*, know everything Nietzsche knew about it . . . and more? We shall begin our reflection on this question with a passage following Mrs. Khokhlakov's declaration that "no one" worries about immortality any more. Another local liberal landowner, Miusov, repeats views on immortality expressed recently by Ivan Karamazov at a local gathering, "predominantly of ladies," one of whom was very likely Mrs. Khokhlakov herself:

> He solemnly announced in the discussion that there is decidedly nothing in the whole world that would make men love their fellow men; that there exists no law of nature that man should love mankind, and that if there is and has been any love on earth up to now, it has come not from natural law but solely from people's belief in their immortality. Ivan Fyodorovich added parenthetically that that is what all natural law consists of, so that were mankind's belief in its immortality to be destroyed, not only love but also any living power to continue the life of the world would at once dry up in it. Not only that, but then nothing would be immoral any longer, everything would be permitted, even anthropophagy. And even that is not all: he ended with the assertion that for every separate person, like ourselves for instance, who believes neither in God nor in his own immortality, the moral law of nature ought to change immediately into the exact opposite of the former religious law, and that egoism, even to the point of evil-doing, should not only be permitted to man but should be acknowledged as the necessary, the most reasonable, and all but the noblest result of his situation. (69–70)

Leaving aside for now the question of whether, or to what extent, Dostoevsky himself might agree with Ivan's words, let us consider what sort of knowledge they convey. At the most obvious level, they express the knowledge that belief in immortality is a powerful incentive for moral behavior; indeed, the passage can be taken as the long version of Ivan's formula for the dependence of morality and love of humanity on religious faith. Though lacking Nietzsche's genealogical analysis, Ivan's "solemn announcement" expresses clearly enough the knowledge that the idea of immortality can be closely connected with a morality based on divine reward and punishment.

The all-too-human desire for consolation and accusation, moreover, figures prominently in various discussions of immortality throughout *The Brothers Karamazov*. It is noteworthy, though, that it is invariably the skeptics of the novel who voice notions of eternal reward and punishment. Ivan's disciple, lackey, and bastard half-brother, Smerdyakov, parrots a shallow version of Voltairean skepticism, allied with Jesuitical casuistry, in his "theological disputation" with the old Orthodox servant, Grigory. In reference to a recent episode involving a Russian soldier captured by Muslim insurgents in the Caucasus, who died under torture rather than renounce his Christian faith, Smerdyakov presents the following moral calculation:

> If I am taken captive by the tormenters of Christian people, and they demand that I curse God's name and renounce my holy baptism, then I'm quite authorized to do it by my own reason, because there wouldn't be any sin in it . . . . Because as soon as I say to my tormenters, "No, I'm not a Christian and I curse my true God," then at once, by the higher divine judgement, I immediately and specifically become anathema, I'm cursed and completely excommunicated from the Holy Church like a heathener . . . so that even at that very moment, sir, not as soon as I say, but as soon as I just think of saying it . . . I'm excommunicated . . . . And since I'm no longer a Christian, it follows that I'm not lying to my tormenters when they ask am I a Christian or not, since God himself has already deprived me of my Christianity, for the sole reason of my intention and before I even had time to say a word to my tormenters. And if I'm already demoted, then in what way, with what sort of justice can they call me to account in the other world, as if I were a Christian? . . . But then it wouldn't even come to torments, sir, for if at that moment I were to say unto that mountain: "move and crush my tormentor," it would move and in that same moment crush him like a cockroach . . . But if precisely at that moment I tried all that, and deliberately cried out to that mountain: "Crush my tormentors"—and it didn't crush them, then how, tell me, should I not doubt then, in such a terrible hour of great mortal fear? I'd know . . . that I wasn't going to reach the fullness of the Kingdom of Heaven (because the mountain didn't move at my word, so they must not trust in my faith there, and no very great reward awaits me in the other world), so why, on top of that, should I let myself be flayed to no purpose? . . . And so, why should I come out looking so especially to blame, if, seeing no profit or reward here or there, I at least keep my skin on? (128–131)

In response to Smerdyakov's cunning calculation, Fyodor Karamazov, who is also very fond of aping the skepticism of Enlightenment philosophes, declares:

"What nonsense! For that you'll go straight to hell and be roasted there like mutton." This old sensualist, "enlightened" though he is, appears to be seriously preoccupied by the prospect of hell, half afraid of the retribution that he ridicules in a conversation with Alyosha early in the novel: "Surely it's impossible, I think, that the devils will forget to drag me down to their place with their hooks when I die. . . . If there are no hooks, the whole thing falls apart . . . because if they don't drag me down, what then, and where is there any justice in the world . . . because you have no idea . . . what a stinker I am!" (24) To what extent will the reader of this passage feel the stirring of a desire for accusation at the thought that a reprobate like Fyodor Karamazov could indeed get off the hook of eternal retribution? And if Fyodor might finally elicit some sympathy from the reader, if only for the humor he provides, what of the torturers of children described by Ivan? Not only is Dostoevsky aware of the connection between belief in immortality and the desire to punish; he goes further than Nietzsche in not permitting his readers to avoid the recognition that this desire can be strong within us all.[46]

As we move from the shallow skeptics of the novel to Ivan (who is able to quote Voltaire without getting it wrong), we encounter far more subtlety in the discussion of heaven and hell. Ivan speaks of immortality in terms of an "eternal harmony, in which we are all supposed to merge" (235), thereby acknowledging that Christian faith in its higher expressions can involve something more than the self-interested calculus of reward and punishment. Nevertheless, he insists that Christianity cannot dispense with the notion of punishment altogether; for an eternal harmony without hell would be an eternal harmony without justice—but then, "where is the harmony if there is hell?" Ivan's Euclidean mind discovers what seems an irresolvable contradiction in Christianity between forgiveness and justice; the Christian idea of immortality, even if true, would be incoherent. This incoherence, from Ivan's point of view, is most pronounced just where Christianity shows itself at its best: among those who, like him, thirst for justice ("I need retribution, otherwise I will destroy myself") at the same time as they are too compassionate to accept the spectacle of the suffering of others, even if deserved ("I want to forgive and I want to embrace, I don't want more suffering") (244–245).

Even as he rejects the truth and the coherence of the idea of immortality, Ivan nevertheless regards it as an idea that, properly employed, could serve human happiness and justice on earth. In the words of the Grand Inquisitor, speaking of his flock: "For their own happiness we will entice them with a heavenly and eternal reward"[51]. The enticement of personal immortality is an important feature of the noble lie that elicits the voluntary sacrifice of individual freedom in the Inquisitor's totalitarian order. This emphasis on belief in immortality as a restraint on individual egoism is also evident in the "solemn pronouncement" of Ivan, reported by Miusov: "For every person . . . who believes neither in God nor in his own immortality . . . egoism, even to the point of evildoing . . . should be acknowledged as the most reasonable . . . result of his situation." Yet for Nietzsche the idea of immortality is the *expression* of egoism, a colossally presumptuous egoism. The difference between the two is not, however, as significant as it might appear: According to Nietzsche, the idea of immortality is an expression of egoism; according to Ivan, it is a constraint on egoism that nevertheless must ultimately become an expression of egoism, since there is no other "law of nature." It might be said that, according to Ivan's reasoning, egoism learns to curb itself by means of belief in God and immortality, and it does so from egoistic motives. Without such restraining beliefs, "the life of the world" could not continue; human life would descend into "anthropophagy." This reasoning finds its counterpart in Nietzsche's noting of the capacity of the will to power to "spiritualize" itself, furthering its ends by means of moral and religious beliefs that only appear to deny it.[47]

Any who doubt Dostoevsky's awareness of the egoistic possibilities inherent in the idea of immortality can be referred to that grotesque tale *Bobok*, in which we eavesdrop on the conversation of an entire cemetery of corpses that have discovered that death is not "really" death. The conversation confirms the extension, even into the life after death, of the same preoccupations that governed the lives of these people while they were "up above." For instance, a former businessman complains about the debts owed him by certain other denizens of the cemetery (they retort that he always overcharged them, anyway); a bureaucrat with the rank of State Councillor wakes up and at once begins discussing with a General a project for setting up a new departmental subcommittee and the probable transfer of officials in connection with it; and another elderly gentleman confesses his desire for a "nice little blonde . . . about fifteen years old . . . in circumstances just like these."[48] Thankfully, this depressing spectacle of petty egoism and base desire is not perpetual; to borrow from Nietzsche, who could stand such a thought? As has been explained by the cemetery philosopher with the evocative name of Platon (Russian for Plato), the extension of life is concentrated only in the consciousness and is of finite duration: "This is—I don't know quite how to put it—a continuation of life as if by inertia . . . . For two or three months . . . sometimes even for half a year . . . . We have one person here, for instance, whose body has almost entirely decomposed, but every six weeks or so he will still suddenly mumble one word—meaningless of course—about a bean or something: 'Bobok, bobok.' . . . We have two or three months of life and then, finally—*bobok*."[49] According to Platon, these two or three months have been given as a gift, an opportunity for the soul to reach a new moral awareness. However, the inhabitants of the cemetery, at the urging of a "charming rascal" from the "pseudo-upper class," opt instead to use this opportunity to abandon all sense of shame, since the appearance of moral rectitude is no longer necessary or profitable.

The appalled narrator-eavesdropper cannot accept this "debauchery of . . . final hopes" and he resolves to continue visiting cemeteries, listening everywhere for something more comforting.[50] And there is, indeed, something other than the meaningless "bobok" to be heard spoken from beyond the grave in Dostoevsky's art. There is also the hope expressed by the peasant-pilgrim Makar in the novel *The Adolescent:* "There's a limit to how long a man is remembered on this earth . . . . Grass will grow over his grave in the cemetery, the white stone over him will crumble, and everyone will forget him, including his own descendants because only very few names remain in people's memory. So, that's all right. . . . Yes, go on, forget me dear ones, but me, I'll go on loving you even from my grave . . . . Live for some time yet in the sunlight and enjoy yourselves while I pray for you . . . . Death doesn't make any difference, for there's love after death too!"[51]

Dostoevsky's knowledge of the all-too-human egoism underlying the idea of immortality includes within its scope something *more* besides—the possibility that the love of others, too, is a motivating factor. This possibility, absent in Nietzsche, can have a subtly transformative effect on the images of heaven and hell in Dostoevsky's fiction. In *The Brothers Karamazov,* for instance, the Inquisitor's image of heaven as an enticing reward appealing to self-love is offset by the evocation of the post-resurrection life in the last lines of the novel, in the dialogue between Alyosha and the boys. Here the emphasis is entirely on the joy of loving others; in Kolya's words, the joy of seeing "one another again, and everyone, and Ilyushechka" (776). Love for the dead boy, Ilyushechka, fuels this hope of resurrection and to some degree restores him to life in the memory of his friends. Here we have Makar's "love after death," but in this instance moving in the other direction, from the living toward the dead. In either case, the possibility is raised that the hope for immortality can be inspired by the strength of our love for others, a love unwilling to acknowledge the finality of death.

The image of hell can be transformed by love in an even more striking manner. The hell with hooks for dragging down "stinkers" like Fyodor Pavlovich is offset by Zosima's definition of hell as "the suffering of being no longer able to love." As he explains:

Once, in infinite existence . . . a certain spiritual being, through his appearance on earth, was granted the ability to say to himself: "I am and I love." . . . Once only, he was given a moment of active, *living* love . . . . And what then? This fortunate being rejected the invaluable gift, did not value it . . . was left unmoved by it. This being, having departed the earth . . . sees clearly and says to himself: "Now I have knowledge, and though I thirst to love, there will be no great deed in my love, no sacrifice,

for my earthly life is over . . . . Though I would gladly give my life for others, it is
not possible now, for the life I could have sacrificed for love is gone." (322)

Zosima's words need careful attention if misunderstanding is to be avoided. He
(and Dostoevsky through him) is not proposing an amiable, sentimentalized
Christianity in which hell is redefined out of existence. He does not eschew the
possibility of "torment" for some. Although he wants to speak of "spiritual" torment rather than the crudely material "hooks" and "flames" imagined by Fyodor
Karamazov, the former is nonetheless real, and even "far more terrible." Yet the
distinction between material and spiritual suffering still does not take us to the
heart of the difference between Zosima's and Fyodor's images of hell. The issue is
not the reality or even the form of the suffering but its source; Zosima proposes
that we understand it as a self-induced inner state—the state of those confronted
by the love they have refused—rather than as externally imposed punishment. In
Zosima's vision of immortality, justice and love are brought together, as in the
words of the seventh-century monk, St. Isaac the Syrian: "The sorrow which takes
hold of the heart which has sinned against love is more piercing than any other
pain. It is not right to say that the sinners in hell are deprived of the love of God
. . . . But love acts in two different ways, as suffering in the reproved, and as joy in
the blessed."[52]
    Zosima's understanding of hell in terms of love and the free refusal of love re-
moves the suspicious traces of deliberate revenge. The suffering here is entirely
self-inflicted rather than divinely administered; the spectacle of this suffering,
moreover, elicits nothing of that satisfaction on the part of the righteous that
Nietzsche detects in Aquinas. According to Zosima, on the contrary, the righteous
would call the others to themselves, "loving them boundlessly," perhaps even
bringing them thereby some relief (322–323).
    Ivan's formula, "There is no virtue if there is no immortality," can no doubt be
interpreted as a concise summary of a morality of divine command, founded on
eternal reward and punishment. If there is no transcendent source of command,
no divine guarantor of eternal reward and punishment, if there is no God, then
"everything is permitted." The formula is all too frequently interpreted solely
along these lines by readers of Dostoevsky and by certain of Dostoevsky's characters—Smerdyakov most notably. Usually Ivan also appears to understand it in
this manner, but not always or entirely. Careful note should be taken of this sentence in the words reported by Miusov: "Were mankind's belief in its immortality to be destroyed, not only love but also any living power to continue the life of
the world would at once dry up in it." The connection made here between love
and immortality hints at an interpretation of the formula as expressing not so
much a morality of divine command as a morality flowing spontaneously from

love. An understanding of virtue as the outcome of love rather than the desire for reward and fear of punishment is discernible in Dmitri's variation on Ivan's formula: "How is [man] going to be virtuous without God? A good question! . . . Because whom will he love then—man, I mean?" (592) For Dmitri, the question is decidedly not "Whom will he fear then?"[53]

With this transformative impact of love on notions of immortality and virtue in Dostoevsky's art, we have a response to the modern suspicion that the idea of immortality merely serves an egoism desirous of eternal reward and punishment. But what of the second reason we have noted for the uncongeniality of immortality to the modern sensibility? Nietzsche's more fundamental indictment of the idea of immortality is that it serves an impulse to devalue this life, functioning as a means of "befouling the Here and Now." Beside this identification of immortality with otherworldliness, let us place, once again, Ivan's words: "Not only love but also *any living power to continue the life of the world*." These words, contrary to Nietzsche's view, imply that the affirmation of life in this world *depends on* the idea of immortality. The phrase "depends on," moreover, does not do justice to the boldness with which Dostoevsky himself actually *identifies* immortality and "living life"; in *A Writer's Diary*, to offer one explicit instance, he asserts that "the idea of immortality *is* life itself—'living life'" (*zhivaya zhizn'*).[54]

## Immortality and the Affirmation of Life

Dostoevsky's assertion in *A Writer's Diary* confronts us with what is so strikingly distinctive in his treatment of the themes both of immortality and of life. I think, too, that it takes us to the heart of his religious vision, and therefore requires close consideration. The identification of immortality with "living life" is made within the context of an article entitled "Unsubstantiated Statements"—which, brief though it is, constitutes Dostoevsky's most explicit account of what the idea of immortality signifies for him. This article can be seen as a philosophical foreword to the question posed by Fyodor Karamazov over cognac, the question embodied poetically throughout *The Brothers Karamazov*.

Dostoevsky's "unsubstantiated statements" about immortality are made in response to the written confession of a "logical suicide" (almost certainly penned by Dostoevsky himself).[55] He aims, by means of this vivid first-person confession, to place the reader imaginatively within the consciousness of someone who knows and experiences life as having its end in annihilation. The focus at first is on the consequence for the "I" of the vision of the finality of becoming: All that "I" know with certainty, upon the renunciation of any consoling religious or metaphysical interpretation of my situation, is that without my willing it I have come into being and must also one day cease to be, and that my consciousness of this fact is a source of suffering. The existence of the universe, and of human consciousness within it, appears to be the outcome of nothing but accident, in combination with "dead laws of Nature." Yet even if there were some point to it all, some sort of "harmony of the whole," this means nothing to the "I" facing annihilation: "But as regards the whole and its harmony, once *I* have been annihilated, I haven't the least concern if this whole with its harmony remains after I am gone or is annihilated at the same instant as I am." This self-centered complaint only appears to corroborate Nietzsche's observation that the desire for immortality is explicable as an expression of egoism. However, the logical suicide's meditation does not end on this note. He considers the possibility of finding some meaning, some "reconciliation" with the brute facticity of his situation, in the less self-centered thought that if not "I" as an individual, then perhaps humanity as a whole might attain a future happiness; my life can become meaningful through a love for humanity issuing in constructive historical struggle. Yet, here again, the thought of the finality of becoming, which applies to the species as much as to the individual, has a deadening impact: "Well, suppose I were to die but humanity were to remain eternal in my place; then, perhaps, I might still find some comfort in it. But our planet, after all, is not eternal, and humanity's allotted span is just such a moment as has been allotted to me. And no matter how . . . joyously, righteously, and blessedly humanity might organize itself on earth, it will all be equated tomorrow to that same empty zero."[56]

The logical suicide denies the possibility of finding meaning in a love for other human beings whom one knows to be destined for nothing but pointless extinction, despite all their hopes and their suffering. In his commentary on this suicide's confession, Dostoevsky observes that the compassionate indignation aroused in the lover of humanity by the spectacle of pointless human suffering within an indifferent universe can be subtly transformed into an actual hatred of humanity: "In just the same fashion, it more than once has been noted how, in a family dying of starvation the father or mother, toward the end when the sufferings of the children have become unbearable, will begin to hate those same children whom they had previously loved so much, precisely because their suffering has become *unbearable*."[57] The psychological possibility of such a grim transformation is discernible to those who are sensitive, as Dostoevsky surely was, to the complex dynamics of compassion and suffering. It is a transformation embodied poetically in the transition from the tone of indignant compassion expressed in Ivan's stories of suffering children to the tone of contempt conveyed through the Inquisitor's words about his "flock."

The logical suicide's consciousness of the futility of human existence fosters within him a hatred of life, and suicide becomes his protest against having to endure a mute and indifferent tyranny "in which there is no guilty party." This act is meant to illustrate, in extreme and dramatic fashion, the principal point Dostoevsky wishes to make in his "Unsubstantiated Statements"—that the idea of immortality binds people "all the more firmly to the earth." This statement, he acknowledges, would seem to be a contradiction. Why should the promise of eternal life lead one to affirm this life? This apparent contradiction, however, points to the truth that without the idea of immortality, human existence becomes "unnatural, unthinkable, and unbearable." The conviction of immortality, then, is essential for human existence, and so, not surprisingly, it has been the norm among human beings; "and if that is the case, then the very immortality of the human soul *exists with certainty.*" Dostoevsky then concludes with the statement that the idea of immortality is "life itself, living life."[58]

Leaving aside the logical validity of Dostoevsky's conclusion about the "certain" existence of immortality, I want to comment on two matters arising from his "Unsubstantiated Statements." First, despite Dostoevsky's frequent use of the phrase *immortality of the soul,* it would be out of place to conclude that he therefore understands immortality more in the manner of Plato than Paul. The difference in emphasis between the symbols of "immortal soul" and "resurrected spiritual body" might indeed be significant; but for Dostoevsky, such a difference is minimal in the face of the notion that all human lives end in "that same empty zero." His language is not intended to specify a theoretical position on the nature of immortality but merely to assert its reality as against the "empty zero." In making this assertion, he employs the terms of philosophy rather than biblical faith because his "unsubstantiated statements" are a response to the argument of a "logical suicide." Dostoevsky's concern here, as in the novels, is to conduct a dialogue with atheism that is immediately accessible to all those willing to enter thoughtfully into it. Upon closer scrutiny, it becomes apparent that his favored phrase *immortality of the soul* functions as a kind of shorthand for an affirmation about human existence also expressed, in the space of a few pages, in such phrases as "higher idea," "higher ideal of existence," "the whole higher meaning and significance of life," and the "higher sense of life." One could add to these phrases Zosima's evocation of the "sense of our bond with the higher heavenly world." Dostoevsky's primary concern in the face of the modern reduction of human existence to an entirely naturalistic explanation is to affirm, nevertheless, a higher level of reality to which human beings have experiential access. Of the various words and phrases that might be used to express this affirmation—*God, the other world, the higher sense of life, the immortality of the soul*—he gives preference in his article in *A Writer's Diary* to the last, perhaps because it symbolizes at once the higher reality and its relation to the human individual: "There is *only one* higher idea on earth, and it is the idea of the immortality of the human soul, for all other 'higher ideas' of life by which humans might live *derive from that idea alone.* Others may dispute this point with me (about the unity of the source of all higher things . . . ), but I am not going to get into an argument just yet and simply set forth my idea in unsubstantiated form. It cannot be explained all at once, and it will be better to do it little by little. There will be time to do this in the future."[59]

My second comment concerns Dostoevsky's assertion that the idea of immortality "binds people all the more firmly to earth." This might indeed seem to be a "contradiction," as Dostoevsky himself acknowledges; but the contradiction disappears if in fact human beings are beings that cannot live happily on the earth without a sense of the "higher meaning and significance of life." The human need for meaning is the theme of a haunting image found in *The House of the Dead* (the novel-memoir based on Dostoevsky's experience in a Siberian labor camp)—an image evocative of the myth of Sisyphus:

> The thought once occurred to me that if one wanted to crush and destroy a man entirely, to mete out to him the most terrible punishment, one at which the most fearsome murderer would tremble, shrinking from it in advance, all one would have to do would be to make him do work that was completely and utterly devoid of usefulness and meaning . . . . If, let us say, he were forced to pour water from one tub into another and back again, time after time, to pound sand, to carry a heap of soil from one spot to another and back again—I think that such a convict would hang himself within a few days or commit a thousand offences in order to die, to escape from such degradation, shame, and torment.[60]

This vision of the unendurable absurdity of forced labor without aim or purpose can be taken as an analogue for metaphysical absurdity.

The manner in which the idea of immortality can confer higher meaning on the universe—a meaning sympathetic to the deepest human aspirations—is important to Dostoevsky's identification of "living life" with immortality. However, such an explanation still remains too much on the level of theory, as though the need for meaning were primarily an intellectual need, to be satisfied by the advancing of theoretical propositions to which mental consent is given or denied. Underlying the logical argumentation of the suicide's "sentence" against life is something else, as he acknowledges: "I cannot be happy under the condition of the nothingness that threatens tomorrow. This is a feeling, a direct feeling, and I cannot overcome it." In his commentary on this "sentence," Dostoevsky speaks of the loss of a "higher meaning in life" as a loss experienced in the form of "unconscious anguish."[61] References to "unconscious anguish" and to "feelings" that cannot be overcome are undeniably (and perhaps necessarily) imprecise, but they suffice to make clear that for Dostoevsky the question of immortality is something more than a matter of theory or doctrine. To reduce religious faith, or its absence, to a matter of belief or unbelief in propositions is to commit the same error Smerdyakov commits in his preposterous theological disputation with the old servant Grigory. Even as he disputes the doctrinal propositions (which are secondary), he remains oblivious to the primary experience that the doctrines symbolize. The entire disputation, like much of the modern debate between belief and unbelief, moves within a realm of insubstantial shadows, within what Eric Voegelin has called the "subfield of doctrinaire existence."[62] For Dostoevsky, faith in immortality is not a doctrinal belief held in the mind; it is an experience of the heart. Similarly, in identifying immortality with "living life," he is not advancing a theoretical proposition but is appealing to an experience of the whole human being.[63]

Yet, is it not a paradox to speak of the *experience* of immortality? No more paradoxical than speaking of immortality as *living life*; and if it is indeed so, then one would expect intimations of immortality to be vouchsafed within human life-experience. It is precisely such intimations that Dostoevsky attempts to convey through his art—for instance (and especially), in the experience of love. We are brought back yet again to the relationship in Dostoevsky between immortality and love. Having already explored the manner in which the *idea* of immortality can be transformed in his work by love, we must now consider how the experience of love points to the *reality* of immortality.[64]

In response to Mrs. Khokhlakov's "devastating" worry about immortality, Zosima has this to say: "No doubt it is devastating. One cannot prove anything here, but it is possible to be convinced . . . by the experience of active love. Try to love your neighbors actively and tirelessly. The more you succeed in loving, the more you'll be convinced of the existence of God and the immortality of your soul" (56). Ivan's formula emphasizes the dependence of love of neighbor on belief in immortality; but here Zosima reverses the terms. It is this possibility—that the conviction of immortality can depend on the practice of love of others—that seems most alien to what Nietzsche knows. For what he knows is that "by prescribing 'love of the neighbor,' the ascetic priest prescribes fundamentally an excitement of the strongest . . . drive, even if in the most cautious doses—namely, of the will to power."[65] According to Nietzsche's suspicious interpretation, in all our doing good to others, we are actually experiencing the pleasure of our superiority.

Nietzsche's discussions of love invariably become discussions of power. For him, the struggle between love and egoism is an unequal one, and this holds true whether it is a matter of agape or eros, the latter being only a more ingenuous expression of egoism. The following observation is representative: "Sexual love betrays itself most clearly as a lust for possession: the lover desires unconditional

and sole possession of the person for whom he longs; he desires equally unconditional power over the soul and over the body of the beloved."[66] Nietzsche does
not believe even in the capacity of eros to enable us, at least temporarily, to transcend self-love toward love of the other.

Dostoevsky, too, is far from sanguine about the human capacity for selfless
love. Even Mrs. Khokhlakov has the sense to realize that the active love advocated
by Zosima is no easy matter, for she is sensitive to her own need for gratitude
from those she would help. Zosima, too, speaks of love of neighbor as a serious
struggle and a "whole science," and above all, as something that gains reality only
through active expression "in the flesh"; so long as it remains merely an easily
available, abstract sentiment, it has no more reality than a "phantom" (56–57). In
the realm of eros as well as that of agape, Dostoevsky's art is painfully alive to the
permutations of power and egoism that can so closely accompany love. Indeed,
*Notes from the Underground* can be read as an artistic case-study of sexual love as
lust for possession. The *Underground* man bears stark witness to the struggle between egoism and love in his words: "I was no longer capable of . . . love because
. . . in my terms love meant tyranny and moral superiority. All my life I've been
unable even to imagine any other kind of love and I've reached the point where
at times I think that love consists of the right to tyrannize that the loved one
freely gives the lover." He bears witness to the struggle also in his shocking action
at the decisive moment in the story when the gift of love is offered him by the
prostitute Liza:

> I was humiliated and so I wanted to humiliate someone else; I had had my face
> rubbed in the mud, and so I wanted to show my power . . . . She was sitting on the
> floor, leaning her head against the bed, and she must have been crying . . . . By now
> she already knew everything. I had thoroughly insulted her, but . . . there's no need
> to go into that. She had guessed that my fit of passion was simply revenge, a new
> humiliation for her . . . . She fully understood that I was not in a condition to love
> her.[67]

We are a long way here from the selfless love preached by Zosima, though we are
still within the realm of what Dostoevsky knew, and knew thoroughly.

Dostoevsky's writings compel us to ask: What does the experience of love reveal, *except* the power of human egoism? And this question brings us firmly back
to what Nietzsche knows: that the *Underground* man's experience of love as
tyranny and submission reflects truthfully, albeit crudely, *any* possible experience
of love. Crudely, because Nietzsche valued highly those phenomena of life—love
among them—that signify a "spiritualization" of more primal drives. Giving due
weight to the importance he ascribes to this spiritualizing process, we must nev-

ertheless conclude that his interpretation of love is reductive; what is "higher" is understood ultimately in terms of what is "lower." For Nietzsche, the most fundamental drive, of which all other drives "are only developments," is the will to power. There is, in his words, no other "psychic force" at work within us; there cannot be, since there is no other force at work within life itself.[68] To quote Nietzsche's most explicit summary of his position, in *Beyond Good and Evil:* "Life itself is *essentially* appropriation . . . overpowering of what is alien and weaker . . . imposition of one's own forms, incorporation and at least, at its mildest, exploitation . . . because life simply *is* will to power."[69] The all-too-human egoism underlying the genesis and the appeal of the idea of immortality is a fundamental expression of life itself. Because the idea of immortality arises out of the suffering of a weak will to power revenging itself against life, it presents us with the spectacle of life turning against life. In the face of this spectacle, Zarathustra urges his listeners to turn away from the illusion of other, higher worlds, and to love this earth.

Perhaps we can thus define the truly fundamental point of divergence between Nietzsche and Dostoevsky: For Dostoevsky, the experience of love can, in the end, be an experience of *love;* it is not always reducible to some lower reality of which it signifies a "spiritualization." The struggle between egoism and love depicted in his work (e.g., in *Notes from the Underground*) cannot be interpreted away as a conflict of more or less spiritualized "drives" or "affects" culminating in the victory of the strongest one.[70] The *Underground* man himself, and Dostoevsky with him, insists on his freedom—a real freedom, situated among real alternatives. The *Underground* man's failure to accept and to give love is a reflection on him rather than on the essence of life itself. For Dostoevsky, the authentic experience of love, in spite of our egoism, remains possible because love has an independent reality. Or to put it more precisely: Love's source is not in something less than love but in the perfection of love. Against the tendency exemplified in Nietzsche to explain what is higher in terms of what is lower, Dostoevsky through Zosima insists on explaining what is already high by what is *yet higher:* "The roots of our thoughts and feelings are not here but in other worlds. . . . God took seeds from other worlds and sowed them on this earth . . . and everything that could sprout sprouted, but it lives and grows only through its sense of being in touch with other mysterious worlds; if this sense is weakened or destroyed in you . . . then you become indifferent to life, and even come to hate it" (320).

That other, higher world of which Zosima speaks is not aloof from or opposed to this earth; rather, the whole of creation is pervaded by divine love and divine life. That is why the experience of love can be an intimation of other worlds, or of immortality. And that is why "living life" and "immortality" are so closely identified with one another in Dostoevsky's vision. The category of "otherworldliness," with its attendant charge that there has been a devaluing of this world, is plainly inadequate in the face of Dostoevsky's sense of immortality.

Let us recall the general method of Nietzsche's critique of the "immortal-soul-hypothesis." Acknowledging that we cannot have logical certainty concerning its truth or falsity, he undertakes to expose its suspicious associations—with a morality based on egoistic incentives of eternal reward and punishment, and with an otherworldly orientation that functions as a covert revenge taken by the weak, unhappy, and disappointed against life itself. As we have seen, Dostoevsky was acutely aware of the possibility of such a critique, and moreover, of its justifiability—but only up to a point. His art evinces a clear distinction between more and less deficient modes of Christian understanding of immortality; it witnesses, furthermore, to a Christianity of love rather than of egoism, and of life-affirmation rather than life-denial. Nor is this a matter of some private Christianity of Dostoevsky's own concoction; Zosima is, as we have already noted,[71] carefully situated within a living, historically visible tradition. Dostoevsky's Christian art demonstrates a capacity to share, and then to transcend, Nietzsche's suspicious analysis.

Yet the same openness does not characterize Nietzsche in relation to Dostoevsky's Christian faith. Save the primary distinction between Jesus and Christianity that he makes in *The Anti-Christ,* Nietzsche tends to treat the latter as though it were a monolithic phenomenon existing solely on the level of dogmatic propositions concerning the "sacrificial death," the "Resurrection," the "Second Coming," the "Last Judgment," and "personal immortality."[72] For all his psychologist's subtlety and *délicatesse,* which sometimes hits the mark so perfectly, Nietzsche's critique of Christian faith is highly selective in comparison with Dostoevsky's. Indeed, it appears that Nietzsche contravenes what should be a cardinal rule of the intellectual conscience: that a phenomenon, especially a complex one, be judged according to its higher manifestations as well as its lower ones.

Dostoevsky's idea of immortality not only eludes Nietzsche's charge of "otherworldliness" but also reverses its direction. From the perspective expressed in Zosima's words about being "in touch with other mysterious worlds," the exhortation of Zarathustra to affirm earthly life by turning away from "otherworldly hopes" is a recipe for indifference toward, and even hatred of, life. Although Nietzsche and Dostoevsky know much in common, the former knew life as will to power and the latter knew it as divine creation. In this fundamental difference, their dialogue reaches an impasse. Any attempt at a concluding assessment as to who knows more truthfully is rendered especially problematic by the question mark that Nietzsche has placed beside "truth." In Nietzsche's thought, the value of truth is estimated in relation to the higher priority of "life"—or, more precisely, the "preservation," "enhancement," and "affirmation" of life.[73] In accord, then, with Nietzsche's own highest criterion for assessing the value of a teaching, let us pose this question: Which vision of life—as will to power, or as divine creation—is more conducive to its affirmation? Zosima's exhortation to "kiss the earth and love it . . . insatiably" (322) has its justification in a vision of the world and of human beings that supports and enhances the very love he advocates. Zarathustra's exhortation to be faithful to the earth, in contrast, appears a stark choice of the will, justified—if at all—in a negative manner, as the only alternative there is to nihilism. Yet a nihilist rejection of life remains all too possible. It would seem that Nietzsche has nothing to say to the "logical suicide," save to condemn the weakness of will that has made him weary of the game of life and unable to will himself into the Nietzschean project of deifying becoming and calling it "good."[74]

As for the last word on the question of immortality, let us grant that to a man who is looking death in the face: that loquacious and rather pompous, but strangely lovable representative of liberal humanism, Stepan Trofimovich (in *Demons*), whose final change of heart was discussed in Chapter 3. After administering the sacrament of extreme unction to the dying man, the priest speaks in a decidedly . . . well, "priestly" manner: "In our sinful time . . . faith in the Almighty is mankind's sole refuge from all the trials and tribulations of life, as well as the only hope for eternal bliss, promised to the righteous." Here we have, concisely expressed, the very idea of immortality that is so uncongenial to the modern sensibility. And Stepan's response? "Mon père, je vous remercie . . . mais . . . " ("Thank you, Father, but . . . "). Stepan's *mais* does not imply a rejection of the idea of immortality but a different way of expressing the idea, in which the emphasis is not on blissful reward for the righteous or on the disparagement of life but on the reality of love:

> My immortality is necessary if only because God will not want to do an injustice and utterly extinguish the fire of love for him once kindled in my heart. And what is more precious than love? Love is higher than being, love is the crown of being; and is it possible for being not to bow before it? If I have come to love him and rejoice in my love—is it possible he should extinguish both me and my joy and turn us into nothing? If there is God, then I am immortal! *Voilà ma profession de foi.*[75]

# Notes

1. Fyodor Dostoevsky, *The Unpublished Dostoevsky,* vol. 3, ed. C.R. Proffer (Ann Arbor, Mich.: Ardis, 1973), p. 175.

2. Paul Ricoeur, *The Conflict of Interpretations: Essays in Hermeneutics,* ed. Don Ihde (Evanston, Ill.: Northwestern University Press, 1974), pp. 442–443.

3. Volker Dürr, Reinhold Grimm, and Kathy Harms, eds., *Nietzsche: Literature and Values* (Madison: University of Wisconsin Press, 1988), p. 69.

4. Fyodor Dostoevsky, *Notes from the Underground,* trans. Jane Kentish (Oxford: Oxford University Press, 1991), p. 7.

5. Paul Ricoeur, *Freud and Philosophy: An Essay on Interpretation,* trans. Denis Savage (New Haven: Yale University Press, 1970), p. 33. The italics are Ricoeur's.

6. For Nietzsche's tribute to Dostoevsky as a psychologist, see *Twilight of the Idols,* trans. R.J. Hollingdale (New York: Penguin, 1968), p. 99.

7. For more on this distinction between a reductive and a recollective hermeneutical practice, see Ricoeur, *Freud and Philosophy: An Essay on Interpretation,* pp. 28–32.

8. Fyodor Dostoevsky, *The Notebooks for The Brothers Karamazov,* ed. and trans. Edward Wasiolek (Chicago: University of Chicago Press, 1971), pp. 75, 79.

9. See his letter of 24 August 1879 to Konstantin Pobedonostsev, in *Selected Letters of Fyodor Dostoevsky,* eds. Joseph Frank and David I. Goldstein, trans. Andrew R. MacAndrew (London: Rutgers University Press, 1987), p. 486.

10. William Blake, "The Marriage of Heaven and Hell," in idem, *Complete Writings,* ed. Geoffrey Keynes (Oxford: Oxford University Press, 1966), p. 150.

11. See Albert Camus, *The Rebel,* trans. Anthony Bower (New York: Knopf Books, 1954), pp. 55–61.

12. Søren Kierkegaard, *Training in Christianity,* trans. Walter Lowrie (Princeton: Princeton University Press, 1941), p. 126.

13. Aeschylus, *Prometheus Bound,* trans. Philip Vellacott (New York: Penguin, 1961), p. 24.

14. Friedrich Nietzsche, *Beyond Good and Evil,* trans. Walter Kaufmann (New York: Random House, 1966), p. 32.

15. For more on Nietzsche's reading of Dostoevsky, see Richard Elliott Friedman, *The Hidden Face of God* (San Francisco: Harper, 1995), chapter 7; Mihajlo Mihajlov, *Nietzsche in Russia* (Princeton: Princeton University Press, 1986), pp. 137–139; C.A. Miller, "Nietzsche's 'Discovery' of Dostoevsky," *Nietzsche-Studien,* vol. 2 (1973), pp. 202–257.

16. Friedrich Nietzsche, *The Gay Science,* trans. Walter Kaufmann (New York: Vintage Books, 1974), p. 76.

17. Nietzsche, *Beyond Good and Evil,* p. 72. Concerning the reference to Moses, see Exodus 4:10.

18. Friedrich Nietzsche, *The Anti-Christ,* trans. R.J. Hollingdale (New York: Penguin, 1968), p. 149.

19. Nietzsche, *Twilight of the Idols,* pp. 69–70.

20. The phrase "killing compassion" is used by Stanley Hauerwas in his *Dispatches from the Front: Theological Engagements with the Secular* (Durham, N.C.: Duke University Press, 1994), chapter 10. Speaking particularly of issues being raised through the practice of medicine (euthanasia, for instance), he remarks wryly that "confronted with this kind of killing compassion, one is tempted to literally kill compassion" (Ibid., p. 165). Hauerwas, however, thinks "there is no question that the most compassionate motivation often lays behind calls to eliminate retardation, for helping the old to die without pain, for insuring that no unwanted children are born, and so on" (Ibid., p. 164). Although much depends on how one interprets *often,* this statement seems to underestimate the influence of a popular Nietzscheanism near the heart of ethical decisionmaking on these matters. In their essay on "The Language of Euthanasia," George and Sheila Grant warn of the im-

plications of an innocent-sounding phrase such as "quality of life": "Decisions for euthanasia based on 'quality of life' assume that we are in a position to judge when someone else's life is not worth living . . . . 'Quality of life' has a persuasive ring about it. To repeat, we all want a good life. But where do the implications of the slogan lead? When it is
used so as to imply that some people have the right to judge that others do not have the
right to be, then its political implications lead straight to totalitarianism. It must be remembered that 'quality of life' was made central to political thought by the philosopher
Nietzsche" ("The Language of Euthanasia," in *Technology and Justice* [Toronto: Anansi,
1986], p. 115).

21. Friedrich Nietzsche, *Thus Spoke Zarathustra,* trans. Walter Kaufmann (New York:
Penguin, 1966), pp. 61–62.

22. Ibid., p. 101.

23. Nietzsche, *Beyond Good and Evil,* p. 201.

24. Albert Camus, *Resistance, Rebellion, and Death,* trans. Justin O'Brien (New York:
Random House, 1974), p. 69.

25. Cf. Nietzsche, *Thus Spoke Zarathustra,* pp. 85–86.

26. Nietzsche, *Beyond Good and Evil,* p. 83.

27. Ibid., pp. 41–42.

28. See, for instance, Robert Belknap, *The Genesis of The Brothers Karamazov* (Evanston,
Ill.: Northwestern University Press, 1990), chapter 8; Nina Perlina, *Varieties of Poetic Utterance: Quotation in The Brothers Karamazov* (New York: University Press of America),
pp. 90–95, 134–135, 160–161.

29. For an illuminating discussion of the merits and the limits of Bakhtin's approach to
reading Dostoevsky, see Jacques Catteau, *Dostoevsky and the Process of Literary Creation*
(Cambridge: Cambridge University Press, 1989), pp. 332–334. Catteau argues persuasively
that "polyphony has its limits and does not explain everything."

30. Samuel Beckett, *Waiting for Godot* (New York: Grove Press, 1954), p. 28. See also
Joseph C. McLelland, *Prometheus Rebound: The Irony of Atheism* (Waterloo, Ont.: Wilfrid
Laurier University Press, 1988), pp. 50–62; and Paul Ricoeur, *The Conflict of Interpretations,* p. 445. McLelland speaks of the God of "classical theism"; Ricoeur, following Heidegger, speaks of the God of "onto-theology."

31. Nietzsche, *Beyond Good and Evil,* p. 66.

32. Dostoevsky, *The Notebooks for The Brothers Karamazov,* p. 76. The italics are Dostoevsky's.

33. See the article of December 1876, "Unsubstantiated Statements," in Fyodor Dostoevsky, *A Writer's Diary,* trans. Kenneth Lantz (Evanston, Ill.: Northwestern University
Press, 1994), which is discussed in detail later in this chapter.

34. Friedman, *The Hidden Face of God,* p. 210.

35. For a more detailed religio-historical situating of Zosima, see the discussion in
Chapter 3 under the subhead "Speaking for Christ: The Elder Zosima's Account of Meaning in History."

36. See, for instance, Dostoevsky's letter of 25 August 1879 to Konstantin Pobedonostsev, in *Selected Letters of Fyodor Dostoevsky,* pp. 485–487. Instead of providing a point-for-
point response, however, Dostoevsky informs Pobedonostsev that he intends to present
Zosima's teaching as an alternative vision, "in an artistic picture."

37. This is Rakitin's wording in his attack on Ivan's formula. Although a "seminarist,"
Rakitin is also a "careerist" who does not hesitate to mouth the fashionable platitudes of

secular liberalism: "And did you hear his [Ivan's] stupid theory just now: 'If there is no immortality of the soul, then there is no virtue, and therefore everything is permitted.'. . . His whole theory is squalid. Mankind will find strength in itself to live for virtue, even without believing in the immortality of the soul! Find it in the love of liberty, equality, fraternity" (82).

38. Dostoevsky, *The Notebooks for The Brothers Karamazov*, pp. 74, 82.

39. Hans Jonas, *Mortality and Morality: A Search for the Good After Auschwitz* (Evanston, Ill.: Northwestern University Press, 1996), p. 115.

40. See Victor Terras, *A Karamazov Companion* (Madison: University of Wisconsin Press, 1981), p. 259.

41. Nietzsche, *Thus Spoke Zarathustra*, pp. 13, 31. The italics are Nietzsche's.

42. For a clear, judicious account of Nietzsche's method and style of argumentation in regard to the "God-hypothesis" or the "soul-hypothesis," see Richard Schacht, *Nietzsche* (London: Routledge and Kegan Paul, 1983), pp. 122–130. Jonas's approach, though by way of defending the idea of immortality, is similar to Nietzsche's in distinguishing between the existence of immortality (unknowable) and the meaning of the idea for human beings: "As transcendental, the object of the idea—immortality itself—is beyond proof or disproof; it is not an object of knowledge. But the idea of it is. Therefore the intrinsic merits of its meaning become the sole measure of its credibility" (*Mortality and Morality*, p. 115).

43. Friedrich Nietzsche, *On the Genealogy of Morals*, trans. Walter Kaufmann (New York: Random House, 1967), p. 49. The italics are Nietzsche's.

44. Ibid., p. 144. The implication of Nietzsche's statement—that even if there were a God, he would certainly not "give a damn" about the moral guilt and aspirations of his pious followers—brings to mind the Inquisitor's statement that even if there *were* "anything in the next world, it would not, of course, be for such as they"[51].

45. Nietzsche, *Twilight of the Idols*, p. 87.

46. Alyosha himself is susceptible to this desire to punish (just as he is susceptible to the whole range of human "broadness" described by Dmitri; see 108–109). Here, for instance, is his immediate response to Ivan's harrowing account of the retired general who set his dogs on an eight-year-old serf-boy, in front of the boy's mother: "'Shoot him!' Alyosha said softly, looking up at his brother with a sort of pale, twisted smile." To which Ivan responds: "'A fine monk you are! See what a little devil is sitting in your heart, Alyoshka Karamazov!'" (242–243). For Zarathustra's warning against those "in whom the impulse to punish is powerful," see *Thus Spoke Zarathustra*, pp. 100–101. Zarathustra associates this impulse particularly with the modern "preachers of equality." Given the political context of Ivan's story about the serf-boy, it would seem that Dostoevsky, like Nietzsche, is especially sensitive to the role played by the desire to punish in the modern ideologies of the left. In this context, the reader might wish to refer to Chapter 6 for a discussion of the "retributive" versus the "restorative" visions of justice. The former is clearly associated with Ivan.

47. See, for instance, *On The Genealogy of Morals*, pp. 84–85: "The entire inner world, originally as thin as if it were stretched between two membranes, expanded and extended itself, acquired depth, breadth and height, in the same measure as outward discharge was *inhibited* . . . . Let us add at once that . . . the existence on earth of an animal soul turned against itself, taking sides against itself, was something so new, profound, unheard of, enigmatic, *and pregnant with a future* that the aspect of the earth was essentially altered."

48. Dostoevsky, *A Writer's Diary*, vol. 1, pp. 178–181.

49. Ibid., p. 182.

50. Ibid., p. 185.

51. Fyodor Dostoevsky, *The Adolescent,* trans. Andrew R. MacAndrew (New York: Doubleday, 1972), pp. 358–359.

52. St. Isaac is quoted in Vladimir Lossky, *The Mystical Theology of the Eastern Church* (London: James Clarke, 1957), p. 234. Reflection on this observation of St. Isaac's could act as a helpful corrective to the common view that Christianity must be faced with the either-or of placing the emphasis on moral judgment (risking harshness) or on love (risking bland sentimentalism).

53. Again, this emphasis on virtue prompted and sustained by love, rather than by fear and desire, should not be regarded as a modern sentimentalizing of Christianity (Ferapont's charge against his monastic rival Zosima). Compare, for instance, Dmitri's words to those of Martin Luther in his *Treatise on Good Works,* "The First Commandment of the Second Table of Moses," no. 17 in *Selected Writings of Martin Luther,* ed. T. G. Tappert (Philadelphia: Fortress, 1967).

54. Dostoevsky, *A Writer's Diary,* vol. 1, p. 736.

55. For the written confession of the "logical suicide" and Dostoevsky's "unsubstantiated statements" in response, see Dostoevsky, *A Writer's Diary,* vol. 1, pp. 653–656, 732–736.

56. Ibid., pp. 654–655.

57. Ibid., p. 735. In a similar vein, note these remarks by Stanley Hauerwas: "A kind of madness erupts in our modern souls when we confront the suffering of our world. How do you work to care for some when not all can be cared for? We thus work to save starving children, and by keeping them alive they have even more children who cannot be fed. Thus compassion perpetrates cruelty, and we are driven mad by such knowledge. Some in their madness turn to strategies that require them to sacrifice present generations in the hope of securing a better future for those who are left. All in the name of compassion" (*Dispatches From the Front,* p. 165).

58. Dostoevsky, *A Writer's Diary,* vol. 1, pp. 656, 733, 736. The italics are Dostoevsky's.

59. Ibid., p. 734. The italics are in the original. Dostoevsky himself, as well as the fictional narrators of his novels, are given to promising further elaborations or explanations, which never come. However, we can justifiably regard *The Brothers Karamazov* itself as the intended future substantiation of Dostoevsky's claims.

60. Fyodor Dostoevsky, *The House of the Dead,* trans. David McDuff (New York: Penguin, 1985), p. 43.

61. Dostoevsky, *A Writer's Diary,* vol. 1, pp. 654, 736.

62. It is wonderfully illuminating to read the "disputation" between Smerdyakov and Grigory (book 3, chap. 7) in conjunction with Eric Voegelin's analysis of the sequential phenomena of "original account, dogmatic exposition, and skeptical argument" in "Immortality: Experience and Symbol," in *The Collected Works of Eric Voegelin XII,* ed. Ellis Sandoz (Baton Rouge: Louisiana State University Press, 1990). The remark about the "subfield of doctrinaire existence" is found on p. 67. In the light of Voegelin's account, an immensely amusing interchange shows itself to be also an immensely serious parody of the manner in which much intellectual debate concerning religious questions, on the part of people with far more formal education than these servants possess, can miss the point entirely. Note also Prince Myshkin's reflections on his conversation with "a very learned" atheist, in *The Idiot:* "I was glad of the opportunity of talking to a real scholar. He is, more-

over, an exceedingly well-bred person, and he talked to me as though I were his equal in knowledge and ideas. He doesn't believe in God. One thing struck me, though: he didn't seem to be talking about that at all the whole time . . . . Before, too, whenever I met unbelievers and however many of their books I read, I could not help feeling that they were not talking or writing about that at all, though they may appear to do so . . . . The essence of religious feeling . . . is something entirely different and it will always be so; it is something our atheists will always overlook and they will never talk about *that*" (Fyodor Dostoevsky, *The Idiot*, trans. David Magarshack [New York: Penguin, 1955], pp. 251–253).

63. Dostoevsky's view of the relationship between reason and religious faith is often misunderstood. He tends to be regarded as a proponent of a radical cleavage between the two, whereas his actual view is that the human being's sense of God and immortality is dependent upon a capacity of a different order than reason, rather than simply opposed to it—a spiritual capacity, which he called the "heart." For a detailed discussion of his understanding and use of the word *heart* in distinction from *reason,* and of the philosophical and theological sources from which he drew, see Bruce Ward, *Dostoyevsky's Critique of the West: The Quest for the Earthly Paradise* (Waterloo, Ont.: Wilfrid Laurier University Press, 1986), pp. 136–139.

64. On the subject of intimations of immortality vouchsafed in living experience, one might point to the sort of "mystical" experience to which Kirillov attests in *Demons:* "There are seconds, they come only five or six at a time, and you suddenly feel the presence of eternal harmony, fully achieved. It is nothing earthly; not that it's heavenly, but man cannot endure it in his earthly state . . . . The feeling is clear and indisputable. As if you suddenly sense the whole of nature and suddenly say: yes, this is true . . . . This . . . this is not tenderheartedness, but simply joy . . . . What's most frightening is that it's so terribly clear, and there's such joy. If it were longer than five seconds—the soul couldn't endure it and would vanish. In those five seconds I live my life through, and for them I would give my whole life, because it's worth it" (Fyodor Dostoevsky, *Demons,* trans. Richard Pevear and Larissa Volokhonsky [New York: Alfred A. Knopf, 1994], pp. 590–592). However, Shatov, in response to Kirillov's account of his mystical experience, warns him that "this is precisely how the falling sickness starts." Myshkin, in *The Idiot,* is also an epileptic, and he describes a transient experience of "eternal harmony" very similar to Kirillov's. He also acknowledges that this intuition of eternity is rendered suspect by its close association with disease (see *The Idiot,* pp. 258–259). As is well known, Dostoevsky himself suffered from epilepsy, and it is likely that Myshkin's doubts convey his own. Such an intimation of immortality is all too susceptible to the suspicion of the modern psychologist; and it is noteworthy that in the novel most devoted to the subject of immortality, Dostoevsky makes his appeal to "active love" rather than to mystical experience. It is worth noting, by way of comparison, that Jonas's defense of the idea of immortality eschews as evidence "unsolicitable encounters of love" that cannot be claimed by everyone in favor of what we all experience in the "call of conscience" (Jonas, *Mortality and Morality,* pp. 120, 125). For Dostoevsky, however, it is precisely the characteristic of active love (as distinct from "love in dreams") that it *is* open to all, despite its difficulty. Dostoevsky, like Jonas, also attaches enormous importance to the "call of conscience." The lackey Smerdyakov notes with a mixture of surprise and contempt Ivan's inability to master the guilt he feels for his complicity in parricide: "You used to be brave once, sir, you used to say 'Everything is permitted,' sir, and now you've got so frightened!" (625). Ivan's three "meetings" with Smerdyakov are indeed a compelling case study of the conflict between nihilist theoretical insight and the "call of conscience." Ivan suffers so acutely from this conflict that it seems

possible he will find resolution only in madness or suicide. The agony of conscience alone cannot save him, because it cannot overcome his theoretical insight into the nature of conscience itself: "What is conscience? I make it up myself. Why do I suffer then? Out of habit. Out of universal human habit over seven thousand years. So let us get out of the habit, and we shall be gods!" (653). Significant though it is, Ivan's suffering of moral guilt is still less decisive in regard to any possibility of redemption than, for instance, his love for Alyosha: "'So, Alyosha,' Ivan spoke in a firm voice, 'if, indeed, I hold out for the sticky little leaves, I shall love them only remembering you. It's enough for me that you are here somewhere, and I shall not stop wanting to live. Is that enough for you? If you wish, you can take it as a declaration of love'" (263–264).

65. Nietzsche, *On the Genealogy of Morals,* p. 135.

66. See Nietzsche's aphorism, entitled "The things people call love," in *The Gay Science,* pp. 88–89.

67. Dostoevsky, *Notes from the Underground,* pp. 115, 118–119.

68. See Friedrich Nietzsche, *The Will to Power,* trans. Walter Kaufmann and R. J. Hollingdale (New York: Random House, 1967), p. 366.

69. Nietzsche, *Beyond Good and Evil,* p. 203.

70. Cf. Nietzsche's analysis of the "popular prejudice" known as "freedom of the will," in ibid., pp. 25–27.

71. See the section in Chapter 3 of this book, subheaded "Speaking for Christ: The Elder Zosima's Account of Meaning in History."

72. See, for instance, Nietzsche, *The Anti-Christ,* p. 154.

73. For instance, Nietzsche, *Beyond Good and Evil,* p. 11; and idem, *The Will to Power,* p. 380: "The standpoint of 'value' is the standpoint of conditions of preservation and enhancement for complex forms of relative life-duration within the flux of becoming."

74. Nietzsche, *The Will to Power,* p. 319 (585 A). Cf. the criticism of Nietzsche's "return to Nature" offered by Daniel W. Conway, "Nietzsche's *Götterdämmerung,*" in *Nietzsche: A Critical Reader,* ed. Peter R. Sedgwick (Oxford: Blackwell, 1995). See also Richard Schacht, *Nietzsche,* p. 398.

75. Dostoevsky, *Demons,* p. 663.

# six

# *The Third Temptation*
## *God, Immortality, and Political Ethics*

Dostoevsky anticipated a backlash in response to his Pushkin speech, especially from liberal Westernizers looking to enlightened, humane, scientific Europe for progressive answers to Russia's "social problem"; and the backlash was not long in coming. Alexander Gradovsky, a prominent political scientist and liberal critic, published a widely circulated critique of the speech that focused on what he viewed as its author's political naïveté. Gradovsky rightly suggests that the core of Dostoevsky's answer to the "perennial questions" both in the Pushkin speech and in *The Brothers Karamazov* may be identified in the phrase: "Humble thyself, O haughty man."[1] States Gradovsky: "In these words Mr. Dostoevsky has expressed the 'holy of holies' of his convictions, that which at once represents the strength and the weakness of the author of *The Brothers Karamazov*. These words contain a great *religious* ideal, a powerful homily on *personal* morality, but they bear not even a hint of *social* ideals."[2] That is to say, Dostoevsky might be right to criticize the personal ethics of "wanderers" like Aleko and Onegin (or Miusov or Ivan) on Christian moral grounds; but that is no reason to reject the civic institutions of Western modernity toward which these personages are oriented and which alone will enable Russia to overcome its miserable serfdom and develop into a great nation. Gradovsky points to the embarrassing example of the Apostle Paul's acceptance of the immoral institution of slavery to make his case that personal ethics and institutional political morality are two different things, and that they are insufficiently differentiated in Dostoevsky's naive Christian vision.

In his reply, Dostoevsky clearly rejects Gradovsky's liberal moral dualism. Were people to take seriously Paul's Christian vision of serving love, slavery would disappear. True, Christian perfection has not yet appeared, but then neither has the perfect civil social order, and a good social order of any kind is dependent upon the personal practice of civic virtue by the citizens. There is no magic here, though the political economy of the good society remains a mystery to human calculation and engineering. Dostoevsky asserts: "Please be aware, my learned professor, that there are no social, civic ideals as such, ones that are not linked organically with moral ideals but exist independently as separate halves sliced off from the whole by your scholarly scalpel; there are no such ideals that, at last, can be taken from outside and transplanted successfully into the spot of your choosing in the form of distinct 'institutions.'"[3]

There is no magical, scientific, or instinctual social formula for human beings. Social orders originate in ideas organically linked to religious and moral conceptions of human nature and fulfillment, and personal betterment cannot be separated from civic institutions. A political society based on survival and on fear cannot maintain unity for long. And in such a society: "What . . . can an 'institution' as such, taken on its own, save? If there were brothers, then there would be brotherhood. If there are no brothers, then you will not achieve any sort of brotherhood through any sort of 'institution.'"[4] European institutions cannot save Russia, precisely because they have already split asunder what must be organically united: personal morality and social ethics. Dostoevsky then repeats what he presents poetically in *The Brothers Karamazov:* The official Roman Catholicism of the West essentially agreed to this split in accepting the Roman state and law as the legitimate civic expression of its spirituality and "brotherhood."

If atheistic socialism is the "other end" of God and immortality in the Russian context, then the French Revolution is the "other end" of Roman Catholicism in the European context—and Dostoevsky sees little difference between the two political philosophies. To adopt such ideas would be to become the lackey of modern Europe and its moribund scientific humanism, which is ultimately a denial of human brotherhood. *The Brothers Karamazov* explores the alternative: not a Russian caesaropapist messianism (as Eric Voegelin and others mistakenly assert[5]) but the monastic Christianity of the Russian peasantry. John Meyendorff points out that caesaropapism never became the official principle of Byzantine theology, largely because of the powerful monastic witness to the church's freedom, which resisted both any compromise with the state and the renaissance of secular humanism.[6] In contrast to the Latin West, the Byzantine East did not develop a juridical agreement defining the institutional division of realms between church and state, religious and secular authority, or personal and social ethics.[7] Dostoevsky, in keeping with the monastic theology of the

East, therefore rejects both caesaropapism and the separation of church and state in order to develop a vision of political order rooted in the crucified, cosmic Christ whose worldly presence in word and sacrament orients the life and practice of the worshiping community on earth. This is the foundation of justice, revealed in John's Apocalypse, the central symbols of which also pervade Dostoevsky's political theology.

In this chapter, we explore the implications for political ethics of the Inquisitor's interpretation of the third temptation, in which he proposes the establishment of a homogeneous, totalitarian state as the solution to the problem of human justice. This solution is a parodic mimesis of the heavenly city imaged poetically in the book of Revelation. Dostoevsky, like the author of the biblical apocalypse, is engaging in a prophetic, poetic critique of ecumenical, imperial politics from the standpoint of "God and immortality"—a hidden divine justice founded upon the "slain Lamb" who rules in the heavenly city and whose rule on earth is mediated in the suffering servant church. These conflicting political theologies with their attendant moral logics inhabit the same worldly space; the only question concerns which is true and which is founded upon a lie. The questions of whom to worship and which conception of political authority and justice is true are fundamentally related in Dostoevsky's writings with reference to the image of the slain Lamb, as they are in the book of Revelation. Our exploration begins, then, with the vivid political pro and contra apocalyptically displayed in Ivan's parodic prose poem. In the novel *The Brothers Karamazov*, the parodied truth is not displayed in a brilliant rhetorical rejoinder but in the contrasting contexts of Russian justice—the modern courtroom (with its rules of forensic evidence, standards of judgment, narrative techniques, and procedural rituals in the administration of retributive justice) versus the traditional monastic cell (with its icons, cycle of prayer and worship, and appeal to conscience rooted in the biblical narrative and in its vision of restorative justice). Alyosha, commissioned by his elder, takes the vision and practices of restorative justice into the world, helping to transform the community of children from a gang of conflicting rivals into brothers. This is Dostoevsky's prophetic word for modern politics: There is one true city made up of diverse peoples whose true rule—one that can preserve harmony in difference—is revealed in the slain Lamb who overcomes the tribulations of worldly, disordered desire and establishes true peace by the sword of the liberating Word. The sword is not a weapon of vengeance used to destroy enemies. It is the active embodiment of serving love that extends even to one's enemies, a posture of death to egoism that makes possible communal life under divine rule, as is expressed in the epigraph to *The Brothers Karamazov* (John 12:24).

# The Third Temptation by the Devil

We suggested in Chapter 3 that Ivan's "staging" of "The Grand Inquisitor" is important to interpreting its meaning. The same may be said of the poem's political context, established by Ivan in his literary preface. The visitation of Christ to medieval
Seville is framed with reference to John's gospel account of the triumphal entry into
Jerusalem ([41];* cf. John 12), where Jesus is welcomed into the city as the messianic
king who will establish the just rule of God. Ivan, of course, adapts this frame to his
own purposes, parodying the gospel account.[8] In this case the parody is especially
noteworthy since it refers to the very biblical passage from which Dostoevsky takes
the epigraph for the entire novel, John 12:24: "Verily, verily, I say unto you, Except a
corn of wheat fall into the earth and die, it abideth alone; but if it die, it bringeth
forth much fruit." Ivan pays no attention to this part of the passage; quite the contrary. The reason given in John 12 for the crowd of people gathered to greet Jesus as
the triumphal king is that they have heard of an impressive "sign" or miracle performed by Jesus (12:9, 17–18)—the raising of Lazarus from the dead. This gives Jesus popular appeal, as the Pharisees recognize: "You see that you can do nothing;
look, the whole world *(kosmos)* has gone after him" (12:19). Jesus responds to this ac-
clamation by saying, "The hour has come for the Son of Man to be glorified" (12:23).
But his glorification is not to be understood in terms of overtly political conquest or
externally visible power, for he follows this statement with the words of John 12:24.

John's gospel emphasizes that the meaning of Jesus' kingship, the mediation of
God's purposes in the world, and the revelation of the truth about the cosmos
and the real structure of worldly human existence are found in death and resurrection—that is, in both judgment and salvation: "Now is the judgment *(krisis)* of
this world *(kosmos),* now shall the ruler *(archon)* of this world be cast out; and I,
when I am lifted up from the earth, will draw all people *(pantas)* to myself"
(12:31–32). How does this cosmic king draw all to himself and thus to God? Not
by the power of external signs and wonders or military action or political control
or brilliant rhetoric, but by dying. There is no conventional power struggle here
but rather a revelation of the ultimate direction of the human search for reconciliation and harmony—for the divine order of truth. This is the word that saves,
in John's gospel—not "Father, save me from this hour" but rather "Father, glorify
thy name" (12:27–28). To respond to the divine drawing is to die to one's own
mortality and its relative claims, to be humbled and emptied in order to experience the fullness of divine completion. By performing these acts, Christ mediates
not only the divine will but also the pattern of human mediation given to human

---

*Here and below, page number references appearing inside square brackets pertain to Dosto-
evsky's "The Grand Inquisitor," reprinted in Chapter 2 of this volume.

beings "in the beginning"—in the royal mandate to have dominion over the earth as God's vice-regents (Genesis 1:26f.). It is a mandate parodied by human beings who seek instead to mediate their own purposes and interests in the world, to secure and complete themselves above all by the exercise of their own power (see, for example, the story of the tower of Babel in Genesis 11 as a symbol of totalitarian political order). In Christ, according to Johannine theology, the true focus of the royal mandate is restored by the recognition that God alone is good and able to judge goodness. Human beings render God's purpose present in the world insofar as they participate in the divine reality, emptying themselves in order to be filled by the outpouring of divine love. This kenotic pattern is the very incarnation of divine love, by which true community is established.

Instead of developing this Johannine theme, Ivan (whose name mimics the New Testament John's) takes it in the opposite direction. In his literary preface he combines the Johannine triumphal entry with the miracle story of the raising from the dead of Jairus's daughter in Mark 5:35–43. The only words of Jesus that Ivan quotes in "The Grand Inquisitor" are the Aramaic words Jesus spoke to the girl, *Talitha cumi* ("Damsel arise").[9] We note, first, that the miraculous raising of one presumed dead here occurs in response to the crowd's royal greeting, and in the most public of settings—the cathedral square. In Mark's story the miracle is *hidden* from public view;[10] Jesus sends everyone out and goes in to the child alone. Afterward he strictly charges the people there to tell no one about it. In the retelling, Ivan has Christ performing a very public, theatrical miracle, displaying his power to fulfill the earthly desires of people without considering the spiritual meaning or end of those desires.

At issue here are the nature and meaning of the power, authority, and purpose of life as revealed in Christ's teaching and ministry. And indeed, these questions become the focus of the Inquisitor's prosecution of Christ. They are a test of Messianic authority and agency, and are thus related to the Lamb/atonement imagery and death and resurrection symbolism that we have already noted. Whose understanding of human freedom and happiness, of evil rebellion and the successful establishment of just order, is truer to reality? John's visions on the island of Patmos are described as a cosmic revelation from the God "who is and who was and who is to come," the beginning and the end, Alpha and Omega (Revelation 1:4, 8), the agent of whose cosmic purpose is the crucified and risen Messiah (1:17–18). When John in his vision is ushered through the door of the heavenly vault into the throne room of the Creator, he describes two central symbols—the rainbow, representing divine mercy,[11] and the lightning and thunder issuing from the throne, representing divine sovereignty and holy righteousness (the giving of the Law). We are thus, as G. B. Caird points out, introduced to a central problem in theology: "How can God, in a sinful world, do equal justice to his sovereignty and his mercy?"[12]

John of Patmos has the answer, as revealed in Revelation 5, in the vision of the sealed scroll that contains the hidden meaning and destiny of history. No one is worthy to open the scroll, and God will not break the seals—human destiny and with it the destiny of all creation is mediated in the world by human freedom. God does not act unilaterally or in magical interventions.[13] John begins to weep: How will God's purposes for this alienated creation be realized? Who is worthy to be the agent of redemptive justice and reconciling harmony in the world? The revealed answer is given (5:5f.) in an amazing conjunction of images. The elder *says* to John, "The *Lion* of the tribe of Judah, the Root of David, has conquered, so that he can open the scroll and its seven seals"—an image of the Messianic warrior-king. What John *sees*, however, is "a *Lamb*, standing, as though it had been slain"—the Messianic conquering of evil is accomplished by death. The Messianic agency that draws all creation to its fulfilling completion is the power of suffering love, which exhausts the strength of evil by patient martyrdom. It is a pattern of witness also imitated by the followers of the Lamb (Revelation 11; cf. 6:9f.; 12:11; 20:4). This in turn calls for an alternative vision of political order (represented by a "new song," 5:9–10, 12) founded on the worthiness of the slain Lamb.[14]

The question at stake in the "Pro and Contra" section of the novel is which image will orient the thought and action of human character and thus "authorize" political judgment and order. It is clear that both the Inquisitor and Christ in Ivan's prose poem understand this to be a spiritual question, not merely a material one. As the Inquisitor puts it, "The universal and everlasting anguish of man as an individual being, and of the whole of mankind together" is found in the question, "before whom shall I bow down?"[45]. Religious worship and political order are inextricably joined, and this conjunction is chiefly expressed, says the Inquisitor, in the "conscience" or in the self-conscious soul, where moral judgment occurs. Here the Inquisitor's anthropology coincides with the Christian vision of elder Zosima, which is expressed early in the novel in response to Ivan's article on ecclesiastical courts and their political jurisdiction. At stake in that article, as in the poem, is the question of justice and how it pertains spiritually and institutionally to political order. Ivan's article argues against the separation of church and state, suggesting that these two institutions do not represent two different spheres (e.g., the personal and the political, or the private and the public) but two different, fundamentally incompatible forms of rule and authority. Any attempt to mix these forms by arranging an institutional compromise between them represents "a lie at the very basis of the matter" (61).* The church, in contrast to the pagan state, appeals to conscience in its judgment of criminals and

---

*Here and below, page number references inside parentheses, unless otherwise indicated, pertain to Fyodor Dostoevsky, *The Brothers Karamazov,* trans. Richard Pevear and Larissa Volokhonsky (New York: Vintage, 1990).

seeks their spiritual regeneration in a manner that preserves their freedom. It is not focused on the mechanical preservation of external social order, as are statist forms of coercive punishment. The elder concurs with Ivan's argument, suggesting that this cosmic truth is authoritative: "In reality it is so even now. . . . If it were not for Christ's church, indeed there would be no restraint on the criminal in his evildoing, and no punishment for it later, real punishment . . . which lies in the consciousness of one's own conscience" (64). It is in the conscience that the law of Christ (and hence the true order of justice) reigns, and it is a law ordered above all by active, reconciling love—not only in some future harmony but even now, *on the earth.*[15]

A true judgment, which sees clearly the cause of the crime and how the criminal might be transformed, cannot "essentially and morally be combined with any other judgment, even in a temporary compromise. Here it is not possible to strike any bargains" (65). Hence the elder pronounces his judgment on the "false consciousness" of all "establishment" churches of Western Christendom, in which the church's authorizing image (the law of Christ) has in some manner been falsely externalized and replaced by another form of rule (the juridical state).[16] This, adds Father Paissy, "is the third temptation of the devil" (66).

As we know, Ivan's argument in the article is "two-edged" (60): Everything depends on whose authority (and which authorizing image—anthropological, sociopolitical, or cosmological) is real and true. Ivan's Inquisitor overtly opposes the authority of Christ in order to establish an external judicial and political order that nevertheless claims the name of Christ. This is the "lie" that founds his earthly rule. It is a noble lie, claims the Inquisitor, premised on a true image of human nature and history, which reverses the claims of the slain Lamb: Earthly bread is more important than the spiritual word of God; religious worship is more a matter of dazzling, external displays of power than the love of a free heart; the sword of Caesar is a more effective and benign instrument of political justice and earthly peace than the rule of conscience and suffering love. It will free the *massa damnata* from the tormenting tyranny of a free but guilty conscience that breeds only resentful rebellion and disorder.

This noble lie, however, is also consciously recognized by the Inquisitor to be a "lie in the soul" (*Republic* 382)—the "true lie" that willfully distorts a true understanding of the highest things, and that uses false images, speeches, and signs to create ignorance within the self and within society. In contrast to Plato's Socrates and in contrast to the Christ of the New Testament, the Inquisitor believes such lies can be politically useful. And the Inquisitor, as a spiritual man, is prepared to pay the spiritual price. He will take on the burden of his sinful rebellion against divine rule and suffer the torments of a divided conscience in order to use his power to relieve the spiritual burden of others—that is, the burden of their own sinful rebellion and guilty consciences. How will he do this? In a parodic reversal of Christ's path of atonement, the Inquisitor will be a miracle-working, sword-wielding Messiah of an earthly kingdom, mediating a worldly happiness of material gratification without conscience.

The secret of this rule, admits the Inquisitor to Christ, is that "we are not with you but with *him*"[49]—that is, with the "great dragon" identified in Revelation 12 as "that ancient serpent, who is called the Devil and Satan, the deceiver of the whole world" (12:9). This "secret" is premised on a reversal of the Christian understanding of life and death; it assumes the ultimate *unreality* of resurrection and the heavenly city in which the slain Lamb rules. "Beyond the grave," asserts the Inquisitor, human beings "will find only death"[51]; but he will use religious constructs of eternal life and happiness in order to create a purely temporal political substitute for conscience. And here again the Inquisitor reveals his disdain for the weak, vain rebels he claims so to love: "For even if there were anything in the next world, it would not, of course, be for such as they." Human beings, then, are not created in God's image—they are merely clever beasts. We see reflected in this comment the psychological anatomy of the liar traced earlier in the novel, by elder Zosima (44, 58). Lying to oneself leads to a loss of discernment of truth, both within oneself and in the world. This leads in turn to contempt, fear, and disrespect—both of oneself and of others—and the inability to love. Such a self becomes the slave of changing passions and abstract, self-glorifying fantasies that can reach "complete bestiality."

It is no accident, then, that the beasts of John's Apocalypse appear in all three temptations of Ivan's prose poem, and most explicitly in the third temptation, which concerns the kingdom of tamed beasts. The premise of the Inquisitor's anthropology is that human beings are not created in the image of God and therefore cannot be guided in freedom by the image of the crucified Lamb. This same premise accounts for the political realism of the third temptation—the use of Caesar's sword and imperial power (the threat of bodily death) to eradicate rebellion. Ironically, in this vision human rebellion will be eradicated in rebellion against the Creator and his purposes. The third temptation—the creation of a universal, homogeneous state held together by the external authority of technological, need-gratifying wonders and the immediate justice of corporal and capital punishment—is a parody of the loving, spiritual unity in the kingdom of God and the *pax Christi*. Dostoevsky follows the cosmic grammar of the Apocalypse here, with his references to the tower of Babel and the Whore of Babylon[49]. The completion of the Inquisitor's project is indeed an image of the biblical vision of the unholy city that has seduced the nations to the worship of what is not God—in particular, to the powers of commercial wealth, dazzling intrigue, and military empire (Revelation 17–18). In the book of Revelation this burlesque parody of the true splendor of the heavenly Jerusalem (which is the pure Bride of the Lamb) is identified with Rome. In "The Grand Inquisitor" the great harlot is the Holy Roman Empire, revived in the papal alliance with the Frankish empire.[17] Whatever the particular historical references, the spiritual principles remain consistent—the mutually destructive passions of Beast and Whore represent a parody of the marriage between Christ and the Church (the Lamb and the heavenly Bride).

The mystery of the woman and the beast are spelled out in Revelation 17 by the angel, who seeks to disenchant the bedazzled prophet who "greatly marvels" at the sight of the mother of harlots and earthly abominations, drunk with the blood of the martyrs.[18] The angel reveals that the name of the beast is an empty parody of the divine name; the antichrist "was, and is not, and is to ascend from the bottomless pit and go to perdition" (17:8; cf. 1:4, 8, 18; 2:8). The true representative of the divine name is Christ, the Lamb who is slain in the earthly world but is alive to the eternal God. The beast is dead to God's world and therefore truly dead, even though he appears to be powerfully alive in the world. The slain truth (the true, eternal image of God) thus conquers the living lie. Those who participate in this reign of and by deception are also dead, though what they seek is to preserve their earthly lives at all costs—which means they will lose them eternally. By contrast the martyrs "who follow the Lamb wherever he goes" (14:4–5) conquer the authority of earthly death "for they loved not their own lives even unto death" (12:11). The parallels here to John 12:24f. and the epigraph of *The Brothers Karamazov* are clear.

The united powers of idolatry—the beast and the harlot—are finally revealed to be nothing in John's vision, even though they are worshiped as gods in the world. The self-destructiveness of evil as the power that distorts the good is revealed in the various images of divine judgment in Revelation. The cup that sends the harlot staggering to her destruction is one she herself has mixed (17:6; 18:6f.), and she is killed by the very beast on whom she sits, enthroned in unholy alliance. The final destruction of the beast, in turn, is accompanied by many violent and deadly plagues. It is important to note that these cosmic images of evil and of mythical demonic powers do not operate independently of human agency.[19] Human beings mediate in the world that which they worship.

The question for Ivan is, will he let his isolated intellect descend into his heart (as Theophanes the Recluse put it) and thus be raised up to paradise? The latter cannot occur without a death—not only an intellectual death to Euclidean, earthly logic but also a spiritual death to the desire for juridical retribution. We know how this is resolved for the Inquisitor, whose last words to the kiss of Christ parody the final words of Revelation: "Go and do not come again . . . do not come at all . . . never, never" (compare this with Revelation 22:20, *Marana tha* [Come, our Lord]). The kiss burns in his heart, but the old man willfully rejects the seeing of the heart in order to hold to his own "idea"[54]. The spiritual death required is also depicted in Zosima's words: "All are guilty for all ... personally, each one of us, for all people and for each person on this earth" (164). Only such a confession of penitential solidarity can reverse the "lie" of juridical guilt that isolates and punishes. Only the practice of such solidarity ("all are responsible for all") will reverse the perverse and destructive freedom expressed in Ivan's parody of Paul's slogan in I Corinthians, "all is permitted."[20] Only such a death to the "puffed up" self who sticks to his shrunken "gnosis" will make possible the loving freedom that "builds up" the spiritual body politic, in which is found the "true security" of the "wholeness of humanity" (304, 320).

It would be possible, though ironic, to reduce all of this to the "ideological level," focusing on the origins of Dostoevsky's borrowed political ideas and how they are used dramatically by characters in the novel in order to stage a kind of sociopolitical critique of ideologies. That would be to miss the novel's dramatic placement of ideas and characters into certain significant political-institutional settings, two of the most important of which are the traditional (though unconventional) Russian monastery and the modern Russian courtroom. The traditional monastic institution of elders is no mere ideological device for Dostoevsky—it is the site where a particular Christian vision of justice is embodied and enacted, a vision that can be extended into the wider world only if one pays attention to the disciplines and practices cultivated in the monastic life. The monastic cell of elder Zosima is not only the setting for an abstract discussion about Ivan's academic article on ecclesiastical and secular courts; it also provides the occasion for attempting to settle a familial dispute over inheritance matters and property accounts. In it the elder offers his opinions on the topic of crime and punishment and enacts a series of prophetic judgments rooted in a penitential vision of restorative justice. Juxtaposed with the monastery, and the elder's cell in particular, is the modern Russian courtroom that embodies the secularizing Judicial Reform Act of 1864. This is the site of Mitya's strange trial in which the factual details of the crime are variously interpreted and construed. It is also the locus of the retributive model of justice, with its mechanical rules of evidence and its clever practitioners who seek to win their case by means of rhetorical speeches. Paying close attention to these settings can tell us much about Dostoevsky's Christian vision of political ethics.

# The Elder's Cell:
## Restorative Versus Retributive Justice

It is not only Ivan's article on the ecclesiastical courts that is described as "double-edged" in the novel. The institution of elders and their powerful authority is also described as a "double-edged weapon" (29) that can lead to moral regeneration and perfection in humility and freedom, or to satanic pride and bondage.[21] So also the psychological analysis used by lawyers in the modern Russian courtroom is described as a "stick with two ends" (book 12, chapter 10). It seems that the very subject of justice and authority is double-edged, posing the question: How are justice and moral goodness established on the earth, and how might one discern and judge them? The duality represented here is neither institutional nor a division between personal and social ethics; it is psychological—a question of conscience. It begins in the soul and moves through all social relationships of spiritual and moral order, from the household to religious and civic communities, to the cosmic struggle between God and the Devil that frames Dostoevsky's novel. The discernment of conscience lies at the heart of Dostoevsky's political vision of justice—an insight shared but differently resolved by the two central ascetic figures in the novel, the Grand Inquisitor and the elder Zosima. Richard Peace comments astutely on these two figures and what they represent:

> The living refutation of what the Grand Inquisitor represents can be seen in Zosima himself. Both are old men on the verge of death; both are monks and ascetics; but whereas the Grand Inquisitor embodies the legend of the Church turned State, Zosima is the prophet of the State turned Church. . . . The Grand Inquisitor rules by 'mystery, miracle and authority', but for Zosima mystery is not an instrument of rule, it is nature; it is life itself. Miracles too, he teaches, only stem from faith; they cannot inspire it. Moreover authority for Zosima is spiritual authority—the voluntary submission of a novice to his elder—it is not the physically imposed will of a despotic 'benefactor'; for the mainspring of Zosima's authority is not pride but humility. . . . The Grand Inquisitor solves the problem of crime by eliminating the criminal with incarceration, torture and fire—this is the external and purely mechanical form of justice deplored by Zosima in the discussion in the cell. To the *autos da fe* of the Grand Inquisitor are opposed the open confessions of Zosima; for he points to the individual conscience as the only true instrument of punishment.[22]

As we have seen, it is precisely the suffering of conscience that the Grand Inquisitor seeks to relieve in his regime of external power. According to the elder, such relief is not a human prerogative, since conscience is not only socially constituted, or guided by the conventional norms and authorities of a community. Conscience is a knowledge constituted also "before God," whose divine law measures human beings. For the elder, *pace* Peace, conscience is neither simply "individual" nor "instrumental"—punishment is not extrinsic to the relational, embodied life of human society. Nor is conscience simply the "mnemotechnical" internalization of contractual power relations rooted in rituals of pain (as Nietzsche has it).[23] The pain and punishment of conscience is rooted in the memory or consciousness of divine love, which exposes one's separation from its fullness and one's own completion. Pain is an important symptom of a deeper illness—one ignores or dulls it at peril of death. As such, conscience cannot work mechanically or instrumentally. Indeed, to treat conscience in such a manner "only chafes the heart in most cases," says the elder (64). The judgment of conscience cannot be linked to the external authority of any office or institution but only to the "law of Christ" that seeks the restoration of all the guilty in the reconciled community of God. The entrance requirement here is not "paying one's dues" or somehow erasing the deeds that have caused suffering. The entrance requirement is penance, the free confession that "each of us is guilty before everyone and for everyone," for only thereby does one gain consciousness of the true cosmic solidarity of human beings and thus exit the isolation of disunion from the whole.

Of course, such a penitential consciousness does not come naturally or without practice and community discipline. Penance is but a first step; it must be followed by the "monastic way" of life—obedience to spiritual authority, fasting to overcome slavery to superfluous needs, and education in prayer. The practice of prayer plays an especially important role in the novel—particularly in the lives of the two transformed brothers Karamazov. From Alyosha's memory of his mother's frenzied pleading for him before the icon of the Mother of God (18–19) to Mitya's frantic prayers after his violent attack on Grigory and his retrospective acknowledgment that he was saved from a more heinous crime (412, 437; 472, 592), prayer is displayed as a significant causal power in the novel. It links human beings to one another through the divine spirit and through consciousness, in a manner that decisively affects action and "builds up" communion. For the elder, the practice of prayer (as confession and "keeping company with the heart"; see 164, 318f.) is closely tied to the practice of active love as the antidote to lying and its isolating fears and fantasies. Prayer is the cultivation of the presence of God in the whole of one's life. In particular it gives rise to divine discernment in relation to sin and to the consequences of human alienation from God that trigger the ongoing cycles of offense, violence, and revenge in familial and social relations. As Zosima puts it:

Brothers, do not be afraid of men's sin, love man also in his sin, for this likeness of God's love is the height of love on earth. Love all of God's creation, both the whole of it and every grain of sand. Love every leaf, every ray of God's light. Love animals, love plants, love each thing. If you love each thing, you will perceive the mystery of God in things. Once you have perceived it, you will begin tirelessly to perceive more and more of it every day. And you will come at last to love the whole world with an entire, universal love.

. . . My young brother asked forgiveness of the birds: it seems senseless, yet it is right, for all is like an ocean, all flows and connects; touch it in one place and it echoes at the other end of the world. . . .

. . . My friends, ask gladness from God. Be glad as children, as birds in the sky. And let man's sin not disturb you in your efforts, do not fear that it will dampen your endeavor and keep it from being fulfilled, do not say, "Sin is strong, impiety is strong, the bad environment is strong, and we are lonely and powerless . . . ." Flee from such despondency my children! There is only one salvation for you: take yourself up, and make yourself responsible for all the sins of men. For indeed it is so, my friend, and the moment you make yourself sincerely responsible for everything and everyone, you will see at once that it is really so. . . . Whereas by shifting your own laziness and powerlessness onto others, you will end by sharing in Satan's pride and murmuring against God. I think thus of Satan's pride: it is difficult for us on earth to comprehend it, and therefore, how easy it is to fall into error and partake of it, thinking, moreover, that we are doing something great and beautiful. . . . But on earth we are indeed wandering, as it were, and did we not have the precious image of Christ before us, we would perish and be altogether lost. . . . Much on earth is concealed from us, but in place of it we have been granted a secret, mysterious sense of our living bond with the other world, with the higher heavenly world, and the roots of our thoughts and feelings are not here but in other worlds. That is why philosophers say it is impossible on earth to conceive the essence of things. God took seeds from other worlds and sowed them on this earth, and raised up his garden . . . if this sense is weakened or destroyed in you, that which has grown up in you dies. Then you become indifferent to life, and even come to hate it. So I think. (318–320)

We cite the elder's words as recorded in Alyosha's "Life" at length because of their importance in the novel's vision of social justice. The extended reflection (g) "Of prayer, love, and touching other worlds" is followed by section (h) on judgment: "Remember especially that you cannot be the judge of anyone. For there can be no judge of a criminal on earth until the judge knows that he, too, is a criminal, exactly the same as the one who stands before him . . . " (320). The only adequate response to the criminal is not retributive justice (for the elder, the desire for vengeance upon the wicked is to be feared most of all) but taking upon oneself the crime of the criminal and sharing in his suffering.

Precisely such a posture of discernment is displayed by the elder in the opening scenes of the novel, and it is a posture of spiritual and political authority that stands in stark contrast to the Grand Inquisitor's. The context of the monastery in which the elder resides is described in explicitly political terms by the narrator. The institution of elders is itself controversial within Russian Orthodoxy, "an unheard-of innovation" reintroduced by Paissy Velichkovsky at the end of the eighteenth century, and the elder Zosima is not without opposition from certain monks of renown within his own monastery. The opposition is clearly due to the personal authority that resides in the "office" of the elder, and, in particular, to the elder's informal—or better, existential—treatment of the sacrament of confession and penance, where "the people" (monks and laypersons, common folk and nobility) come to the elder in order to confess their doubts, sins, and sufferings and to seek advice and admonition. "Seeing which, the opponents of the elders shouted, among other accusations, that here the sacrament of confession was being arbitrarily and frivolously degraded" (28).[24] Indeed, the "office" of elder is not allocated by any mechanical or instrumental means but is a recognition of the spiritual maturity and discernment practiced by a monk, of the kind enacted by elder Zosima in parts 1 and 2 of *The Brothers Karamazov.*

The gathering of the Karamazovs in the elder's cell, in contrast to most other such audiences, the narrator tells us, has a false pretext. The conflict over inheritance money between Fyodor and Dmitri has intensified, rendering their relations sharp and unbearable. Apparently as a joke, Fyodor suggests they gather in the elder's cell—not for direct mediation but to see whether the "dignity and personality of the elder might be somehow influential and conciliatory" (32). Also attending the gathering is the relative of Fyodor's first wife and an early guardian of Mitya's, Pyotr Alexandrovich Miusov, a liberal, freethinking atheist who is engaged in a lawsuit with the monastery (which borders his estate) over property and logging and fishing rights. He is curious to visit the monastery and the elder, so "he hastened to take advantage of this meeting under the pretext of an intention to settle everything with the Father Superior and end all their controversies amicably" (32).[25] Neither Alyosha (who suspects the motives of these various "quarrelers and litigants") nor the elder is keen on the visit, but in the end the elder agrees, citing (with a smile) the words of Luke 12:14—"Who made me a divider over them?" (Jesus' response to a request that he settle an inheritance dispute between brothers). The visit therefore has a definite litigious and juridical context—although the visitors are not sincere in their stated purpose of obtaining justice.

The meeting is to immediately follow the late morning liturgy, and of course the guests show up *after* the liturgy. None but Alyosha truly orders his life under the authority of Christ or the disciplines of the Church, and as Alyosha has feared, no reverence or deep respect is paid either to the monastery or to the elder by Alyosha's family members. Indeed, to the contrary, Fyodor's blasphemous buffoonery combined with Miusov's offended liberal vanity leads to a quintessentially Dostoevskian scandal scene. Zosima is not offended by the antics of his guests but addresses the discerned causes of their behavior—shame, pride, false honor—and offers his interpretation as well as a prescribed cure: "Above all, do not lie to yourself" (44). This evokes an exaggerated, self-parodying "confession" from Fyodor: "I've lied decidedly all my life, every day and every hour. Verily, I am a lie and the father of a lie! Or maybe not the father of a lie, I always get my texts mixed up; let's say the son of a lie, that will do just as well!" (44).

Fyodor's confused outburst parodies the words of John 8:44f., set in a lengthy controversy scene regarding the origin of Jesus' authority and how the witness of his words and his life is to be judged. Jesus tells his opponents: "You judge according to the flesh, I judge no one. Yet even if I do judge, my judgment is true, for it is not I alone that judge, but I and he [the Father] who sent me" (8:15–16). Judgment *(krisis)* here has to do with discernment or the knowledge of God, since Jesus' claim is that his speech and his deeds bear witness to divine truth and its authority. If only his opponents "knew" the Father (God) they would also "know" the origin of his identity and authority. This is the context of the "double-edged" words of judgment spoken by Jesus in John 8:42f.:

> If God were your Father, you would love me, for I proceeded and came forth from God. . . . Why do you not understand what I say? It is because you cannot bear to hear my word. You are of your father the devil, and your will is to do your father's desires. He was a murderer from the beginning, and has nothing to do with the truth, because there is no truth in him. When he lies, he speaks according to his own nature, for he is a liar and the father of lies.

Love, desire, knowledge, truth, will, nature—these are bound together existentially and can only be discerned in the prophetic pattern of spiritual causality, which is here tied to language of "fatherhood" and, one could say, "inheritance." Here Jesus echoes the understanding of the Hebrew prophets: Lack of knowledge of God is not primarily a noetic deficiency but a failure to acknowledge God in proper invocation and worship, which involves the whole of life and entails certain ethical markers, such as the practice of justice.[26] Freedom for John (and for the elder Zosima) is dependent upon knowledge of the truth (8:32), that which is truly real and truly alive in the world—in other words, the eternal God of love whose real presence is mediated in the world by the incarnate *logos*. The opposite, slavery to the things of the flesh, which lies to itself about the origin and end of life, can only end up in the desire to murder the truth that judges it a lie. The desire of the several sons of Fyodor to murder their father is a desire, presumably, they have inherited from their father himself. The elder prophetically discerns this as well.

The prophetic discernment exercised by the elder in relation to each of the three legitimate sons of Fyodor present at the gathering in his cell is preceded, however, by another display of the elder's authority that confirms the connections between faith and deed in the "knowledge" of God and divine immortality. The elder has a special reputation among the people (and women especially) as a healer and "miracle-worker," and at a certain point he leaves his guests in order to greet the people awaiting him outside his cell. The narrator comments that the elder's healings are not magical but quite "natural"—if one takes spiritual causality of illness into account. Nor are the elder's interactions with the people theatrical displays of religious power; they are, rather, deeply personal and intimate encounters that seek to address the particular afflictions and concerns of body and soul expressed by the people themselves. The elder's discernment is fully coherent with his penitential theology—penitence and humility are closely tied to the experience and insight of divine love. This becomes especially evident in his conversation with the "lady of little faith," Madame Khokhlakov, who is plagued by doubts about "life after death." According to the elder, such doubt is not simply an intellectual matter, and it certainly has nothing to do with "proof" in a scientific sense. Yet, says the elder, it is possible to be convinced by the experience of active love: "Try to love your neighbors actively and tirelessly. The more you succeed in loving, the more you'll be convinced of the existence of God and the immortality of your soul. And if you reach complete selflessness in the love of your neighbor, then undoubtedly you will believe, and no doubt will even be able to enter your soul" (56). This is precisely the issue that plagues Ivan, as he confesses to Alyosha in the conversation leading up to the tale of the Grand Inquisitor:

> I must make an admission. . . . I never could understand how it's possible to love one's neighbors. In my opinion, it is precisely one's neighbors that one cannot possibly love. Perhaps if they weren't so nigh . . . I read sometime, somewhere about "John the Merciful" (some saint) that when a hungry and frozen passerby came to him and asked to be made warm, he lay down with him in bed, embraced him, and began breathing into his mouth, which was foul and festering with some terrible disease. I'm convinced that he did it with the strain of a lie, out of love enforced by duty, out of self-imposed penance. (236–237)

Clearly the question of moral interpretation is related to the measure of truth and of lie that is being used.[27] The elder discerns precisely this struggle going on in Ivan's conscience, and also in the conscience of his brother Mitya. The forms of the struggle, although quite different in each brother, are intimately related.

The elder's prophetic acts of discernment in relation to the brothers follow Miusov's vindictive attempt to expose Ivan's hypocrisy in writing the article on the ecclesiastical courts. Miusov finds the article offensive to his liberal sensibilities, and feels insulted by Ivan's comment that he, Miusov, has misunderstood the theological and political logic of the article as but another ideological debate about worldly power. Initially (and rather humorously) Miusov mislabels the ecclesial political vision of traditional Orthodox monasticism "sheer ultramontanism," thus betraying his Parisian outlook on nineteenth-century Roman Catholic church-state politics.[28] He then dismisses Zosima's long discourse on the Church's position on crime and punishment with a Parisian anecdote concerning the dangers of Christian socialism. Ivan simply points out Miusov's confusion in applying liberal European categories to a debate that calls those categories themselves critically into question, and Miusov then responds with another anecdote—this time about Ivan's lack of faith. At a recent local gathering Ivan has argued that human love for fellow humans is not based on natural law but on the belief in immortality. Were that belief in God and immortality to be destroyed, the moral law of love would no longer hold; indeed, "the moral law of nature ought to change into the exact opposite of the former religious law, and egoism, even to the point of crime" would be the logical result, a situation in which "all is permitted" (69).

The elder strangely and suddenly questions Ivan himself about this: "Can it be that you really hold this conviction about the consequences of the exhaustion of men's faith in the immortality of their souls?" Ivan responds that he does: "There is no virtue if there is no immortality"; to which the elder responds, "You are blessed if you believe so, or else most unhappy!" (70). Ivan's response to the elder's insight is a sudden and strange confession of the ambivalence that the elder has identified, the lack of resolution of this idea in his heart. This division, the elder tells him, demands resolution:

> "But can it be resolved in myself? Resolved in a positive way?" Ivan Fyodorovich continued asking strangely. . . .
>
> "Even if it cannot be resolved in a positive way, it will never be resolved in the negative way either—you yourself know this property of your heart, and therein lies the whole of its torment. But thank the Creator that he has given you a lofty heart, capable of being tormented by such a torment, 'to set your mind on things that are above, for our true homeland is in heaven.' May God grant that your heart's decision overtake you still on earth, and may God bless your path!" (70)

Zosima's conviction that conscience's call to unity has an eschatological orientation is signaled by his biblical quotation, which conflates Colossians 3:2—"Set your minds on things that are above"—with Philippians 3:20—"But our commonwealth *(politeuma)* is in heaven"—or perhaps Hebrews 11, where the people who live by faith as strangers and exiles on the earth seek a "higher homeland," a *polis* built by God (11:10, 13–16; cf. 13:14). The elder's discernment of Ivan's tormented conscience is of a piece with his political theology, that the authority of

divine rule is already present in Christ's law of love, which will ultimately transfigure worldly life, including society itself, into the city of God. This eschatological orientation, like Ivan's formulation "There is no virtue if there is no immortality," is not merely a doctrinal question of belief or an ideological program. It is
an existential orientation tied to a cosmic drama that also has political implications for the practical achievement of justice on the earth.[29]

The response of the elder to Dmitri is yet more dramatic. The elder's exchange
with Ivan is followed by an increasingly revealing and violent set of charges and
countercharges between Fyodor and Dmitri, prefaced by Fyodor's bombastic
charge to the elder about the purpose of this gathering in his cell: "Judge us and
save us! It's not just your prayers we need, but your prophecies!" (71). The dispute between father and son about money quickly turns into open conflict over
their shared love interest, Grushenka, and degenerates into talk of duels and parricide.[30] The ugly scene ends very unexpectedly when the elder kneels deeply before Dmitri, even touching the floor with his forehead, and then begging forgiveness of all his guests. It is a gesture no one understands, but it evokes different
responses in the various characters—Dmitri flees with his face in his hands, and
Miusov takes the gesture as a display of religious madness. Zosima explains his
"prophetic" gesture to Alyosha later: "I bowed yesterday to his great future suffering," in response to what he detected in Dmitri's eyes:

> Yesterday I seemed to see something terrible . . . as if his eyes yesterday expressed
> his whole fate. He had a certain look . . . so that I was immediately horrified in my
> heart at what this man was preparing for himself. Once or twice I've seen people
> with the same expression in their faces . . . as if it portrayed the whole fate of the
> person, and that fate, alas, came about. (285)

He then repeats his specific earlier injunction to "be near your brothers" (77,
cf. 170), thinking that Alyosha's "brotherly countenance" will help them. This
specific injunction is set in the context of Zosima's general commissioning of
Alyosha, immediately following the scandalous gathering: "I give you my blessing
for a great obedience in the world. . . . Christ is with you. Keep him, and he will
keep you. You will behold great sorrow, and in this sorrow you will be happy.
Here is a commandment for you: seek happiness in sorrow. Work, work tirelessly" (77). The elder's prophetic commissioning of Alyosha is reinforced during
a later conversation: "You will go forth from these walls, but you will sojourn in
the world like a monk. You will have many opponents, but your very enemies will
love you. Life will bring you many misfortunes, but through them you will be
happy, and you will bless life and cause others to bless it—which is the most important thing" (285).

In keeping with our suggestion that the monastic pattern is recognized by Dostoevsky as a political theology that seeks to overcome the hellish isolation of sin by humble, penitent service of one's neighbor, and that this is nourished by a spiritual joy increased through active love and the disciplines of prayer, we will explore in the final section of this chapter how Alyosha begins the practice of restorative justice in the gang of children; for it is here that he most clearly replicates, in his own unique manner, the spiritual and moral authority of his elder in a social setting. But first we consider the novel's lengthy depiction of a stark alternative vision of justice: the retributive justice enacted in the modern liberal courtroom.

## The Courtroom:
## Adversarial Retribution on Stage

It is painfully ironic that Alyosha fails to remember his elder's specific injunction to visit Dmitri in those fateful hours prior to the parricide, when his "brotherly countenance" is most desperately needed. This "forgetting" is closely related to Ivan's recitation of his prose poem—a vision that has deeply shaken and saddened Alyosha, so that he feels a special urgency to return to the monastery and his "Pater Seraphicus,"[31] as Ivan has called the elder. Immediately prior to his "conversion," Alyosha too is a "divided man" whose conscience is not yet formed in the unifying vision required to enact the elder's commission. His genuine but naive faith in his elder still focuses largely on external authority; he has not yet appropriated the elder's spiritual discernment for himself. Hence he flees the disturbing conversation with Ivan about the justice of God and human evil-doing, forgetting completely about his brother Dmitri. Similarly, when the venerated elder dies and his inner righteousness is called into question by an external sign (the preternatural putrefaction of the elder's body), Alyosha's "wounded heart" becomes obsessed with the problem of retributive justice. For Alyosha, this is a "fatal and confused" moment during which two images or impressions flash through his mind: a "tormenting and evil impression from the recollection of the previous day's conversation with his brother Ivan" (340), and the image of his brother Dmitri, which "reminded him of something, some urgent business, which could not be put off even a moment longer, some duty, some terrible responsibility" (342). However, the first impression, with its rebellious anger against God's unjust world, has already taken hold of Alyosha's heart so that the latter image "did not reach his heart, it flitted through his memory and was forgotten." Later, Alyosha will remember this with regret.

It is precisely the need for external vindication of righteousness (what Kierkegaard calls the worldly transparency for the eternal) to which Alyosha must die in order to be reborn into the elder's Christ image of restorative justice. But in the meantime his neglect of this image and its call to responsibility in his conscience parallels and contributes to Dmitri's isolated struggle with his feelings of vengeful anger in Fyodor's garden. It is Mitya who will face the full force of retributive justice in the crime of parricide—for which all three legitimate brothers bear some responsibility, but which the illegitimate brother Smerdyakov carries out. That Mitya should be the one charged with the crime represents a kind of poetic justice, since he is the passionate sensualist most controlled by his desires. This gets him into trouble not only with women—the subject of his basest secret (the dishonorable dealings with Katya)—but causes him to abuse violently three central "fathers" in the novel: Fyodor, Snegiryov, and the servant Grigory. Given this past, his unrestrained speech about his hatred and violent intentions toward Fyodor, and Grigory's blood on his hands, it is not surprising that his protestation of innocence is not believed by the police investigators. Yet book 12, which details the courtroom trial of Dmitri, is entitled "A Judicial Error," and concerns not only a conventional miscarriage of justice on technical grounds but a display of the erroneous measure of justice embodied in the modern liberal judicial process, which stands in stark contrast with the spiritual discernment of the elder.[32]

The focus of the trial is described by the narrator as the public spectacle of a sensational crime and what promises to be an interesting forensic contest—lawyers arrive "from all over," and chairs are set up for various dignitaries. Among the many spectators, the narrator reports, there is an especially large number of ladies whose faces exhibit "hysterical, greedy, almost morbid curiosity" (657). Mitya, of course, has a reputation as a "conqueror of women's hearts," and the trial promises the appearance of the two women rivals, Katerina and Grushenka—the latter being the explicit occasion behind the crime of passion. The ladies tend to favor Mitya's acquittal. The male spectators, in contrast, unanimously desire his conviction and punishment, some with considerable vindictiveness. The rivalries sensationally displayed in the crime are vicariously experienced by the spectators of the courtroom drama. The legal performance will consciously exploit these dispositions and desires, though the lawyers are not interested in them for truly moral reasons. Their interest is focused on the contemporary legal and social significance of the case, to which their careers and reputations are attached. No one is really in doubt about Mitya's guilt, the evidence being what it is. The legal process is viewed as largely a performative matter, the interesting question being what the witnesses will say (especially under examination), what kinds of arguments will be offered to interpret the evidence, and what kinds of considerations will go into the adjudication. The ladies share Madame Khokhlakov's conviction regarding the "blessing of the new courts" (577), believ-

ing that Mitya will be acquitted "because of humaneness, because of the new
ideas, because of the new feelings going around nowadays" (663). That is, according to the new legal criteria, medical evidence may be used to argue, in Mme.
Khokhlakov's words, "a legal fit of passion . . . for which they forgive everything."
The men, on the other hand, are more interested in the struggle between legal rivals, the local prosecutor (with all the evidence on his side) and the famous Petersburg defense attorney, Fetyukovich, whose brilliant legal reputation is
renowned.

It is important to note that the trial is not the locus of a dispute between Westernizers and Slavophiles on the "social question": Mitya's trial is sensational because it involves a case of parricide in which the son is accused of murdering the
father over a love rivalry, and thus it highlights a breakdown in traditional "family values"; but all of the legal actors share a commitment to Westernizing legal
reforms. Though both prosecutor and defense attorney in arguing their case appropriate Christian language pertaining to the family, it is clear that this is a fundamentally liberal debate over "Christian values" and which kind of Russian
"progressivism" they will support. The presiding judge, an educated humanist
"with the most modern ideas," is also a party to this dispute:

> His chief goal in life was to be a progressive man. . . . He took, as it turned out later,
> a rather passionate view of the Karamazov case, but only in a general sense. He was
> concerned with the phenomenon, its classification, seeing it as a product of our so-
> cial principles, as characteristic of the Russian element, and so on and so forth. But
> his attitude towards the personal character of the case, its tragedy, as well as the per-
> sons of the participants, beginning with the defendant, was rather indifferent and
> abstract, as, by the way, it perhaps ought to have been. (659)

The detached, scientific exactitude of the secular, progressivist judge stands in
sharp contrast to the engaged spiritual disposition of the elder toward matters of
justice.

The ideological line of the prosecution, expressed early in the testimony by
Rakitin, portrays the tragedy of the case as the result of ingrained habits of serfdom and the current disorder of a Russia in need of "proper institutions" (667),
presumably of the sort provided by the new law and courts. The medical exper-
tise, however, and its presumed importance as a "blessing of the new courts,"
turns out not to have a decisive role in the trial, partly because of the comical disagreement among experts about Mitya's psychological condition.[33] More crucial
is the demented confession of Ivan, which incites the hysterical outburst by Katerina, the "mathematical proof" she offers as evidence, and the vengeful testimony
against Mitya, painfully extracted from her by the judge and the prosecutor. Both

unexpected, "raving" testimonies by Ivan and Katya are ruled admissible, and Katya's letter is added to the table of material evidence (under which, Ivan has said, the devil is sitting). Katya's letter is treated as a mathematical, Euclidean "proof"—but as we know, "facts" too are appearances; their causality is not transparently evident in them. The disjuncture between courtroom evidence and the real relations of the human beings involved, and their psychological and moral meaning, is nowhere more clearly displayed than in the concluding speeches by the two lawyers.

Like Katya, Ippolit Kirillovich the prosecutor seeks "revenge"—not for a violated personal honor[34] but for the violated honor of the Russian society he so desires to save (693). His statement for the prosecution is an eloquent commentary on "civic" matters, and situates the significance of Mitya's crime in relation to the "accursed questions"—the spiritual and social principles and the future of Russian society. It is, therefore, a prophetic speech—"the chef d'oeuvre of his whole life, his swan song," as Ippolit himself considered it (693). The crime of parricide in the "nice little family" Karamazov evinces certain "signs of the times," signs that foretell the future of Russia's unrestrained social order, galloping, like Gogol's "bold Russian troika," toward an unknown goal (695). Ippolit will interpret those signs of the times by prophetically linking the psychology of Russian crime to the social question in general. Compared with the ridiculously narrow positivist psychology of the medical expert from Moscow, Ippolit's social psychology is highly astute and illuminating. Victor Terras suggests that his treatment of these questions is very like Dostoevsky's own in *Diary of a Writer*.[35] Yet although some of Ippolit's language is similar to Dostoevsky's, the overall interpretation is radically different. More importantly for our purposes here, the "judgment" (it is not really discernment) Ippolit pronounces upon the various brothers and the crime diverges markedly from elder Zosima's.

Here, then, is the prosecutor's account: Fyodor, the unfortunate victim, who begins as "a poor little sponger," turns into an opportunistic and skillful capitalist whose sensualism and "extraordinary thirst for life" over time are crudely and cynically reduced to vulgar self-gratification—"the whole spiritual side has been scrapped" (696), including any notion of fatherly duty. Such a "modern-day" father will not only evoke outrage in his children but also will instill in them crude moral ideas and practices that lead toward parricide. Ivan, for example, is a modern intellectual whose spiritual unrestraint is captured in his thesis "all is permitted," a horrifying teaching that will further corrupt others.[36] This teaching, claims the prosecutor, represents a deformed understanding of European enlightenment. Alyosha, by contrast, is still an innocent and pious youth who "clings to 'popular foundations,' so to speak" (697)—namely, the monastic life—an action, says Ippolit, manifesting an unconscious "timid despair" in the face of the depraved cynicism of his father and brothers. His escapist path ("like children frightened by ghosts" who run to the "motherly embrace of the native earth") portends an even greater danger to Russia than does Ivan's distorted enlightenment philosophy, since it so often turns into "dark mysticism on the moral side, and witless chauvinism on the civic side."[37]

It is the figure of Mitya, however, that most fully represents "ingenuous Russia": Neither fully enlightened in the European sense nor tied to the popular monastic foundations of traditional Russian piety, Mitya represents a volatile and unresolved mixture of influences both good and evil. Ippolit's portrait recapitulates significant features of Mitya's own earlier romantic "confession" to Alyosha: the love of nature, of beauty, of Schiller, combined with lustful disorder that falls "head down and heels up" into the abyss of vulgar, violent passion (107). There is a duality in the Russian makeup, claims Ippolit, that is well demonstrated in the breadth of nature of the Karamazovs, which is "capable of containing all possible opposites and of contemplating both abysses at once, the abyss above us, an abyss of lofty ideals, and the abyss beneath us, an abyss of the lowest and foulest degradation" (699). Mitya's parricidal "fit of passion," then, is in no way "unnatural"; given his bitter anxieties about money (exacerbated by Fyodor's cynical dealings) and the frenzied erotic rivalry with his father over Grushenka, it is a predictable outcome. It is not the factual details of the crime, finally, that interest the civic-minded prosecutor, so much as the general Russian malaise to which it points and to which he returns at the end of his speech.

In the chapter entitled "Psychology at Full Steam: The Galloping Troika," the prosecutor's civic-minded moralism and its terms of reference become clear. He believes he has captured the complexity of Mitya's character with the "two abysses" of conscience, but like the pre-conversion Mitya, he has assigned them a purely romantic meaning—rooted in the passions and their worldly objects (money and erotic love): Mitya goes to Mokroye to "finish the *poema*" with a memorable suicide, which is averted by his discovery that Grushenka loves him after all. Here too the "state of the criminal's soul," though no doubt tormented by the revenge of outraged nature, overcomes the suicide plan—not through the Hamletian perception of "what lies beyond"[38] but through slavish submission to the prospect of more immediate gratification of desire and the invention of an escape plan. So he hides the extremity of his situation from himself through drunken fantasy and monetary calculation. Mitya's subsequent arrest and the journey of his soul through the torments of inquisition are reduced to an "animal thirst for self-salvation" (719), and his answers to the investigators are therefore filled with subtle and indeed artistic cunning. Despite this vulgar, highly rhetorical reductionism of Mitya's soul and conscience, the prosecutor ends his speech with an impassioned charge to the jury (made up largely of local peasants) not to allow the defense attorney's rhetoric to manipulate their emotions:

> Remember still that at this moment you are in the sanctuary of our justice. Remember that you are the defenders of our truth, the defenders of our holy Russia, of her foundations, of her family, of all that is holy in her! Yes, here, at this moment, you represent Russia, and your verdict will resound not only in this courtroom but for all of Russia, and all of Russia will listen to you as to her defenders and judges, and will be either heartened or discouraged by your verdict. Then do not torment Russia and her expectations, our fateful troika is racing headlong, perhaps to its destruction. (722)

It is difficult to imagine a less consistent rhetorical appeal, given the prosecutor's initial depiction of the Russian character and its flaws. So it is not surprising that he ends his speech with a threat—the threat that the enlightened European forces of civilization may not stand aside as the troika races along but may instead seek to halt this mad course of unrestraint, out of love for humanity. Ippolit implores the jurors not to tempt European alarm or "add to their ever-increasing hatred with a verdict justifying the murder of a father by his own son!" Retributive justice must be done, not only to restore just order in Russia but also to ensure that modern liberal justice is seen to be done by enlightened Europeans, lest Russia be forced to turn over the reins of its own destiny.

The retributive inquisition conducted by Ippolit has yielded no real insight either into the facts of the case (which he completely misconstrues) or into Mitya's psychological condition, his conscience. One could say of Ippolit, as he says of Mitya, "there is a good deal of posturing here, of romantic frenzy, of . . . sentimentality" (716). And indeed Fetyukovich the defense lawyer will cruelly and repeatedly tar Ippolit with his own rhetorical brush, accusing him (as Ippolit has Mitya) of indulging in a cunning artistic game, "the creation of a novel" (*roman*— a play on words, since the Russian can also mean "romance") of his own in the display of his considerable rhetorical and psychological gifts. Fetyukovich disingenuously suggests that he cannot compete with the prosecutor as rhetorician and psychologist (i.e., as "novelist") but that he brings a judicial detachment and objectivity to the case that are locally lacking. The defense attorney—as he did in his skillful cross-examination of local witnesses—craftily introduces a doubt about the local population's ability to judge Mitya's case without "prejudice," though he will later shamelessly exploit their presumed religious prejudices, when his summation for the defense takes a highly rhetorical and bathetic turn.

First, however, Fetyukovich will show that psychology, though profound, is nonetheless "a stick with two ends." One can construe the evidence, each pertinent fact, in exactly the opposite light to that suggested by the prosecutor if one takes "the same psychology" and applies it "from the other end" (727). That is, if one assumes that Mitya did not commit the parricide and was acting with a "clear conscience," one can make out a quite different account: "I myself, gentlemen of the jury, have resorted to psychology now, in order to demonstrate that one can draw whatever conclusions one likes from it. It all depends on whose hands it is in" (728). He then proceeds to lay out an account of the facts that is exactly correct—not only with regard to Mitya's actions and motivations but also in its characterization of Smerdyakov. Contrary to the prosecutor's impression that Smerdyakov is a sick and timid victim, Fetyukovich finds him spiteful, mistrustful, ambitious, vengeful, and burning with envy behind his mask of naïveté—and quite cunning in his testimony. As for the prosecutor's argument that Smerdyakov had "enough conscience" to write a suicide note "so as not to blame anybody" (712), and thus could easily have added a confession to the crime, Fetyukovich begs to differ:

> Excuse me, but conscience implies repentance, and it may be that the suicide was not repentant but simply in despair. Despair and repentance are two totally different things. Despair can be malicious and implacable, and the suicide, as he was taking his life, may at that moment have felt twice as much hatred for those whom he had envied all his life. Gentlemen of the jury, beware of a judicial error! (740)

Up to this point the defense attorney's account has achieved the truth,[39] and he himself proceeds to "swear by all that's holy" that he completely believes this explanation of the facts. And yet the reader already knows that Mitya has no such assurance regarding what his lawyer believes. He has told Alyosha: "Forget the lawyer! I talked with him about everything [Fetyukovich's true account is really Mitya's own]. He's a smooth Petersburg swindler. A Bernard! He just doesn't believe a pennyworth of what I say. He thinks I killed him, can you imagine?" (593). Consequently, at the end of his summation, Fetyukovich's tone changes dramatically, and he extends his appeal to the jury beyond the issue of judicial error: "Remember, you are given an immense power, the power to bind and to loose," citing the words of the Gospel (Matthew 16:19; 18:18).[40] One is reminded of the prosecutor's "sanctuary of justice" and "defenders of holy Russia and her holy foundations" language; but such rhetorical excesses are "an adultery of thought" in the argument of the smooth Petersburg swindler. Ironically, the words of Jesus on binding and loosing pertain not at all to secular courts of law but to relationships in the church community—in particular, to the spiritual power of moral discernment and intended reconciliation between divided members of a community.[41] The procedure outlined in the Gospel stands in stark contrast to the judicial decision of a courtroom jury. In the Biblical text, indeed, the power to bind and to loose is not attached in any way to a formal office, and the intention is not retributive but rather restorative. It is in fact related precisely to the elder's language of conscience as "the law of Christ," a phrase that appears in Galatians 6: "My friends, if anyone is detected in a transgression, you who have received the Spirit should restore such a one in a spirit of gentleness. Take care that you yourselves are not tempted. Bear one another's burdens, and in this way you will fulfill the law of Christ" (6:1–2). Restorative justice, for St. Paul as for the elder, requires a penitential consciousness, the awareness of one's own weakness and solidarity in guilt. It becomes clear that the pious lawyer understands neither his own Biblical language nor the profundity of his earlier observations on the difference between repentance and despair.

Fetyukovich begins his "adultery in thought" with the seductive rhetoric of sincerity: "I have it in my heart to speak out something more to you, for I also sense a great struggle in your hearts and minds . . . Let us all be sincere" (741). He will address the "prejudice" of the jurors and the local populace with regard to the crime of parricide. The prejudice is rooted in spiritual Christianity and its mystical elevation of filiation in traditional trinitarian language about God the Father and God the Son. The authority of such language, implies the prosecutor, should not be accepted blindly and should not be allowed in this case to influence the judgment of Mitya's crime—at least, not negatively. So, gentlemen of the jury, what is a real father, what "great idea" is contained in fatherhood? Precisely the kind of loving care and sacrificial attention that are so conspicuously absent in Fyodor Karamazov. Indeed, if anyone is responsible for the "wild beast" that Mitya has become, it is his neglectful, cynical, and perverse father who does not deserve to be called a father. And yet, despite this, the evidence also shows that Mitya has a passionate and noble, sensitive heart. Such a heart should be treated with gentleness, not cruel vindictiveness, in keeping with "the crucified lover of mankind" who gave his life for his sheep. Here the "swindling" begins, as Fetyukovich cites the New Testament and uses Christian language to distort the teachings of Christ.[42] He rejects the teachings of traditional, "mystical" Christianity in order to develop a progressive, rational account of fatherhood and filial love: "Love that is not justified by the father is an absurdity, an impossibility," and therefore only those who are worthy fathers may be considered true fathers. It is our Christian duty here "to foster only those convictions that are justified by reason and experience, that have passed through the crucible of analysis." Hence, the only way to establish fatherhood is as follows:

> Let the son stand before the father and ask him reasonably: "Father, tell me why should I love you? Father, prove to me that I should love you"—and if the father

can, if he is able to answer and give him proof, then we have a real, normal family, established not just on mystical prejudice, but on reasonable, self-accountable, and strictly humane foundations. In the opposite case, if the father can give no proof— the family is finished then and there: he is not a father to his son, and the son is free and has the right henceforth to look upon his father as a stranger and even as his enemy. (745–746)

Mitya's murderous deed, therefore, was an involuntary, unrestrained, but natural "fit of passion" for avenging the evil deeds of an enemy—"like all things in nature." But such a murder is not a parricide; indeed, it is not even a murder. It could be so considered only "out of prejudice."

Fetyukovich here puts not only Fyodor but fatherhood itself on trial (using language similar to that in Ivan's "Rebellion" against God's world). He justifies a lie in the soul in order to hide real guilt. Definitions of parricide and murder, as well as moral norms governing filial and familial relations, are matters of social convention, and therefore must be justified rationally within the terms of this world (even if one wishes to appeal to religious sanctions for rhetorical or political reasons). As Fyodor did not fulfill his parental duties, he does not deserve to be called a father. As he was a perverse and evil man, not only neglecting but deliberately provoking his sensitive son to wrath, the murder was not a truly evil act but a natural and reasonable consequence. In case the peasants in the jury box still stand behind their traditional prejudices, however, Fetyukovich will conclude with yet another twisted rhetorical appeal—this time parodying the words both of Matthew 25 (a judgment scene) and of Zosima concerning guilt and the punishment of conscience. If Mitya is condemned, he will justly be confirmed in his bitterness toward his fellow citizens. He will say: They did nothing to relieve the misery of my childhood or to make me a better man, they did not give me to eat and drink, did not visit me in prison, and now they have exiled me to penal servitude. Such a verdict will destroy what natural goodness is left in him, thus easing his conscience even while chafing his heart. The true, restorative punishment would be to "overwhelm him with your mercy" by a great act of compassion. He will then be overwhelmed with repentance and his debt to society, and his soul will expand in tender gratitude. This will represent a vindication of Russia as a "majestic Russian chariot" guided by its salvific civil justice, not a mad, mystical troika: "It is for me, insignificant as I am, to remind you that the Russian courts exist not only for punishment but also for the salvation of the ruined man! Let other nations have the letter and punishment, we have the spirit and meaning, the salvation and regeneration of the lost. And if so, if such indeed are Russia and her courts, then—onward Russia!" (747–748).

Though Fetyukovich's plea for mercy, for a punishment of conscience, bears a superficial resemblance to the ideas of elder Zosima, it is not a plea (Richard Peace to the contrary[43]) that Zosima—or Dostoevsky—could accept. Yet just as some of Ippolit's language can be identified with Dostoevsky's own in spite of basic substantive differences, so too can the defense attorney's. Language, like psychology and various forms of authority, is obviously "two-ended." In 1877, Dostoevsky played a highly publicized role (in print) in the criminal trials of a pregnant stepmother named Kornilova, who in a fit of passion directed at her husband, threw her stepdaughter out of a window.[44] In his comments on the eventual acquittal of this woman, who confessed to and showed remorse for her crime of child abuse, Dostoevsky takes up the issue of "mercy" in terms comparable to Fetyukovich's appeal for Mitya. In doing so he is accused in print by a critic of being too "impressionable," too soft on crime, for not having adequate concern for victims, in this case helpless children, and the deterrence of further such crimes. Dostoevsky's comments show that his own understanding of mercy differs crucially from Fetyukovich's, in that this understanding is premised on an awareness of *true guilt*, not on medical or environmental or other "rational" excuses for crime. In cases where there is genuine repentance, mercy can lead to a higher happiness and clarity of conscience (which also bears a measure of suffering in it) precisely because it does not deny guilt. Such mercy also places an obligation on the soul, not through punitive measures but through the more powerful motivation of love: "And so the whole question in the Kornilova case amounts merely to the kind of soil in which the seed fell"—if on good soil, the truly penitent heart, she will be restored to life.[45]

Fetyukovich's dramatic but twisted rhetorical display evokes a rapturous tide of enthusiasm in the courtroom. The prosecutor seeks to stem the tide by rebutting this "novel upon novel" offered by Fetyukovich: that this murder is not really a murder, that parricide is a mere prejudice, that Christ's language of "measure for measure" justifies the murder of those who offend us rather than the cheek-turning forgiveness even of our enemies. But with this last point, and his subsequent appeal to the high Christology of "the whole of Orthodox Russia," which Fetyukovich has so distorted, the prosecutor also unwittingly subverts his own retributive argument—though he does not see it. It is clear that his appeal to traditional beliefs and family values is simply in the service of a conventional moralism that separates personal morality (of the sort advocated in the gospels) from social institutions (which are guided by liberal progressivist notions of order). He seeks here strategically to impugn the personal piety of his legal rival and the inexcusable behavior of Mitya—not in order to apply the spiritual truth of Christ to his own line of argument on civic order and justice (it has no place there), but in order to win the case. What we have in these two legal representatives are differing ideological rhetorics (one "conservative" or "reactionary," and the other a kind of revolutionary romanticism) on the common ground of liberal progressivism. Social salvation for both lawyers lies in the modern courts, though they disagree on the best juridical and political methods to attain such an enlightened society—a hard-line "law and order" approach based on the protection of individual rights, the logic of deterrence, and the security of the family (Ippolit); or radical social engineering and the exercise of "social compassion" (Fetyukovich). Of course, this is to put the best construal on what could simply be interpreted as the crass manipulation of rhetorical images, designed to win the case for personal glory.

A frequent observer of criminal trials, Dostoevsky believed this to be an inherent problem in modern adversarial justice, which assumes that a distorting construal of the facts and exaggerated arguments on each side will somehow lead to the truth that presumably lies somewhere in between.[46] Not only was Dostoevsky suspicious of such assumptions (namely, that "ultimately, the truth does emerge from all this and emerges even mechanically, so to say, through a most devious process," 1167); he also believed that public processes and practices of this kind breed cynicism and lack of discernment not only in the lawyers but also in the public watching the spectacle: "People no longer yearn for truth but for talent, so long as it can amuse and divert them." He argued that these mechanisms of adversarial justice, which cater to appearance and spectacle, should be replaced by the disciplined pursuit of and argument for the truth. In *The Brothers Karamazov,* such an alternative approach to social and political justice is offered in the practical institution of elders and the ascetic practices of the church. Alyosha bears witness to the manner in which this alternative vision may be taken out of the monastery and into the world.

## The Political Danger of a Nonpolitical Ideal: An Arendtian Objection

Before we examine Alyosha's penitential political practice in the concluding pages of *The Brothers Karamazov,* let us consider briefly an important objection to public appeals to mercy and compassion, whether Christian or socialist. When Dostoevsky suggests that the politics of the French Revolution and of Russian socialism[47] address the Christian questions "from the other end," it is important to see exactly what he means to say, since this is explicitly at issue in the crucial exchanges between Alyosha and Kolya, in book 10. In order to clarify this, let us consider Hannah Arendt's interesting comments on "The Social Question" in her book, *On Revolution,* in which she explicitly refers to Dostoevsky's "Grand Inquisitor." Arendt asserts that *le peuple* is the key word for understanding the

French Revolution, and that its definition was born out of compassion by those exposed to the spectacle of suffering and misery on the part of *le peuple toujours malheureux,* in which they did not themselves share.[48] This politics of compassion, argues Arendt, is misguided from the outset because by its true nature it must be evoked by and directed toward the particular—it has no capacity for generalization. When it becomes generalized, seeking the liberation, equality, and brotherhood of all in a social *volonté génerale,* it quickly becomes totalitarian—a spiritual unity of will rather than of shared worldly institutions.[49] Dostoevsky's poetic depiction of the Grand Inquisitor is designed to point up the stark contrast between the apolitical spirit of true compassion represented in Christ and the tragic and self-defeating politics of distorted compassion represented by the prophetic words of the Inquisitor. According to Arendt, Dostoevsky's point is to show the impossibility of turning Christ's teachings and deeds of compassion into a political order of rational law:

> To Dostoevsky, the sign of Jesus' divinity clearly was his ability to have compassion with all men in their singularity, that is, without lumping them together into some such entity as one suffering mankind. The greatness of the story, apart from its theological implications, lies in that we are made to feel how false the idealistic, high-flown phrases of the most exquisite pity sound the moment they are confronted with compassion.[50]

To Arendt, the silence of Christ in Ivan's poem is the very language of compassion, listening attentively to the suffering Inquisitor and responding finally not in speech but in a personal gesture, the kiss. This compassion expresses the very image of God portrayed by Rousseau, as one "who could understand the passions of men without feeling any of them,"[51] but in Arendt's view it cannot become a political model without grotesque distortion. True compassion abolishes the worldly space between human beings—the very space where political speech and affairs occur. It cannot establish lasting worldly institutions (legislative and legal), even as it cannot engage in the argument, negotiation, and compromise of political reason and law. Were such pure compassion, such "absolute goodness," to take political action in the world, it could only do so with the "swift and direct" (one might say "apocalyptic") application of destruction so as to establish the terms of goodness without compromise.[52] This is so, says Arendt, because it is rooted in a "goodness that is beyond virtue, and hence beyond temptation, ignorant of the argumentative reasoning by which man fends off temptations."[53]

It is ironic indeed, then, that "The Grand Inquisitor" is structured as a trial in which Christ's responses to the three temptations are called into question. Arendt's claim, it would seem, is the exact opposite of Dostoevsky's. For her

Cain's murder of Abel remains paradigmatic for politics and law in a fallen world. The only other *political* possibility she can see is—like Rousseau and the French revolutionists—to reverse the primordial crime by having Abel kill Cain. This deed of violence in the name of "original goodness" would unleash the same chain of evildoing as did original sin, but it would also erase the clear distinction between good and evil. In other words, perhaps a politics of pure love could exist in heaven, where no evil and no suffering block it, but it cannot build real communities of justice on the earth. In this at least, it would seem, the Grand Inquisitor is right.

In order to discern how exactly Dostoevsky's conception of Christian politics differs from Arendt's interpretation, it is necessary to explore Arendt's understanding of "public virtue," which is the only sort of speech and action she considers appropriate to politics. The term "public," she maintains, signifies two related phenomena: the widest possible "appearance" or publicity; and the common, visible artifacts and institutions that gather human beings into a common world.[54] Christian charity fails the test on both counts. As a virtue, love is private and "worldless"—especially the Christian love taught by Jesus, which seeks to hide its good deeds from view (see Matthew 6).[55] Nor can the bond of "brotherly love" found a truly public political community, says Arendt, although "it is admirably fit to carry a group of essentially worldless people through the world, a group of saints or a group of criminals [a group of martyrs or a group of inquisitors], provided only that it is understood that the world itself is doomed."[56] Indeed, the very language used by Christians to describe community—"a 'body,' whose members were to be related to each other like brothers of a family"[57]—is "unpolitical" and "nonpublic," indeed even "antipolitical." According to Arendt, the only communities in which the principle of charity became the basis for some sort of political order were the monastic orders, in which excellence viewed as a source of pride constantly undermined the building up of a lasting public life or memory (an "earthly immortality"). A politics of compassion could truly exist only in heaven. Substantively, though not ideologically, Arendt's position on Christianity parallels Gradovsky's.

However, such an analysis of politics assumes a discontinuity between earth and heaven, this world and the "other world," public and private, that Dostoevsky's Christian vision rejects. The kingdom of God and its justice (*dikaiosyne*; see Matthew 6:33), although not fully apparent to the external eye, are nevertheless present on the earth and are not unaware of earthly needs. Furthermore, their action is not unworldly but is precisely the subject matter for a generative political memory, the paradigmatic story of Jesus and the narrative of the New Testament, and the subsequent witness of the church in time as the embodied enactment of that pattern. The immortality that Christians seek is not purely "otherworldly," as if it has no connection with this world; rather, the telos of history in the "new Jerusalem" that "comes down out of heaven" is intimately connected to actions in this world and to the "power" or "authority" depicted in the person of Jesus, the slain Lamb.

# "Like Children":
# Educating the Russian Boys

Dostoevsky displays his approach to the "social question" from the "other end," in the educative exchange between Alyosha and the leader of the gang of boys, Kolya Krasotkin. Robert Belknap has suggested that Kolya is a parody of both Ivan and the Grand Inquisitor, educated as he has been by Ivan's intellectual sidekick Rakitin.[58] But "parody" may not be exactly the right term, since Kolya is a highly precocious student and an intimidatingly accomplished, charismatic leader of other children. He is more like a double whose mimetic enactment (as a fatherless only child) of these models of desire becomes the occasion, in the novel, for revealing the capacity of Alyosha's contrasting "authority," modeled after the elder's, to engage and reorder the stance of the "Russian boys" on the eternal questions.

When the brothers Ivan and Alyosha "get acquainted" in the tavern conversation leading up to Ivan's recitation of his prose poem, it is clear that they are drawn to one another not only by blood and shared childhood memories but by shared interest in the perennial questions—an interest shared by "all of young Russia" (233). The question of how the ever-youthful erotic love of life is related to its meaning in the order of things is the subject of this discussion by these two "Russian boys," who want to get acquainted with one another.[59] Ivan sees that this modern Russian discussion is dominated by European hypotheses—that "most precious graveyard" of ideas summed up in Voltaire's aphorism: *S'il n'existait pas Dieu, il faudrait l'inventer* [If God did not exist, it would be necessary to invent him] (234). Enlightened European hypotheses (as Nietzsche also prophetically recognized) all revolve around the death of God—that is, the self-conscious recognition that ideas of God are human inventions used in support of certain moral and political conventions of order. Ivan goes on to make an important observation about the "Russian boys"—namely that "what is a hypothesis there [in Europe] immediately becomes an axiom [i.e., a basis for action] for a Russian boy" (235). He then makes his "confession" to Alyosha about his "essence," his "thesis"—that it is not God but this world of God's, created by God, that he cannot accept on the grounds of its injustice. For Ivan this is no abstract intellectual hypothesis but rather a practical question of how to live; hence, he says, he has begun (as Russian conversations of this sort all do) "as stupidly as possible" (236). Why? Because whereas "reason is a scoundrel, stupidity is direct and honest," and it gets straight to the existential point. The point of Ivan's "stupid" confession to his pious brother is "not that I want to corrupt you and push you off your foundation; perhaps I want to be healed by you"—and he suddenly smiles like a little boy.

What is the illness of which Ivan seeks healing? We have seen Alyosha's later diagnosis of it as "the torments of . . . a deep conscience" (655); here, Ivan calls it "my despair" (236). Kierkegaard's exposition of Christian psychology helps us understand Ivan's spiritual illness as the self's inability to relate to the eternal God (of which it is a reflection), and therefore its inability to reflect accurately upon itself—in other words, as impaired self-consciousness.[60] This relation is indeed the ground of human spiritual freedom, the ability to transcend the immediacy of one's external, temporal environment through reflection on various possibilities for action and becoming a certain sort of person before God. Despair, defined in Christian terms, is the inability to act upon this spiritual freedom to be (or to become) a self within time yet also in relation to eternity. In effect it is a person's desire "to tear his self away from the power that established it."[61] According to Kierkegaard there are various forms of despair, correlative to the level of spiritual self-consciousness a person has. Ivan, Alyosha says, is "deep." His acceptance of "secular" European hypotheses is not smooth and unself-conscious—he is tormented by the reduction of human life to Euclidean finitude, to the "earthy force of Karamazov baseness" without the brooding presence of the Holy Spirit (220; cf. 230, 263). He realizes that to actualize himself in such a manner will lead to suicide of one sort or another—such an expenditure of the erotic thirst for life will not keep despair at bay, he speculates, past the age of thirty. On the other hand, he cannot understand or accept the world as it is, with its unjust and arbitrary suffering—especially the suffering of children who are punished for the sins of their base fathers, which is, says Ivan, "reasoning from another world; for the human heart here on earth it is incomprehensible" (238). Such a world and such a God are impossible to love.

In Ivan, then, the despair of the human condition divided from God is not unconscious but rather highly developed. He is a man not of immediacy but of what Kierkegaard calls "inclosing reserve,"[62] a self trapped within its inner division and yet unable to repent of it by entering into relation with God. Ivan understands that he is taking his stand on his own ground: "I've made up my mind to stick to the fact . . . "; "Oh, with my pathetic, earthly, Euclidean mind, I know only . . . "; "I need retribution . . . "; "I want to see with my own eyes . . . "; "while I am on the earth, I hasten to take my own measures . . . "; "I absolutely renounce all higher harmony . . . "; "I want to remain with unrequited suffering . . . and my unquenched indignation, *even if I am wrong*" (243–245). Ivan ends his long lament, punctuated throughout by the first person *I*, with his rejection of the "too high"

price to be paid for admission to the divine harmony game. His profound intellectual and moral honesty requires him to "most respectfully" return his admission ticket to God. "That is rebellion," says Alyosha, and even here Ivan is conscious of the spiritual implication: "Rebellion? I don't like hearing such word from
you . . . One cannot live by rebellion, and I want to live" (245). Even here Ivan is
fully conscious. He understands that suicide is the most despairing attempt of the
spirit to escape its existence before God.[63] Yet there is another form of despair,
which actively wills to live even in that rebellion by which one cannot live—this is
the politics of rebellious despair depicted in Ivan's prose poem. "This kind of despair is rarely seen in the world," says Kierkegaard. "Such characters really appear
only in the poets, the real ones, who always lend 'demonic' ideality . . . to their creations."[64] Ivan is such a poet; and it is important to see that the politics of "The
Grand Inquisitor" is not separated or separable from the state of consciousness—
from the inclosing reserve—that it represents. It is the consistent outworking in
the world of the separation from God that represents parodic self-contradiction—
the fact that only the spiritual cover of seeming faith can hide this height of rebellion against the relation of faith, from oneself and from others. This is the lie in the
soul enacted as public "order," which is truly in violent rebellion against divine
harmony. It can only intensify the suffering and division that give rise to it in the
first place, even as they claim to overcome it.

We will consider this poetic, idealized form of despair in its disclosure before
the silent Christ more fully in the next chapter. For the moment we are interested
in the boyish "double" of the despairing Ivan and his legendary Inquisitor—
Kolya Krasotkin, who practices the politics of enlightened despotism as leader of
the gang of Russian boys. Kolya is a hyper-self-conscious almost-fourteen-year-
old who is well-read, a show-off, and above all, "extremely vain."[65] Because of
this, although he is obviously possessed of deep feelings, he sternly shuns all
forms of what he calls "sentimental slop" so as to cultivate a disciplined regime of
obedient children—much as he trains dogs. The basis of Kolya's rule parallels the
Inquisitor's parodic correction of Christ's relation to the "three earthly powers"—miracle, mystery, and authority. His dazzling stunts of death-defying
bravado gain him a reputation as a "desperado" even among older children; and
his mysterious secret regarding "who founded Troy," a derivative bit of hidden information taken from one of his dead father's books, is used to create the impression that he has a superior intellect and could even "show up the teacher."[66]
His authority is exercised as a patronizing, protective "love" that rewards and
threatens by turns, so as to instill his strict code of discipline and loyalty in others. One can see this in Kolya's treatment of the "squirts" he babysits, in the peasants he meets, and above all in the schoolboys—Ilyusha, in particular.

Kolya already has a well-developed (for a child) "inclosing reserve"[67]—he hates sentimentalities and prides himself on his superior knowledge of human nature and the honorable ideals served by his disciplined pedagogy. He boasts to Alyosha about having saved Ilyusha, Snegiryov's small, weak, but proud boy, from his bullying classmates:

> I beat them up—and they adore me, do you know that Karamazov? . . . And I like kids generally. . . . So, after that they stopped beating Ilyusha, and I took him under my protection. I saw he was a proud boy, I can tell you how proud he is, but in the end he gave himself up to me like a slave, obeyed my every order, listened to me as though I were God, tried to copy me. . . . I was teaching him, developing him. . . . I noticed that a sort of tenderness, sensitivity, was developing in the boy, and, you know, I am decidedly the enemy of all sentimental slop. . . . Moreover, there were contradictions: he was proud, but devoted to me like a slave—devoted to me like a slave, yet suddenly his eyes would flash and he wouldn't even want to agree with me, he'd argue, beat on the wall. . . . It wasn't that he disagreed with the ideas, I could see that he was simply rebelling against me personally, because I responded coldly to his sentimentalities. And so, the more sentimental he became, the colder I was, in order to season him; I did it on purpose, because it's my conviction. I had in mind to discipline his character, to shape him up, to create a person. (534)

Two events then coincided to break Ilyusha's spirit, each tied to negative forms of spiritual causality and pointing to the close connection between the personal (or psychological) and the social or political levels. Smerdyakov had befriended Ilyusha and taught him a "beastly trick"—they stuck a pin into a piece of bread and tossed it to a hungry "yard dog" Zhuchka, who swallowed it and started squealing, running in circles, and finally disappearing, obviously in pain. Ilyusha, full of remorse, "confesses" his deed to Kolya, and Kolya sees an opportunity to discipline him and break his pride. And so he temporarily "breaks relations" with Ilyusha, whom he accuses of being a scoundrel. It is an excommunication that "struck [Ilyusha] terribly," and he rebels against Kolya. Kolya says to Alyosha: "I confess, I cheated here, I pretended to be more indignant than maybe I really was. . . . Secretly I just meant to give him the silent treatment for a few days, and then, seeing his repentance, to offer my hand again." However, Ilyusha has already repented—not only in his heart but to his mentor Kolya. It is not surprising then that he should rebel against this gratuitous external punishment imposed by Kolya, which chafes his heart. Kolya's punitive act not only fails to discern Ilyusha's heart; it reveals Kolya's perverse desire to play God in a grotesquely abusive parody of "binding and loosing." Instead of repenting of his excess when Ilyusha rebels, however, Kolya seeks to break his "free little spirit" by "showing complete contempt for him, turning away whenever I met him, or smiling ironically" (535).

At the same time, Ilyusha's father is publicly humiliated in the town tavern by Mitya, after which the schoolboys mercilessly tease the now unprotected Ilyusha—occasioning the violent attack on Kolya by Ilyusha (sticking him with a penknife) and the stone-throwing incident during which Alyosha first becomes involved with the children and with the Snegiryov family. All this is enough to make sickly Ilyusha deathly ill; but even then Kolya is unwilling to reconcile with him, for his own egotistical "special reasons." Kolya's ordering authority is detached from love and affection, rooted in a self-glorifying, godlike protection that tries to mold others in his superior image for their own good, which he alone can judge. Ilyusha's rebellion against this order is rooted in a higher conscience, which he will not renounce—not even to gain reacceptance into the good graces of the acclaimed Kolya—and also in the name of his publicly humiliated but loving and affectionate father, to whom he is passionately and loyally devoted.

Ilyusha, however, is dying, and he is also suffering from a guilty conscience for the mean trick he and Smerdyakov played on the dog. As Alyosha sorrowfully reports to Kolya, "Would you believe that three times, since [Ilyusha] got sick, I've heard him say in tears to his father: 'I'm sick because I killed Zhuchka, papa, God is punishing me for it'—and he won't give up the idea!" (536). Alyosha has quietly and unostentatiously brought the other boys together with Ilyusha in reconciliation, so as to ease the boy's suffering. In contrast, Kolya, who has actually managed to find Zhuchka, keeps this "resurrecting" news from Ilyusha, in order to prepare a show: For several weeks Kolya secretly trains the dog (which he renames *Perezvon*) in order to pull off a "real stunt," a theatrical performance in which the dead Zhuchka (trained by Kolya to play dead) will be miraculously raised back to life. During this time Kolya has also avoided the gathering of boys, which he considers "sentimentalizing." When he finally goes to give his performance, he makes it clear to his sidekick Smurov that "I am going on my own, because such is my will, while you were dragged there by Alexei Karamazov, so there's a difference" (526). Smurov denies this. Alyosha's reconciling act has been done in such a way that the boys have experienced it as their own, as the narrator makes clear:

> His whole art in this case lay in getting them together one by one, without "sentimental slop," but as if quite unintentionally and inadvertently. And this brought enormous relief to Ilyusha in his suffering. Seeing an almost tender friendship and concern for him in all these boys, his former enemies, he was very touched. Only Krasotkin was missing, and this lay as a terrible burden on his heart. (539)

Alyosha has also sought indirectly (through Smurov) to encourage Kolya to come, but at no point does he impose himself on Kolya. It is clear that this sense of freedom intrigues Kolya—that, and the attractive stories he has heard about Alyosha from the other boys, though he always displays an air of "scornful indifference" and critical distance—and so he very much wants to make Alyosha's acquaintance. Finally he is ready to make his dramatic appearance.

The contrast between the authority of Kolya and that of Alyosha is starkly depicted in this gathering at the bedside of the dying Ilyusha, and again the setting is given a political description. As Robert Belknap nicely shows, Kolya's poses imitate the prescribed attitudes and ideas of nineteenth-century Russian radicalism,[68] many of which he has learned from his "remarkable" teacher, Rakitin. "I am a socialist, Smurov," Kolya pronounces sententiously: "'And what is a socialist?' asked Smurov. 'It's when everyone is equal, everyone has property in common, there are no marriages, and each one has whatever religion and laws he likes, and all the rest. You're not grown up enough for that yet, you're too young'" (527).

And yet, having just admonished Smurov never to stoop to lying—"not even for a good cause" (525), as when Smurov suggests that he pass off Perezvon as Zhuchka in order to comfort Ilyusha—Kolya proceeds to lie brazenly to a peasant they encounter about the practice of being whipped at school:

> "I like talking with the people, and am always glad to do them justice."
> "Why did you lie about them whipping us at school?" asked Smurov.
> "But I had to comfort him."
> "How so?"
> "You know, Smurov, I don't like it when people keep asking questions, when they don't understand the first time. . . . A peasant's notion is that schoolboys are whipped and ought to be whipped: what kind of schoolboy is he if he isn't whipped? And if I were suddenly to tell him that they don't whip us in school, it would upset him. Anyway, you don't understand these things. One has to know how to talk with the people" (528).[69]

Kolya, by virtue of his superior knowledge and special insight, is clearly not under the same moral obligations he imposes on his followers. He exercises the prerogative of the "noble lie" even though he requires the absolute honesty and accountability of his followers. The rhetoric of equality and "the people" masks the profound vanity that underlies Kolya's dictatorial rule.

Alyosha's responses to Kolya stand in sharp contrast to Kolya's arrogant posturing and intellectual bullying. When Kolya and Smurov arrive at the Snegiryov house, Kolya sends Smurov in to call Alyosha to meet him outside in the freezing cold. Alyosha, who already has reason to be angry and offended by Kolya's cruel behavior, rushes out to meet him with genuine affection, holding out his hand and saying, "Here you are at last, we've been waiting for you so!" (533). The eagerness of each to make the acquaintance of the other is reminiscent of the earlier meeting between Ivan and Alyosha. But Alyosha has clearly changed since that conversation in the tavern—not only in dress (he has changed his cassock for secular clothes) but in manner. No longer timid or tentative, he has begun his monastic sojourn in the world as a "steadfast fighter" (363)—or, to use Kierkegaard's fitting terminology, a "knight of faith."[70] The elder, in addressing that "lady of little faith," Madame Khokhlakov (who at this point in the novel has lost even what little faith she had[71]), had recommended "the labor and perseverance" of active love as a cure for lack of faith. Such love, if it is to be real and not a mere dream or passing fantasy about "mankind in general," entails a death to the immediacy of love's reward, to the impatient desire to see love temporally vindicated. It entails a dying to the finite self and its claims in order to be reborn into the spiritual causality of divine immortality, in which the community of love is built up through humble servanthood. As Kierkegaard points out, however, what distinguishes the knight of faith from the (Platonic) "knight of infinite resignation," who also dies to the temporal vindication of love by dwelling in the higher sufficiency of the love of the eternal, is the knight's faith that even as he gives up the worldly objects of his love through self-relinquishment, he will get them back again by divine gift. That is, the objects of earthly love are relinquished and yet continue to be fully loved and joyfully embraced and cared for—without ironic detachment or resigned sorrow—in the lived hope that all loving worldly relations will be consummated (or "resurrected") on the basis of mysterious, divine possibility. Such a faith is, humanly speaking, absurd, since it gives itself completely to an outcome that cannot be calculated on the basis of immanent physical, psychological, or sociohistorical causality. Calculation of this kind is impossible, not only because there are too many finite factors and variables but more importantly because faith's love participates in the eternal agency of God, who is also an actor in the worldly drama. Faith's love is thus, as Kierkegaard's meditation on Abraham's sacrifice of Isaac shows, an *ordeal* of love that requires that one abandon all possessive or proprietary claims on the objects of love (whether that be son or elder, lover or friend), at the same time being fully open to receiving and fully enjoying the return of the loved one as God's gift.

Alyosha has learned from love's ordeal, relinquishing his egoistic hold upon and proprietary hopes for elder Zosima's earthly vindication, only to see a transfigured ("miraculous") vindication in the heart-shaking but oh-so-earthly encounter with Grushenka. He expresses a selfless yet completely engaged and earthly love for Lise (to whom he is informally betrothed), which enables him to relate to her with complete, caring candor despite her destructive erotic games and sadomasochistic fantasies. It also enables him to break the cycle of erotic rivalry among the brothers—not only Grushenka's attempted seduction but also Lise's flirtatious and twisted relationship with Ivan. Instead of taking offense, Alyosha discerns the sickness that fuels their mutually destructive dalliance, and he seeks to address it therapeutically in each.[72]

This selfless yet completely engaged love is given political expression in Alyosha's response to Kolya and the gang of boys. Alyosha makes no attempt to control the free response of the schoolboys to Ilyusha, nor to make them feel a duty imposed by guilt. When Kolya finally shows up on his own swaggering terms, Alyosha makes no effort to deflate the pretension by showing up Kolya's self-important ideas (which he could easily do) or by lecturing him. He neither judges Kolya nor flatters him (as Snegiryov does) but rather treats him as an equal, listening to his views and responding to them in open, vulnerable honesty. Interestingly, it is precisely this nonjudgmental, affectionate openness that unsettles Kolya—he feels his vain posturing to be judged by it—and completely disarms him.

In order to develop the contrast between the Christlike authority of the knight of faith Alyosha and the Inquisitorial authority of the despotic Kolya, we might examine the uses made by each of the death and resurrection symbolism that pervades the novel. Kolya's secret project, his "special reasons" for avoiding the gathering of boys and for showing up unannounced, is to stage the glorious resurrection of the dog Zhuchka, whose presumed death has weighed so heavily on the dying Ilyusha's conscience. Kolya's reason for staging the event has little to do with easing Ilyusha's torment. Indeed, he not only intensifies Ilyusha's suffering by keeping silent about the found dog for weeks; but when he finally arrives, he torments Ilyusha with the question, "Do you remember Zhuchka, old man?" (543), and mercilessly prolongs Ilyusha's agony before revealing the dog, in order more dramatically and impressively to show off his own glory in having brought the dog back to life, and thus to relieve the suffering to which he has hideously contributed. Ilyusha's evil deed and suffering have become the "manure" for Kolya's godlike orchestration, played in praise of Kolya's glory (compare Ivan's accusations against God, 244). Here is the answer to Ivan's question regarding what children have to do with it: There is solidarity not only in suffering but also in sin.

Kolya's egoism prevents him from seeing the intense suffering he is causing Ilyusha. When he finally calls in his dog and Ilyusha recognizes him as Zhuchka, Kolya reveals that he found him by the marks described by Ilyusha during his confession to Kolya: "I found him by those marks! I found him right then, very quickly" (544). The other boys are dutifully impressed—"Bravo, Krasotkin!" and much applause. Kolya, however, has more to show—"what counts is how it happened, not anything else!" (545). He has taught the dog clever tricks, and a particularly amusing one is the way he "plays dead," with all four legs in the air. Ilyusha watches it all "with the same suffering smile," and Alyosha alone realizes the "killing effect" of the moment: "'And can it be, can it be that you refused to come all this time only in order to train the dog!' Alyosha exclaimed with involuntary reproach. 'That's precisely the reason,' Kolya shouted in the most naive way. 'I wanted to show him in all his glory!'" (545). Kolya follows up this glorious display with another symbol of the power he wields—a little toy cannon that fires real shot. It is a gift for Ilyusha: "You're already happy as it is, well, here's some more happiness for you!"—Kolya is ecstatic. This display is followed by Kolya's rehearsal of the shared "memories" of his deeds of power—the train, the goose, and the secret knowledge about "who founded Troy."

Aside from the one involuntary reproach, Alyosha has remained silent during Kolya's triumphal entry, and his silence "gradually began to rankle the vain boy" (550). He begins to worry that Alyosha despises him, and his pronouncements grow increasingly outrageous and pretentious. Alyosha, however, refuses to publicly embarrass Kolya, simply questioning him on his views. It is during their private conversation outside Ilyusha's room that Alyosha at last punctures the pretension—not so much by his direct responses to Kolya's ideological posturing as by the manner of his engagement. Kolya begins the private conversation awkwardly, expressing his respect for the "rare person" in Alyosha but at the same time dismissing his mystical monasticism as an illness that "the touch of reality" will cure. The illness, claims Kolya, is the belief in God and the host of prejudices and forms of social oppression that go along with traditional Christian faith. He confesses (following his mentor Rakitin), "I'm a socialist, Karamazov, I am an incorrigible socialist" (554)—and "I have no prejudices" (555). Alyosha, however, does not enter into an ideological debate or impose his intellectual superiority—he responds "softly, restrainedly, and quite naturally, as if he were talking to someone of the same age or even older than himself," and Kolya is struck by Alyosha's openness in leaving it "precisely up to him, little Kolya, to resolve the question" (554). This makes it possible for Kolya finally to confess at a deeper level: "Tell me, Karamazov, do you despise me terribly?" (555), and then Kolya's admission: "I'm insecure. Stupidly insecure, crudely insecure" (556). Alyosha, however, does not despise the boy but loves him and his "lovely nature," though it has, he suggests, been perverted. The cure, as Kolya himself sees without having to be told, is penitence: "Oh, how sorry I am and how I scold myself for not coming sooner!"

This penitential confession follows a shift in the conversation from ideological matters to the unhappy Snegiryov family—not only the dying Ilyusha but also his

crippled sister Ninochka. Kolya says, "I like that Ninochka. . . . I think she's terribly kind and pathetic," and Alyosha concurs: "'Yes, yes! When you've come more
often, you'll see what sort of being she is. It's very good for you to get to know
such beings, in order to learn to value many other things besides, which you will
learn precisely from knowing these beings. . . . That will remake you more than
anything" (556). With this reference we are brought back to the spiritual source
of Alyosha's authority: the cruciform wisdom and power of God displayed in
foolishness, weakness, and lowliness (I Corinthians 1:18–31). The power of this
unveiling of divine glory cannot be discerned in the vain displays of human wisdom, the "debaters of this age." The authority of divine wisdom is not a matter of
human cleverness, rhetorical skill, or dialectical brilliance—or any other grounds
for "human boasting." The authority of divine power and wisdom is embodied in
humble servanthood, not magisterial splendor. Alyosha bears witness to this
truth, not by trying to persuade Kolya through eloquent rhetoric or dialectical
argument but by actions pointing to the embodiment of this power, which can
only be spiritually discerned. The requirement for such discernment is humble
repentance, as Kolya finally sees: "It was vanity that kept me from coming, egoistic vanity and base despotism, which I haven't been able to get rid of all my life,
though all my life I've been trying to break myself. I'm a scoundrel in many ways,
Karamazov, I see it now!" (556–557).

Of course, to talk of curing oneself of this illness is still to dwell within the
proud isolation of the divided self; and we see in Ivan where such efforts lead—
to "brain fever," madness. The cure comes from beyond any human self, as the
gift of God. This gift cannot be possessed as if it were just another human teaching or cure or power. And yet for the knight of faith it is embodied in human
form and it is present in the shared "mind of Christ," which makes true discernment possible. In the act of confession to Alyosha, Kolya has taken a decisive step
out of the inclosing reserve of his vanity, and in this he finds a strange comfort.
"You know, Karamazov, our talk is something like a declaration of love," a relation that binds brothers together in the humble love of mutual confession. The
shared mind of Christ is thus attached to a stone of stumbling, a *skandalon,*
which is also the foundation of "the edifice"—the crucifixion of Christ, the slain
Lamb. How this act may found a new political community is expressed in
Alyosha's first public speech, to the community of twelve boys surrounding
"Ilyusha's stone" on the day of the funeral. Several interpreters[73] have linked this
reference to the stone of Matthew 16:18, where Christ plays on Peter's name in
"founding" the church: "And I tell you, you are *Petros,* and on this rock *[petra]* I
will build my church, and the powers of death shall not prevail against it." Interestingly, this is also the setting in Matthew where the church is given "the keys of
the kingdom of heaven," the power to bind and to loose. This power or authority

is related to the recognition of Jesus' messianic identity, which is also the basis of Jesus' blessing of Peter in Matthew 16:17: "Blessed are you, Simon Bar-Jona! For flesh and blood has not revealed this to you, but my Father who is in heaven." And yet Peter has not yet understood the revelation he has received—as the subsequent verses in Matthew 16 show. Jesus begins to show his disciples that the messianic path is one of suffering and death, and Peter resists this: "God forbid, Lord! This shall never happen to you." Jesus then addresses Peter in very different terms: "Get behind me, Satan! You are a *skandalon* to me; for you are not on the side of God, but of men" (16:22–23). The path of the Messiah is the path of the cross; and if anyone wishes to share in this revealed form of the heavenly Father's rule and the community it founds, Christ says, "let him deny himself and take up his cross and follow me" (16:24). The path of restorative, suffering love entails the renunciation of the devil's illusory power of idolatry, rooted in vengeance and violence.[74] Only when Jesus' followers are able to appropriate this vision for themselves and in themselves—this internalization of the power to forgive—can it become the basis for a different political pattern.

Ilyusha's stone is therefore also a reference to the various "stone" images gathered together in I Peter 2:4–8:

> Come to him, to that living stone, rejected by men but in God's sight chosen and precious; and like living stones be yourselves built into a spiritual house, to be a holy priesthood, to offer spiritual sacrifices acceptable to God through Jesus Christ. For it stands in scripture: "Behold, I am laying in Zion a stone, a cornerstone chosen and precious, and he who believes in him will not be put to shame."[75] To you therefore who believe, he is precious, but for those who do not believe, "The very stone which the builders rejected has become the head of the corner,"[76] and "a stone that will make men stumble, a rock that will make them fall"[77]; for they stumble because they disobey the word.

Ilyusha's death is the unjustified suffering of a child, to which suffering the gathered boys have all contributed, and Alyosha in his word asks that all of them remember it: "Let us always remember how we buried the poor boy, whom we threw stones at—remember, there by the little bridge?—and whom afterwards we all came to love so much" (774). Their newfound brotherhood has a new foundation: forgiveness. In the case of Ilyusha, of course, the victim is not "innocent"—he too threw stones, stuck Kolya with a penknife, bit Alyosha's finger to the bone. And yet his life bears witness to the reconciling power of forgiveness, in a harmony that does not, however, forget or annul the suffering but that transfigures it beyond the violent counterclaims of victim and offender. To those trapped within the framework of retributive justice, such a remembered witness is a scandal, for it can only continue to point offensively to the cycle of unwarranted violence of which it is a part. For Alyosha and the boys, however, it is not a scandal but a spiritual sanctuary, an edifice founded on the living stone, who is no victim but rather the conqueror and cornerstone of the heavenly city, which is present also on the earth in the lives of those who remember.

Let us consider this more carefully. Alyosha is prompted to give his speech on memory and on the educative power of sacred memories that the elder calls "seeds" of the word of God (290f.), because his soul has been shaken by a memory (774). His soul-shaking memory is triggered by Ilyusha's stone, as Alyosha recollects the "whole picture" of what Snegiryov has told him there (book 4, chapter 7)—Snegiryov's own memory of the suffering, loving exchange between himself and his son at the stone. This incident occurs at the end of book 4, entitled "Strains" or *Nadryv* (sometimes translated "Lacerations").[78] The various forms of *nadryv* encountered in book 4 and throughout the novel share a common root—self-isolating pride, and as Robert Belknap points out, a twisted response to offered gifts or offered love; the lacerating inability to enter into the vulnerability of humble love. In effect, the forms of *nadryv* are really forms of despair or offense[79] experienced by those who are locked in the tormenting retributive cycle of pain and revenge, who are despairing of forgiveness and thus also unwilling either to repent or to forgive.

Perhaps the most heartrending *nadryv* is that experienced by the child Ilyusha in response to the public humiliation of his father at Dmitri's hand. As Dmitri is dragging Snegiryov around the town square by his "whiskbroom" beard, Ilyusha and the schoolboys are just getting out of school. Snegiryov tells Alyosha of his son's distress:

> "When he saw me in such a state, sir, he rushed up to me: 'Papa,' he cried, 'papa!' He caught hold of me, hugged me, tried to pull me away, crying to my offender: 'Let go, let go, it's my papa, my papa, forgive him'—that was what he cried: 'Forgive him!' And he took hold of him, too, with his little hands, and kissed his hand, that very hand, sir . . . I remember his face at that moment, I have not forgotten it, sir, and I will not forget it . . . !" (204)

Dmitri pays no attention to the boy's plea, but challenges the humiliated, impoverished father of three to a duel. (Ilyusha has two sisters—one a crippled hunchback, and the other a "too-smart" student now helping out at home—and a crippled, deranged mother). Such "public honor" is well beyond the former captain's means—for his family's sake he cannot afford to be killed or maimed in a duel. This "genealogical family picture," Snegiryov fears, has imprinted itself in the memory of Ilyusha's soul—his father will be despised also as a coward.

Ilyusha suffers, for despite the fact that his father is publicly humiliated and a laughingstock, an abject failure, Ilyusha knows him to be a loving, compassionate, and responsible papa. Not only do Ilyusha's pleas for mercy go unheeded, but his own honorable and loving deed becomes the occasion for merciless teasing by the schoolboys: "'Whiskbroom,' they shouted at him, 'your father was dragged out of the tavern by his whiskbroom, and you ran along asking for forgiveness'" (206). Just as he was publicly punished and isolated by Kolya for his personal penitential confession of the pin-and-bread prank, so he is publicly humiliated for nobly standing up for his father. The boy cannot face this crushing truth, and he comes down with the fever that eventually kills him.

More intense than the fever, however, is the desire for revenge that grows in the offended child. He dreams of challenging Dmitri to a duel himself, with a sword: "Papa . . . don't make peace with him. . . . I'll throw him down when I'm big, I'll knock the sword out of his hand with my sword, I'll rush at him, throw him down, hold my sword over him and say: 'I could kill you now, but I forgive you, so there!'" (207). Snegiryov suffers with his son's suffering, fearing the destructive bitterness growing in young Ilyusha's heart. He tries to comfort the boy, and at the stone Ilyusha finally breaks down in "great grief" and they sit there, holding each other, weeping, expressing their love. Yet that is not the end of the story. Ilyusha's story is finally one of making peace through the forgiveness of sins—a lived experience ordered by the consciousness that "all are guilty for all" and "all are responsible for all." As Alyosha suggests at the stone, this is indeed to be educated by a sacred memory, a truth "not of this world" and not conceived in any human heart. It is a truth revealed in the slain Lamb who "draws all" through the humiliation and offense of the cross, to a community of life and light that lives in brotherhood, beyond the isolation of offense. Ilyusha's suffering brings the children together as penitents and peacemakers who are liberated from self-assertion to declare their love one for another in word and in deed. This story of suffering becomes for them, like the story of Job for the elder, a precious memory that enables the soul to "seek out what is precious" (290), and to practice the discernment of a conscience that is not divided by the judgmental knowledge of good and evil but that is penitential and is united to the reconciling community of divine love. The elder was about the same age as Ilyusha when he "consciously received the first seed of the word of God" in his soul, in the story of Job and of the inwardness built up in the experience of suffering and spiritual trial endured by this servant of God:

> But what is great here is this very mystery—that the passing earthly image and eternal truth here touched each other. In the face of earthly truth [pravda],[80] the enacting of eternal truth is accomplished. Here the Creator, as in the first days of cre-

ation, crowning each day with praise: 'That which I have created is good,' looks at Job and again praises his creation. And Job, praising God, does not only serve him, but will also serve his whole creation, from generation to generation and unto ages of ages. (292)

The Epilogue of *The Brothers Karamazov* is thus an icon of the community or *polis* ordered by the memory of Christ as the slain Lamb—an earthly community that enacts the eternal truth that the slain Lamb is indeed worthy to rule. His rule is by the sword of the word that pierces the heart and evokes either offense or faith. The politics of Christian faith, however, is not just inner or private. All politics is tied to consciousness; the real question is which form of consciousness is embodied in the world. Types of community or political order, as Plato recognized long ago, are types of (shared) soul. The politics of Ivan and the Grand Inquisitor are rooted in the divided consciousness that seeks retributive justice in order to alleviate the destructive consequences for fallen humanity of its separation from God. This consciousness possesses a measure of truth: In a fallen world, people do act in a vicious cycle of self-assertion, offense, violation, retribution, claim, and counterclaim. The earthly city is built by the progeny of Cain, where the suffering of violence proliferates.

The stone that bruises Ilyusha "in the chest, over the heart" (205) plays its role in the illness that leads to his death. But it is clear in his case (as in the case of Ivan's "brain fever") that the physical symptoms are also closely linked to spiritual factors. This stone represents the stone of stumbling—the vicious and merciless treatment of others (and especially of children—see Matthew 18[81]) by those who embody the consciousness of Cain in the world, those who kill their brothers out of envy and resentful, rivalrous anger, or out of disordered, fallen, sinful desire. Such actions are truly stones of stumbling, temptations to sin and to take offense—woe to the one who is responsible for such a stumbling block (Matthew 18:7). And yet, as Kierkegaard points out, the possible *skandalon* or offense of Christianity lies in the paradox that the prescribed cure seems infinitely worse than the sickness.[82] For the Christian consciousness, everything turns on how one responds to life-destroying deeds of offense. Christ's response in Matthew 18, which launches the extensive discussion of *skandala,* is in answer to the disciples' question, "Who is greatest in the kingdom of heaven?" He points to a child with the comment: "Truly, I tell you, unless you turn and become like children, you will never enter the kingdom of heaven. Whoever becomes humble like this child is the greatest in the kingdom of heaven" (18:3–4).

Christ's appeal to humility is also at the center of Dostoevsky's poetic and prophetic politics, which offends political theorists such as Gradovsky—even as it offends Ivan, the Grand Inquisitor, and Hannah Arendt. Greatness is not found in a name or family genealogy or reputation that glorifies itself. Rather it is found in the humble love that builds up the community of servants in the world, a love that must pass through the forgiveness of sins. The divine drawing to which Jesus refers in John 12:31–32, by which the heavenly Father's name is glorified, and by which the "ruler *(archon)* of this world *(kosmos)*" is overcome, is tied to the power of the cross. The work of divine drawing, which has not ceased since the crucifixion, converges (says Kierkegaard) on a single point: "the consciousness of sin; through that goes *the way* along which [Christ] draws a person, the penitent, to himself."[83] This is the fully voluntary, courageous path that actively embodies the restorative power of humble, forgiving love to reverse violence and to end victimization.

Also in Matthew 18, Jesus clarifies the real political meaning of the power of the keys so recently given to *Petros* that "founds" the church—the practice of binding and loosing (18:15–20). The founding authority of the church is not tied to papal splendor and official duties but rather to the personal, embodied practice of restorative justice wherever two or three (or ten or twelve) are gathered. Not surprisingly, the *Petros* who is still struggling to understand what exactly was revealed to him and then given to him as a great authority—against the very "powers of death" (or "gates of Hades")—comes to Jesus with a question: "Lord, if my brother sins against me, how often should I forgive? As many as seven times?" (18:21). Jesus' response ("seventy-seven times") goes beyond the seven-fold vengeance of Cain to address the seventy-sevenfold vengeance of Lamech (Cain's great-great-great grandson) in his boasting song of violence sung to his wives.[84] The power of God's rule counters violence with self-denying forgiveness.

Jesus' teaching and embodiment of forgiveness are not an abstract doctrine and a unique, perhaps praiseworthy, but never-to-be repeated forensic act. His scandalous practice of forgiving sins exemplifies a way of life that is to be imitated and a consciousness or "mind" that is to be cultivated in and by the church, as the earthly enactment of eternal truth. Those attached politically to the body of Christ are therefore participants in a drama that is both human and divine, earthly and heavenly, bodily and spiritual, individual and social. This drama is a source of possible offense in its prophetic witness to the God-man who remains the slain Lamb: It is witness to a truth that, even as it is publicly enacted on the earth, cannot be communicated directly (not even in miracles). It can be seen only by the free and obedient decision of the heart; and it will continue to cause scandal and offense to those stuck in scandal, who cannot and will not believe that Jesus reveals the authority of divine rule and that the community he founds can effectively counter Cain's killing of his brother (much less the violence of Cain's sons of later generations) through the embodied practice of restorative justice. Yet Dostoevsky ends his novel in a celebration of the realism of this very faith: that the Spirit of God does indeed move over the earthy forces of Karama-zovian baseness, raising the erotic love of life, and all worldly loves, to suffering, celebratory completion in the "all in all."

# Notes

1. For the initial reference in the Pushkin speech, see Fyodor Dostoevsky, *A Writer's Diary,* trans. Kenneth Lantz (Evanston, Ill.: Northwestern University Press, 1994), vol. 2, p. 1284; for Dostoevsky's quotation of and response to Gradovsky's article, see ibid., pp. 1296–1328 (especially pp. 1307, 1323f.). In *The Brothers Karamazov* the "eternal questions" concern the relationship of truth and politics, centered around the question of the existence of God and immortality. If there is no God and no immortality, then socialism becomes the logical alternative, answering the same questions from the "other end" (Fyodor Dostoevsky, *The Brothers Karamazov,* trans. Richard Pevear and Larissa Volokhonsky [New York: Vintage, 1990], p. 234). The narrator comments on Alyosha's decision to set out upon the monastic path: "As soon as he reflected seriously and was struck by the conviction that immortality and God exist, he naturally said at once to himself: 'I want to live for immortality, and I reject any halfway compromise.' In just the same way, if he had decided that immortality and God do not exist, he would immediately have joined the atheists and socialists (for socialism is not only the labor question or the question of the so-called fourth estate, but first of all the question of atheism, the question of the modern embodiment of atheism, the question of the Tower of Babel built precisely without God, not to go from earth to heaven but to bring heaven down to earth)" (Ibid., p. 26). With regard to the teaching on humility, see the elder's discussion on "Masters and Servants" and "whether it is possible for them to become brothers in spirit" ("Talks and Homilies," section f). Such a social order, claims the elder, cannot be derived from scientific reason (which is oriented to bodily needs and external relations). It can only be found in the image of God as revealed by Christ, and this requires humility. Thus Russia's social salvation must come from the Christian piety of the people, "for Russia is great in her humility." "Equality is only in man's spiritual dignity. . . . Where there are brothers, there will be brotherhood; but before brotherhood they will never share among themselves. Let us preserve the image of Christ, that it may shine forth like a precious diamond to the whole world . . . So be it, so be it!" (Ibid., p. 316). "Great human communion" is realized only in mutual servanthood, according to the elder.

2. Dostoevsky, *A Writer's Diary,* vol. 2, p. 1307; cf. the discussion—with conclusions that differ greatly from the ones arrived at here—by Sven Linner, *Starets Zosima in The Brothers Karamazov: A Study in the Mimesis of Virtue* (Stockholm: Almqvist and Wiksell, 1975), chapter 8.

3. Dostoevsky, *A Writer's Diary,* vol. 2, pp. 1316–1317.

4. Ibid., p. 1319.

5. See Eric Voegelin, *The New Science of Politics* (Chicago: University of Chicago Press, 1952), p. 17; and the critical response developed by Bruce Ward in *Dostoyevsky's Critique of the West: The Quest for the Earthly Paradise* (Waterloo, Ont.: Wilfrid Laurier University Press, 1986), chapter 6.

6. See John Meyendorff, *Byzantine Theology: Historical Trends and Doctrinal Themes* (New York: Fordham University Press, 1974), pp. 6, 73, 213f.

7. See Vigen Guroian, *Incarnate Love: Essays in Orthodox Ethics* (Notre Dame, Ind.: Notre Dame University Press, 1987), part 3; and Alexander Schmemann, *Church, World, Mission* (Crestwood, N.Y.: St. Vladimir's Seminary Press, 1979).

8. Diane Oenning Thompson provides extensive documentation and illuminating analysis of Ivan's "obsessive negations, distortions and corruptions of the Gospels" (Thompson, *The Brothers Karamazov and the Poetics of Memory* [Cambridge: Cambridge University Press, 1991], p. 149; cf. pp. 179f., 280f.), though she misses this example. Perhaps the most significant distortion in Ivan's romanticized portrait of Jesus is that he is immediately recognized by everyone, in what Ivan considers "one of the best passages in the poem, I mean, why it is exactly that they recognize him. People are drawn to him by an invincible force. . . . He passes silently among them with a quiet smile of infinite compassion. The sun of love shines in his heart, rays of Light, Enlightenment, and Power stream from his eyes"[41]. This is a fantastic, sentimental, and idolatrous picture that blatantly disregards the New Testament portrait of the necessary hiddenness of Jesus' true identity. As Kierkegaard says: "Spirit is the denial of direct immediacy. If Christ is true God, then he also must be unrecognizable, attired in unrecognizability, which is the denial of all straightforwardness. Direct recognizability is specifically characteristic of the idol. But this is what people make Christ into, and this is supposed to be earnestness. They take the direct statement and fantastically form a character corresponding to it (preferably sentimental, with the gentle look, the friendly eye, or whatever else such a foolish pastor can hit upon), and then it is *directly* altogether certain that Christ is God" (Søren Kierkegaard, *Practice in Christianity,* eds. and trans. Howard Hong and Edna Hong [Princeton: Princeton University Press, 1991], p. 136). Of course, Ivan is not a pastor, but he knows how to manipulate sentimental pastoral images for his own purposes.

9. Helen Canniff de Alvarez makes the following astute observation about this scene: "Because Ivan's Christ speaks only once in his prose poem and in conjunction with his theatrical miracle, Ivan effectively places Christ's importance . . . in his power to fulfill the earthly wants of men" (de Alvarez, "The Augustinian Basis of Dostoevsky's *The Brothers Karamazov,*" unpublished dissertation, University of Dallas, 1977, p. 140). This serves as an effective rhetorical trick, distorting the picture of Christ by establishing superficial similarities between miracle stories and their meanings.

10. In Mark's gospel, the messianic secret is tied to the mystery of the kingdom of God (see Joel Marcus, *The Mystery of the Kingdom of God* [Atlanta: Scholars Press, 1986]; and Chapter 1 in the present volume).

11. Divine mercy is also represented by the "sea of glass" (Revelation 4:6), the primordial deep conquered by God in the creation myth, bringing order out of chaos and light out of darkness. In Revelation 13:1 the beast arises out of it (cf. 15:2–3, where the sea is connected with a new exodus in which the liberated ones sing the song of Moses and the song of the Lamb, the song acclaiming divine justice, which Ivan finds so loathsome); and in Revelation 21:1, in the final revelation of the new heaven and new earth "the sea was no more"—it has been ultimately defeated and thus allows the heavenly Jerusalem to come down out of heaven from God, symbolizing the harmonious and fulfilling dwelling of God with humankind.

12. G. B. Caird, *The Revelation of St. John the Divine* (New York: Harper and Row, 1966), pp. 291–292.

13. This is the heart of what is at stake in "The Grand Inquisitor": "Nothing has ever been more insufferable for man and for human society than freedom!"[44]; "There is

nothing more seductive for man than the freedom of his conscience, but there is nothing more tormenting either. . . . Instead of taking over men's freedom, you increased it and forever burdened the kingdom of the human soul with its torments. . . . Thus you yourself laid the foundation for the destruction of your own kingdom"[46–47]. The references to the centrality of this human problem are abundant, not only in the poem but throughout the novel.

14. This model of suffering martyrdom is extended in Revelation 6:9f. to the souls of slaughtered saints under the heavenly altar, whose lives are offered as atoning sacrifices, grounded in the overcoming blood of the Lamb (cf. 12:11). Farrer states: "The blood of Christ both atones and cries, uttering better words than Abel's: here the blood of the martyrs cries, as Enoch says of Abel, for the extirpation of the race of Cain: it also atones for saints on the altar of sacrifice" (Austin Farrer, *A Rebirth of Images: The Making of St. John's Apocalypse* [Boston: Beacon Press, 1949], p. 110). The cry for retributive justice here requires further waiting for the completion of divine salvation through the patient exercise of suffering love, which will be publicly vindicated only at the end.

15. As Robert Belknap accurately notes, Father Zosima's "answer" to the Grand Inquisitor is rooted in a counter-ontology no less cosmic than that of the materialists: "I mean the doctrine of universal causal connections, the belief that all things in the world are interconnected, that no event occurs without its causes and its effects in this world, that if we knew enough we would see the world as a seamless web of causes and effects" (Belknap, *The Genesis of The Brothers Karamazov: The Aesthetics, Ideology, and Psychology of Making a Text* [Evanston, Ill.: Northwestern University Press, 1990], p. 140). One is an external bodily account of causality (the seeing of which is a matter of "nerves in the brain"), the other a spiritual account seen by "keeping company" with the image of Christ in the heart.

16. We might note here that this anthropology also underlies Dostoevsky's artistic realism: "With utter realism to *find the man in man.*. . . They call me a *psychologist;* this is *not true.* I am merely a realist *in the higher sense,* that is, I portray all the *depths of the human soul*" (Dostoevsky in his notebook, as quoted in Mikhail Bakhtin, *Problems of Dostoevsky's Poetics,* ed. and trans. Caryl Emerson [Minneapolis: University of Minnesota Press, 1984], p. 60). Later in the chapter we will contrast Dostoevsky's dialogical and participatory visualization of the inner life of his characters with the nondialogical, clinical, and reified juridical model of courtroom psychology (which is also dramatized in book 12 of *The Brothers Karamazov* as "a stick with two ends").

17. The highly symbolic coronation of Charlemagne by Pope Leo III at St. Peter's on Christmas Day A.D. 800 is alluded to in the following words of the Inquisitor: "Listen, then: we are not with you, but with *him,* that is our secret! For a long time now—eight centuries already—we have not been with you but with *him.* Exactly eight centuries ago we took from him what you so indignantly rejected, that last gift he offered you when he showed you all the kingdoms of the earth"[49].

18. It bears notice that in Revelation even John the author, at the climax of the vision exposing the world's idolatry, must two times be warned against false worship and directed to worship only God (Revelation 19:10 and 22:8–9).

19. See the good discussion of this in Caird, *Revelation,* pp. 90f., 293f.; Farrer, *Rebirth of Images,* pp. 33f., 296f.

20. See Paul's slogan *panta moi exestin* (I Corinthians 6:12; 10:23), which more literally translated means "all things are in my power." Ivan omits Paul's consistent qualification of the slogan: "but not all things are helpful"; "but I will not be enslaved by anything"; "but

not all things build up." The focus of freedom in Paul's vision is not the individual power to act but the discernment of love, unbound by external rules and doctrinal formulas, for the building up of the community of love and the good of one's sisters and brothers. This is the very meaning of the "law of Christ" that liberates the self from isolating partiality for participation in the fullness of divine agape (see the four *pantas* of I Corinthians 13:7).

21. The institution of elders is given the following description: "What, then, is an elder? An elder is one who takes your soul, your will into his soul and into his will. Having chosen an elder, you renounce your will and give it to him under total obedience and with total self-renunciation. A man who dooms himself to this trial, this terrible school of life, does so voluntarily, in the hope that after the long trial he will achieve self-conquest, self-mastery to such a degree that he will, finally, through a whole life's obedience, attain to perfect freedom—that is, freedom from himself—and avoid the lot of those who live their whole lives without finding themselves in themselves. This invention—that is, the institution of elders—is not a theoretical one, but grew in the East out of a practice that in our time is already more than a thousand years old" (27–28). This raises, in a very different context from the poem of the Grand Inquisitor, the central question of freedom (conscience) and authority. Obedience to the elder's spiritual authority places tremendous responsibility and power in the hands of the elder, the purpose of which is not to lessen the burden of freedom on the disciple but to build it up through strenuous discipline. This is a filial model of authority and education based on Jesus' relation to his disciples in the New Testament, and it is clearly a risky institution, since its integrity demands that the whole of the character of both elder and disciple be oriented toward the *mimesis* of the humble love incarnated by Christ. The discovery of oneself in freedom thus entails the disciplined pursuit of complete selflessness.

22. Richard Peace, *Dostoyevsky: An Examination of the Major Novels* (Cambridge: Cambridge University Press, 1971), p. 276. Peace's analysis is rich in interpretive literary insight, but he fails at crucial points to discern Dostoevsky's apocalyptic grammar of spiritual causality. The agricultural metaphors of seed and earth that pervade the novel and are crucial to understanding its central transformations are considered "heretical ideas" by Peace, who argues that Zosima weds Christian teachings to a more prominently pagan "cult of the earth" (*Dostoevsky,* p. 285f.). He suggests that Zosima's deep bow to Dmitri (whose name links him to Demeter, and who will also be regenerated by a "cult of the earth") confirms this. We have argued in Chapter 3 that the direction of transformation is precisely the opposite: from pagan fertility cult and nature romanticism toward an apocalyptic transformation of all creation through the incarnate spiritual agency of Christ. This is not a movement that leaves material creation behind; to the contrary, the resurrection of the body is central to the Christian moral vision of the elder and of the novel as a whole. Only a gnostic, Westernized interpretation of Christianity could fail to see this.

23. According to Nietzsche, the history of human "answerability" (*Verantwortlichkeit*) is tied to the human animal's evolutionary development of the faculty of *memory*—promises made for calculable action in the future, a necessary feature of ordered human communities of speech. The beginning of the inner life of moral consciousness in which instinctual drives are countered and controlled, then, is dictated by social needs and is imprinted not by love but by pain. The cruelest of these rituals of pain are religious, codified in penal customs. But the social origin of the guilty conscience is above all *economic,* as is evident in the German word *Schuld* (see Friedrich Nietzsche, *On the Genealogy of Morals,* trans. Walter Kaufmann [New York: Vintage, 1987; Random House, 1989], part 2). This

connection between economic and religious language in the retributive understanding of conscience is also present in Ivan's lament, where suffering "buys harmony" and "buys truth" at too great a price. Ivan adds to the mix the language of "manure," thus anticipating not only Nietzsche but Freud. Dostoevsky offers a fundamentally different account of the origins of moral memory, of conscience and responsibility. It originates in the human soul's ordering relation to divine love.

24. This is also evident in the malicious rumors about Zosima that quickly circulate, beginning with the oppositional monks, upon the premature odor of corruption emanating from the elder's corpse. The narrator attributes much of this to "envy of the dead man's holiness" and the spiritual authority and influence it generated (331). The denunciations include charges of heresy, such as not accepting the material fire of hell (see the elder's spiritual treatment, 322f.); lack of ascetic rigor ("he was not strict in fasting, allowed himself sweets, had cherry preserve with his tea, and liked it very much"); and from "the most ardent opponents of the institution of elders . . . and among these were some of the oldest and most strictly pious of the monks," the charge that "he abused the sacrament of confession" (333). Given the pervasive importance of existential confession in the novel as the embodiment of spiritual humility, Dostoevsky is clearly suggesting that the elder (whose example in this regard is clear) truly understands and exemplifies the meaning of the sacrament.

25. Miusov, it should be noted, got himself appointed as Mitya's co-guardian when the young boy was left virtually abandoned by his dissolute father. But Miusov also abandoned young Mitya when, having returned to Paris for a lengthy stay, he got caught up in the 1848 revolution (in which he "almost" took part "on the barricades," one of the delightful memories of his youth that "so struck his imagination that he was unable to forget it for the rest of his life"; 10f.), and simply "forgot" the child. Miusov, the narrator tells us, was "enlightened, metropolitan, cosmopolitan, a lifelong European," who "had relations with many of the most liberal people of his epoch, both in Russia and abroad; he knew Proudhon and Bakunin personally," and so he considered his lawsuit against the "clericals" his "civic and enlightened duty." The narrator makes it clear, therefore, that Miusov's interest in the monastery visit was mere curiosity, which he paraded as "good intentions" partly to ensure himself a dignified, deferential reception.

26. See the helpful discussion of "Knowledge of God" in C.H. Dodd, *The Interpretation of the Fourth Gospel* (Cambridge: Cambridge University Press, 1953), chapter 3.

27. Ivan asserts: "In my opinion, Christ's love for people is in its kind a miracle impossible on earth. True, he was God. But we are not gods" (237). Here Ivan clearly dismisses the Orthodox monastic teaching on *theosis*, the possibility that the image of Christ is not an impossible otherworldly ideal but rather the ground for human deification and the existential mediation of the Kingdom of God in the world even now (as in the elder's teaching that paradise is present here and now in life itself, a gift of the divine presence; 298–299).

28. To which Father Iosef nicely replies, "Ah, but we don't even have any mountains." In the nineteenth century, *ultramontanism* refers to Roman Catholic opposition to "the new liberal and anti-Christian movements of which the French Revolution of 1789 was the logical and most systematic expression." See *The Oxford Dictionary of the Christian Church*, 2d ed., eds. F. L. Cross and E. A. Livingston (Oxford: Oxford University Press, 1974), p. 1405. The stages of the "triumph" of ultramontanism in that century are identified as follows: 1814—revival of the Jesuit order loyal to the Pope alone; 1864—Pius IX is-

sues his antiliberal *Syllabus;* 1870—Vatican I declares papal infallibility on *ex cathedra* pronouncements concerning faith and morals. It is clear, then, that Dostoevsky, like Miusov, rejects the ultramontanist agenda, though for very different reasons. Miusov represents the extension of the French Revolution in nineteenth-century politics to which ultramontanism is the reaction. Dostoevsky views both as corrupted forms of power politics.

29. Rakitin, the liberal seminarian, does not buy this, calling Ivan's theory "stupid" and "squalid," "a tempting theory for scoundrels": "Mankind will find strength in itself to live for virtue, even without believing in the immortality of the soul! Find it in the love of liberty, equality, fraternity" (82). On the perspective of the novel, however, Rakitin is a confused Christian socialist without spiritual insight—everything becomes grist for his egoistic (and careerist) ideological mill.

30. Dmitri's earlier response to Miusov's anecdote about Ivan's theory was immediate and intense: "Allow me . . . to be sure I've heard correctly: 'Evildoing [crime] should not only be permitted but even should be acknowledged as the most necessary and most intelligent solution for the situation of every godless person'!" (69) "I'll remember," he says—a statement that others besides Mitya will later recall.

31. The reference here is to Goethe's *Faust*, Part II, Act V, lines 11890f. Alyosha is uncertain of the origin of Ivan's somewhat derisive appellation for the elder ("Pater Seraphicus—he got that name from somewhere—but where?"), but he accepts it as true: "Yes, yes, that's him, Pater Seraphicus, he will save me . . . from him, and forever!"[56]. In *Faust* the Pater Seraphicus inhabits the "middle region" between the upper (Pater Ecstaticus—love's glowing, eternal height: *"ewiger Wonnebrand, glühendes Liebeband . . . schäumende Gotteslust"*) and nether (Pater Profundus—love's creative, reaching abyss) regions. He teaches the chorus of blessed boys the ways of the earth by taking them into himself so they might see through his eyes. The boys are overwhelmed by the power and darkness of what they see and beg to be released, so the Pater Seraphicus leads them to a higher region through the growth made possible by God's strengthening presence, and finally a revelation of eternal love that opens out into blessedness *(Seligkeit)*. The name turns out to be prophetic, but not in the sense apprehended by the "pre-crisis" Alyosha.

32. The title itself, of course, is taken from the speech of the defense attorney Fetyukovich, that "smooth Petersburg swindler" (as Ivan calls him; 593), in his charge to the jury to "beware of a judicial error!" (740). It is an ironic charge, given the famous lawyer's cynical tactics.

33. It is of course the visiting expert hired by Katerina from Moscow who, in contrast to the more "commonsense" testimony of the two local doctors, speaks at length in technical terms about "mania" and "morbid fit of passion" and adduces as evidence for his "abnormal psychological condition" statements and behavior fully in keeping with Mitya's character, as is obvious to all who know him.

34. However, this is not entirely clear, as the narrator hints that Ippolit is a vain, consumptive, and bitter man who "had always thought himself injured by someone, because his talents were not properly appreciated" (658), and that his depiction of Ivan was prompted by an "indelicate feeling" at having been snubbed by Ivan once or twice in argument (697). The desire for revenge in the novel is never "pure"—it is always to some extent rooted in egoism and vanity, despite the noble-sounding speeches trumpeting love for humanity or civic redemption. This is of course in keeping with the inner-outer spiritual causality that informs the novel.

35. See Victor Terras, *A Karamazov Companion: Commentary on the Genesis, Language, and Style of Dostoevsky's Novel* (Madison: University of Wisconsin Press, 1981), p. 412. Terras makes a good observation about the two opposing lawyers: "Ironically, Ippolit Kirillovich, who spends his effort in a miscarriage of justice, is right about some fundamental issues (from Dostoevsky's viewpoint, that is), while Fetyukovich, whose philosophy is odious to Dostoevsky, is right about the facts of the case." Or perhaps, is right about some of the facts of the case. Both lawyers lack the quality displayed in the elder Zosima's discernment, which integrates the outer details and the inner reality of a "case" into a personal, living whole—not in order to "judge" but in order discerningly to serve the common good of those involved.

36. The prosecutor cites the poor, sick Smerdyakov as one such "victim" of Ivan's ideology, and meaningfully quotes Smerdyakov's remark that Ivan, of all the Karamazov brothers, "most resembles Fyodor Pavlovich in character" (697).

37. Terras points out that "mysticism" and "chauvinism" were precisely the terms used to characterize Dostoevsky by progressivist liberal critics (Terras, *A Karamazov Companion*, p. 416).

38. Of such spiritual heights, claims Ippolit, neither Mitya Karamazov nor the majority of modern Russian young men are capable (716; cf. 694).

39. Indeed, as Terras comments, this last observation on the difference between penitence and despair is profound: "Smerdyakov's suicide note ('I destroy my life of my own will and desire, not to blame anyone') contains a diabolic irony: by destroying himself, he assures Dmitri's conviction and deprives Ivan of a chance to relieve himself of his guilt" (Terras, *A Karamazov Companion*, p. 429). We might note here also Smerdyakov's cynical discussion of penitence and forgiveness early on in the novel, in his disputation with Grigory (127f., 130f.).

40. The power of binding and loosing is also claimed by the Grand Inquisitor as a "right": "You promised, you established with your word, you gave us the right to bind and loose, and surely you cannot even think of taking this right away from us"[43]. This power is later parodied as a surveillance technique in the Inquisitor's grotesque use of atonement language: "And they will have no secrets from us. We will allow or forbid them to live with their wives and mistresses, to have or not to have children—all depending on their obedience—and they will submit to us gladly and joyfully. The most tormenting secrets of their conscience—all, all they will bring to us, and we will decide all things"[51].

41. The extended passage in Matthew 18:15–20 details the procedure entailed in the practice. See the fine discussion by John Howard Yoder, *Body Politics: Five Practices of the Christian Community Before the Watching World* (Nashville: Discipleship Resources, 1992), chapter 1; idem, "Binding and Loosing," in *The Royal Priesthood: Essays Ecclesiological and Ecumenical*, ed. Michael Cartwright (Grand Rapids, Mich.: William B. Eerdmans, 1994), pp. 323–358.

42. Ivan's Devil comments on this Russian form of swindling in connection with the "new man" to whom, as a man-god who self-consciously takes the place of God and therefore of law-making, "all is permitted": "It's all very nice; only if one wants to swindle, why, I wonder, should one also need the sanction of truth? But such is the modern little Russian man: without such a sanction, he doesn't even dare to swindle, so much does he love the truth" (649). Here the Devil gets carried away by his own eloquence. His speech reminds us of Nietzsche's assessment of "wir Erkennenden" in *On the Genealogy of Morals* (pt. 3, section 24), who are still "far from being *free* spirits: *for they still have faith in the*

*truth.*" This too must be called into question in the liberating process of *Selbstaufhebung* that will go beyond the moral law of justice toward the freedom of mercy and self-legislation enjoyed by those with the courage of the will to power (Nietzsche, *On the Genealogy of Morals*, pt. 2, section 10; pt. 3, section 27). In the terms of both Nietzsche and Ivan's devil, the bourgeois Petersburg lawyer lacks this courage, appealing to a sanction (Christian belief and Christian morality) in which he himself does not believe.

43. Peace, *Dostoevsky*, p. 281.

44. See Dostoevsky, *A Writer's Diary*, December 1877, pp. 1221–1244.

45. Ibid., p. 1244.

46. See, for example, Dostoevsky's reflections in *A Writer's Diary*, October 1877, entitled "Lies Are Indispensable for Truth. A Lie Times a Lie Equals Truth. Is That True?" (pp. 1163–1168); and his extensive discussion of the Kornilova case, in which trial his own published reflections played a role (December 1877, pp. 1221–1244).

47. Bruce Ward elaborates Dostoevsky's views on the European liberal-socialist tradition under Dostoevsky's own rubric, the "Geneva" idea—that is, the traditions inspired by Rousseau and embodied in the slogan of the French Revolution—*liberté, égalité, fraternité*—and in its theoretical elaborations: "Broadly speaking, this would include French liberalism, the French socialism which appeared at the same time, and the German philosophical commentary on these movements. More specifically, 'Geneva' thinkers would include such figures as Rousseau, Saint-Just, Saint-Simon, Fourier, Kant, Hegel, Feuerbach, and Marx" (Ward, *Dostoyevsky's Critique of the West*, pp. 45–46). Ward's book provides an account of Dostoevsky's relation to modern politics and political philosophy.

48. Hannah Arendt, *On Revolution* (New York: Penguin, 1963), p. 75.

49. It is tempting to take a lengthy detour here comparing Jean-Jacques Rousseau and the Grand Inquisitor, but we will content ourselves with a few remarks: The fundamental human and social problem for Rousseau, as for the Inquisitor, is the problem of freedom—"Man was born free, and he is everywhere in chains" (Jean-Jacques Rousseau, *The Social Contract*, trans. M. Cranston [New York: Penguin, 1968], book 1, chapter 1). The only way to liberate human beings from destructive forms of social enslavement, which are always particular and arbitrary (including the tyranny of the church in matters of conscience) is to establish an enlightened social order as a "sacred right." It is to give one's particular freedom to the general will so as to overcome particular (and prejudicial) forms of dependence, and thus to be "reborn" into a community, committed to a single body politic. As Rousseau puts it: "In order that the social pact shall not be an empty formula, it is tacitly implied in that commitment—which alone can give force to all others—that whoever refuses to obey the general will shall be constrained to do so by the whole body, which means nothing other than that he shall be forced to be free; for this is the condition which, by giving each citizen to the nation, secures him against all personal dependence, it is the condition which shapes both the design and the working of the political machine" (bk. 1, chap. 7; cf. bk. 2, chap. 7). Such a rebirth lifts unhappy people from the animal "state of nature" and its physical, passionate dependencies into a rational civil liberty limited by the general will. Of course, the general will (and its gifts of liberty, equality before the law, and fraternity of the whole) requires an ordering power, a lawgiver, a "sovereign" who gives the body politic coherent movement and will by legislation (bk. 2, chap. 6). This act of "founding" requires divine intelligence because it entails a transformation of human nature into a spiritual whole in which each can do nothing except through social cooperation. Hence the appeal to divine intervention in all acts of political founding, says

Rousseau: "But it is not for every man to make the Gods speak. . . . The lawgiver's great soul is the true miracle which must vindicate his mission" (bk. 2, chap. 7). Vindication is confirmed by the extent of social harmony achieved, that is, the extent to which the relations among members of the body are as limited as possible and relations with the whole body as extensive as possible ("in order that each citizen shall be at the same time perfectly independent of all his fellow citizens and excessively dependent on the republic"; bk. 2, chap. 12). This cannot simply be external, mechanical justice—it requires the "hearts of the citizens," a common morality, and "above all, belief." Such common belief will eliminate disagreement, dissent, rebellion, and all other signs that the enslaving prejudice of particular wills is undermining the liberating dominance of the general will (bk. 4, chap. 2). This common belief, then, will entail a "civil religion" (bk. 4, chap. 8)—with which Rousseau ends *The Social Contract*. This civil religion will "correct" the work of Jesus, who "came to establish a spiritual kingdom on earth; this kingdom, by separating the theological system from the political, meant that the state ceased to be a unity, and it caused those intestine divisions which have never ceased to disturb Christian peoples." The conflict of jurisdictions in Christian states has rendered harmonious political order impossible, since people have never known whether to obey the civil rule or the priest. Religious conflict must be eliminated: "Everything that destroys social unity is worthless; and all institutions that set man at odds with himself are worthless." The Christianity of the Gospel, of course, is "altogether different," emphasizing as it does the brotherhood of all—but it is private and its bonds of union otherworldly; indeed, "a society of true Christians would not be a society of men." Here, of course, we have the agreement of Ivan, the Inquisitor, and also, ironically, Hannah Arendt—as we shall see. Dostoevsky's novel calls this assumption radically into question. What Rousseau proposes in place of Christianity is a civil religion of toleration, stripped of dogma, in which the "sentiments of sociability" and moral duties are enshrined in a purely civil and rational profession of faith. Whoever does not believe them may be banished not for impiety but "as an antisocial being, as one unable sincerely to love law and justice. . . . If anyone, after having publicly acknowledged these same dogmas, behaves as if he did not believe in them, then let him be put to death, for he has committed the greatest crime, that of lying before the law." Although Rousseau is anti-Catholic and the Grand Inquisitor represents a form of Catholicism, their political positions are similar in many respects.

50. Arendt, *On Revolution*, p. 85.

51. Rousseau, *The Social Contract*, bk. 2, chap. 7.

52. Arendt says (*On Revolution*, pp. 86–87): "As a rule, it is not compassion which sets out to change worldly conditions in order to ease human suffering, but if it does, it will shun the drawn-out wearisome processes of persuasion, negotiation, and compromise, which are the processes of law and politics, and lend its voice to the suffering itself, which must claim for swift and direct action, that is, for action with the means of violence."

53. Arendt, *On Revolution*, p. 87.

54. Hannah Arendt, *The Human Condition* (Chicago: University of Chicago Press, 1958), p. 50f.

55. Ibid., pp. 74–75.

56. Ibid., p. 53.

57. Ibid. Arendt claims that this terminology is uniquely Christian, and that the Greek term *soma* is never used politically outside of Christianity. The metaphor appears for the first time in Paul's writings (I Corinthians 12). Strangely, Arendt here overlooks the most

famous work of ancient political philosophy, Plato's *Republic*. There Plato uses the language of body in a manner so similar to Paul's that one can imagine Paul borrowing it from Plato: "Then is that city best governed which is most like a single human being? For example, when one of us wounds a finger, presumably the entire community—that community tying the body together toward the soul *[pasa he koinonia he kata to soma pros ten psychen tetamene]* in a single arrangement under the ruler within it—is aware of the fact, and all of it is in pain as a whole along with the afflicted part" (462cd). Plato's reference to the Phoenician tale, which uses the language of "brothers" *(adelphoi)* born of a common mother earth (414de), serves as a crucial metaphor for the kind of body politic that is held together by a common good not reducible to an external, somatic unity (i.e., a unity such as Socrates's comic diversion on women and men exercising naked together, and the elaborate eugenics program that so fascinates Glaucon). A society focused on external goods, says Socrates, would be crammed full of lawyers and doctors (always a bad sign, as Dostoevsky also believed), and would need many drugs—that is, lies, numbing illusions, and feel-good diversions. The only true remedy for the problem of injustice and the founding of a good city "in speech" is for the soul to be "turned around" toward the good, the pattern laid "in heaven" *(en ourano*, 592b) that can nevertheless be enacted on the earth among "brothers" or "friends" wherever the virtue of prudence is exercised. We do not have the space to pursue it here, but the parallels with Dostoevsky's Christian understanding of politics are evident. In any case, it is not surprising that the model for politics chosen by Arendt from antiquity is not that of Plato or other Greeks but rather that of the Romans.

58. Belknap, *The Genesis of The Brothers Karamazov*, pp. 148–155. See also the fine discussion in Robin Feuer Miller, *The Brothers Karamazov: Worlds of the Novel* (New York: Twayne, 1992), chapter 7. Miller suggests that in Kolya, Dostoevsky "offers a new refraction of aspects of Mitya, Ivan, and the Grand Inquisitor" (Miller, *The Brothers Karamazov*, p. 101).

59. Ivan tells Alyosha: "I want to get acquainted with you once and for all, and I want you to get acquainted with me. . . . I saw how you kept looking at me all these three months, there was a certain ceaseless expectation in your eyes, and that is something I cannot bear, which is why I never approached you. But in the end I learned to respect you: this little man stands his ground, I thought. . . . I love people who stand their ground, whatever they may stand upon, and even if they're such little boys as you are." Alyosha responds with a declaration of love and the statement that although he still finds Ivan to be a riddle, he has come to understand something about him: "That you are just a young man, exactly like all other young men of twenty-three—yes, a young, very young, fresh and nice boy, still green, in fact!" (229). Their talk continues to make reference to "green youths" and "little boys," in ways that later resonate with Alyosha's dealings with the schoolchildren and particularly with Kolya.

60. The following comments are based on Søren Kierkegaard, *The Sickness Unto Death: A Christian Psychological Exposition for Upbuilding and Awakening*, eds. and trans. Howard Hong and Edna Hong (Princeton: Princeton University Press, 1980).

61. Ibid., p. 20.

62. Ibid., p. 63f.; cf. Søren Kierkegaard, *The Concept of Anxiety: A Simple Psychologically Orienting Deliberation on the Dogmatic Issue of Hereditary Sin*, eds. and trans. R. Thomte and A. Anderson (Princeton: Princeton University Press, 1980), pp. 123–135. "Ivan is a grave," says Dmitri, presumably commenting on Ivan's self-enclosed reserve (110, 229);

later he repeats this to Alyosha: "Brother Ivan is a sphinx; he's silent, silent all the time" (592, 593). Indeed, it would seem that Ivan confesses only to Alyosha, the "devil" . . . and Smerdyakov—the latter "confessions," and they are related, immediately precede his "madness."

63. Kierkegaard suggests: "If this inclosing reserve is maintained completely, . . . then his greatest danger is suicide. . . . But if he opens up to one single person, he probably will become so relaxed, or so let down, that suicide will not result from inclosing reserve. . . . However, it may happen that just because he has opened himself to another person he will despair over having done so; it may seem to him that he might have held out far, far longer in silence rather than to have a confidant. . . . In a poetic treatment, the denouement . . . could be designed so that the confidant is killed. It is possible to imagine a demonic tyrant like that, one who craves to speak with someone about his torment and then successively consumes a considerable number of people, for to become his confidant means certain death" (*Sickness Unto Death,* p. 66). How this is displayed in Ivan's poetic creation, the Grand Inquisitor, will be brought into focus in the next chapter, which treats "the silence of Christ." Ivan, although he is less inclosed than the Inquisitor, has his regrets as well: "He even hated Alyosha, recalling that day's conversation; at moments he hated himself very much as well" (276).

64. Kierkegaard, *Sickness Unto Death,* p. 72.

65. Kolya is introduced in book 10, chapter 1 ("Boys").

66. *Who founded Troy?* Kolya once asked the teacher. "Dardanelov gave only a general answer about peoples, their movements and migrations, about the remoteness of the times, about fable telling, but who precisely had founded Troy—that is, precisely which persons—he could not say, and even found the question for some reason an idle and groundless one. But this only left the boys convinced that Dardanelov did not know who had founded Troy. As for Kolya, he had learned about the founders of Troy in Smaragov, whose history was in the bookcase left by his father. The upshot of it was that all the boys became interested finally in who precisely had founded Troy, but Krasotkin would not give away his secret, and the glory of his knowledge remained unshakeably his own" (518). That the secret should concern the question of a political "founding" of a community is surely not accidental.

67. A particularly revealing example of this is his changed relation to his mother following a dangerous stunt in which he lay down between the railroad tracks and let a train pass over him. His doting mother is hysterical when she learns of this, and Kolya himself, already shaken by the prank, tearfully swears (on his knees before an icon and by his father's memory) never to do such a thing again. Regretting his "feelings," "the next day Kolya woke up as 'unfeeling' as ever, yet he grew more silent, more modest, more stern, more thoughtful" (518)—and more despotic.

68. See Belknap, *The Genesis of The Brothers Karamazov,* pp. 148–155.

69. Later, when boasting about his exploit in the marketplace (which involved a goose and a peasant), he again pronounces on "the people": "I never reject the people, you know. I like to be with the people . . . We lag behind the people—that is an axiom" (548). Of course, the incident with the peasant reveals Kolya's disdainful superiority over gullible peasants. When brought before the judge for his role in killing the goose, he argues "with complete equanimity" that he "had merely stated the basic idea and was speaking only hypothetically" (549)—exactly the manner in which Ivan tells Smerdyakov that "all is permitted."

70. See Søren Kierkegaard, *Fear and Trembling,* trans. Alasdair Hannay (New York: Penguin, 1985). For a superb commentary, see Edward F. Mooney, *Knights of Faith and Resignation: Reading Kierkegaard's Fear and Trembling* (Albany: State University of New York Press, 1991).

71. It becomes clear in book 8, chapter 3 ("Gold Mines") that as a result of the scandalous stench of the elder's dead body, Mme. Khokhlakov has given up her naive, admiring faith in the elder's miraculous powers: "I'm all for realism now, I've been taught a good lesson about miracles," she tells Dmitri (384). It appears she has now become "an experienced doctor of souls" based on the evidence of natural science—"after all that story in the monastery, which upset me so, I'm a complete realist, and want to throw myself into practical activity. I am cured" (385). Her daughter Lise will now become "a modern girl, educated and without prejudices," a "new woman" (387).

72. That Lise has a private relationship with Ivan is revealed in her comment, "I don't like your brother Ivan Fyodorovich, Alyosha," in the chapter entitled "A Betrothal" (220). Alyosha notes the comment with silent surprise, and later discovers that Ivan has been secretly visiting Lise (and that Mme. Khokhlakov is suspicious of these visits; 578–579). The mutually destructive character of their relation becomes clear in the chapter "A Little Demon" (book 11, chapter 3); and yet, despite this, Alyosha willingly takes a letter from Lise to Ivan (600). To anyone interpreting this scene in terms of erotic immediacy, Alyosha's actions here would be viewed as either ridiculously naive or perversely self-sacrificing. In terms of the "double movement" of the knight of faith (the renunciation of proprietary claims, as well as complete care for the other) that constitutes active, serving love, it is neither. Rather, it makes possible Alyosha's discernment into the illness that both Lise and Ivan bring to their distorted relation, and enables him to address it with frank speech that is undermined neither by despair nor resentment.

73. See, for example, Terras, *A Karamazov Companion,* p. 443 (note 55); and Miller, *The Brothers Karamazov,* p. 133.

74. There is a fascinating discussion of this dynamic in René Girard, *Things Hidden Since the Foundation of the World* (Stanford: Stanford University Press, 1987), pp. 416–431. Girard understands the language of *scandalon* to refer to the obstacle model of mimetic rivalry—the exact, demonic opposite to the model of Christian love, which removes scandal and seeks to restore proper vision so that no one will stumble. The cross is a scandal only to those whose vision is already caught in the trap of the scandal model and the cycle of desire for domination and revenge. Girard puts it this way: "There is an element of idolatry and scandal in the type of ascendancy that Jesus holds over his disciples before the Resurrection. That is why they never appreciate what the real issues are. They still credit Jesus with the worldly prestige of a great chief, a 'leader of men' or a 'master thinker'. The disciples see Jesus as being invulnerable—they see him as master of a superior form of power. They are his followers so that they can take part in this invulnerability—so they can become godlike according to the logic of violence. So it is inevitable that they be scandalized" (Ibid., pp. 418–419). Satan is therefore the mimetic model of scandal par excellence, the master of mimetic tricks—"the violent principle underlying all forms of earthly domination and all forms of idolatry, who tries to divert toward himself the adoration that is strictly due to God alone" (Ibid., p. 419). Thus, Paul recognizes the cross as the ultimate scandal, because it is presented as the ultimate victory—and those scandalized "fail to understand what this victory could possibly consist in" (Ibid., p. 428).

75. The quotation is from Isaiah 28:16, where the cornerstone is the sure foundation of truth against lies, of justice and righteousness against false judgment and the "covenant with death."

76. This quotation is taken from Psalm 118:22; cf. Matthew 21:42.

77. This quotation is from Isaiah 8:14–15, where it is spoken of the "Lord of hosts," who is to be regarded as holy: "Let him be your fear, and let him be your dread, And he will become a sanctuary, and a stone of offense." The context of this passage is that the politics in dialogue with the holy God differs from the power politics of idolatry—those who fear God do not fear what idolaters fear, namely temporal power. What is a sanctuary for the prophet, then, becomes a stumbling block for those who do not fear God. I have discussed this passage in "The Theological Politics of Plato and Isaiah: A Debate Rejoined," *Journal of Religion* 73/1 (January 1993):16–30.

78. Robert Belknap comments: "*Nadryv* . . . is hard to translate. It has been rendered as 'laceration', and is derived from *rvat'*, to 'rend', 'tear', 'burst', 'split', as is shown in the translations, 'heartbreak', or 'hysterics'. . . . The adjective derived from it can almost always be translated 'heartrending'" (Robert Belknap, *The Structure of The Brothers Karamazov* [The Hague: Mouton, 1967], p. 47).

79. Kierkegaard discusses the various forms of offense or *skandalon* in *Sickness Unto Death* (pp. 113–131); and in *Practice in Christianity* (eds. and trans. Howard Hong and Edna Hong [Princeton: Princeton University Press, 1991]), "Blessed Is He Who Is Not Offended at Me."

80. The Russian word *pravda* means both truth and justice (righteousness, veracity, integrity); it is the exact opposite of the lie.

81. Both Smerdyakov and Dmitri cause young Ilyusha to stumble; Ivan does the same with the child Lise and his younger brother Alyosha; and their father Fyodor causes all his children to stumble.

82. Kierkegaard, *Practice in Christianity*, p. 110f. In Matthew 18, that "crucial passage about offense in general" (note the physicality of Jesus' language: millstones for drowning, cutting off limbs, plucking out eyes, the hell of fire), "Christ is speaking about offense, but see, Christianly understood, the possibility of offense (the possibility of real offense, that which is related to becoming Christian) really emerges first in the second place: in the remedy that Christ recommends in order to be saved from the offense."

83. Kierkegaard, *Practice in Christianity*, p. 155. Let us again recall elder Zosima's understanding of the "crown of the monk's path, and of every man's path on earth," that moves the heart to insatiable love of the world (Dostoevsky, *The Brothers Karamazov*, p. 164).

84. See Genesis 4. It is also relevant to the brothers, fathers and sons, genealogy and inheritance motifs in *The Brothers Karamazov* to note that Lamech is not only tied to the progeny of proliferating violence; he is also the father of Noah, according to the Genesis genealogy.

# seven

# Christ in "The Grand Inquisitor"

## Identifying the Silent Christ:
## Sources, Parallels, and Contrasts

In Dostoevsky's notebooks for *The Brothers Karamazov* we find the following allusion to John's account (John 18:33–38) of the encounter between Christ and Pilate: "The clever Pilate . . . had reflected on truth. . . . What is the Truth? It stood before him, Truth himself."[1] The trial of Christ before Pilate signified in dramatic fashion for Dostoevsky the collision between two radically opposed ideas of the meaning and purpose of human existence—indeed, "the two most completely opposed ideas that could exist on earth."[2] The idea of the man-god (Pilate as image of Caesar) confronted the God-man. "The Grand Inquisitor" hearkens back to this ancient confrontation and at the same time anticipates that it will define also the future *krisis* (Greek, meaning "decision") of modernity. The entire prophetic point of Dostoevsky's art is given its encapsulating dramatic expression in the encounter between the Inquisitor and his silent prisoner.

The words about the "clever" Pilate being faced by "Truth himself" are given to Zosima, in that section of the notes for the novel corresponding to book 6, "The Russian Monk," which Dostoevsky designated as his explicit response to the argument of Ivan in book 5. This reference to the trial of Christ before Pilate suggests, however, that Dostoevsky's response is *already* present in the silent Christ-figure of Ivan's prose poem. The manner in which the truth of Christ is articulated through the characters of the novel—directly in the words and actions of Zosima and Alyosha, indirectly in the self-betraying words and actions of Ivan and his Inquisitor—has been the subject of reflection in this book. Yet Christ himself is also a character in *The Brothers Karamazov*, and a compelling one, although he does not speak; his silence challenges us to a more explicit consideration. The first requirement of such a consideration is to bear in mind that the Christ of "The Grand Inquisitor" is both Ivan Karamazov's "character" and Dostoevsky's "Truth." It is necessary, therefore, both to distinguish between the two Christs and to understand how they are related.

## Ivan's Christ

In the introduction to his "poem," Ivan offers a number of literary precedents, medieval and modern, Western and Russian, for bringing "higher powers down to earth." His poem, in which God "in his infinite mercy . . . once more walked among men in the semblance of man as he had walked among men for thirty-three years fifteen centuries ago," has its antecedents in Dante, in Victor Hugo's *Notre Dame de Paris*, in an Eastern Orthodox monastery poem, and in the nineteenth-century Russian poet, Fyodor Ivanovich Tyutchev. Like Tyutchev's Christ, who traversed the Russian land "in slavish garb," Ivan's Christ appears in the streets of sixteenth-century Seville "quietly, inconspicuously." Nevertheless, the people recognize him: "[They] are drawn to him by an invincible force, they flock to him, surround him, follow him. He passes silently among them with a quiet smile of infinite compassion. The sun of love shines in his heart, rays of Light, Enlightenment, and Power stream from his eyes and, pouring over the people, shake their hearts with responding love." Ivan suggests that this miracle of recognition by ordinary people of the divine in their midst might well constitute one of the "best passages" in his poem. He is right in this, and not only from a literary standpoint; for he demonstrates an acute theological sensitivity in his emphasis that this recognition, being already granted, is therefore not compelled by the subsequent public miracle of the raising of the little girl on the cathedral steps[40–42].*

All this is, however, in Ivan's own words, just a "literary preface" to what he really wants to say. The merely pro forma nature of this bringing "higher powers down to earth" reveals itself readily enough in Ivan's response to Alyosha's perplexed questioning as to the real identity of the prisoner: "Of course . . . the man is ninety years old, and might have lost his mind long ago over his idea. He might have been struck by the prisoner's appearance. It might, finally, have been simple delirium, the vision of a ninety-year-old man nearing death. . . . But isn't it all the

---

*Here and below, page number references appearing inside square brackets pertain to Dostoevsky's "The Grand Inquisitor," reprinted in Chapter 2 of this volume. Page numbers appearing inside parentheses, unless otherwise indicated, pertain to Fyodor Dostoevsky, *The Brothers Karamazov*, trans. Richard Pevear and Larissa Volokhonsky (New York: Vintage, 1990).

same to you and me whether it's *qui pro quo* or boundless fantasy? The only thing is that the old man needs to speak out, that finally after all his ninety years, he speaks out"[42]. Ivan appears at this point not to be particularly interested in the exact identity of the prisoner, suggesting that he is only something of a literary device, a catalyst for the Inquisitor's self-revelatory monologue. However, we come to see that this initial indifference is a pose; Ivan is as much concerned with the nature of the silent prisoner as he is with the Inquisitor's speaking out. Under Alyosha's further questioning after the recitation of his poem, he reveals that if the prisoner is not divinity brought down to earth, as his literary preface would have it, neither is he merely an old man's fantasy. He is, rather, the "great idealist" (*velikii idealist*)[53].

The most significant source for Ivan's Christ is one he does not name explicitly: The title of "great idealist" alludes in all probability to Ernest Renan's *Life of Jesus*. This probability becomes a virtual certainty when one considers Ivan's poem about the return of Christ to sixteenth-century Spain in the light of Dostoevsky's own recollection, in *A Writer's Diary*, of an actual conversation in which he was involved during the period of his life (in the 1840s) when he was under the influence of Vissarion Belinsky's left-Hegelian socialism. The subject of this conversation also was Christ's return to earth, but in the modern era of secular progressivism. Dostoevsky's reminiscence offers an illuminating background to "The Grand Inquisitor," and it is therefore worth quoting at length:

> For the most part, Belinsky was not a self-reflective person; he was always, throughout his life, a wholehearted enthusiast . . . . At the time of our first acquaintance he attached himself to me with all his heart, and at once . . . he threw himself into converting me to his faith . . . . I found him to be a passionate socialist, and in speaking to me he began directly with atheism . . . . As a socialist he first had to dethrone Christianity. He knew that the revolution must necessarily begin with atheism. He had to dethrone the religion that provided the moral foundation of the society he was rejecting. He radically rejected the family, private property, and the moral responsibility of the individual . . . but he believed with all his being that socialism not only would not destroy personal freedom but would, to the contrary, restore it to unheard-of grandeur, but on a new . . . foundation.
>
> There remained, however, the radiant personality of Christ himself, which was most difficult to contend with. Belinsky, as a socialist, was absolutely bound to destroy Christ's teachings; to label them false and uninformed philanthropy, proscribed by contemporary science and economic principles. Still there remained the most radiant image of the God-man, its moral unattainability, its marvelous and miraculous beauty. But Belinsky . . . in his unflagging enthusiasm, did not pause even before this insurmountable obstacle, as did Renan when he proclaimed in his

*Life of Jesus,* a book filled with unbelief, that Christ is still the ideal of human beauty, an unattainable type, never to be repeated in the future.

"But do you know," Belinsky screeched one evening (sometimes, if he was very excited, he would screech) as he turned to me, "Do you know that man's sins cannot be counted against him and that he cannot be laden down with obligations and with turning the other cheek when society is set up in such a mean fashion that a man cannot help but do wrong; economic factors alone lead him to do wrong, and it is absurd and cruel to demand from a man something which the very laws of nature make it impossible for him to carry out . . . "

"It's touching just to look at him," said Belinsky, suddenly breaking off his furious exclamations and turning to his friend as he pointed to me. "I no sooner mention the name of Christ than his whole face changes, just as if he were going to cry . . . . But believe me, you naïve fellow," he said, attacking me again, "Believe me, that your Christ, were he born in our time, would be the most undistinguished and ordinary of men; he would be utterly eclipsed by today's science and by those forces that now advance humanity."

"Oh, I think not," interrupted Belinsky's friend (I recall that we were sitting while Belinsky was pacing back and forth around the room). "I think not. If Christ appeared now he would join the socialist movement and take his place at its head . . . "

"He would indeed," Belinsky agreed suddenly with surprising haste. "He certainly would join the socialists and follow them."[3]

Dostoevsky penned this reminiscence of his relationship with Belinsky in 1873, during the period in which he was preparing to write *The Brothers Karamazov.*[4] Renan's *Life of Jesus* had already been on his mind for almost a decade, as is evident from the numerous allusions to it in his notebooks for *The Idiot* and for *Demons.*[5] In *The Brothers Karamazov,* Ivan's reference to the "great idealist" is one of several echoes of Renan distributed among characters such as the devil of Ivan's "nightmare," and the liberal defense lawyer from St. Petersburg, Fetyukovich, who speaks of "the crucified lover of humanity" (648, 743).[6]

Although Fetyukovich's "crucified lover of humanity" is evidently the Jesus of Renan and not the Christ of the Orthodox Church, to say that Dostoevsky simply repudiates the former in favor of the latter would be to oversimplify.[7] I have argued elsewhere in this book that although Dostoevsky judges modern "liberal idealism" inadequate, especially in its inability to withstand the nihilism that it engenders, he does not condemn it entirely. His final estimation of Renan's portrait of Jesus should be considered in the light of his attitude toward the "liberal idealism" of Stepan Verkhovensky in *Demons.* He evidently wishes to "redeem" a Stepan who has attained self-awareness through the suffering brought on by his own way of thinking. Stepan's liberalism generates nihilist offspring, but his adherence to the "Great Thought" does leave him open in the end to the acknowledgment of divine reality.[8] This treatment of Stepan might well offer us a key to understanding how the "great idealist" of Ivan's poem might at the same time point to Dostoevsky's "Truth."

Dostoevsky's frequent allusions to Renan indicate that he was struck especially by two features of the liberal French scholar's treatment of Jesus: the denial of Jesus' divinity, and yet at the same time, the exaltation of Jesus as a model, *the* bearer of the ideal of human perfection. For Dostoevsky, Renan is the "unbeliever" who nevertheless cannot help betraying a sense of awe before the sheer beauty of the "unattainable type" signified by Christ. Indeed, the case of Renan appears to confirm Dostoevsky's conviction that no amount of analysis and reduction of the image of Christ according to rational and historical "truth" will eclipse the radiance of this image as a perpetually compelling ideal for humanity. This conviction is expressed with defiance in the well-known letter written shortly after his release from the Siberian labor camp in which he had "accepted Christ into his soul":

> I can tell you about myself that I am a child of this century, a child of doubt and disbelief . . . and shall ever be (that I know), until they close the lid of my coffin. . . . And, despite all this, God sends me moments of great tranquillity . . . and it was during such a moment that I formed within myself a symbol of faith in which all is clear and sacred for me. This symbol is very simple, and here is what it is: to believe that there is nothing more beautiful, more profound, more sympathetic, more reasonable, more courageous, and more perfect than Christ; and there not only isn't, but I tell myself with a jealous love, there cannot be. More than that—if someone succeeded in proving to me that Christ was outside the truth, and if, *indeed,* the truth was outside Christ, I would sooner remain with Christ than with the truth.[9]

Ivan Karamazov, in accord with Renan (and despite his "literary preface"), treats Christ strictly in accord with "Euclidean" truth, and therefore exclusively as a human being. Moreover, Ivan follows Renan in applying, above all, the category of "idealist" to Jesus; and like Renan also, he means by this something more profound than a "great moralist" or a "benefactor of humanity" in any obviously utilitarian sense.[10] Indeed, it is the Inquisitor's contention that the "perfect idealism" of Jesus, in asking far too much of humanity, constitutes a radical challenge to any realistic solution to the problem of human order, and is thus actually incompatible with the accolade "benefactor of humanity": "If anyone has ever deserved our stake, it is you"[51].

Yet, in the face of the Inquisitor's "realism," the image of the silent prisoner remains strangely compelling. Just as Renan, in a book "filled with unbelief," could not help but "pause" before the "radiant image," so Ivan's poem seems in its effect to deny the intention of its author. As Alyosha observes: "Your poem praises Jesus, it doesn't revile him . . . as you meant it to"[52]. This unlooked-for effect of Ivan's poem is particularly noteworthy in that, unlike Renan, who affirms the "perfect idealism" of Jesus while repudiating his divinity, Ivan is intent on repudiating *both*. Ivan's Jesus is heavily determined by Dostoevsky's encounter with Renan's *Life of Jesus;* but the French author, while recognizing his Jesus in Ivan's portrait, would be appalled at the Inquisitor's declaration that this Jesus deserves the stake. Renan, a liberal humanist, believes in the ideal that his Jesus purportedly bequeathed to humanity: "His perfect idealism is the highest rule of the unblemished and virtuous life. He has created the heaven of pure souls, where is found what we ask for in vain on earth . . . in fine, liberty, which society excludes as an impossibility, and which exists in all its amplitude only in the domain of thought. The great Master of those who take refuge in this ideal Kingdom of God is still Jesus."[11] Ivan's Euclidean rationalism, on the contrary, leads him to reject not only the divinity of Jesus but also the great idealist's affirmation of human freedom and equality. In the charges of Ivan's Grand Inquisitor, the Jesus of liberal humanism is subjected to the hammer blows of nihilism. The Inquisitor's contention that "there are the strong and there are the weak,"[12] and that only the former can handle their freedom, expresses the tendency of Ivan's secular humanism to move into nihilism. Here, as it were, Renan is confronted by Nietzsche. And somehow present in this confrontation, and transcending it, is Dostoevsky's "Truth," which we must now consider.

## Dostoevsky's Christ

Nietzsche has already been introduced into the discussion of Ivan's Christ, and it is to him that we should turn first, in an effort to get a clearer view of Dostoevsky's Christ. In the course of his own treatment of the "psychology of the redeemer," Nietzsche noted that he had in view two modern antecedents especially—Renan and Dostoevsky. Although he is clearly indebted to Renan (more, it would seem, than he is willing to acknowledge) for certain features of his own presentation in *The Anti-Christ* of the type of "the redeemer,"[13] Nietzsche rejects what he takes to be the formative categories of Renan's portrait:

> Monsieur Renan, that buffoon *in psychologis,* has appropriated for his explication of the type Jesus the two *most inapplicable* concepts possible in this case: the concept of the *genius* and the concept of the *hero.* But if anything is unevangelic it is the concept hero. Precisely the opposite of all contending, of all feeling oneself in struggle has here become instinct: the incapacity for resistance here becomes morality

("resist not evil!"; the profoundest saying of the Gospel, its key in a certain sense), blessedness in peace, in gentleness, the *inability* for enmity . . . . To make a *hero* of Jesus!—And what a worse misunderstanding is the word "genius"! Our whole concept, our cultural concept "spirit" had no meaning whatever in the world Jesus lived in. To speak with the precision of the physiologist a quite different word would rather be in place here: the word idiot.[14]

As I have noted elsewhere, Nietzsche did not have the opportunity to read *The Brothers Karamazov,* but he was thoroughly familiar with Dostoevsky's portrait of the Christlike Prince Myshkin in *The Idiot.* That he appropriated the category of "idiot" from Dostoevsky is explicitly acknowledged elsewhere in *The Anti-Christ:*

> That strange and sick world to which the Gospels introduce us—a world like that of the Russian novel, in which refuse of society, neurosis and 'childlike' idiocy seem to make a rendezvous—must in any case have *coarsened* the type . . . . One has to regret that no Dostoevsky lived in the neighborhood of this most interesting *décadent.* I mean someone who could feel the thrilling fascination of such a combination of the sublime, the sick, and the childish.[15]

In Nietzsche's unpublished notebooks there is a passage entitled "Jesus: Dostoevsky," in which he asserts that Dostoevsky has been the only one (before himself) who has properly "figured out" Christ.[16] Coming from Nietzsche, this is high praise indeed; but how helpful is it in our own effort to "figure out" Dostoevsky on Christ? Two questions here need to be addressed: To what extent can Prince Myshkin be identified with Dostoevsky's Christ? Does the portrait of Myshkin actually bear out Nietzsche's juxtaposition of Dostoevsky's "idiot" to Renan's "hero/genius"?

As for the first question, it should be noted that Dostoevsky's explicitly stated intention in writing *The Idiot* was the relatively modest one (though more than ambitious enough in its own right) of depicting the "*perfectly* beautiful" or "good" *(prekrasnyi)* man.[17] It is clear from the notebooks for the novel, however, that for Dostoevsky the model of the "perfectly good man" is Christ himself; this is evident, for instance, in his frequent shorthand identification of the two in the title "Prince-Christ" *(Kniaz' Khristos).*[18] This is not to say that Dostoevsky was intentionally attempting, through his art, to discover and portray the authentic Jesus, but rather the reverse. In his attempt to discover and portray the "perfectly good" human being, he drew on the highest model he knew, the Christ of the Gospels especially,[19] but also the Christ of subsequent Christian (particularly Russian Orthodox) tradition. Since Dostoevsky also drew inspiration from other sources, such as characters in Western literature (Cervantes's Don Quixote and Dickens's Pickwick, most notably),[20] and of course his own experience, observation, and imagination, one must be cautious about claiming simply that Prince Myshkin reflects Dostoevsky's sense of Christ. This caution noted, however, the general correspondence between the two is undeniable at one level: In contemplating the characteristics of Myshkin, we contemplate the sort of human being Dostoevsky likely thought Jesus was. These characteristics include humility, the capacity for forgiveness, a spontaneous love for children, insight into the character of others, remarkable intelligence, and innocence—to indicate some of the more prominent attributes highlighted in the novel and the notebooks.[21]

Let us now consider the second question: Does the portrait of Myshkin actually justify Nietzsche's juxtaposition of "idiot" to "hero/genius"? Nietzsche argues in *The Anti-Christ* that the Gospels present us with two alternative portraits of Jesus: the "mountain, lake and field preacher, whose appearance strikes one as that of a Buddha on a soil very little like that of India"; and the "aggressive fanatic, the mortal enemy of [Jewish] theologian and priest."[22] He identifies the latter as a fabrication of the early Church and the former as the "authentic" Jesus, who is, in his view, the Jesus also of *The Idiot*. Yet if such a distinction is certainly too simple for the Jesus of the Gospels, it is also too simple for Dostoevsky's Myshkin. It misses the element of prophetic judgment in Myshkin—perhaps because Nietzsche understood prophetic judgment only in terms of "aggressive fanaticism." Dostoevsky embodies in Myshkin a different understanding, expressed concisely in these words in his rough notebooks, immediately following a passage in which he emphasizes Myshkin's forgiving and serene nature: "Prophecy. Each one has been illuminated about himself." The presence itself of the "perfectly good" person illuminates the surrounding darkness so that those living within that darkness can see it and judge themselves.[23]

Yet Myshkin's prophetic role can on occasion be more "aggressive," too. He appears anything but "gentle," incapable of "resistance" to the world around him, when at a social gathering of prominent people he launches into a vehement critique of the West:

> Roman Catholicism believes that the Church cannot exist on earth without universal temporal power, and cries: *Non possumus!* . . . They have trifled with the most sacred, truthful, innocent, ardent feelings of the people, have bartered it all for money, for base temporal power. And isn't this the teaching of Antichrist? . . . Socialism, too, is the child of Catholicism. . . . It, too, like its brother atheism, was begotten of despair . . . to quench the spiritual thirst of parched humanity, and save it not by Christ but . . . by violence . . . . By their works ye shall know them—as it is written . . . . We must organize our resistance, and do it now—now! It is necessary

that our Christ should shine forth in opposition to the ideas of the West, our Christ, whom we have preserved and they have never known![24]

If Myshkin's drawing-room speech is any indication, there is room in Dostoevsky's image of Christ for both "mountain, lake, and field" preacher *and* apocalyptic prophet. The contrast might be jarring to readers of *The Idiot*, as indeed to readers of the Gospels; but Dostoevsky was apparently able to contemplate both types within one person.

The key to assessing Nietzsche's interpretation of Myshkin lies in the word he most appreciated in Dostoevsky's novel—*idiocy*. Nietzsche, like Dostoevsky, does not understand "idiocy" in relation to intelligence (or any deficiency thereof). He defines it primarily as a psycho-physiological condition determining a general attitude toward reality:

> We recognize a condition of morbid susceptibility of the *sense of touch* which makes it shrink back in horror from every contact, every grasping of a firm object. Translate such a physiological *habitus* into its ultimate logic—as instinctive hatred of *every* reality, as flight into the 'ungraspable' . . . as antipathy towards everything firm, all that is custom, institution, Church, as being at home in a world undisturbed by reality of any kind, a merely "inner" world.[25]

Now there is certainly a *physiological* element to Myshkin's idiocy; Dostoevsky emphasizes that he has been ill much of his life with epilepsy. To this extent, Nietzsche's reading converges with Dostoevsky's portrait. However, Myshkin's idiocy has for Dostoevsky also a *religious* meaning, and a very specific one, as this observation in the notebooks indicates: "The Prince is downright ill, a *yurodivyi*."[26]

Dostoevsky's use of *yurodivyi* is the most important indicator as to how he himself understands Myshkin's idiocy. The *yurodivyi*, or "holy fool in Christ," is a central figure in the Russian religious consciousness. Byzantine ascetic practice provided the Russians with this model, which they appropriated with special enthusiasm as a suitable expression of their kenotically oriented Christianity. The Russian "holy fool" intended to give dramatic expression to Paul's account in 1 Corinthians (1:18, 1:21, 3:18, 4:10) of the tension between spiritual "foolishness" and worldly "wisdom." As a living sign of this tension, the "holy fool" adopted forms of behavior—poverty, eccentricity, and often feigned madness—that were at once exercises in self-humiliation and an indirect judgment of the "world" and its "common sense."[27] Although Myshkin certainly shares the eccentricity of the *yurodivyi*, there is no serious question of madness in his case, feigned or otherwise; even the worldly characters in the novel who are most disposed to regard him as a bit "touched" quickly come to appreciate the lucidity of his insight. Dostoevsky, being attentive to the modern consciousness, substitutes "illness" (not typically a trait of the "holy fool" as traditionally defined) for "madness" as the concrete correlative of Myshkin's unworldly foolishness.

The judgment of the world embodied in the holy fool could also take a more overtly prophetic form in the Russian tradition. By the sixteenth century, "holy foolishness" had come to acquire an important social and even political meaning. During this period, the Russian Church hierarchy had become noticeably slack in the duty of defending the oppressed and exposing injustice, so that the holy fools increasingly assumed this role of the ancient Church leaders. They also came increasingly to assume the role of the ancient "sainted" princes, who had built the state, and according to tradition, had attempted to realize in it the principles of Christian justice; for the Moscow rulers of the sixteenth century no longer paid even lip service to this princely ideal. With this abdication of moral leadership on the part of the Church leaders and the princes, the needed corrective of the Christian conscience came to be embodied in the holy fools. As the eminent historian of Russian Christianity George Fedotov has noted: "This conscience could pronounce its judgement the more freely and authoritatively, the less it was connected with the world, the more radically it denied the world . . . . At this period holy foolishness was a form of prophetic service, in the ancient Jewish sense."[28] Although the public role of the "holy fool" in Russian culture diminished considerably after the sixteenth century, it was clearly not forgotten by Dostoevsky. Myshkin is both "prince" and "holy fool," and his pronouncing of judgment before the powerful gathered together in General Yepanchin's drawing room is entirely in keeping with the meaning of his character. The views concerning the modern West he so vehemently expresses might well be those of Dostoevsky himself; but the author has not, as some commentators allege,[29] committed an artistic incongruity in order to get those views into the novel. Myshkin's public outburst is faithful to the *yurodivyi* tradition, which combined—albeit, often in different people and at different times—the indirect sign of self-humiliation with the direct speech of admonition.

In his preference for Dostoevsky's category of "idiot" over Renan's "genius/hero," Nietzsche misses the crucial concept that mediates between the two—that of "prophet." For Dostoevsky, the Prince as *yurodivyi* is both idiot and hero, both "absurdly unpolitical" (in Nietzsche's words) and profoundly concerned with the question of social order. In short, even as Dostoevsky is critical of Renan's *Life of Jesus*, he would no more agree with Nietzsche's reasons for esteeming more highly Prince Myshkin as a representation of Jesus. Dostoevsky would find no essential contradiction between *idiot* and *genius/hero* as descriptions of Jesus. He does not reject Renan because of the latter's use of the words *genius, hero,* or even *perfect idealist.*[30] Indeed, Dostoevsky too would affirm that Jesus embodies and expresses "perfect idealism." The problem is not with Renan's terms but with his inadequate understanding of the very ideal that Jesus heroically—and idiotically—brings to the world.

In order to clarify Dostoevsky's view of the deficiencies in this understanding of Jesus, we return to Renan: The idealism of Jesus is, according to Renan, above all an idealism of the free conscience, or "liberty."

> His kingdom of God was . . . probably above all the kingdom of the soul, founded on liberty . . . . It was a pure religion, without forms, without temple, and without priest; it was the moral judgement of the world, delegated to the conscience of the just man . . . . On the one hand, the right of all men to participate in the kingdom of God was proclaimed. On the other, religion was henceforth separated in principle from the state. The rights of conscience, withdrawn from political law, resulted in the constitution of a new power—the "spiritual power" . . . . He was the first to say, "My kingdom is not of this world."[31]

Evidently Jesus endorses, well ahead of his time, the liberal principle of separation of church and state. Renan's Jesus signifies an ideal of individual freedom that stands in opposition to any worldly order that would purport to integrate soul and body. If, as I have suggested, Ivan's "great idealist" is identifiable with Renan's, then the Inquisitor would be justified in regarding this Jesus as having come to the world primarily with a "promise of freedom . . . which you placed above everything"—an individual freedom that in the Inquisitor's view is fundamentally antithetical to the social unity that human beings crave above all. That this exaltation of the "rights of conscience," in separation from the world of political and social existence, is not the proper interpretation of Jesus's "ideal" is signaled by Alyosha's question to Ivan in "The Grand Inquisitor": "Who will believe you about freedom? Is that, is that any way to understand it? It's a far cry from the Orthodox idea"[52]. Alyosha is speaking here on behalf of Dostoevsky. From Dostoevsky's perspective, Renan's understanding of Jesus' perfect idealism is deficient in two respects: in regard to the nature of the ideal itself, and in regard to its realizability.

If setting forth Dostoevsky's perspective were to entail a complete elaboration of the "Orthodox idea" to which Alyosha refers, we would be faced with a large task indeed, and one fraught with complicated questions. It is possible, however, to follow a more direct route to Dostoevsky's Christ by focusing on a document that contains the most explicit albeit informal account we have of his Christology—the remarkable private meditation penned while he kept vigil by the corpse of his first wife. In this meditation, Dostoevsky's thoughts about his unhappy marriage give rise to a struggle to articulate the meaning of Christ, in relation not only to his personal loss but also to the more general questions that preoccupied him as poet-prophet. He indicates how the ideal of Christ shows the way to the overcoming of those perennial contradictions—between egoism and love, individuality and social unity, freedom and equality—which continue to permeate modern thought and practice. In contradistinction to Renan, Dostoevsky's Christ signifies a personal liberty that fulfills itself only by giving itself over to community with others:

*April 16.* Masha is lying on the table. Will I meet again with Masha?

To love a person *as one's own self* according to the commandment of Christ is impossible . . . . The law of individuality on earth is the constraint, "I" is the stumbling block. [But] Christ alone was able to do this, but Christ was eternal, an eternal ideal toward which man strives and should by the laws of nature strive. Meanwhile, after the appearance of Christ, as the *idea of man incarnate,* it became as clear as day that . . . the highest, final development of the individual should attain precisely the point (at the very end of his development, at the very point of reaching the goal) . . . where man might find, recognize and with all the strength of his nature be convinced that the highest use which he can make of his individuality, of the full development of his *I,* is to seemingly annihilate that *I,* to give it wholly to each and every one wholeheartedly and selflessly. And this is the greatest happiness. In this way the law of the *I* merges with the law of humanism, and in the merging both, both the *I* and the *all* (in appearance two extreme opposites) mutually annihilated for each other, at the same time . . . each apart attains the highest goal of his individual development.

This is indeed the paradise of Christ. All history whether of humanity or in part of each man separately is only development, struggle, striving and attainment of that goal . . . .

Christ entered entirely into humanity, and man strives to transform himself into the *I* of Christ or into his own ideal . . . .

And thus on earth mankind strives toward an ideal *opposed* to his nature. When a man has not fulfilled the law of striving towards the ideal, that is, has not *through love* sacrificed his *I* to people or to another person (Masha and I), he suffers and calls this state a sin. And so, man must unceasingly experience a suffering which is compensated for by the heavenly joy of fulfilling the Law, that is, by sacrifice. This is earthly equality. Otherwise earth would be senseless.[32]

It is noteworthy that in this most personal effort at articulating the meaning of Christ, free of the self-consciousness of an author with any audience in mind, Dostoevsky's instinct is to employ the more tentative—and more universally accessible—language of philosophy rather than Christian doctrine. Indeed, the document illustrates clearly how foreign the terms of dogmatic theology are to Dostoevsky's religious thought. He speaks of Christ as "eternal ideal" rather than "Redeemer." Although this language might resemble the liberal discourse of a Renan, Dostoevsky's emphasis on Christ as an ideal or model toward which human beings can and should strive is also in accordance with the Orthodox idea to which Alyosha refers. Orthodox thinking has been deeply influenced by the distinction made by the early Hellenistic theologians, especially Irenaeus, between human beings as created initially in the divine "image" and human beings as moving gradually also into the divine "likeness" through their own free responses. The understanding of Christ as the model of human life in the divine likeness, held out for the emulation of human beings, is in keeping with the Irenaean notion of human moral perfection as the outcome of a development characterized by a synergy of divine grace and human freedom. In speaking of Christ as an "eternal ideal" toward which humanity strives, Dostoevsky reflects the thinking of Irenaeus and the Greek East, even if his language seems closer to that of Renan. Moreover, his interpretation of this ideal as one of self-realization through self-abandonment shares in the Eastern (and especially Russian) emphasis on the way of *kenosis*.[33]

Yet, what are the prospects for the realization of this "eternal ideal" of self-sacrificing love in the face of the "law" of egoism that rules in the world? Renan assumes that the "kingdom of God" preached by Jesus has its realization finally in the private conscience of the individual. As such, it is an inspiring hope but also a continual reminder of the individual's separation from a recalcitrant world that denies freedom and virtue. Dostoevsky certainly preferred Renan's sense of antithesis between the ideal and the real to the rational synthesis promised by Hegel and his epigones. He could affirm in Renan's "perfect idealism," as in Stepan Verkhovensky's devotion to the "Great Thought," the evidence of a longing for transcendence. His own work, moreover, exhibits a vivid sense of the unrelenting indifference of the world, both human and natural, to this longing. Let us recall that in the meditation he speaks of humanity striving "toward an ideal *opposed* to [its] nature." We might also note, for instance, the unforgettable commentary of Ippolit Terentyev in *The Idiot* on Holbein's painting of "The Dead Christ in the Tomb":

> In the picture the face is terribly smashed with blows, swollen, covered with terrible, swollen and blood-stained bruises, the eyes open and squinting; the large, open whites of the eyes have a sort of dead and glassy glint . . . . As one looks at the dead body of this tortured man, one cannot help asking oneself the peculiar and interesting question: if such a corpse (and it must have been just like that) was seen by all his disciples . . . by all who believed in Him and worshipped Him, then how

could they possibly have believed, as they looked at the corpse, that that martyr would rise again? Here one cannot help being struck with the idea that if death is so horrible and if the laws of nature are so powerful, then how can they be overcome? How can they be overcome when even He did not conquer them . . . ? Looking at that picture, you get the impression of nature as some enormous, implacable, and dumb beast, or to put it more correctly, much more correctly . . . as some huge engine of the latest design, which has senselessly seized, cut to pieces, and swallowed up—impassively and unfeelingly—a great and priceless Being, a Being worth the whole of nature and all its laws, worth the entire earth . . . . The picture seems to give expression to the idea of a dark, insolent, and senselessly eternal power, to which everything is subordinated.[34]

Although we know of the devastating impact Holbein's painting had on Dostoevsky himself when he viewed it at the art gallery in Basel,[35] his vision is not identical to that of Ippolit. Whereas Ippolit's Christ (like that of Renan) is the "great idealist" who becomes yet one more human victim of an indifferent or hostile world, Dostoevsky's Christ *is* the "great ideal" itself: "Christ—the great and final ideal of the development of all humanity—which appeared to us . . . incarnate." Elsewhere in his meditation, Dostoevsky speaks of Christ as the "reflection of God on earth."[36] The modern portraits of Christ most closely related to Dostoevsky's Christ—those of Renan, Nietzsche, and Ivan Karamazov—explicitly deny his divinity; and Dostoevsky's own Prince Myshkin must also finally be understood as a representation not of Christ but of Christlikeness, of the human possibility of transformation "into the *I* of Christ." The Christ who is Dostoevsky's "Truth" is (again, in accord with the "Orthodox idea") both human *and* divine, the divine-human God-man *(bogochelovek)*.[37]

As the eternal ideal who appeared in the world "incarnate," Dostoevsky's Christ signifies that the world and human nature are not finally opposed to the ideal of love. Christ himself not only incarnates that ideal in the face of the law of egoism on earth, therein acting as the model for human beings; he also founds a communal order in and through which the world and human behavior might be transformed in practice. This, for Dostoevsky, is the primary significance of the Church. It is an embryonic expression in practice of the merging of the "*I* and the *all*" in a way that allows individuals to find in their unity with others at the same time the highest development of their unique personality.[38] As is well known, Dostoevsky had strong opinions about the relative merits of the institutional churches—Roman Catholic, Protestant, and Orthodox—as faithful preservers of the communal order founded by Christ. Yet when it comes to a concrete depiction in his art of the merging of the "*I* and the *all*," he eschews such grand and tendentious interpretations of history in favor of showing what he means through the tiny, modest community of children founded by Alyosha in the epilogue to *The Brothers Karamazov*.[39]

It was Dostoevsky's hope that the problem of the "*I* and the *all*," would be resolved in the historical future after the model of Christ rather than according to the social formula of the Grand Inquisitor. He recognized that this was a *hope*, not a certainty. Indeed, all that was certain for him was that the full realization of his hope would signify the end of history itself—though not, of course, in the immanentized sense of Kojève, Fukuyama, or the Inquisitor. Referring again to Dostoevsky's meditation: "But if that [that is, the "paradise of Christ," the "merging of the *I* and the *all*"] is the final goal of humanity (and having attained it, it would no longer be necessary to develop . . . to struggle, to glimpse the ideal through all one's falls and eternally strive towards it . . . )—then it follows that man attaining it would also end his earthly existence." This end, however, is not one of annihilation but of transformation into a "heavenly life."[40] The final consummation of the law of love among human beings is enfolded in the "other mysterious worlds" of which Zosima speaks.

Dostoevsky's meditation on love and egoism, individuality and social unity, in relation to the "eternal ideal" of Christ thus becomes a meditation also on the mystery of immortality: "Everything depends on whether Christ is taken for the final ideal on earth . . . . If you believe in Christ, then you believe that you will live eternally."[41] For him, the divinity of Christ implies that he is the "reflection" on earth of both God *and* immortality. Dostoevsky asserts that the "synthetic nature of Christ is wondrous,"[42] and indeed the capacity of his Christ to draw all to himself is evident in the manner in which the central themes and tensions of Dostoevsky's whole religious thought are brought together in this meditation of three pages. Although the language of the meditation tends to be philosophical, the vision is thoroughly biblical: Dostoevsky's Christ is the "light of the world" (John 8:12) who both illumines the darkness of the world and "overcomes" that darkness (John 16:33). Despite Ivan's intentions, the compelling silence of his "great idealist" images forth something of the Christ of the Gospels. The Inquisitor might stick to his idea, and Ivan with him, but the silent prisoner's kiss glows in his heart.

## The Silent Christ: A Theological Coda

What are we to make theologically of the silence of Christ in the poem of the Grand Inquisitor? An intriguing question, with an equally intriguing range of possible answers that connect to the themes of this book. Might it be related to the silence of the slain Lamb of the book of Revelation, in regard to which one commentator has noted, "One rather remarkable feature of the Lamb in Revelation is that *he never speaks*," in contrast to the "beasts" who speak blasphemously (13:5) and "like a dragon" (13:11)?[43] Might it be understood as the embodiment of Christ's kenotic pattern of self-emptying, the dying seed of John 12, or the self-abnegating sower of the parable? Could it be that the Christ figure, like the silent Jesus before Pilate, will not answer the Grand Inquisitor on his own ground, as an argumentative or political rival—the "other" in the mediation of mimetic desire? Is the silent Christ of Ivan's poem perhaps related to Hesychastic (from the Greek, *hesychia*, "silence") monasticism, which strongly influenced the Russian monastic tradition that forms an important backdrop to Dostoevsky's final novel? All of these related answers are plausible, and yet they cannot be given in abstraction from the literary and dramatic setting of the novel itself. Nor should we forget that the silent Christ "answers" the Inquisitor's defiant monologue with a silent gesture, a kiss of intimacy that burns in the Inquisitor's heart. Let us explore this web of associations in order to make some concluding observations about Dostoevsky's prophetic poetics.

To do so, we will first return to the scene of confrontation between the Christ figure and the Grand Inquisitor in Ivan's poetic work. Ellis Sandoz has astutely observed that the Inquisitor is in some respects modeled on John the Baptist.[44] Like John, the Inquisitor "was in the wilderness, and I, too, ate locusts" (260), preparing for martyrdom, until he "awoke" and joined the host seeking to correct Christ's deed. The opening words of the Inquisitor—"Is it you? You?"—to his prisoner echo the question of the imprisoned John the Baptist in Matthew 11, "Are you he who is to come, or shall we look for another?" In Ivan's poem, no answer is given, and the Inquisitor quickly cuts off the possibility of an answer: "Do not answer, be silent." In Matthew's gospel, Jesus's answer is certainly not direct: "Go and tell John what you hear and see: the blind receive their sight and the lame walk, lepers are cleansed and the deaf hear, and the dead are raised up, and the poor have good news preached to them. And blessed is he who takes no offense [is not scandalized] at me" (11:4–6). The issue here is prominently featured in Ivan's literary preface—namely, how is the identity and authority of Christ recognized in the world? The act of recognition, Ivan clearly asserts, can be resolved only with reference to "faith in what the heart tells you." The act of recognition reveals the heart of the realist—as Kierkegaard puts it: either faith or offense.

Ivan's Inquisitor is a John the Baptist figure who takes offense, leaving the wilderness and the prophetic proclamation of repentance in order to prepare a very different path of human blessedness. Whatever the Romantic colorings in Ivan's portrait of the Christ figure, it is nonetheless evident that his intent is to judge the Christ of the New Testament, the one to whom Alyosha has appealed—in response to Ivan's despairing dossier of unrequited tears of innocent suffering children—as having the "right to forgive," who "can forgive everything, forgive all *and for all*" (246). A basic premise of our interpretation of *The Brothers Karamazov* has been to view the poetic whole of Dostoevsky's novel as portraying a situation of "contemporaneity" with Christ, a dramatic enactment of the Christian vision of spiritual causality.[45] Yet in Ivan's "play within a play" it is remarkable that Ivan cannot himself fully risk this challenge—unlike his "nice collection" of antitheodicy anecdotes taken from contemporary news reports, his poetic trial of Christ maintains its critical detachment. It is set, somewhat anachronistically, in the Spanish Inquisition of the Counterreformation,[46] representing everything that modern Europe has rejected in the authoritarian church of Christendom. Expressing one of the more cynical and brutal examples of Christian power politics, it serves to counter but also to highlight the political weakness and powerlessness of the biblical Jesus. Thus it brings into focus the double offense of the God-man—in relation to loftiness (the claim that Jesus embodies divinity) and in relation to lowliness (the one who embodies divinity is powerless to end suffering)[47]—an offense tied above all to Jesus's claim to forgive sins.

The opposite of faith in response to Christ's claim to forgive sin, says Kierkegaard, is not doubt but offense, or the sickness unto death expressed in various conscious and unconscious forms of despair. That is, the response is not determined in relation to a *doctrine* of the God-man or a *doctrine* of Atonement; it is the personal will to accept or willfully reject the life of Christ as paradigmatic both of the divine purpose for the world and of the path to human well-being, the edifice of human happiness. The life of Christ evokes an existential trial, described in Simeon's prophetic blessing in Luke 2:35 as the sword that pierces the soul and reveals the thoughts of the heart. I suggest this is precisely what happens dramatically to the Grand Inquisitor, whose ninety-year silence (250) is broken open in his confrontation with the silent Christ. What we have in Ivan's poem is the defiant self-disclosure of demonic despair. It will help to have Kierkegaard's definition of this despair before us as we consider the Inquisitor:

Demonic despair is the most intensive form of the [spiritual sickness] despair: in despair to will to be oneself . . . in hatred toward existence, it wills to be itself, wills to be itself in accordance with its misery. . . . Rebelling against all existence, it feels that it has obtained evidence against it, against its goodness. The person in despair believes that he himself is the evidence, and that is what he wants to be, and therefore he wants to be himself, himself in his torment, in order to protest against all existence with this torment. . . . Figuratively speaking, it is as if an error slipped into an author's writing and the error became conscious of itself as an error—perhaps it actually was not a mistake but in a much higher sense an essential part of the whole production—and now this error wants to mutiny against the author, out of hatred toward him, forbidding him to correct it and in maniacal defiance saying to him:

No, I refuse to be erased; I will stand as a witness against you, a witness that you are a second-rate author.[48]

For the most part, suggests Kierkegaard, demonic despair keeps itself hidden in a self-inclosing reserve that will not confess its deepest identity. Yet when confronted by the good, a bad conscience cannot endure silence: "The only thing that can constrain inclosing reserve to speak is either a higher demon (for every devil has his day), or the good, which is absolutely able to keep silent."[49] So in the face of the silent Christ the defiant despair of the Inquisitor is brought to involuntary confession in the form of speech that precisely characterizes the spiritual state of such an isolated, tormented self: a monologue.[50] Ivan's poem, like the Inquisitor's monologue, represents the isolated self that will not enter into the free reciprocity of love offered in Christ's forgiveness of sin. It devotes itself rather to proving that happiness and human fulfillment must take away that freedom of conscience, the cost of which is too high, and replace it with the security of mass society presided over by higher humanists, who will correct the botched anthropology of the God-man.

Ivan and the Inquisitor take offense at Christ's claim with reference to his divinity. Early on in "Rebellion," the chapter preceding "The Grand Inquisitor," Ivan admits to Alyosha that in his opinion Christ's love is a "miracle impossible on earth": "True, he was God. But we are not gods" (237). Thus to put forward Christ's love as a model for human imitation is not only a cruel mockery of human incapacity; it incites people to godlike aspirations that create tremendous suffering on earth. To fall from such an elevated ideal leads human beings to demonic excesses. As Ivan puts it, "I think that if the devil does not exist, and man has therefore created him, he has created him in his own image and likeness" (239)—a formulation proven by Ivan's collection of "little facts." So Ivan's Inquisitor accuses Christ of ignoring this insoluble contradiction of human nature and unrealistically elevating the expectations of free conscience by putting himself forward as the image of human fulfillment, able to resist demonic temptations: "Oh, of course, in this you acted proudly and magnificently, like God, but mankind, that weak, rebellious tribe—are they gods?" (255). Such an overestimation of human freedom can only evoke the unhappy, rebellious despair of the majority of human beings, who are not up to the challenge of becoming selves in confession, accepting the offer of forgiveness of sins, and taking up the divine posture of self-sacrificing, serving, humble love—which is, after all, the true, not directly visible miracle of the God-man.

The offense in relation to the loftiness of the God-man has everything to do with his claim as an individual human being to forgive sin, which is something only God can do. Ivan's "humble confession" that he can never understand how the suffering of innocents could ever be forgiven, or how in the whole world there could be a being who would have the "right" to forgive (243f.), is rooted in a refusal to believe the revelation of such a possibility in the incarnation of Christ. His "humility" causes him to "hasten" to take his own human measures and to defend himself against the "higher harmony" of the divine offer of forgiveness of sin. Ivan and the Inquisitor deny the truth of Christ because in human understanding a God's willingness to become human in order to forgive sin is impossible and scandalous.

This leads to the second, related form of offense: that related to the lowliness of the God-man. The offensive lowliness of Christ is the dominant subtext of the Inquisitor's monologue. If he is going to be God, then at least he should have made this directly evident to human beings, evoking their compliant obedience by an overwhelming, public display of divine power and authority, and thereby solving the tormenting problem of personal freedom that leads to such horrific human suffering. To continue to appeal to the free decision of the heart reinforces the paradox of freedom in the divided conscience: Nothing is more seductive and yet nothing is more harmful. The indirect communication of divine love in the lowly, powerless human form of the suffering servant is offensive to human understanding—not least because it requires that human beings model their lives after it as the path to harmony and happiness. Such a paradoxical foundation for the rule of God, accuses the Inquisitor, is destructive of the very conditions for its success. It cannot therefore be the truth, since it is beyond human capacity for comprehension and action.

The irony here is intentional: It is the God-man, after all, who stands in the prisoner's dock and is subjected to human trial. The point is that Christ's revelation of God and the human offends natural human knowledge and expectation of both—both with respect to loftiness (any self-respecting God should remain hidden in mysterious transcendence rather than become overly familiar in particular human form, offering forgiveness of sins as if such a right could be offered to all by one) and with respect to lowliness (human beings cannot be expected to be drawn toward the divine by way of voluntary suffering and death, taking upon themselves even those burdens unjustly imposed by others and being willing to forgive even those who impose these burdens; they cannot be expected to believe that this is the path to the highest happiness). Such a revelation offends natural religious and moral sensibilities by prescribing a cure for the human condition that is more tormenting and difficult than the illness: a pattern of righteousness that flies in the face of natural justice. Ivan and the Inquisitor judge the God-man according to their own, more realistic idea of the nature both of divinity and of humanity. Ivan in particular wants Euclidean proof of divine goodness and trustworthiness, absent which he is not prepared to take on the weak and humble posture of Christlike love. At a minimum, he wants a philosophically respectable Christ who answers the theodicy problem.

The answer to the Inquisitor's monologue given by the Christ figure indicates that Ivan sees what is required. The prisoner remains attentive but silent, and then approaches the old man (still in silence) and kisses him on his lips: "That," says Ivan, "is the whole answer." There is no direct, doctrinal resolution to the offense of the divided human conscience that refuses to enter the divine mystery of incarnate love through the forgiveness of sin. There is no external, rational answer to the problem of suffering. The response required is to hand the self over in an obedient trust that temporally embraces the offering of eternal, divine love, offering in turn to share it actively with others in the superabundant economy of divine fullness. Hence the language of intimacy, the gesture of the kiss, is exactly faithful to the revelation of Christ; it is an invitation to intimacy with God and neighbor by giving up one's tight hold upon the self in order to hand over one's will to a mysterious higher purpose—a handing over that can only be experienced as a death, a complete giving up of control in order to serve what we cannot fully know or resolve.[51] The identity and authority of the God-man cannot be seen or spoken about directly, and one therefore cannot control its meaning or its reception by others in the world. It can only be encountered through the sacrificial self-giving of intimate love, in which the self finds itself and its power to act by emptying itself in service to the other. In effect, it is a pattern that requires dramatic enactment of a possibility that appears to be humanly impossible—to get oneself back by giving it up . . . in love.

This is the spiritual causality disclosed in the "law of Christ"—the law of intimate, divine love that burns in the heart. It is utterly fitting that Alyosha reminds the despairing Ivan of the erotic attachments that move him to love life, asking him: "How will you live, what will you love them with?" (263). Ivan appeals to the force of "Karamazov baseness" and the formula "all is permitted." It is a formula that Ivan will not renounce, and he defies Alyosha to renounce him for it. Instead Alyosha commits his act of "literary theft," silently kissing his brother on the lips. The law of Christ, the kenotic posture of humble love, is not a moral law in conflict with freedom but rather seeks its fulfillment in the purification of desire. "All is permitted," but everything depends on whether one's heart is attuned to the inarticulate embrace of the divine Word that loves through the penitential giving of the self, or to the various self-asserting ideas that judge according to the logic of fallen desire. For Dostoevsky, only the practice of love disclosed in the image of Christ can lead to a recognition of the causal structure of love in reality—a love above all manifested in dying. Handing oneself over to the "not-knowing" of God in a faith that "sees darkly" and therefore seeks actively, in the form of the servant, will involve the self in complex trials of love that cannot be accounted for in direct human speech. Yet it can be represented indirectly, in the dramatic display of the pattern in manifold, particular forms. In *The Brothers Karamazov* Ivan is "answered" by his brothers, Dmitri and Alyosha, who penitentially embrace the scandalous posture of Christ, enacting the words of the elder—"all are guilty for all, all are responsible for all"—and experience the blessedness of "brotherly communion" in the order of self-giving love.

The fundamental but implicit, unexpressed thought that we take with us from this reading of Dostoevsky's novel, then, is the final inability to put into speech the spiritual causality of divine purpose. As Dostoevsky's art shows, insight into the truth of divine purpose is not a matter of rhetorical power or dianoetic virtue, of the various apparatuses of conceptual control devised by human wisdom. It entails the relational risk of obedient trust that relinquishes its hold on causal levers, repents of the attempt to manage reality, and gives itself to the excessive, active love of divine intimacy. Like the New Testament witness, Dostoevsky believes that this kenotic pattern—which scandalizes conventional human wisdom and therefore suffers in the world—represents the path toward the fullness of divine love in which human beings are destined to share. Christ is not only suffering servant but also bridegroom—depicting the relational intimacy of divine love that reveals how our own hopes are tied to the whole of life. The language of immortality in *The Brothers Karamazov*, in keeping with that found in the gospels, is not focused on doctrines of an afterlife or on the nature of the soul. The focus is on the drama of excessive, divine love that through suffering service invites all to participate in God's passionate desire for wholeness—so that all may one day feast together in the marriage banquet of divine consummation, where all particular loves dance for joy because they know face to face even as they are fully known.

# Notes

1. Fyodor Dostoevsky, *The Notebooks for The Brothers Karamazov*, ed. and trans. Edward Wasiolek (Chicago: University of Chicago Press, 1971), p. 102.

2. Fyodor Dostoevsky, *A Writer's Diary*, vol. 2, trans. Kenneth Lantz (Evanston, Ill.: Northwestern University Press, 1994), p. 1322.

3. Dostoevsky, *A Writer's Diary*, vol. 1, pp. 127–129.

4. See Dostoevsky, *Notebooks for The Brothers Karamazov*, p. 7.

5. See, for instance, Fyodor Dostoevsky, *The Notebooks for The Idiot*, ed. Edward Wasiolek, trans. Katherine Strelsky (Chicago: University of Chicago Press, 1967), p. 105; and idem, *The Notebooks for The Possessed [Demons]*, ed. Edward Wasiolek, trans. Victor Terras (Chicago: University of Chicago Press, 1968), pp. 218, 236–237.

6. See also Victor Terras, *A Karamazov Companion* (Madison: University of Wisconsin Press, 1981), pp. 395, 431. Terras suggests that the title of Ivan's other significant poem, the

"Geological Cataclysm," which is outlined by the devil of Ivan's "nightmare," was inspired by a passage from chapter 7 of Renan's *Life of Jesus*.

7. A degree of ambiguity might well be inherent in a discussion such as this; but in what follows an effort has been made to be consistent in using the names *Jesus* in relation to the historical person (especially when the focus is exclusively on his humanity, as it is in the case of, say, Renan), and *Christ* in relation to the God-man of Christian faith.

8. See the discussion of Stepan Verkhovensky in Chapter 5.

9. Letter of 15 February 1854 to Natalya D. Fonvizin, in *Selected Letters of Fyodor Dostoevsky*, eds. Joseph Frank and David I. Goldstein, trans. Andrew R. MacAndrew (London: Rutgers University Press, 1987), p. 68. The italics are Dostoevsky's. See also Dostoevsky, *A Writer's Diary*, vol. 2, p. 1300.

10. Renan was not content, as were many of his liberal contemporaries, merely to admire the "morality of the gospel." In his view, this would be to underestimate seriously the profoundly revolutionary implications of Jesus' teaching: "The idea of Jesus was much more profound; it was the most revolutionary idea ever formed in a human brain." See Ernest Renan, *The Life of Jesus* (New York: Random House, 1955), p. 156.

11. Ibid., p. 383.

12. See Dostoevsky, *Notebooks for The Brothers Karamazov*, p. 82.

13. One of the leading historical analogies by which Nietzsche attempts to get a clear image of Jesus—that of a Buddha on Palestinian soil—appears to follow Renan's suggestion (cf. *The Life of Jesus*, pp. 187, 197).

14. Friedrich Nietzsche, *The Anti-Christ*, trans. R. J. Hollingdale (New York: Penguin, 1968), p. 141. The italics are Nietzsche's. For references in Renan to Jesus as a "hero/genius," see *The Life of Jesus*, pp. 93, 144, 160.

15. Nietzsche, *The Anti-Christ*, pp. 142–143. (The italics are Nietzsche's.) The reader might wish to refer back to the discussion in Chapter 5, for details about Nietzsche's familiarity with Dostoevsky's writings.

16. Friedrich Nietzsche, *Kritische Gesamtausgabe*, eds. Giorgio Colli and Mazzino Montinari (Berlin, 1967–), vol. 8, pt. 3, p. 203.

17. Letter of 31 December 1867 to Apollon N. Maikov, in *Selected Letters of Fyodor Dostoevsky*, p. 262. (The italics are Dostoevsky's.) The Russian word *prekrasnyi* can be translated as either *good* or *beautiful*. In this context, *good* would be the better choice, though its close identification with the *beautiful* should be kept in mind. Here is the more complete text of Dostoevsky's remarks: "For a long time already, there was one idea that had been troubling me, but I was afraid to make a novel out of it because it was a very difficult idea, and I was not ready to tackle it, although it is a fascinating idea and one I am in love with. The idea is—*to portray a perfectly good man*. I believe there can be nothing more difficult than this, especially in our time" (*Selected Letters of Fyodor Dostoevsky*, pp. 269–270; the italics are Dostoevsky's).

18. See, for instance, Dostoevsky, *Notebooks for The Idiot*, p. 198.

19. In a letter of 1 January 1868 to his niece, Sofya A. Ivanov, discussing the idea of *The Idiot*, Dostoevsky writes: "There is only one positively good figure in the world—Christ—so that the phenomenon of that boundlessly, infinitely good figure is already in itself an infinite miracle. (The whole of the Gospel of Saint John is a statement to that effect; he finds the whole miracle in the Incarnation alone, in the manifestation of the good alone)."

20. Ibid.

21. See Fyodor Dostoevsky, *The Idiot,* trans. David Magarshack (New York: Penguin, 1955), pp. 78, 89, 101–104, 116, 325, 347, 376, 378; and idem, *Notebooks for The Idiot,* pp. 181, 191.

22. Nietzsche, *The Anti-Christ,* p. 143.

23. Dostoevsky, *Notebooks for The Idiot,* p. 239. Myshkin can also arouse the hatred of those he helps to self-judgment; this, for instance, is Ganya Ivolgin's reaction to him: "I hate you more than anyone. . . . I understood and hated you long ago, when I first heard of you; I hated you with all the hatred of my heart" (Dostoevsky, *The Idiot,* p. 334). Cf. John 3:20: "For every one who does evil hates the light, and does not come to the light."

24. Dostoevsky, *The Idiot,* pp. 585–586.

25. Nietzsche, *The Anti-Christ,* p. 141. (The italics are Nietzsche's.)

26. Dostoevsky, *Notebooks for The Idiot,* p. 203. For a lengthy reflection on the relation between Myshkin's illness and his spiritual insight, see Dostoevsky, *The Idiot,* pp. 258–259.

27. For a detailed discussion of the *yurodivyi,* see George Fedotov, *The Russian Religious Mind,* vol. 2 (Belmont, Mass.: Nordland, 1975), chap. 12. Fedotov observes (p. 324) that in the cases of several "holy fools," one cannot decide whether one faces "real or fake madness."

28. Ibid., pp. 340–342.

29. One of these commentators was Bruce Ward, in an earlier study of Dostoevsky: See Bruce Ward, *Dostoyevsky's Critique of the West: The Quest for the Earthly Paradise* (Waterloo, Ont.: Wilfrid Laurier University Press, 1986), p. 2.

30. For Renan's reference to Jesus's "perfect idealism," see *The Life of Jesus,* p. 383.

31. Ibid.

32. Fyodor Dostoevsky, *The Unpublished Dostoevsky,* vol. 1, ed. C.R. Proffer (Ann Arbor, Mich.: Ardis, 1973), pp. 39–41. (The italics are Dostoevsky's.)

33. See, for instance, Vladimir Lossky, *The Mystical Theology of the Eastern Church* (London: James Clarke, 1957), pp. 126–127, 143–144. On the subject of the free cooperation of the human with the divine will, Lossky writes: "The concurrence of two wills is necessary; on the one side, there is the divine and deifying will granting grace through the presence of the Holy Spirit in the human person; on the other side there is the human will which submits to the will of God in receiving grace and making it its own, and allowing it to penetrate all its nature" (Ibid., 126–127). For an interesting discussion of the implications for the problem of evil (and hence for Ivan's "Rebellion") of this Eastern emphasis on human free development toward the divine likeness, see John Hick, *Evil and the God of Love* (London: Collins, 1968), pp. 217–224. Lossky writes about the Eastern sense of *kenosis* in terms very much like Dostoevsky's meditation: "As we have said many times, the perfection of the person consists in self-abandonment: the person expresses itself most truly in that it renounces to exist for itself. It is the self-emptying of the Person of the Son, the Divine *kenosis*" (Lossky, *The Mystical Theology,* p. 144). For a discussion of the kenotic ideal in Russian Christianity particularly, see Fedotov, *The Russian Religious Mind,* vol. 1, pp. 390–395.

34. Dostoevsky, *The Idiot,* pp. 446–447.

35. Dostoevsky's wife Anna recounted this story: During the couple's visit to the Kunstmuseum in Basel, her husband had been transfixed by the Holbein painting. After a few moments, Anna, finding the painting too bleak to bear, left him to go through the other rooms. When she returned about twenty minutes later, she found him still gazing at the

*Dead Christ,* as if stunned, now standing on a chair that he had moved under the painting for a closer look. Worried that Dostoevsky might be on the verge of an epileptic fit—"his agitated face had a kind of dread in it"—she led him by the arm out of the room (Anna Dostoevsky, *Reminiscences,* trans. and ed. Beatrice Stillman [New York: Liveright, 1977], pp. 133–134).

36. Dostoevsky, *The Unpublished Dostoevsky,* vol. 1, p. 41.

37. See Lossky, *The Mystical Theology,* p. 143. Lossky simply reaffirms that the Eastern Church has always accepted the Christology of the two natures, human and divine, in one *hypostasis* (person), as this was formulated by the Council of Chalcedon. As I have noted, it is sufficiently clear that on this point also Dostoevsky is in accord with Orthodoxy. Indeed, although the precise degree of "Orthodoxy" in Dostoevsky's understanding of Christ might well remain open to interpretation and debate (even among Eastern Christian scholars), I think that at the very least it can be concluded that his Christ does not depart in any significant way from the Eastern theological tradition. In my view, this is evident from any careful reading of his meditation, in conjunction with, say, Lossky's magisterial account of *The Mystical Theology of the Eastern Church* (especially chapters 6 and 7).

38. Cf. Vladimir Solovyov, "Tri rechi v pamyat' Dostoevskago," in *Sobranie sochinenii,* vol. 3-4, p. 183. Solovyov writes: "This central idea, which Dostoevsky served in all his activities, was the Christian idea of a free ecumenic union of universal brotherhood in the name of Christ. Dostoevsky was preaching this idea when he spoke of the true Church, of ecumenic Orthodoxy."

39. See Dostoevsky, *The Brothers Karamazov,* p. 61, where Father Paissy asserts, "Our Lord Jesus Christ came precisely to establish the Church on earth." The community of children, having its basis in a shared devotion to the memory of the boy Ilyusha Snegiryov, is a microcosm of the order that has its basis in the God-man. The simultaneous affirmation of human beings as unique persons and as manifestations of a common humanity is expressed in Alyosha's speech by Ilyusha's stone: "I give you my word . . . that for my part I will never forget any one of you; each face that is looking at me now, at this moment, I will remember. . . . You are all dear to me. . . . From now on I shall keep you all in my heart, and I ask you to keep me in your hearts, too! Well, and who has united us in this good . . . feeling which we . . . intend to remember always, all our lives, who, if not Ilyushechka . . . that boy dear to us unto ages of ages! Let us never forget him, and may his memory be eternal" (775).

40. Dostoevsky, *The Unpublished Dostoevsky,* vol. 1, pp. 39–40.

41. Ibid., p. 41.

42. Ibid.

43. See David E. Aune, *Revelation 1–5* (Dallas: Word, 1997), p. 373.

44. Ellis Sandoz, *Political Apocalypse: A Study of Dostoevsky's Grand Inquisitor* (Baton Rouge: Louisiana State University Press, 1971), p. 90f.

45. For Kierkegaard's discussion of contemporaneity, see Søren Kierkegaard, *Practice in Christianity,* eds. H. Hong and E. Hong (Princeton: Princeton University Press, 1991), no. 1, especially pp. 36–66. As a Christian poet of spiritual causality, Dostoevsky would have appreciated the following comment by Kierkegaard: "Christ is no play-actor, if I may say this soberly; neither is he a merely historical person, since as the paradox [God-man] he is an extremely unhistorical person. But this is the difference between poetry and actuality: contemporaneity. The difference between poetry and history is surely this, that history is

what *actually* happened, whereas poetry is the possible, the imagined, the poetized. But that which has actually happened (the past) is still not, except in a certain sense (namely, in contrast to poetry), the actual. The qualification that is lacking—which is the qualification of truth (as inwardness) and of all religiousness is—for you. The past is not actuality—for me. Only the contemporary is actuality for me. That with which you are living simultaneously is actuality—for you. Thus every human being is able to become contemporary only with the time in which he is living—and then with one more, with Christ's life upon earth, for Christ's life upon earth, the sacred history, stands alone by itself, outside history" (Ibid., pp. 63–64). This, says Kierkegaard, renders all didactic moralizing about Christ in Christianity the most "un-Christian of all heresies"—a comment with which Dostoevsky's art is in full agreement. Dostoevsky's work as an author, like Kierkegaard's, is devoted to the question of what it means to become a Christian.

46. The Grand Inquisitor is modeled after the notorious Spanish Inquisitor-General, Torquemada, an austere and ascetic Dominican monk whose political powers during the last decade of the fifteenth century were unequaled. For this reason he was heavily armed and lived in extravagant palaces. According to Michael Baigent and Richard Leigh, *The Inquisition* (New York: Viking, 1999), Dostoevsky's portrait is as accurate as any historian's or biographer's. Yet Ivan's setting, although Spanish, implies a Counterreformation context closer to the Papal, or Roman, Inquisition. The latter was modeled on its Spanish counterpart but spearheaded by the Jesuits to ensure the political stability of the papacy and the Roman church in the sixteenth century.

47. See Kierkegaard, *Practice in Christianity*, no. 2.

48. Søren Kierkegaard, *The Sickness Unto Death: A Christian Psychological Exposition for Upbuilding and Awakening*, eds. and trans. Howard Hong and Edna Hong (Princeton: Princeton University Press, 1980), pp. 73–74.

49. Søren Kierkegaard, *The Concept of Anxiety: A Simply Psychologically Orienting Deliberation on the Dogmatic Issue of Hereditary Sin*, eds. and trans. T. Thomte and A. Anderson (Princeton: Princeton University Press, 1980), p. 125.

50. Ibid., p. 128. Buber also characterizes "the demonic You for whom nobody can become a You" as the isolated ego of the monologist, the one who refuses to be a self in relation to the dialogical divine power that establishes it (and others) as a self, and therefore defiantly refuses the freedom of voluntary reciprocity. See Martin Buber, *I and Thou*, trans. W. Kaufmann (New York: Scribners, 1970), p. 117f.

51. See the exquisite meditation on love, death, and the silent Christ in John's gospel, in Paul Gooch, *Reflections on Jesus and Socrates: Word and Silence* (New Haven: Yale University Press, 1996), chapter 6. Gooch's reflections give insight into the Christian spiritual causality that also informs Dostoevsky's art: "Words come to their end in the silence of Jesus, who handed over in obedience his inability to sort out the meaning of the will of the Father and his own motivations. Words reach their limit in prayer, as we take up an elemental relation of address and attention toward God. In our attempts at obedient listening to God, our own words get in the way; we have to quieten our hearts, discern the signs, heed the unconditional call of God even in our suffering. So much of the self is constituted in language that our willingness to hand over all of our scheming and conceptualizing, and to deposit our very beings into the divine care, cannot be better expressed than as a dying. And now I glimpse it: that dying is nothing but prayer, nothing but obedience, nothing but love" (Ibid., p. 304).

# References

## Works By Fyodor Dostoevsky

The definitive Russian-language edition of Fyodor Dostoevsky's complete works is: *Polnoye sobranie sochinenii v tridsati tomakh.* Leningrad: Nauka, 1966–1977.

❧

*The Adolescent.* Trans. Andrew R. MacAndrew. New York: Doubleday, 1972.

*The Brothers Karamazov.* Trans. Richard Pevear and Larissa Volokhonsky. New York: Vintage, 1990.

*Complete Letters.* Vol. 5. Ed. and trans. David Lowe. Ann Arbor, Mich.: Ardis, 1991.

*Crime and Punishment.* Trans. Richard Pevear and Larissa Volokhonsky. New York: Vintage, 1993.

*Demons.* Trans. Richard Pevear and Larissa Volokhonsky. New York: Alfred A. Knopf, 1994.

*The House of the Dead.* Trans. David McDuff. New York: Penguin, 1985.

*The Idiot.* Trans. David Magarshack. New York: Penguin, 1955.

*The Notebooks for The Brothers Karamazov.* Ed. and trans. Edward Wasiolek. Chicago: University of Chicago Press, 1971.

*The Notebooks for Crime and Punishment.* Ed. and trans. Edward Wasiolek. Chicago: University of Chicago Press, 1967.

*The Notebooks for The Idiot.* Ed. Edward Wasiolek, trans. Katherine Strelsky. Chicago: University of Chicago Press, 1967.

*The Notebooks for The Possessed [Demons].* Ed. Edward Wasiolek, trans. Victor Terras. Chicago: University of Chicago Press, 1968.

*The Notebooks for A Raw Youth [The Adolescent].* Ed. Edward Wasiolek, trans. Victor Terras. Chicago: University of Chicago Press, 1969.

*Notes from the Underground.* Trans. Jane Kentish. Oxford: Oxford University Press, 1991.

*Selected Letters of Fyodor Dostoevsky.* Eds. Joseph Frank and David I. Goldstein, trans. Andrew R. MacAndrew. London: Rutgers University Press, 1987.

*The Unpublished Dostoevsky: Diaries and Notebooks (1860–81).* 3 vols. Ed. C. R. Proffer, trans. T. S. Berczynski, B. H. Montu, A. Boyer, and E. Proffer. Ann Arbor, Mich.: Ardis, 1973.

*Winter Notes on Summer Impressions.* Trans. R. L. Renfield. N.p.: Criterion, 1955.

*A Writer's Diary.* 2 vols. Trans. Kenneth Lantz. Evanston, Ill.: Northwestern University Press, 1994.

# Other References

Aeschylus. 1961. *Prometheus Bound.* Trans. Philip Vellacott. New York: Penguin.

Allen, Joseph J. 1994. *Inner Way: Towards a Rebirth of Eastern Christian Spiritual Direction.* Grand Rapids, Mich.: William B. Eerdmans.

de Alvarez, Helen Canniff. 1977. "The Augustinian Basis of Dostoevsky's The Brothers Karamazov." Unpublished dissertation, University of Dallas.

Arendt, Hannah. 1958. *The Human Condition.* Chicago: University of Chicago Press.

_____. 1963. *On Revolution.* New York: Penguin.

_____. 1968. *Between Past and Future: Eight Exercises in Political Thought.* New York: Penguin.

Auerbach, Eric. 1953. *Mimesis: The Representation of Reality in Western Literature.* Trans. Willard Trask. Princeton: Princeton University Press.

_____. 1984. *Scenes from the Drama of European Literature.* Minneapolis: University of Minnesota Press.

Aune, David E. 1997. *Revelation 1–5.* Dallas: Word.

Baigent, Michael, and Richard Leigh. 1999. *The Inquisition.* New York: Viking.

Bakhtin, Mikhail. 1984. *Problems of Dostoevsky's Poetics.* Ed. and trans. Caryl Emerson. Minneapolis: University of Minnesota Press.

Barr, D. L. 1986. "The Apocalypse of John as Oral Enactment." *Interpretation* 40, pp. 243–256.

Bauckham, Richard. 1992. *The Climax of Prophecy: Studies on the Book of Revelation.* Edinburgh: T. & T. Clark.

_____. 1993. *The Theology of the Book of Revelation.* Cambridge: Cambridge University Press.

Beckett, Samuel. 1954. *Waiting for Godot.* New York: Grove Press.

Belinsky, Vissarion G. 1948. *Selected Philosophical Works.* Moscow: Foreign Languages.

Belknap, Robert. 1967. *The Structure of The Brothers Karamazov.* The Hague: Mouton.

_____.1990. *The Genesis of The Brothers Karamazov: The Aesthetics, Ideology, and Psychology of Making a Text.* Evanston, Ill.: Northwestern University Press.

Berdyaev, Nicholas. 1957. *Dostoevsky.* Trans. Donald Attwater. New York: World.

Bonhoeffer, Dietrich. 1955. *Ethics.* Ed. E. Bethge. New York: Macmillan.

Buber, Martin. 1957. "Prophecy, Apocalyptic, and the Historical Hour." In *Pointing the Way,* ed. and trans. M. Friedman. New York: Schocken.

_____. 1970. *I and Thou.* Trans. Walter Kaufmann. New York: Scribners.

Buckle, Henry Thomas. 1885. *History of Civilization in England.* London: Longmans, Green.

Caird, G. B. 1966. *The Revelation of St. John the Divine.* New York: Harper and Row.

_____. 1980. *The Language and Imagery of the Bible.* London: Duckworth.

Camus, Albert. 1954. *The Rebel.* Trans. Anthony Bower. New York: Alfred A. Knopf.

_____. 1962. "Pour Dostoïevski." In *Théâtre, récits, nouvelles.* Paris: Gallimard.

_____. 1974. *Resistance, Rebellion, and Death.* Trans. Justin O'Brien. New York: Random House.

Catteau, Jacques. 1989. *Dostoyevsky and the Process of Literary Creation.* Cambridge: Cambridge University Press.

Cox, Roger L. 1969. *Between Earth and Heaven: Shakespeare, Dostoevsky, and the Meaning of Christian Tragedy.* New York: Holt, Rinehart, and Winston.

Crossan, John Dominic. 1973. *In Parables: The Challenge of the Historical Jesus.* New York: Harper and Row.

_____. 1980. *Cliffs of Fall: Paradox and Polyvalence in the Parables of Jesus.* New York: Seabury.

Dodd, C. H. 1953. *The Interpretation of the Fourth Gospel.* Cambridge: Cambridge University Press.

Dostoevsky, Anna. 1977. *Reminiscences.* Ed. and trans. Beatrice Stillman. New York: Liveright.

Dürr, Volker, Reinhold Grimm, and Kathy Harms, eds. 1988. *Nietzsche: Literature and Values.* Madison: University of Wisconsin Press.

Emerson, Caryl, ed. 1999. *Critical Essays on Mikhail Bakhtin.* New York: G. K. Hall.

Farrer, Austin. 1949. *A Rebirth of Images: The Making of St. John's Apocalypse.* Boston: Beacon Press.

_____. 1964. *The Revelation of St. John the Divine.* Oxford: Clarendon Press.

Fedotov, George. 1975. *The Russian Religious Mind.* 2 vols. Belmont, Mass.: Nordland.

Frank, Joseph. 1986. *Dostoevsky: The Stir of Liberation, 1860–1865.* Princeton: Princeton University Press.

Frei, Hans W. 1974. *The Eclipse of Biblical Narrative: A Study in Eighteenth- and Nineteenth-Century Hermeneutics.* New Haven: Yale University Press.

Friedman, Richard Elliott. 1995. *The Hidden Face of God.* San Francisco: Harper.

Fukuyama, Francis. 1992. *The End of History and the Last Man.* New York: Free Press.

Girard, René. 1965. *Deceit, Desire, and the Novel: Self and Other in Literary Structure.* Trans. Y. Freccero. Baltimore: Johns Hopkins Press.

_____. 1987. *Things Hidden Since the Foundation of the World.* Stanford: Stanford University Press.

_____. 1997. *Resurrection from the Underground: Feodor Dostoevsky.* Ed. and trans. James Williams. New York: Crossroads.

Gooch, Paul. 1996. *Reflections on Jesus and Socrates: Word and Silence.* New Haven: Yale University Press.

Grant, George. 1995. *Time As History.* Toronto: University of Toronto Press.

_____. 1985. *English-Speaking Justice.* Notre Dame, Ind.: University of Notre Dame Press.

Grant, George, and Sheila Grant. 1986. "The Language of Euthanasia." In *Technology and Justice,* by George Grant. Toronto: Anansi.

Grossman, Leonid. 1919. *Biblioteka Dostoevskago.* Odessa: N.p.

Guroian, Vigen. 1987. *Incarnate Love: Essays in Orthodox Ethics.* Notre Dame, Ind.: University of Notre Dame Press.

_____. 1994. *Ethics after Christendom: Toward an Ecclesial Christian Ethic.* Grand Rapids, Mich.: William B. Eerdmans.

Hackel, Sergei. 1989. "The Religious Dimension: Vision or Evasion? Zosima's Discourse in *The Brothers Karamazov.*" In *Fyodor Dostoevsky,* ed. Harold Bloom. New York: Chelsea House.

Hauerwas, Stanley. 1994. *Dispatches from the Front: Theological Engagements with the Secular.* Durham, N.C.: Duke University Press.

Hegel, G.W.F. 1956. *The Philosophy of History*. Trans. J. Sibree. New York: Dover.

Heidegger, Martin. 1949. "Hölderlin and the Essence of Poetry." In *Existence and Being*, ed. Werner Brock, trans. R.F.C. Hull and Alan Crick. Chicago: H. Regnery.

Heschel, Abraham J. 1962. *The Prophets*. 2 vols. New York: Harper and Row.

Hick, John. 1968. *Evil and the God of Love*. London: Collins.

Jackson, Robert Louis. 1981. *The Art of Dostoevsky: Deliriums and Nocturnes*. Princeton: Princeton University Press.

Jeffrey, David. 1990. "How to Read the Hebrew Prophets." In *Mappings of the Biblical Terrain: The Bible as Text*, eds. V. Tollers and J. Maier. Lewisburg, Pa.: Bucknell University Press.

Jeffrey, David Lyle. 1996. *People of the Book: Christian Identity and Literary Culture*. Grand Rapids, Mich.: William B. Eerdmans.

Jonas, Hans. 1996. *Mortality and Morality: A Search for the Good After Auschwitz*. Evanston, Ill.: Northwestern University Press.

Kant, Immanuel. 1963. *On History*. Trans. Lewis White Beck. New York: Bobbs-Merrill.

———. 1964. *Groundwork of the Metaphysic of Morals*. Trans. H. J. Paton. New York: Harper and Row.

Kierkegaard, Søren. 1941. *Training in Christianity*. Trans. Walter Lowrie. Princeton: Princeton University Press.

———. 1980. *The Concept of Anxiety: A Simply Psychologically Orienting Deliberation on the Dogmatic Issue of Hereditary Sin*. Eds. and trans. T. Thomte and A. Anderson. Princeton: Princeton University Press.

———. 1980. *The Sickness Unto Death: A Christian Psychological Exposition for Upbuilding and Awakening*. Eds. and trans. Howard Hong and Edna Hong. Princeton: Princeton University Press.

———. 1991. *Practice in Christianity*. Eds. and trans. Howard Hong and Edna Hong. Princeton: Princeton University Press.

Kjetsaa, Geir. 1984. *Dostoevsky and His New Testament*. Atlantic Highlands, N.J.: Humanities Press.

Knapp, Liza. 1996. *The Annihilation of Inertia: Dostoevsky and Metaphysics*. Evanston, Ill.: Northwestern University Press.

Kroeker, P. Travis. 1993. "The Theological Politics of Plato and Isaiah: A Debate Rejoined." *Journal of Religion* 73/1, January, pp. 16–30.

Linner, Sven. 1975. *Starets Zosima in The Brothers Karamazov: A Study in the Mimesis of Virtue*. Stockholm: Almqvist and Wiksell.

Lossky, Vladimir. 1957. *The Mystical Theology of the Eastern Church*. London: James Clarke.

Löwith, Karl. 1949. *Meaning in History*. Chicago: University of Chicago Press.

Marcus, Joel. 1986. *The Mystery of the Kingdom of God*. Atlanta: Scholars Press.

McLelland, Joseph C. 1988. *Prometheus Rebound: The Irony of Atheism*. Waterloo, Ont.: Wilfrid Laurier University Press.

Meyendorff, John. 1962. *A Study in Gregory Palamas*. London: Faith Press.

———. 1974. *Byzantine Theology: Historical Trends and Doctrinal Themes*. New York: Fordham University Press.

Mihailovic, Alexander. 1997. *Corporeal Words: Mikhail Bakhtin's Theology of Discourse*. Evanston, Ill.: Northwestern University Press.

Mihajlov, Mihajlo. 1986. *Nietzsche in Russia*. Princeton: Princeton University Press.

Miller, C. A. 1973. "Nietzsche's 'Discovery' of Dostoevsky." *Nietzsche-Studien* 2, pp. 202–257.

Miller, Robin Feuer. 1992. *The Brothers Karamazov: Worlds of the Novel.* New York: Twayne.

Minear, Paul S. 1962. "The Cosmology of the Apocalypse." In *Current Issues in New Testament Interpretation,* eds. W. Klassen and G. Snyder. New York: Harper and Row.

Nietzsche, Friedrich. 1966. *Beyond Good and Evil.* Trans. Walter Kaufmann. New York: Random House.

_____. 1967. *The Will to Power.* Trans. Walter Kaufmann and R.J. Hollingdale. New York: Random House.

_____. 1968. *Twilight of the Idols.* Trans. R.J. Hollingdale. New York: Penguin.

_____. 1974. *The Gay Science.* Trans. Walter Kaufmann. New York: Vintage.

_____. 1978. *Thus Spoke Zarathustra.* Trans. Walter Kaufmann. New York: Penguin.

_____. 1989. *On the Genealogy of Morals.* Trans. Walter Kaufmann. New York: Random House.

O'Donovan, Oliver. 1986. *Resurrection and Moral Order.* Grand Rapids, Mich.: William B. Eerdmans.

Panichas, George. 1977. *The Burden of Vision.* Grand Rapids, Mich.: William B. Eerdmans.

Peace, Richard. 1971. *Dostoyevsky: An Examination of the Major Novels.* Cambridge: Cambridge University Press.

Perlina, Nina. *Varieties of Poetic Utterance: Quotation in The Brothers Karamazov.* New York: University Press of America.

Plato. 1968. *The Republic.* Trans. Allan Bloom. New York: Basic Books.

Posner, Richard A. 1998. *Law and Literature.* Rev. ed. Cambridge: Harvard University Press.

Renan, Ernest. 1955. *The Life of Jesus.* New York: Random House.

Ricoeur, Paul. 1970. *Freud and Philosophy: An Essay on Interpretation.* Trans. Denis Savage. New Haven: Yale University Press.

_____. 1974. *The Conflict of Interpretations: Essays in Hermeneutics.* Ed. D. Ihde. Evanston, Ill.: Northwestern University Press.

Robinson, Douglas. 1998. "Literature and Apocalyptic." In *The Encyclopedia of Apocalypticism,* vol. 3. New York: Continuum.

Rousseau, Jean-Jacques. 1968. *The Social Contract.* Trans. M. Cranston. New York: Penguin.

Sandoz, Ellis. 1971. *Political Apocalypse: A Study of Dostoevsky's Grand Inquisitor.* Baton Rouge: Louisiana State University Press.

Schacht, Richard. 1983. *Nietzsche.* London: Routledge and Kegan Paul.

Schmemann, Alexander. 1979. *Church, World, Mission.* Crestwood, N.Y.: St. Vladimir's Seminary Press.

Solovyov, Vladimir. 1948. *Lectures on Godmanhood.* London: D. Dobson.

_____. 1966. "Tri rechi v pamyat' Dostoevskago." In *Sobranie sochinenii.* Vol. 3-4. Brussels.

Steiner, George. 1959. *Tolstoy or Dostoyevsky: An Essay in the Old Criticism.* New York: Penguin.

_____. 1996. *No Passion Spent.* New Haven: Yale University Press.

Strauss, Leo. 1953. *Natural Right and History.* Chicago: University of Chicago Press.

Sutherland, Stewart. 1977. *Atheism and the Rejection of God.* Oxford: Basil Blackwell.

Terras, Victor. 1981. *A Karamazov Companion: Commentary on the Genesis, Language, and Style of Dostoevsky's Novel.* Madison: University of Wisconsin Press.

Thompson, Diane Oenning. 1991. *The Brothers Karamazov and the Poetics of Memory.* Cambridge: Cambridge University Press.

Toole, David. 1998. *Waiting for Godot in Sarajevo: Theological Reflections on Nihilism, Tragedy, and Apocalypse.* Boulder: Westview.

Torrance, T. F. 1957. "Liturgie et Apocalypse." *Verbum Caro* 11, pp. 28–40.

Vassiliadis, Petros. 1997. "Apocalypse and Liturgy." *St. Vladimir's Theological Quarterly* 41/2–3, pp. 95–112.

Voegelin, Eric. 1952. *The New Science of Politics.* Chicago: University of Chicago Press.

_____. 1990. "Immortality: Experience and Symbol." In *The Collected Works of Eric Voegelin,* vol. 12, ed. Ellis Sandoz. Baton Rouge: Louisiana State University Press.

Walicki, Andrzej. 1979. *A History of Russian Thought: From the Enlightenment to Marxism.* Stanford: Stanford University Press.

Ward, Bruce K. 1986. *Dostoyevsky's Critique of the West: The Quest for the Earthly Paradise.* Waterloo, Ont.: Wilfrid Laurier University Press.

_____. 1994. "Dostoevsky and the Problem of Meaning in History." In *Dostoevsky and the Twentieth Century,* ed. Malcolm V. Jones. Nottingham, U.K.: Astra.

Ware, Kallistos. 1974. "The Spiritual Father in Orthodox Christianity." *Cross Currents,* Summer/Fall.

Wellek, Rene, ed. 1962. *Dostoevsky: A Collection of Critical Essays.* Englewood Cliffs, N.J.: Prentice-Hall.

Wright, N. T. 1996. *Jesus and the Victory of God.* Minneapolis: Fortress.

Yoder, John Howard. 1992. *Body Politics: Five Practices of the Christian Community Before the Watching World.* Nashville: Discipleship Resources.

_____. 1994. *The Royal Priesthood: Essays Ecclesiological and Ecumenical.* Ed. Michael Cartwright. Grand Rapids, Mich.: William B. Eerdmans.

# Index

Printed in the United States
116560LV00001BA/61/A